CHILTON'S
REPAIR & TUNE-UP GUIDE
GM X-BODY 1980-85

**All U.S. and Canadian models of BUICK Skylark •
CHEVROLET Citation • OLDSMOBILE Omega • PONTIAC Phoenix**

Senior Vice President	Ronald A. Hoxter
Publisher and Editor-In-Chief	Kerry A. Freeman, S.A.E.
Executive Editors	Dean F. Morgantini, S.A.E., W. Calvin Settle, Jr., S.A.E.
Managing Editor	Nick D'Andrea
Special Products Manager	Ken Grabowski, A.S.E., S.A.E.
Senior Editors	Jacques Gordon, Michael L. Grady, Debra McCall, Kevin M. G. Maher, Richard J. Rivele, S.A.E., Richard T. Smith, Jim Taylor, Ron Webb
Project Managers	Martin J. Gunther, Will Kessler, A.S.E., Richard Schw...
Production Manager	Andrea Steige...
Product Systems Manager	Robert Maxey...
Director of Manufacturing	Mike D'Imper...
Editor	Michael A. N...

CHILTON *BOOK COMPANY*

*ONE OF THE DIVERSIFIED PUBLISHING COMPANIES,
A PART OF CAPITAL CITIES/ABC, INC.*

SAFETY NOTICE

Proper service and repair procedures are vital to the safe, reliable operation of all motor vehicles, as well as the personal safety of those performing repairs. This book outlines procedures for servicing and repairing vehicles using safe, effective methods. The procedures contain many NOTES, CAUTIONS and WARNINGS which should be followed along with standard safety procedures to eliminate the possibility of personal injury or improper service which could damage the vehicle or compromise its safety.

It is important to note that repair procedures and techniques, tools and parts for servicing motor vehicles, as well as the skill and experience of the individual performing the work vary widely. It is not possible to anticipate all of the conceivable ways or conditions under which vehicles may be serviced, or to provide cautions as to all of the possible hazards that may result. Standard and accepted safety precautions and equipment should be used when handling toxic or flammable fluids, and safety goggles or other protection should be used during cutting, grinding, chiseling, prying, or any other process that can cause material removal or projectiles.

Some procedures require the use of tools specially designed for a specific purpose. Before substituting another tool or procedure, you must be completely satisfied that neither your personal safety, nor the performance of the vehicle will be endangered.

Although information in this guide is based on industry sources and is as complete as possible at the time of publication, the possibility exists that the manufacturer made later changes which could not be included here. While striving for total accuracy, Chilton Book Company cannot assume responsibility for any errors, changes, or omissions that may occur in the compilation of this data.

PART NUMBERS

Part numbers listed in this reference are not recommendations by Chilton for any product by brand name. They are references that can be used with interchange manuals and aftermarket supplier catalogs to locate each brand supplier's discrete part number.

ACKNOWLEDGMENTS

The Chilton Book Company expresses its appreciation to the Chevrolet Motor Division, General Motors Corporation, Detroit, Michigan 48202; Oldsmobile Division, General Motors Corporation, Lansing, Michigan 48921; Pontiac Motor Division, General Motors Corporation, Pontiac, Michigan 48053, and the Buick Motor Division, General Motors Corporation, Flint, Michigan 48550 for their generous assistance.
The author would particularly like to thank Fritz Bennetts at Oldsmobile and Ralph Kramer at Chevrolet for their help.

Information has been selected from Chevrolet, Oldsmobile, Pontiac, and Buick shop manuals, owner's manuals, data books, brochures, service bulletins, and technical manuals.

Manufactured in the United States of America
Thirteenth Printing, June, 1996

Chilton's Repair & Tune-Up Guide: GM X-Body 1980–85
ISBN 0-8019-7592-1 Pbk
Library of Congress Catalog Card No. 84-45462

CONTENTS

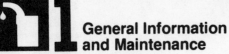

Quick Reference
Specifications For Your Vehicle

Fill in this chart with the most commonly used specifications for your vehicle. Specifications can be found in Chapters 1 through 3 or on the tune-up decal under the hood of the vehicle.

 Tune-Up

Firing Order_____

Spark Plugs:

Type_____

Gap (in.)_____

Point Gap (in.)_____

Dwell Angle (°)_____

Ignition Timing (°)_____

Vacuum (Connected/Disconnected)_____

Valve Clearance (in.)

Intake_____   Exhaust_____

 Capacities

Engine Oil (qts)

With Filter Change_____

Without Filter Change_____

Cooling System (qts)_____

Manual Transmission (pts)_____

Type_____

Automatic Transmission (pts)_____

Type_____

Front Differential (pts)_____

Type_____

Rear Differential (pts)_____

Type_____

Transfer Case (pts)_____

Type_____

FREQUENTLY REPLACED PARTS
Use these spaces to record the part numbers of frequently replaced parts.

PCV VALVE

Manufacturer_____

Part No._____

OIL FILTER

Manufacturer_____

Part No._____

AIR FILTER

Manufacturer_____

Part No._____

General Information and Maintenance

HOW TO USE THIS BOOK

All General Motors 1980–85 X-Body cars—the Chevrolet Citation, Oldsmobile Omega, Pontiac Phoenix, and Buick Skylark—are covered in this book, with procedures specifically labeled as to the particular division when it makes a difference. The purpose of this book is to cover maintenance and repair procedures that the owner can perform without special tools or equipment. A lot of attention is given to the type of jobs on which the owner can save labor charges and time by doing it him or herself. Jobs which absolutely require special tools, such as transaxle overhaul, or which the beginner is unlikely to get right the first time, such as differential adjustment, are purposely not covered.

To use the book properly, each operation must be approached logically, with a clear understanding of the theory behind the work involved. The procedures should be read completely and understood thoroughly before any work is begun. The required tools and supplies should be on hand and a clean, uncluttered place to work should be available. There is nothing more frustrating than finding yourself one metric bolt short in the middle of your Sunday afternoon repair. So read ahead and plan ahead. To avoid confusion, it is best to complete one job at a time, so that results can be independently evaluated.

When reference is made in this book to the "right side" or "left side" of the car, it should be understood that these positions are to be viewed from the front seat. Thus, the left side of the car is always the driver's side, even when one is facing the car, as when working on the engine.

We have attempted to eliminate the use of special tools wherever possible, substituting more readily available hand tools. However, in some cases the special tools are necessary.

These can be purchased from your G.M. dealer, or from an automotive parts store.

Always be conscious of the need for safety in your work. Never crawl under your car unless it is firmly supported by jackstands or ramps. Never smoke near or allow flame to get near the battery or fuel system. Keep your clothing, hands and hair clear of the fan and pulleys when working near the engine, if it is running. Most importantly, try to be patient, even in the midst of a problem such as a particularly stubborn bolt; reaching for the largest hammer in the garage is usually a cause for later regret and more extensive repair. As you gain confidence and experience, working on your car will become a source of pride and satisfaction.

TOOLS AND EQUIPMENT

The service procedures in this book presuppose a familiarity with hand tools and their proper use. However, it is possible that you may have a limited amount of experience with the sort of equipment needed to work on an automobile. This section is designed to help you assemble a basic set of tools that will handle most of the jobs you may undertake.

In addition to the normal assortment of screwdrivers and pliers, automotive service work requires an investment in wrenches, sockets and the handles needed to drive them, and various measuring tools such as torque wrenches and feeler gauges.

You will find that virtually every nut and bolt on your X-Body car is metric. Therefore, despite various close size similarities, standard inch-size tools will not fit and must not be used. You will need a set of metric wrenches as your most basic tool kit, ranging from about 6 mm to 17 mm in size. High quality forged wrenches are available in three styles: open end, box end, and combination open/box end. The combination tools are generally the most desirable as a starter set; the wrenches shown in the accompanying illustration are of the combination type.

The other set of tools inevitably required is a ratchet handle and socket set. This set should have the same size range as your wrench set. The ratchet, extension, and flex drives for the sockets are available in many sizes; it is advisable to choose a ⅜ inch drive set initially. One break in the inch/metric sizing war is that metric-sized sockets sold in the U.S. have inch-sized drive (¼, ⅜, ½, etc.). Thus, if you already have an inch-size socket set, you need only buy new metric sockets in the sizes needed. Sockets are available in six and twelve point versions; six point types are generally cheaper and are a good choice for a first set. The choice of a drive handle for the sockets should be made with some care. If this is your first set, take the plunge and invest in a flex-head ratchet; it will get into many places otherwise accessible only through a long chain of universal joints, extensions, and adapters. An alternative is a flex handle, which lacks the ratcheting feature but has a head which pivots 180°; such a tool is shown below the ratchet handle in the illustration. In addition to the range of sockets mentioned, a rubber-lined spark plug socket should be purchased. The correct size for the plugs in your X-Body car's engine is ⅝ inch.

The most important thing to consider when purchasing hand tools is quality. Don't be misled by the low cost of "bargain" tools. Forged wrenches, tempered screwdriver blades, and fine tooth ratchets are much better investments than their less expensive counterparts. The skinned knuckles and frustration inflicted by poor quality tools make any job an unhappy chore. Another consideration is that quality tools come with an on-the-spot replacement quarantee—if the tool breaks, you get a new one, no questions asked.

Most jobs can be accomplished using the tools on the accompanying lists. There will be an occasional need for a special tool, such as snap ring pliers; that need will be mentioned in the text. It would not be wise to buy a large assortment of tools on the premise that someday they will be needed. Instead, the tools should be acquired one at a time, each for a specific job, both to avoid unnecessary expense and to be certain that you have the right tool.

The tools needed for basic maintenance jobs, in addition to the wrenches and sockets mentioned, include:

1. Jackstands, for support;
2. Oil filter wrench;
3. Oil filler spout or funnel;
4. Grease gun;
5. Battery terminal and clamp cleaner;
6. Container for draining oil;
7. Many rags for the inevitable spills.

In addition to these items there are several others which are not absolutely necessary, but handy to have around. These include a transmission funnel and filler tube, a drop (trouble) light on a long cord, an adjustable wrench (crescent wrench), and slip joint pliers.

A more advanced list of tools suitable for tune-up work, can be drawn up easily. While the tools involved are slightly more sophisticated, they need not be outrageously expensive. The key to these purchases is to make them with an eye towards adaptability and wide range. A basic list of tune-up tools could include:

1. Tachometer;
2. Spark plug gauge and gapping tool;
3. Timing light.

In this list, the choice of a timing light should be made carefully. A light which works on the DC current supplied by the car battery is the best choice; it should have a xenon tube for brightness. The X-Body cars have electronic ignition, and thus the light should have an inductive pick-up (the timing light illustrated has one of these).

In addition to these basic tools, there are several other tools and gauges you may find useful. These include:

1. A compression gauge. The screw-in type is slower to use, but eliminates the possibility of a faulty reading due to escaping pressure;
2. A manifold vacuum gauge;
3. A test light;
4. An induction meter. This is used to determine whether or not there is current flowing in a wire, and thus is extremely helpful in electrical troubleshooting.

Finally, you will probably find a torque wrench necessary for all but the most basic of work. The beam type models are perfectly adequate. The newer click (breakaway) type torque wrenches are more accurate, but are much more expensive, and must be periodically recalibrated.

SERVICING YOUR CAR SAFELY

It is virtually impossible to anticipate all of the hazards involved with automotive maintenance and service, but care and common sense will prevent most accidents.

The rules of safety for mechanics range from "don't smoke around gasoline," to "use the proper tool for the job." The trick to avoiding

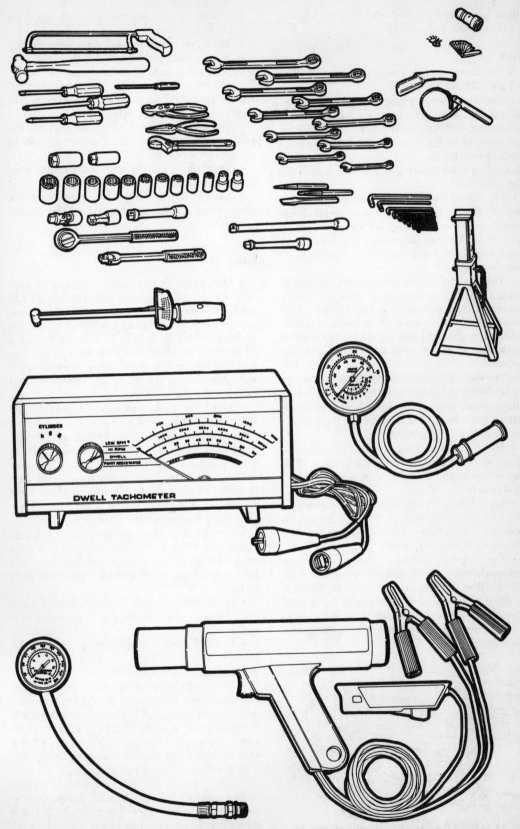

You need only a basic assortment of hand tools for most maintenance and repair jobs

injuries is to develop safe work habits and take every possible precaution.

Dos

• Do keep a fire extinguisher and first aid kit within easy reach.

• Do wear safety glasses or goggles when cutting, drilling, grinding or prying, even if you have 20–20 vision. If you wear glasses for the sake of vision, they should be made of hardened glass that can serve also as safety glasses, or wear safety goggles over your regular glasses.

• Do shield your eyes whenever you work around the battery. Batteries contain sulphuric acid. In case of contact with the eyes or skin, flush the area with water or a mixture of water and baking soda and get medical attention immediately.

• Do use safety stands for any undercar service. Jacks are for raising vehicles; safety stands are for making sure the vehicle stays raised until you want it to come down. Whenever the car is raised, block the wheels remaining on the ground and set the parking brake.

• Do use adequate ventilation when working with any chemicals or hazardous materials. Like carbon monoxide, the asbestos dust resulting from brake lining wear can be poisonous in sufficient quantities.

• Do disconnect the negative battery cable when working on the electrical system. The secondary ignition system can contain up to 40,000 volts.

• Do follow manufacturer's directions whenever working with potentially hazardous materials. Both brake fluid and antifreeze are poisonous if taken internally.

• Do properly maintain your tools. Loose hammerheads, mushroomed punches and chisels, frayed or poorly grounded electrical cords, excessively worn screwdrivers, spread wrenches (open end), cracked sockets, slipping ratchets, or faulty droplight sockets can cause accidents.

Always support the car securely with jackstands; don't use cinder blocks, tire-changing jacks, or the like

• Do use the proper size and type of tool for the job being done.

• Do when possible, pull on a wrench handle rather than push on it, and adjust your stance to prevent a fall.

• Do be sure that adjustable wrenches are tightly closed on the nut or bolt and pulled so that the face is on the side of the fixed jaw.

• Do select a wrench or socket that fits the nut or bolt. The wrench or socket should sit straight, not cocked.

• Do strike squarely with a hammer; avoid glancing blows.

• Do set the parking brake and block the drive wheels if the work requires the engine running.

Don'ts

• Don't run an engine in a garage or anywhere else without proper ventilation—EVER! Carbon monoxide is poisonous; it takes a long time to leave the human body and you can build up a deadly supply of it in your system by simply breathing in a little every day. You may not realize you are slowly poisoning yourself. Always use power vents, windows, fans or open the garage doors.

• Don't work around moving parts while wearing a necktie or other loose clothing. Short sleeves are much safer than long, loose sleeves; hard-toed shoes with neoprene soles protect your toes and give a better grip on slippery surfaces. Jewelry such as watches, fancy belt buckles, beads or body adornment of any kind is not safe working around a car. Long hair should be hidden under a hat or cap.

• Don't use pockets for toolboxes. A fall or bump can drive a screwdriver deep into your body. Even a wiping cloth hanging from the back pocket can wrap around a spinning shaft or fan.

• Don't smoke when working around gasoline, cleaning solvent or other flammable material.

• Don't smoke when working around the battery. When the battery is being charged, it gives off explosive hydrogen gas.

• Don't use gasoline to wash your hands; there are excellent soaps available. Gasoline may contain lead, and lead can enter the body through a cut, accumulating in the body until you are very ill. Gasoline also removes all the natural oils from the skin so that bone dry hands will suck up oil and grease.

• Don't service the air conditioning system unless you are equipped with the necessary tools and training. The refrigerant, R-12, is extremely cold when compressed, and when released into the air will instantly freeze any surface it contacts, including your eyes. Although the refrigerant is normally non-toxic, R-12 becomes a deadly poisonous gas in the presence of an open flame. One good whiff of the vapors from burning refrigerant can be fatal.

HISTORY

Planning for the 1980 G.M. X-Body cars began in the Chevrolet advance design studios in April, 1974. Five principal objectives were outlined: the car would have to be fuel-efficient, roomy, comfortable, safe, and durable.

Four months later, in August, 1974, a group met to consider the proposals advanced. From the beginning, it was decided that a front wheel drive, transverse-engined car would be the most efficient design possible, and could most easily meet the objectives established. Work began on prototypes, mostly re-worked versions of front-drive Volkswagens and Fiats. Soon it was decided to make the X-Body car a corporate undertaking. Pontiac joined the project in the latter half of 1975, and Buick and Oldsmobile divisions began work in February, 1976. By this time, the Chevrolet pre-prototype Citations were nearly completed (each at a cost of over $650,000) and ready for evaluation. Styling was finalized in July, 1976, four phases of prototypes were built between February, 1977, and January, 1978, and 141 pilotline cars were built between February and July, 1978.

The X-Body car was originally scheduled to make its debut at the start of the 1979 model year, but this introduction was postponed to iron out final wrinkles (mostly problems with supply of never before produced components). The April, 1979, introduction of the car as a certified 1980 model also meant that it could be produced for seventeen months before having to undergo emissions recertification with the Environmental Protection Agency, a costly and time-consuming process. Finally, of course, the 1980 designation was a symbolic one—as the "first G.M. car for the '80s," the new X-Body models demonstrated the efficient and thoughtful direction for the corporation over the next difficult decade.

The result of all this work is a car which is almost 800 pounds lighter than the car it replaces, but has more interior space and luggage room, and better fuel economy, performance, and handling.

Most of these improvements can be credited to the use of the transverse-engine, front wheel drive configuration. By packaging the entire drive train in the front "box" of the car, the rest is left for people and their possessions, an eminently sensible arrangement, although one which had been the exclusive province of European and Japanese carmakers until the introduction of the X-car.

The do-it-yourselfer should be pleased to discover that designing a completely new car gave G.M. engineers an opportunity to either reduce or eliminate most servicing headaches. For example, the X-Bodies have a self-adjusting clutch, a "maintenance-free" battery, and sealed and lubricated for life front and rear wheel bearings which require no periodic adjustment. There are many other aids to scheduled maintenance which make working on these cars a much more enjoyable and less time-consuming task than it has been in the past.

The X-Bodies are the first of a new range of G.M. front-drive cars. They will be followed by larger and smaller versions, each to suit specific needs and whims. But the X-Bodies are truly the first G.M. cars of the '80s, and, as the owner of one of these cars, you are helping to create a little bit of history yourself.

A Note About Terminology

There are a few descriptive words used in connection with the X-Body cars which may be new to you.

First, of course, is the term "X-Body" itself. The explanation for this, used to collectively describe the Citation, Omega, Phoenix, and Skylark, is quite simple. All General Motors cars have code names, used within the corporation to designate a body size series. For example, the full-size Impala, Eighty-Eight, LeSabre, and Bonneville are known within G.M. as "B-Bodies." The 1972 Nova was the first "X-Body," and all cars built on that floorpan since have been known by the term.

If this is your first front wheel drive car, you may not be familiar with the terms "transaxle," "halfshaft," or "constant velocity joint."

In a front wheel drive car, the transmission and differential share a common housing, and the front axles (halfshafts) are driven directly by this unit. Thus, a "transaxle" is a combination transmission/differential/drive axle. The X-Body cars use a manual transaxle as standard equipment and an automatic transaxle as an option.

"Halfshafts" are drive axles. The term came about as a way to describe the two shafts which emerge from the transaxle case and connect to the front wheels, transmitting power from one to the other. In a conventional front engine/rear drive car, a driveshaft is used to transmit power from the transmission to the drive axle. Thus, in a front wheel drive car, where there are two driveshafts, each one becomes half of a driveshaft, or a halfshaft. The halfshafts are also known as "drive axles."

A "constant velocity joint" is a variation on a conventional universal joint. Differences between them lie in the greater flexibility of the constant velocity joint, and its ability to transmit power at an angle without fluctuations in speed (thus, "constant velocity"). Two constant velocity joints are used on each halfshaft.

Because the X-Body is an all-metric car, there are a few metric terms with which you should be familiar, if only so that you won't become annoyed by the constant references to them in this book. Newton-meters are the metric equivalent of foot-pounds, a measurement of torque. Thus, the "Nm."s you see in these pages are torque values in Newton-meters. Millimeters are abbreviated to "mm"; liters are "L". Celcius temperature measurements are of course abbreviated to "C." In all cases, conventional English equivalents are given in the text along with the metric value.

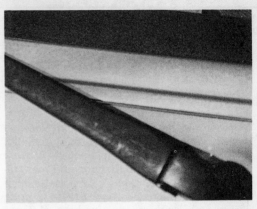

The V.I.N. plate is visible through the windshield

SERIAL NUMBER IDENTIFICATION

It is important for servicing and ordering parts to be certain of vehicle and engine identification.

Vehicle Identification Number (VIN)

The VIN (Vehicle Identification Number) is a 13 or 17 digit number visible through the windshield on the driver's side of the dash and contains the vehicle and engine identification codes. It can be interpreted in the following charts:

Engine

The four cylinder engine VIN code is also stamped on a pad at the right front of the cylinder block below the cylinder head. The V6 VIN code is stamped on a pad at the left front of the cylinder block below the cylinder head.

Transaxle

The manual transaxle identification number is stamped on a pad on the forward side of the transaxle case, next to the middle transaxle-to-engine attaching bolt. The automatic transaxle identification number is stamped on the oil flange pad to the right of the oil dipstick, at the rear of the transaxle. The automatic transaxle model code tag is on top of the case, next to the shift lever.

ROUTINE MAINTENANCE

Routine maintenance is the self-explanatory term used to describe the sort of periodic work

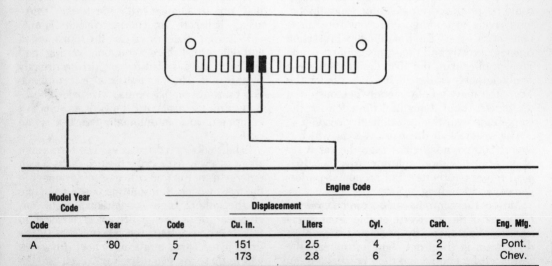

Model Year Code		Engine Code					
			Displacement				
Code	Year	Code	Cu. in.	Liters	Cyl.	Carb.	Eng. Mfg.
A	'80	5	151	2.5	4	2	Pont.
		7	173	2.8	6	2	Chev.

The thirteen digit Vehicle Identification Number can be used to determine engine application and model year. The 6th digit indicates the model year, and the 5th digit identifies the factory installed engine.

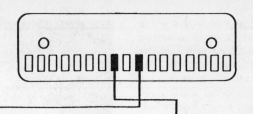

Model Year Code		Engine Code				
Code	Year	Code	Displacement Cu. In. (Liters)	Cyl.	Fuel Delivery System	Eng. Mfg.
B	'81	5	151 (2.5)	4	2-bbl.	Pontiac
		X	173 (2.8)	6	2-bbl.	Chevrolet
		Z	173 (2.8) HO	6	2-bbl.	Chevrolet
C	'82	R	151 (2.5)	4	T.B.I.	Pontiac
		5	151 (2.5)	4	2-bbl.	Pontiac
		X	173 (2.8)	6	2-bbl.	Chevrolet
		Z	173 (2.8) HO	6	2-bbl.	Chevrolet
D	'83	R	151 (2.5)	4	T.B.I.	Pontiac
		X	173 (2.8)	6	2-bbl.	Chevrolet
		Z	173 (2.8) HO	6	2-bbl.	Chevrolet
E	'84	R	151 (2.5)	4	T.B.I.	Pontiac
		5	151 (2.5)	4	2-bbl.	Pontiac
		X	173 (2.8)	6	2-bbl.	Chevrolet
		Z,W	173 (2.8) HO	6	2-bbl.	Chevrolet
F	'85	R	151 (2.5)	4	T.B.I.	Pontiac
		5	151 (2.5)	4	2-bbl.	Pontiac
		X	173 (2.8)	6	2-bbl.	Chevrolet
		Z,W	173 (2.8) HO	6	2-bbl.	Chevrolet

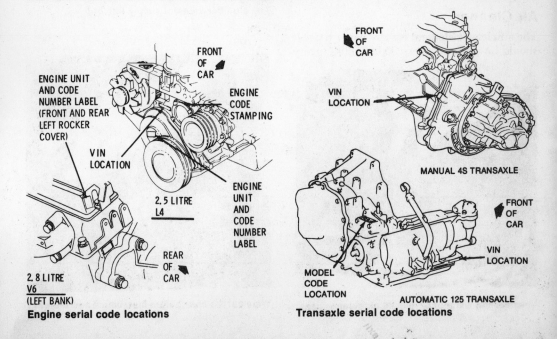

Engine serial code locations

Transaxle serial code locations

necessary to keep a car in safe and reliable working order. A regular program aimed at monitoring essential systems ensures that the car's components are functioning correctly (and will continue to do so until the next inspection, one hopes), and can prevent small problems from developing into major headaches. Routine maintenance also pays off big dividends in keeping major repair costs at a minimum, extending the life of the car, and enhancing resale value, should you ever desire to part with your X-car.

The Citation, Omega, Phoenix, and Skylark require less in the way of routine maintenance than any cars in recent memory. However, a very definite maintenance schedule is provided by General Motors, and must be followed, not only to keep the new car warranty in effect, but also to keep the car working properly. The "Maintenance Intervals" chart in this chapter outlines the routine maintenance which must be performed according to intervals based on either accumulated mileage or time. Your X-Body car also came with a maintenance schedule provided by G.M. Adherence to these schedules will result in a longer life for your car, and will, over the long run, save you money and time.

The checks and adjustments in the following sections generally require only a few minutes of attention every few weeks; the services to be performed can be easily accomplished in a morning. The most important part of any maintenance program is regularity. The few minutes or occasional morning spent on these seemingly trivial tasks will forestall or eliminate major problems later.

Air Cleaner

The air cleaner element is a dry paper type. It should be replaced every 30,000 miles (every

Remove the two nuts on the four cylinder air cleaner case

The old filter element simply lifts out

Unscrew the wingnut on the V6 air cleaner case

Wipe out the case before installing a new element

15,000 miles if the car is used in extremely dusty conditions) as follows:

1. Remove the wing nut (V6) or bolts (four cylinder) on top of the air cleaner housing which sits on top of the carburetor.

2. Remove the housing lid.

3. Lift out the old filter.

4. Before installing the new filter, wipe out the housing with a damp cloth. Check the lid gasket for a tight seal.

5. Install a new filter into the housing. Replace the lid and wing nut or bolts.

PCV Valve

The Positive Crankcase Ventilation (PCV) valve must be replaced every 30,000 miles (48,000 km.). Details on the PCV system, including system tests, are given in Chapter Four.

The valve is located in a rubber grommet in the valve cover, connected to the air cleaner housing by a large diameter rubber hose. To replace the valve:

1. Pull the valve (with the hose attached) from the rubber grommet in the valve cover.

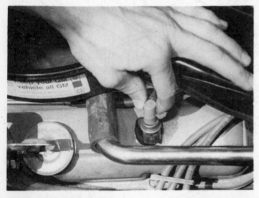

V6 PCV valve location

Four cylinder PCV valve location

Slide the clip on the outside of the air cleaner case to the right to release the four cylinder PCV filter

2. Remove the valve from the hose.
3. Install the new valve into the hose.
4. Install the valve in the grommet.

PCV FILTER

Four cylinder engines have a PCV filter located in the air cleaner housing which must be replaced at 30,000 mile (48,000 km.) intervals.

1. Remove the air cleaner housing lid.
2. Slide back the filter retaining clip.
3. Pull the old filter from the hose.
4. Install the new filter, replace the clip, and replace the lid.

Evaporation Control System Canister Filter

All models have a charcoal canister located in the engine compartment as part of the Evaporation Control System (ECS). Details on this system can be found in Chapter Four. Every 30,000 miles, or 24 months, the filter on the bottom of the charcoal canister must be changed. Cut the interval in half if the car is driven under extremely dusty conditions.

1. Locate the canister in the right front of

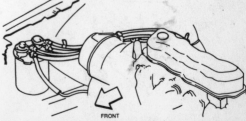

FRONT

The charcoal canister is located in the right front of the engine compartment

the engine compartment. It is held at the base by two bolts. Unbolt and lift the canister without disconnecting any of the hoses.

NOTE: *If there is not enough slack in the hoses to allow you to get at the filter, label them before removal. It is important to reconnect them properly.*

2. Turn the canister over. The filter, installed in the bottom, can simply be pulled out.

3. Install a new filter into the bottom of the canister.

4. Install the canister.

The ECS hoses should be inspected for cracks, kinks, or breaks at the time of filter replacement. If replacement hoses are necessary, use only hose designed for the purpose, which is usually marked "EVAP". This hose is available from your dealer or an automotive parts store.

Battery

The Citation, Omega, Phoenix and Skylark have a "maintenance free" battery as standard equipment, eliminating the need for fluid level checks and the possibility of specific gravity tests. Never-the-less, the battery does require some attention.

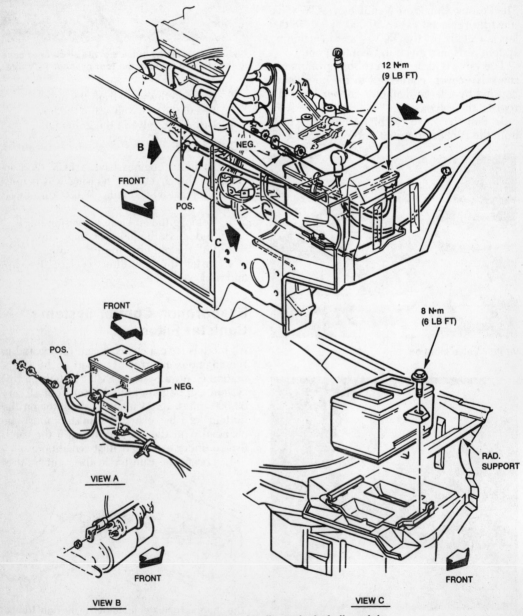

Battery installation details, typical of all models

Once a year, the battery terminals and the cable clamps should be cleaned. Remove the side terminal bolts and the cables, negative cable first. Clean the cable clamps and the battery terminals with a wire brush until all corrosion, grease, etc. is removed and the metal is shiny. It is especially important to clean the inside of the clamp thoroughly, since a small deposit of foreign material or oxidation there will prevent a sound electrical connection and inhabit either starting or charging. Special tools are available for cleaning the side terminal clamps and terminals.

Before installing the cables, loosen the battery hold-down clamp, remove the battery, and check the battery tray. Clear it of any debris and check it for soundness. Rust should be wire-brushed away, and the metal given a coat of anti-rust paint. Replace the battery and tighten the hold-down clamp securely, but be careful not to overtighten, which will crack the battery case.

After the clamps and terminals are clean, reinstall the cables, negative cable last. Give the clamps and terminals a thin external coat of grease after installation, to retard corrosion.

Check the cables at the same time that the terminals are cleaned. If the cable insulation is cracked or broken, or if the ends are frayed, the cable should be replaced with a new cable of the same length and gauge.

NOTE: *Keep flame or sparks away from the battery; it gives off explosive hydrogen gas. Battery electrolyte contains sulphuric acid. If you should get any on your skin or in your eyes, flush the affected areas with plenty of clear water; if it lands in your eyes, get medical help immediately.*

EFE Valve (Heat Riser)

The EFE valve, or heat riser, is part of the Early Fuel Evaporation system, described in Chapter Four. It is only used on the 1980 V6 engine. The EFE valve is a thermostatically-controlled, vacuum-operated valve in the right exhaust pipe (near the firewall). It closes when the engine is cold, to direct hot exhaust gases to the intake manifold, in order to preheat the incoming air/fuel mixture. If it sticks open, the result will be frequent stalling during warm-up, especially in cold and damp weather. If it sticks shut, the result will be a rough idle after the engine is warm.

The EFE valve should move freely. It can easily be checked when the engine is cold by pulling the actuating arm next to the vacuum motor to open and shut the valve. If the valve is sticking or binding, a quick shot of solvent especially made for the purpose should free it up. The EFE valve shaft is more easily reached from under the car. The solvent should be applied after the first 6 months or 7,500 miles, and then every 24 months or 30,000 miles thereafter—more often if sticking or binding problems occur.

If the valve is still stuck after application of the solvent, sometimes rapping the end of the shaft lightly with a hammer will break it loose. Otherwise, the components will have to be removed for further repairs.

NOTE: *The 1981 V6 engines continue to utilize the EFE system, but have replaced the valve with an electric heater insulator on the carburetor. There is no periodic maintenance other than replacement.*

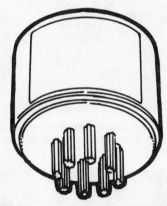

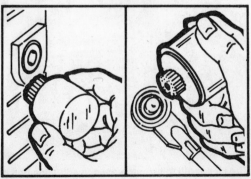

A special tool is available for cleaning the side terminals and clamps

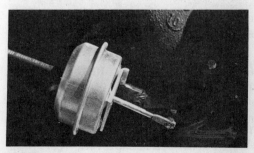

V6 EFE valve

Drive Belts

BELT TENSION

Every 12 months or 15,000 miles, check the water pump, alternator, power steering pump (if so equipped), and air conditioning compressor (if so equipped) drive belts for proper tension. Also look for signs of wear, fraying, separation, glazing and so on, and replace the belts as required.

Belt tension should be checked with a gauge made for the purpose. If a gauge is not available, tension can be checked with moderate thumb pressure applied to the belt at its longest span midway between pulleys. If the belt has a free span less than twelve inches, it should deflect approximately ⅛–¼ inch. If the span is longer than twelve inches, deflection can range between ⅛ and ⅜ inches.

1. Loosen the driven accessory's pivot and mounting bolts.

2. Move the accessory toward or away from the engine until the tension is correct. You can use a wooden hammer handle or a broomstick as a lever, but do not use anything metallic.

3. Tighten the bolts and recheck the tension. If new belts have been installed, run the engine for a few minutes, then recheck and readjust as necessary.

It is better to have belts too loose than too tight, because overtight belts will lead to bearing failure, particularly in the water pump and alternator. However, loose belts place an extremely high impact load on the driven component due to the whipping action of the belt.

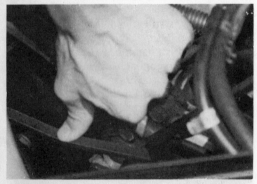
Belt tension can be checked with your thumb, but a gauge is recommended

Air Conditioning System

The air conditioning system requires no routine maintenance, except for belt tension adjustment periodically, as outlined previously. The air conditioning system should be operated for about five minutes each week, even in winter. This will circulate lubricating oil within the system to prevent the various seals from drying out.

The factory-installed air conditioning unit has no sight glass for system checks. It is recommended that all air conditioning service work be entrusted to a qualified mechanic. The system is a potentially hazardous one.

CAUTION: *Do not attempt to charge or discharge the refrigerant system unless you are thoroughly familiar with its operation and the hazards involved. The compressed refrigerant used in the air conditioning system expands and evaporates (boils) into the atmosphere at a temperature of $-21.7°F$ ($-29.8°C$) or less. This will freeze any surface that it contacts, including your eyes. In addition, the refrigerant decomposes into a poisonous gas in the presence of flame.*

All accessories have a slotted mount to adjust belt tension; this one belongs to the four cylinder's alternator

The air conditioning compressor's adjusting bolt is above the left arrow. You can lever the compressor in or out by inserting a ½ in. drive rachet into the square hole above the arrow on the right

HOW TO SPOT WORN V-BELTS

V-Belts are vital to efficient engine operation—they drive the fan, water pump and other accessories. They require little maintenance (occasional tightening) but they will not last forever. Slipping or failure of the V-belt will lead to overheating. If your V-belt looks like any of these, it should be replaced.

This belt has deep cracks, which cause it to flex. Too much flexing leads to heat build-up and premature failure. These cracks can be caused by using the belt on a pulley that is too small. Notched belts are available for small diameter pulleys.

Cracking or weathering

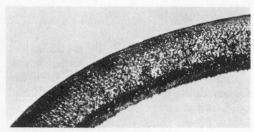

Oil and grease on a belt can cause the belt's rubber compounds to soften and separate from the reinforcing cords that hold the belt together. The belt will first slip, then finally fail altogether.

Softening (grease and oil)

Glazing is caused by a belt that is slipping. A slipping belt can cause a run-down battery, erratic power steering, overheating or poor accessory performance. The more the belt slips, the more glazing will be built up on the surface of the belt. The more the belt is glazed, the more it will slip. If the glazing is light, tighten the belt.

Glazing

The cover of this belt is worn off and is peeling away. The reinforcing cords will begin to wear and the belt will shortly break. When the belt cover wears in spots or has a rough jagged appearance, check the pulley grooves for roughness.

Worn cover

This belt is on the verge of breaking and leaving you stranded. The layers of the belt are separating and the reinforcing cords are exposed. It's just a matter of time before it breaks completely.

Separation

HOW TO SPOT BAD HOSES

Both the upper and lower radiator hoses are called upon to perform difficult jobs in an inhospitable environment. They are subject to nearly 18 psi at under hood temperatures often over 280°F., and must circulate nearly 7500 gallons of coolant an hour—3 good reasons to have good hoses.

A good test for any hose is to feel it for soft or spongy spots. Frequently these will appear as swollen areas of the hose. The most likely cause is oil soaking. This hose could burst at any time, when hot or under pressure.

Swollen hose

Cracked hoses can usually be seen but feel the hoses to be sure they have not hardened; a prime cause of cracking. This hose has cracked down to the reinforcing cords and could split at any of the cracks.

Cracked hose

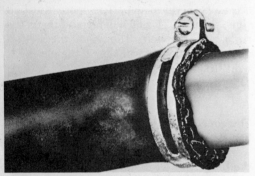

Weakened clamps frequently are the cause of hose and cooling system failure. The connection between the pipe and hose has deteriorated enough to allow coolant to escape when the engine is hot.

Frayed hose end (due to weak clamp)

Debris, rust and scale in the cooling system can cause the inside of a hose to weaken. This can usually be felt on the outside of the hose as soft or thinner areas.

Debris in cooling system

Windshield Wipers

For maximum effectiveness and longest element life, the windshield and wiper blades should be kept clean. Dirt, tree sap, road tar and so on will cause streaking, smearing and blade deterioration if left on the glass. It is advisable to wash the windshield carefully with a commercial glass cleaner at least once a month. Wipe off the rubber blades with the wet rag afterwards.

If the blades are found to be cracked, broken or torn, they should be replaced immediately. Replacement intervals will vary with usage, although ozone deterioration usually limits blade life to about one year. If the wiper pattern is smeared or streaked, or if the blade chatters across the glass, the elements should be replaced. It is easiest and most sensible to replace the elements in pairs.

The wiper blades are retained to the wiper arms by one of two methods. One uses a press-type release tab, which, when depressed, allows the blade to be separated from the arm. The other uses a coil spring retainer. By inserting a screwdriver on top of the spring and pressing downward, the blade can be separated from the arm.

The rubber wiper element can be replaced separately from the blade, which is usually less expensive than replacing both blade and element. As with the blades, two methods are used to retain the rubber element to the blade. On one, a press-type button is used which, when depressed, releases the element, which can be slid off the blade. On the other, a squeeze clip is used; squeezing the clip allows the element to be pulled from the blade. Replacements are simply slid back into place; be sure all the arms are engaged.

Tires

Tires should be checked weekly for proper air pressure. A chart, located at the left front door edge, gives the recommended inflation pressures. Maximum fuel economy and tire life will result if the pressure is maintained at the highest figure given on the chart. The tires should be checked before driving since pressure can increase as much as six pounds per square inch (psi) due to heat buildup. It is a good idea to have your own accurate pressure gauge, because not all gauges on service station air pumps can be trusted. When checking pressures, do not neglect the spare tire. Note

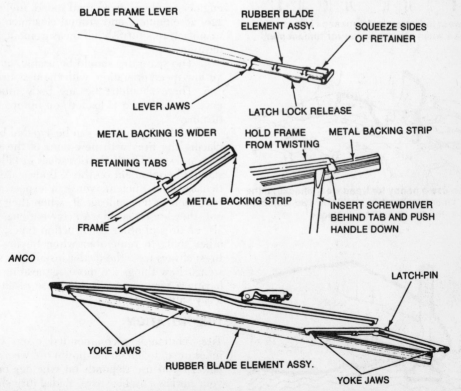

The rubber element can be changed without replacing the entire blade assembly; your X-car may have either one of these types of blades

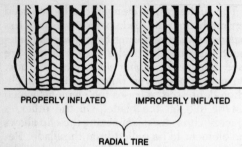

PROPERLY INFLATED   IMPROPERLY INFLATED

RADIAL TIRE

Don't judge a radial tire's pressure by its appearance. An improperly inflated radial tire looks similar to a properly inflated one

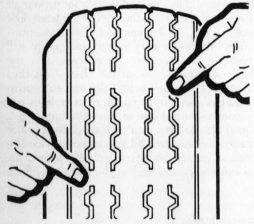

Tread wear indicators will appear as bands across the tread when the tire is due for replacement

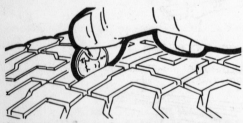

You can use a penny for tread wear checks; if the top of Lincoln's head is visible in two adjacent grooves, the tire should be replaced

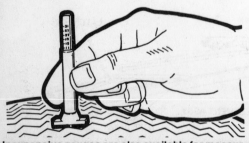

Inexpensive gauges are also available for measuring tread wear

that some spare tires require pressures considerably higher than those used in the other tires.

While you are about the task of checking air pressure, inspect the tire treads for cuts, bruises, and other damage. Check the air valves to be sure that they are tight. Replace any missing valve caps.

Check the tires for uneven wear that might indicate the need for front end alignment or tire rotation. Tires should be replaced when a tread wear indicator appears as a solid band across the tread.

When buying new tires, give some thought to the following points, especially if you are considering a switch to larger tires or a different profile series:

1. All four tires should be of the same construction type. Radial, bias, or bias-belted tires should not be mixed.

2. The wheels must be the correct width for the tire. Tire dealers have charts of tire and wheel rim compatibility. A mismatch can cause sloppy handling and rapid tread wear. The tread width should match the rim width (inside bead to inside bead) within an inch. For radial tires, the rim width should be 80% or less of the tire (not tread) width.

3. The height (mounted diameter) of the new tires can change speedometer accuracy, engine speed per given road speed, fuel mileage, acceleration, and ground clearance. Tire manufacturers furnish full measurement specifications.

4. The spare tire should be usable, at least for low speed operation, with the new tires.

5. There shouldn't be any body interference when the car is loaded, on bumps or in turning.

All of these problems can be avoided by replacing the tires with new ones of the same type and size. The P-metric radials installed as standard equipment on the X-Bodies are particularly fuel-efficient; you can expect some reduction in fuel mileage if, when they wear out, they are replaced with conventional radials, or tires of other construction types. One other thing to remember when buying new tires: always have the dealer install new valve stems. Few things are more aggravating than having a new tire go flat because of an old, leaky valve stem.

TIRE ROTATION

Tire rotation is recommended every 6,000 miles or so, to obtain maximum tire wear. The pattern you use depends on whether or not your car has a usable spare. Radial tires should not be cross-switched (from one side of the car to the other); they last longer if their direction

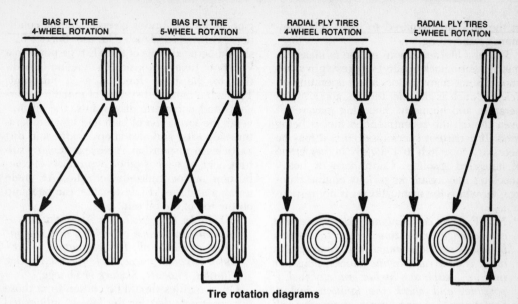

| BIAS PLY TIRE 4-WHEEL ROTATION | BIAS PLY TIRE 5-WHEEL ROTATION | RADIAL PLY TIRES 4-WHEEL ROTATION | RADIAL PLY TIRES 5-WHEEL ROTATION |

Tire rotation diagrams

of rotation is not changed. Snow tires sometimes have directional arrows molded into the side of the carcass; the arrow shows the direction of rotation. They will wear very rapidly if their rotation is reversed. Studded tires will lose their studs if their rotational direction is reversed. Mark the wheel position or direction of rotation on radial tires or studded snow tires before removing them to avoid these problems.

Fuel Filter

CARBURETTED ENGINES

All models have a fuel filter located within the carburetor body. The fuel filter has a check valve to prevent fuel spillage in the event of an accident. When the filter is replaced, make sure the new one is of the same type. All fil-ters are of the paper element type. Replace the filter every 15,000 miles.

1. Place a few absorbent rags underneath the fuel line where it joins the carburetor.

2. Disconnect the fuel line connection at the fuel inlet nut.

3. Unscrew the fuel inlet nut from the carburetor. As the nut is removed, the filter will be pushed partway out by spring pressure.

4. Remove the filter and spring.

5. Install the new spring and filter. The hole in the filter faces the nut.

6. Install a new gasket on the inlet nut and install the nut into the carburetor. Tighten securely.

7. Install the fuel line. Tighten the connector to 18 ft. lbs. (24 Nm.) while holding the inlet nut with a wrench.

8. Start the engine and check for leaks.

FUEL INJECTED ENGINES

The filter is an inline unit ahead of the TBI unit. To remove the filter, make sure the engine is cold, unclamp and remove the fuel hose, then unscrew the filter from the steel fuel line. Installation is the reverse of removal.

FLUIDS AND LUBRICANTS

Fuel Recommendations

All G.M. X-Body cars must use unleaded fuel. The use of leaded fuel will plug the catalyst rendering it inoperative, and will increase the exhaust back pressure to the point where engine output will be severely reduced. The minimum octane for both the four cylinder and V6 engines is 91 RON. All unleaded fuels sold

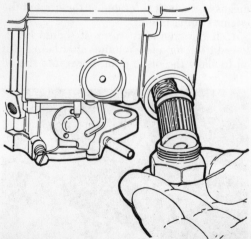

The fuel filter is located behind the fuel inlet nut in the carburetor body

in the U.S. are required to meet this minimum octane rating.

Use of a fuel too low in octane (a measurement of anti-knock quality) will result in spark knock. Since many factors affect operating efficiency, such as altitude, terrain, and air temperature and humidity, knocking may result even though the recommended fuel is being used. If persistent knocking occurs, it may be necessary to switch to a slightly higher grade of unleaded gasoline. Continuous or heavy knocking may result in serious engine damage, for which the manufacturer is not responsible.

NOTE: *Your car's engine fuel requirement can change with time, due to carbon buildup, which changes the compression ratio. If your car's engine knocks, pings, or runs on, switch to a higher grade of fuel, if possible, and check the ignition timing. Sometimes changing brands of gasoline will cure the problem. If it is necessary to retard timing from specifications, don't change it more than a few degrees. Retarded timing will reduce power output and fuel mileage, and will increase engine temperature.*

Engine

OIL RECOMMENDATION

The SAE (Society of Automotive Engineers) grade number indicates the viscosity of the engine oil, and thus its ability to lubricate at a given temperature. The lower the SAE grade number, the lighter the oil; the lower the viscosity, the easier it is to crank the engine in cold weather.

The API (American Petroleum Institute) designation indicates the classification of engine oil for use under given operating conditions. Only oils designated for use "Service SE" should be used. Oils of the SE type perform a variety of functions inside the engine in addition to the basic function as a lubricant. Through a balanced system of metallic detergents and polymeric dispersants, the oil prevents the formation of high and low temperature deposits, and also keeps sludge and dirt particles in suspension. Acids, particularly sulfuric acid, as well as other byproducts of combustion, are neutralized. Both the SAE grade number and the API designation can be found on the top of the oil can.

NOTE: *In late 1980, the American Petroleum Institute came out with a new classification of motor oil. Its designation is "SF" and it is equally acceptable for use in your Citation, Phoenix, Skylark or Omega.*

Oil viscosities should be chosen from those oils recommended for the lowest anticipated temperatures during the oil change interval.

Multi-viscosity oils offer the important advantage of being adaptable to temperature extremes. They allow easy starting at low temperatures, yet give good protection at high speeds and engine temperatures. This is a decided advantage in changeable climates or in long distance touring.

OIL LEVEL CHECK

The engine oil level should be checked at every fuel stop, or once a week, whichever occurs more regularly. The best time to check is when the engine is warm, although checking immediately after the engine has been shut off will result in an inaccurate reading, since it takes a few minutes for all of the oil to drain back down into the crankcase. If the engine is cold, the engine should not be run before the level is checked. The oil level is checked by means of a dipstick, located at the front of the engine compartment:

1. If the engine is warm, it should be allowed to sit for a few minutes after being shut off to allow the oil to drain down into the oil

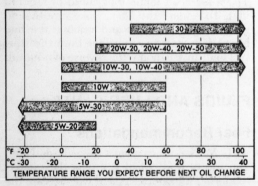

USE THESE SAE VISCOSITY GRADES

| 30 |
| 20W-20, 20W-40, 20W-50 |
| 10W-30, 10W-40 |
| 10W |
| 5W-30 |
| 5W-20 |

°F -20 0 20 40 60 80 100
°C -30 -20 -10 0 10 20 30 40
TEMPERATURE RANGE YOU EXPECT BEFORE NEXT OIL CHANGE

NOTICE: DO NOT USE SAE 5W-20 OILS FOR CONTINUOUS HIGH-SPEED DRIVING. 5W-30 OILS MAY BE USED UP TO 100°F (38°C)

Oil viscosity chart; multi-viscosity oils offer greater temperature latitude

V6 oil dipstick location

pan. The car should be parked on a level surface.

2. Pull the dipstick out from its holder, wipe it clean with a rag, and reinsert it firmly. Be sure it is pushed all the way home, or the reading you're about to take will be incorrect.

3. Pull the dipstick again and hold it horizontally to prevent the oil from running. The dipstick on the four cylinder engine is marked with "Add" and "Full" lines. The V6 engine dipstick is marked "Add 1 Qt." and "Full." The oil level should be above the "Add" line.

4. Reinstall the dipstick.

If oil is needed, it is added through the capped opening in the engine valve cover. One

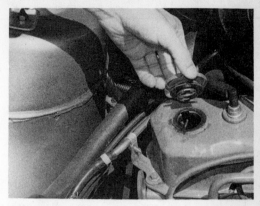

Four cylinder oil filler location

Four cylinder oil dipstick location

Keep the oil level between the "Add" and "Full" marks

V6 oil filler location

quart of oil will raise the level from "Add" to "Full". Only oils labeled "SE" or "SF" should be used; select a viscosity that will be compatible with the temperatures expected until the next drain interval. See the "Oil and Fuel Recommendations" section later in this chapter if you are not sure what type of oil to use. Check the oil level again after any additions. Be careful not to overfill, which will lead to leakage and seal damage.

CHANGING OIL AND FILTER

If you purchased your X-Body car new, the engine oil and filter should be changed at the first 7,500 miles or 12 months (whichever comes first), and every 7,500 miles or 12 months thereafter. You should make it a practice to change the oil filter at every oil change; otherwise, a quart of dirty oil remains in the engine every other time the oil is changed. The change interval should be halved when the car is driven under severe conditions, such as in extremely dusty weather, or when the car is used for trailer towing, prolonged high speed driving, or repeated short trips in freezing weather.

1. Drive the car until the engine is at normal operating temperature. A run to the parts store for oil and a filter should accomplish this. If the engine is not hot when the oil is changed, most of the acids and contaminants will remain inside the engine.

2. Shut off the engine, and slide a pan of at least six quarts capacity under the oil pan. Throw-away aluminum roasting pans can be used for this.

3. Remove the drain plug from the engine oil pan, after wiping the plug area clean. The drain plug is the bolt inserted at an angle into the lowest point of the oil pan.

4. The oil from the engine will be HOT. It will probably not be possible to hold onto

the drain plug. You may have to let it fall into the pan and fish it out later. Allow all the oil to drain completely. This will take a few minutes.

5. Wipe off the drain plug, removing any traces of metal particles. Pay particular attention to the threads. Replace it, and tighten it snugly.

6. The oil filter for the V6 engine is right up front, just behind the radiator. The four cylinder oil filter is at the back of the engine. It is impossible to reach from above, and almost as inaccessible from below. It may be easiest to remove the right front wheel and reach through the fender opening to get at the four cylinder oil filter. Use an oil filter strap wrench to loosen the oil filter; these are available at auto parts stores. It is recommended that you purchase one with as thin a strap as possible, to get into tight areas. Place the drain pan on the ground, under the filter. Unscrew and discard the old filter. It will be VERY HOT, so be careful.

7. If the oil filter is on so tightly that it collapses under pressure from the wrench, drive a long punch or a nail through it, across the diameter and as close to the base as possible, and use this as a lever to unscrew it. Make sure you are turning it counterclockwise.

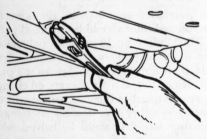

The oil drain plug is located at the lowest point of the oil pan

The V6 oil filter is right up front

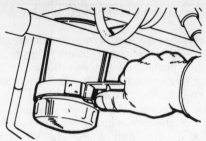

Use an oil filter strap wrench to remove the oil filter; install the new filter by hand

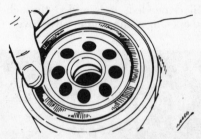

Apply a thin film of clean oil to the new filter gasket to prevent it from tearing upon installation

8. Clean off the oil filter mounting surface with a rag. Apply a thin film of clean engine oil to the filter gasket.

9. Screw the filter on by hand until the gasket makes contact. Then tighten it by hand an additional ½ to ¾ of a turn. *Do not overtighten.*

10. Remove the filler cap on the rocker (valve) cover, after wiping the area clean.

11. Add the correct number of quarts of oil specified in the "Capacities" chart. If you don't have an oil can spout, you will need a funnel. Be certain you do not overfill the engine, which can cause serious damage. Replace the cap.

Recommended Lubricants

Lubricant	Classification
Engine Oil	API SE
Manual Transaxle	DEXRON® II
Automatic Transaxle	DEXRON® II
Power Steering	Power Steering Fluid
Chassis Grease	EP Grease meeting G.M. specification 6031-M
Brake Fluid	DOT 3
Antifreeze	Ethylene Glycol
Clutch Linkage Pivot points Push rod to fork joint	Engine Oil Chassis Grease
Transaxle Shift Linkage	Engine Oil

12. Check the oil level on the dipstick. It is normal for the level to be a bit above the full mark. Start the engine and allow it to idle for a few minutes.

CAUTION: *Do not run the engine above idle speed until it has built up oil pressure, indicated when the oil light goes out.*
Check around the filter and drain plug for any leaks.

13. Shut off the engine, allow the oil to drain for a minute, and check the oil level.

After completing this job, you will have several quarts of filthy oil to dispose of. The best thing to do with it is to funnel it into old plastic milk containers or bleach bottles. Then, you can either pour it into the recycling barrel at the gas station (if you're on good terms with the attendant), or put the containers into the trash.

Transaxle

FLUID RECOMMENDATION AND LEVEL CHECK

Manual

The fluid level in the manual transaxle should be checked every 12 months or 7,500 miles, whichever comes first.

1. Park the car on a level surface. The transaxle should be cool to the touch. If it is hot, check the level later, when it has cooled.

2. Slowly remove the filler hole plug from the left side of the transaxle. If lubricant trickles out as the plug is removed, the fluid level is correct. If not, stick in your finger (watch out for sharp threads); the lubricant should be right up to the edge of the filler hole.

3. If lubricant is needed, add DEXRON® II automatic transmission fluid until the level is correct. The use of a manual transmission lubricant is specifically *not* recommended.

4. When the level is correct, install the filler plug and tighten until snug.

Automatic

The fluid level in the automatic transaxle should be checked every 12 months or 7,500 miles, whichever comes first. The transaxle has a dipstick for fluid level checks.

1. Drive the car until it is at normal operating temperature. The level should not be checked immediately after the car has been driven for a long time at high speed, or in city traffic in hot weather; in those cases, the transaxle should be given a half hour to cool down.

2. Stop the car, apply the parking brake, then shift slowly through all gear positions, ending in Park. Let the engine idle for about five minutes with the transmission in Park. The car should be on a level surface.

3. With the engine still running, remove the dipstick, wipe it clean, then reinsert it, pushing it fully home.

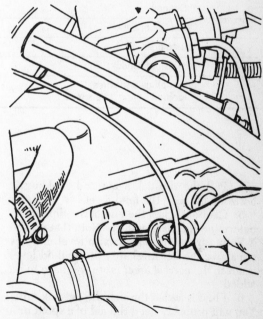

Automatic transaxle fluid dipstick and filler hole location

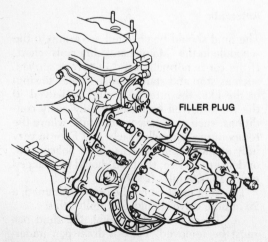

FILLER PLUG

Manual transaxle filler plug

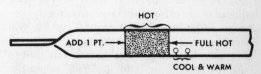

Automatic transaxle dipstick markings

Maintenance Intervals Chart

Intervals are for number of months or thousands of miles, whichever comes first.

NOTE: *Heavy-duty operation (trailer towing, prolonged idling, severe stop and start driving) should be accompanied by a 50% increase in maintenance. Cut the interval in half for these conditions.*

Maintenance	Service Interval
Air cleaner (Replace)	30,000 mi. (48,000 km.)
PCV filter element (Replace)	30,000 mi. 48,000 km.)
PCV valve (Replace)	30,000 mi. (48,000 km.)
Carbon canister filter (Replace)	30,000 mi. (48,000 km.)
EFE system check	6 mo/7,500 mi. (12,000 km.), then every 24 mo/30,000 mi (48,000 km.)
Belt tension (Adjust)	12 mo/15,000 mi. (24,000 km.)
Engine oil and filter (Change)	12 mo/7,500 mi. (12,000 km.)
Fuel filter (Change)	15,000 mi. (24,000 km.)
Manual transaxle Check Change	 12 mo/7,500 mi. (12,000 km.) 100,000 mi. (160,000 km.)
Automatic transaxle Check Change (including filter)	 12 mo/7,500 mi. (12,000 km.) 100,000 mi. (160,000 km.)
Engine coolant Check Change	 Weekly 12 mo/15,000 mi. (24,000 km.)
Chassis lubrication	12 mo/7,500 mi. (12,000 km.)
Rotate tires	7,500 mi. (12,000 km.)
Brake fluid (Check)	12 mo/7,500 mi. (12,000 km.)
Spark plugs and wires, ignition timing, idle speed	30,000 mi. (48,000 Km.) See Chapter Two

4. Pull the dipstick again and, holding it horizontally, read the fluid level.

5. Cautiously feel the end of the dipstick to determine the temperature. Note that on the X-Body cars the cool and warm level dimples are above the hot level area. If the fluid level is not in the correct area, more will have to be added.

6. Fluid is added through the dipstick tube. You will probably need the aid of a spout or a long-necked funnel. Be sure that whatever you pour through is perfectly clean and dry. Use an automatic transmission fluid marked "DEXRON® II." Add fluid slowly, and in small amounts, checking the level frequently between additions. Do not overfill, which will cause foaming, fluid loss, slippage, and possible transaxle damage. It takes only one pint to raise the level from "Add" to "Full" when the transaxle is hot.

DRAIN AND REFILL

Automatic

The fluid should be changed according to the schedule in the "Maintenance Intervals" chart. If the car is normally used in severe service, such as stop and start driving, trailer towing, or the like, the interval should be halved. If the car is driven under especially nasty conditions, such as in heavy city traffic where the temperature normally reaches 90°F, or in very hilly or mountainous areas, or in police, taxi, or delivery service, the fluid should be changed every 15,000 miles (24,000 km.).

The fluid must be hot before it is drained; a 20 minute drive should accomplish this.

1. There is no drain plug; the fluid pan must be removed. Place a drain pan underneath the transaxle pan and remove the pan

attaching bolts at the front and sides of the pan.

2. Loosen the rear pan attaching bolts approximately four turns each.

3. Very carefully pry the pan loose. You can use a screwdriver for this if you work CAREFULLY. Do not distort the pan flange, or score the mating surface of the transaxle case. You'll be very sorry later if you do. As the pan is pried loose, all of the fluid is going to come pouring out.

4. Remove the remaining bolts and remove the pan and gasket. Throw away the gasket.

5. Clean the pan with solvent and allow it to air dry. If you use a rag to wipe out the pan, you risk leaving bits of lint behind, which will

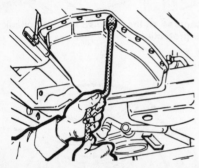

Many late model vehicles have no drain plug. Loosen the pan bolts and allow one corner of the pan to tilt slightly to drain the fluid

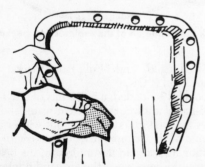

Clean the pan thoroughly with gasoline and allow to air dry completely

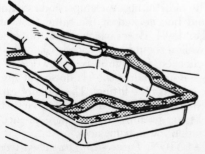

Install a new gasket on the pan

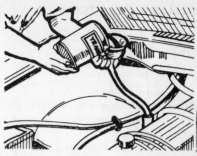

Fill the transmission with the required amount of fluid. Do not overfill. Start the engine and shift through all gears. Check the fluid level and add fluid if necessary

clog the dinky hydraulic passages in the transaxle.

6. Remove and discard the filter and the O-ring seal.

7. Install a new filter and O-ring, locating the filter against the dipstick stop.

8. Install a new gasket on the pan and install the pan. Tighten the bolts evenly and in rotation to 12 ft. lbs. (16 Nm.). Do not overtighten.

9. Add approximately 4 qts. (2.8 L) of DEXRON® II automatic transmission fluid to the transaxle through the dipstick tube. You will need a long necked funnel, or a funnel and tube to do this.

10. With the transaxle in Park, put on the parking brake, block the front wheels, start the engine and let it idle. DO NOT RACE THE ENGINE. DO NOT MOVE THE LEVER THROUGH ITS RANGES.

11. With the lever in Park, check the fluid level. If it's ok, take the car out for a short drive, park on a level surface, and check the level again, as outlined earlier in this chapter. Add more fluid if necessary. Be careful not to overfill, which will cause foaming and fluid loss.

NOTE: *If the drained fluid is discolored (brown or black), thick, or smells burnt, serious transmission troubles, probably due to overheating, should be suspected. Your car's transaxle should be inspected by a reliable transmission specialist to determine the problem.*

Manual

The fluid in the manual transaxle should be changed at the interval specified in the "Maintenance Intervals" chart, or more often if the car is used under severe conditions. You may also want to change it if you have purchased your X-car used, or if it has been driven in water deep enough to reach the transaxle case.

1. The fluid should be hot before it is drained. If the car is driven until the engine is

at normal operating temperature, the fluid should be hot enough.

2. Remove the filler plug from the left side of the transaxle to provide a vent.

3. The drain plug is located on the bottom of the transaxle case. Place a pan under the drain plug and remove it.

CAUTION: *The fluid will be HOT. Push up against the threads as you unscrew the plug to prevent leakage.*

4. Allow the fluid to drain completely. Check the condition of the plug gasket, and replace it if necessary. It will probably be ok. Clean off the plug and replace, tightening until snug.

5. Fill the transaxle with fluid through the filler hole in the left side. Use only DEXRON® II automatic transmission fluid to fill the transaxle. DO NOT use conventional manual transmission lubricants. You will need the aid of a long necked funnel or a funnel and a hose to pour through. Lubricant capacity is only three quarts (2.8 L); do not overfill.

6. The fluid should come right up to the edge of the filler hole. You can stick your finger in to verify this. Watch out for sharp threads.

7. Replace the filler plug. Dispose of the old fluid in the same manner as old engine oil. Take a drive in your car, stop on a level surface, and check the fluid level.

Coolant

FLUID RECOMMENDATIONS AND LEVEL CHECK

Once a month, the engine coolant level should be checked. This is quickly accomplished by observing the level of coolant in the recovery tank, which is the translucent tank mounted to the right of the radiator, and connected to the radiator filler neck by a length of hose. As long as coolant is visible in the tank between

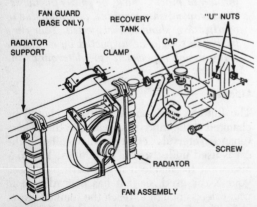

FAN GUARD (BASE ONLY)   RECOVERY TANK   "U" NUTS
RADIATOR SUPPORT   CAP
CLAMP
SCREW
RADIATOR
FAN ASSEMBLY

The coolant recovery tank is at the right front of the engine compartment

You can use an inexpensive tester to check antifreeze protection

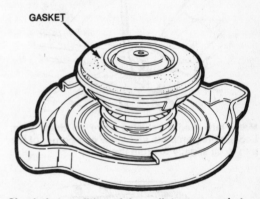

GASKET

Check the condition of the radiator cap gasket

the "Full Cold" and "Full Hot" marks, the coolant level is OK.

If coolant is needed, a 50/50 mix of ethylene glycol-based antifreeze and clear water should always be used for additions, both winter and summer. This is imperative on cars with air conditioning; without the antifreeze, the heater core could freeze when the air conditioning is used. Add coolant to the recovery tank through the capped opening; make additions only when the engine is cool.

The radiator hoses, clamps, and radiator cap should be checked at the same time as the coolant level. Hoses which are brittle, cracked, or swollen should be replaced. Clamps should be checked for tightness (screwdriver tight only—do not allow the clamp to cut into the hose or crush the fitting). The radiator cap gasket should be checked for any obvious tears, cracks, or swelling, or any signs of incorrect seating in the radiator neck.

CAUTION: *To avoid injury when working with a hot engine, cover the radiator cap*

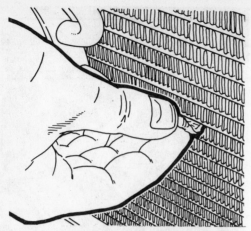

Clean the front of the radiator of any bugs, leaves, or other debris at every yearly coolant change

with a thick cloth. Wear a heavy glove to protect your hand. Turn the radiator cap slowly to the first stop, and allow all the pressure to vent (indicated when the hissing noise stops). When the pressure has been released, press down and remove the cap the rest of the way.

DRAIN SYSTEM, FLUSH AND REFILL

The cooling system should be drained, flushed and refilled every two years or 30,000 miles, according to the manufacturer's recommendations. However, many mechanics prefer to change the coolant every year; it is cheap insurance against corrosion, overheating or freezing.

1. Remove the radiator cap when the engine is cool. See the preceding "CAUTION" about removing the cap.
2. With the radiator cap removed, run the engine until heat can be felt in the upper hose, indicating that the thermostat is open. The heater should be turned on to its maximum heat position, so that the core is flushed out.
3. Shut off the engine and open the drain cock in the bottom of the radiator.
4. Close the drain cock and fill the system with clear water. A cooling system flushing additive can be added, if desired.
5. Run the engine until it is hot again.
6. Drain the system, then flush with water until it runs clear.
7. Clean out the coolant recovery tank: remove the cap leaving the hoses in place. Remove the tank and drain it of any coolant. Clean it out with soap and water, empty it, and install it.
8. Close the drain cock and fill the radiator with a 50/50 mix of ethylene glycol base antifreeze and water to the base of the radiator filler neck. Fill the coolant recovery tank with

the same solution to the "Full Hot" mark. Install the recovery tank cap.

9. Run the engine until the upper radiator hose is hot again (radiator cap still off). With the engine idling, add the 50/50 mix of antifreeze and water to the radiator until the level reaches the bottom of the filler neck. Shut off the engine and install the radiator cap, aligning the arrows with the overflow tube. Turn off the heater.

Master Cylinder

FLUID RECOMMENDATION AND LEVEL CHECK

Once a month, the fluid level in the brake master cylinder should be checked.

1. Park the car on a level surface.
2. Clean off the master cylinder cover before removal.
3. The cover simply snaps onto the master cylinder body. Use your thumbs to press up on the two tabs on the side of the cover to unsnap it. Remove the cover, being careful not

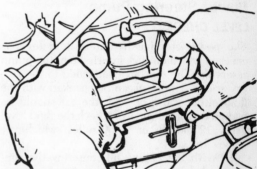

Use thumb pressure to remove the brake master cylinder cover

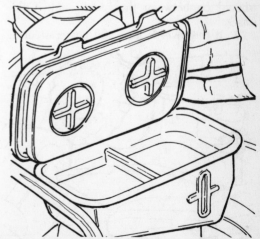

Proper brake fluid level; non-power brakes do not have the see-through window on the side of the reservoir

to drop or tear the rubber diaphragm underneath. Be careful also not to drip any brake fluid on painted surfaces; the stuff eats paint.

NOTE: *Brake fluid absorbs moisture from the air, which reduces effectiveness, and will corrode brake parts once in the system. Never leave the master cylinder or the brake fluid container uncovered for any longer than necessary.*

4. The fluid level should be about ¼ inch below the lip of the master cylinder well.

5. If fluid addition is necessary, use only extra heavy duty disc brake fluid meeting DOT 3 specifications. The fluid should be reasonably fresh because brake fluid deteriorates with age.

6. Replace the cover, making sure that the diaphragm is correctly seated.

If the brake fluid level is constantly low, the system should be checked for leaks. However, it is normal for the fluid level to fall gradually as the disc brake pads wear; expect the fluid level to drop not more than ⅛ inch for every 10,000 miles of wear.

Power Steering Pump

LEVEL CHECK

The power steering hydraulic fluid level is checked with a dipstick inserted into the pump reservoir. The dipstick is attached to the reservoir cap. The level can be checked with the fluid either warm or cold; the car should be parked on a level surface. Check the fluid level every 12 months or 7,500 miles, whichever comes first.

1. With the engine off, unscrew the dipstick and check the level. If the engine is warm, the level should be between the "Hot" and "Cold" marks. If the engine is cold, the level should be between the "Add" and "Cold" marks.

2. If the level is low, add power steering

The V6 power steering reservoir is at the right rear of the engine compartment. We couldn't get a photograph of it with the engine in the car, but don't let its inaccessibility prevent you from checking it regularly

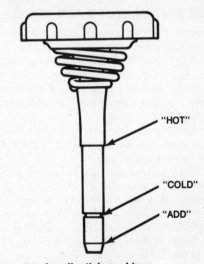

Power steering dipstick markings

fluid until correct. Be careful not to overfill, which will cause fluid loss and seal damage.

Steering Gear

The rack and pinion steering gear used on the X-Body cars is a sealed unit; no fluid level checks or additions are ever necessary.

Chassis Greasing

There are only two areas which require regular chassis greasing: the front suspension components and the steering linkage. These parts should be greased every 12 months or 7,500

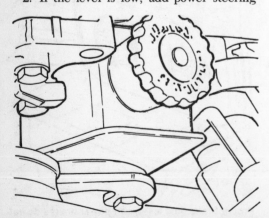

The power steering reservoir dipstick is attached to the cap; the four cylinder reservoir is right up front, behind the radiator

Capacities

Year	Engine Displacement Cu In.	Crankcase Quarts		Transaxle Pints		Gas Tank Gal	Cooling System Qts	
		w/filter	wo/filter	4 speed	Auto		w/heater	w/AC
1980–83	151	3.0	3.0	6.0	10.0	14.0	9.5	9.75
	173	4.0	4.0	6.0	10.0	14.0	11.5	11.75
1984–85	151	4.0	3.0	6.0	10.5	14.6	8¾	9
	173	5.0	4.0	6.0	10.5	15.1	10½	11

miles (12,000 Km.) with an EP grease meeting G.M. specification 6031M.

If you choose to do this job yourself, you will need to purchase a hand operated grease gun, if you do not own one already, and a long flexible extension hose to reach the various grease fittings. You will also need a cartridge of the appropriate grease.

Press the fitting on the grease gun hose onto the grease fitting on the suspension or steering linkage component. Pump a few shots of grease into the fitting, until the rubber boot on the joint begins to expand, indicating that the joint is full. Remove the gun from the fitting. Be careful not to overfill the joints, which will rupture the rubber boots, allowing the entry of dirt. You can keep the grease fittings clean by covering them with a small square of tin foil.

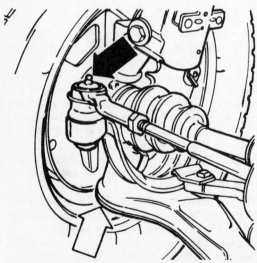

Grease the steering linkage at the knuckle (black arrow) and the ball joint at the lower arm (above the white arrow)

Body Lubrication

Every 12 months or 7,500 miles (12,000 km.), the various linkages and hinges on the chassis and body should be lubricated, as follows:

TRANSAXLE SHIFT LINKAGE

Lubricate the manual transaxle shift linkage contact points with the EP grease used for chassis greasing, which should meet G.M. specification 6031M. The automatic transaxle linkage should be lubricated with clean engine oil.

HOOD LATCH AND HINGES

Clean the latch surfaces and apply clean engine oil to the latch pilot bolts and the spring anchor. Use the engine oil to lubricate the hood hinges as well. Use a chassis grease to lubricate all the pivot points in the latch release mechanism.

DOOR HINGES

The gas tank filler door, car door, and rear hatch or trunk lid hinges should be wiped clean and lubricated with clean engine oil. Silicone spray also works well on these parts, but must be applied more often. Use engine oil to lubricate the trunk or hatch lock mechanism and the lock bolt and striker. The door lock cylinders can be lubricated easily with a shot of silicone spray or one of the many dry penetrating lubricants commercially available.

PARKING BRAKE LINKAGE

Use chassis grease on the parking brake cable where it contacts the guides, links, levers, and pulleys. The grease should be a water resistant one for durability under the car.

ACCELERATOR LINKAGE

Lubricate the carburetor stud, carburetor lever, and the accelerator pedal lever at the support inside the car with clean engine oil.

Wheel Bearings

The front wheel bearings are sealed, non-adjustable units which require no periodic attention. They are bolted to the steering knuckle by means of an integral flange.

PUSHING AND TOWING

The X-Body cars may not be pushed or towed to start, because doing so may cause the catalytic converter to explode. If the battery is weak, the engine may be jump started, using the procedure outlined in the following section.

Your Citation, Omega, Phoenix, or Skylark may be towed on all four wheels at speeds less than 35 mph (60 km/h) for distances up to 50 miles (80 km). The driveline and steering must be normally operable. If either one is damaged, the car may not be flat-towed. If the car is flat-towed (on all four wheels), the steering must be unlocked, the transaxle shifted to Neutral, and the parking brake released. Towing attachment must be made to the main structural members of the chassis, not to the bumpers or sheetmetal.

The car may be towed on its rear wheels by a wrecker; make sure that safety chains are used. X-Body cars with manual transaxles may be towed on their front wheels, for short distances and at low speeds. Be sure the transaxle is in Neutral. Cars with automatic transaxles should not be towed on their front wheels; transaxle damage may result. If it is impossible to tow the car on its rear wheels, place the front wheels on a dolly.

JUMP STARTING

Jump starting is the only way to start an automatic transaxle model with a weak battery, and the best method for a manual transaxle model.

CAUTION: *Do not attempt this procedure on a frozen battery; it will probably explode.*

The battery in the other vehicle must be a 12 volt, negatively grounded one. Do not attempt to jump start your car with a 24 volt power source; serious electrical damage will result.

1. Turn off all electrical equipment. Place the automatic transaxle in Park or the manual in Neutral and set the parking brake.

2. Make sure that the two vehicles are not touching. It is a good idea to keep the engine running in the booster vehicle.

3. Remove the caps from both batteries and cover the openings with cloths. This step can be ignored with "maintenance free" batteries.

4. Attach one end of a jumper cable to the positive (+) terminal of the booster battery. The red cable is usually positive. Attach the other end to the positive terminal of the discharged battery.

CAUTION: *Be very careful about these*

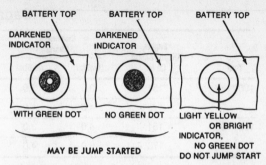

Check the appearance of the charge indicator on top of the battery before attempting a jump start; if it's not green or dark, do not jump start the car

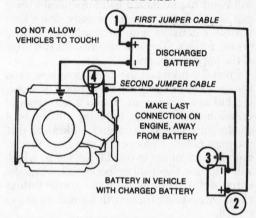

Cable connections for jump starting

connections. An alternator and regulator can be destroyed in a remarkably short time if battery polarity is reversed.

5. Attach one end of the other cable (the black one) to the negative (−) terminal of the booster battery. Attach the other end to a ground point such as the alternator bracket on the engine of the car being started. Do not connect it to the battery.

CAUTION: *Be careful not to lean over the battery while making this last connection.*

6. If the engine will not start, disconnect the batteries as soon as possible. If this is not done, the two batteries will soon reach a state of equilibrium, with both too weak to start an engine. This is no problem if the engine of the booster vehicle is running fast enough to keep up the charge. Lengthy cranking can also damage the starter.

7. Reverse the procedure exactly to remove the jumper cables. Discard the rags, because they may have acid on them.

NOTE: *It is recognized that some or all of the precautions outlined in this procedure are often ignored with no harmful results.*

However, the procedure outlined is the only fully safe, foolproof one.

JACKING AND HOISTING

The X-Body cars are supplied with a jack for changing tires. This is a bumper jack, engaging slots in the bumpers by means of a hook. This jack is satisfactory for its intended purpose; it is not meant to support the car while you go crawling around underneath it. *Never crawl under the car when it is supported by only the bumper jack.*

The car may also be jacked at the rear axle between the spring seats, or at the front end at the engine cradle crossbar or lower control arm. The car must never be lifted by the rear lower control arms.

The car can be raised on a four point hoist which contacts the chassis at points just behind the front wheels and just ahead of the rear wheels, as shown in the accompanying diagram. Be certain that the lift pads do not contact the catalytic converter.

It is imperative that strict safety precautions be observed both while raising the car and in the subsequent support after the car is raised. If a jack is used to raise the car, the transaxle should be shifted to Park (automatic) or First (manual), the parking brake should be set, and the opposite wheel should be blocked. Jacking should only be attempted on a hard level surface.

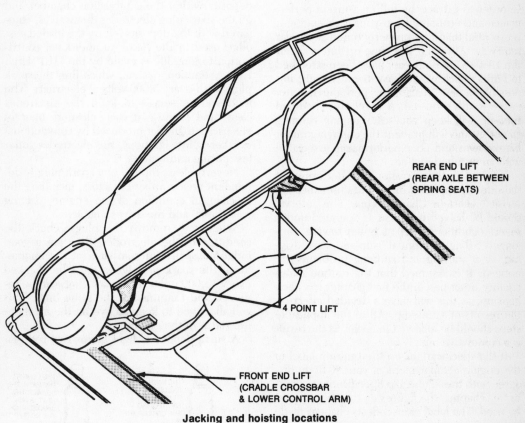

REAR END LIFT (REAR AXLE BETWEEN SPRING SEATS)

4 POINT LIFT

FRONT END LIFT (CRADLE CROSSBAR & LOWER CONTROL ARM)

Jacking and hoisting locations

Tune-Up and Performance Maintenance

TUNE-UP PROCEDURES

In order to extract the full measure of performance and economy from your car's engine it is essential that it be properly tuned at regular intervals. Although the tune-up intervals for the 1980–83 X-Body cars have been stretched to limits which would have been thought impossible a few years ago, periodic maintenance is still required. A regularly scheduled tune-up will keep your car's engine running smoothly and will prevent the annoying minor breakdowns and poor performance associated with an untuned engine.

A complete tune-up should be performed at the interval specified in the "Maintenance Intervals" chart in Chapter One. This interval should be halved if the car is operated under severe conditions, such as trailer towing, prolonged idling, continual stop-and-start driving, or if starting and running problems are noticed. It is assumed that the routine maintenance described in the first chapter has been kept up, as this will have a decided effect on the results of a tune-up. All of the applicable steps should be followed in order, as the result is a cumulative one.

If the specifications on the tune-up label in the engine compartment of your X-Body disagree with the "Tune-Up Specifications" chart in this chapter, the figures on the sticker must be used. The label often reflects changes made during the production run.

Spark Plugs

Spark plugs ignite the air and fuel mixture in the cylinder as the piston reaches the top of the compression stroke. The controlled explosion that results forces the piston down, turning the crankshaft and the rest of the drive train.

The average life of a spark plug in an X-Body car is 30,000 miles. Part of the reason for this extraordinarily long life is the exclusive use of unleaded fuel, which reduces the amount of deposits within the combustion chamber and on the spark plug electrodes themselves, compared with the deposits left by the leaded gasoline used in the past. An additional contribution to long life is made by the HEI (High Energy Ignition) System, which fires the spark plugs with over 35,000 volts of electricity. The high voltage serves to keep the electrodes clear, and because it is a "cleaner" blast of electricity than that produced by conventional breaker-points ignitions, the electrodes suffer less pitting and wear.

Nevertheless, the life of a spark plug is dependent on a number of factors, including the mechanical condition of the engine, driving conditions, and the driver's habits.

When you remove the plugs, check the condition of the electrodes; they are a good indicator of the internal state of the engine. Since the spark plug wires must be checked every 15,000 miles, the spark plugs can be removed and examined at the same time. This will allow you to keep an eye on the mechanical status of the engine.

A small deposit of light tan or rust-red ma-

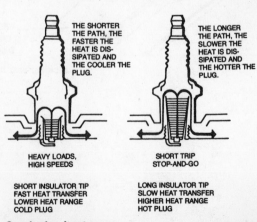

THE SHORTER THE PATH, THE FASTER THE HEAT IS DISSIPATED AND THE COOLER THE PLUG.

THE LONGER THE PATH, THE SLOWER THE HEAT IS DISSIPATED AND THE HOTTER THE PLUG.

HEAVY LOADS, HIGH SPEEDS

SHORT TRIP STOP-AND-GO

SHORT INSULATOR TIP
FAST HEAT TRANSFER
LOWER HEAT RANGE
COLD PLUG

LONG INSULATOR TIP
SLOW HEAT TRANSFER
HIGHER HEAT RANGE
HOT PLUG

Spark plug heat range

Tune-Up Specifications

When analyzing compression test results, look for uniformity among cylinders rather than specific pressures.

Year	Engine			Spark Plugs		Distributor		Ignition Timing (deg)▲●		Valves Intake Opens (deg)■	Fuel Pump Pressure (psi)	Idle Speed (rpm)▲	
	V.I.N. Code	No. Cyl Displacement (cu in.)	hp	Orig Type	Gap (in.)	Point Dwell (deg)	Point Gap (in.)	Man Trans	Auto Trans			Man Trans●	Auto Trans●
1980	5	4-151	90	R-43TSX	0.060	Electronic		10B(12B)	10B	33	6.5–8.0	1000	650
	X	6-173	110	R-44TS	0.045	Electronic		2B(6B)	6B(10B)	25	6.0–7.5	1050(1100)	650(700)
1981	5	4-151	90	R-44TSX	0.060	Electronic		4B	4B	33	6.5–8.0	1000	675
	X	6-173	110	R-44TS	0.045	Electronic		6B	10B	25	6.0–7.5	850	850 ①
	Z	6-173 HO	135	R-42TS	0.045	Electronic		10B	10B	31	6.0–7.5	700	700
'82–85	5,R	4-151 Pont.	90	R-44TSX	0.060	Electronic		8B	8B	33	6.0–8.0	950 ②	750 ③
	X	6-173 Chev.	112	R-43TS	0.045	Electronic		10B	10B	25	6.0–7.5	800	600
	Z	6-173 Chev. HO	135	R-42TS	0.045	Electronic		6B	10B	31	6.0–7.5	850 ④	750

NOTE: The underhood specifications sticker often reflects tune-up specification changes made in production. Sticker figures must be used if they disagree with those in this chart.

▲ See text for producedure

● Figure in parenthesis indicates California and High Altitude engine

■ All figures Before Top Dead Center

B Before Top Dead Center

Part numbers in this chart are not recommendations by Chilton for any product by brand name.

① With A/C: 900
② Without A/C: 850
③ Without A/C: 680
④ Calif.: 750

terial on a spark plug that has been used for any period of time is to be considered normal. Any other color, or abnormal amounts of wear or deposits, indicates that there is something amiss in the engine.

The gap between the center electrode and the side or ground electrode can be expected to increase not more than 0.001 in. every 1,000 miles under normal conditions.

When a spark plug is functioning normally or, more accurately, when the plug is installed in an engine that is functioning properly, the plugs can be taken out, cleaned, regapped, and reinstalled in the engine without doing the engine any harm.

When, and if, a plug fouls and begins to misfire, you will have to investigate, correct the cause of the fouling, and either clean or replace the plug.

There are several reasons why a spark plug will foul and you can learn which is at fault by just looking at the plug. A few of the most common reasons for plug fouling, and a description of the fouled plug's appearance, are listed in Chapter Nine, which also offers solutions to the problems. Also see the "Color Insert" section of Chapter Four.

Spark plugs suitable for use in your car's engine are offered in a number of different heat ranges. The amount of heat which the plug absorbs is determined by the length of the lower insulator. The longer the insulator, the hotter the plug will operate; the shorter the insulator, the cooler it will operate. A spark plug that absorbs (or retains) little heat and remains too cool will accumulate deposits of oil and carbon, because it is not hot enough to burn them off. This leads to fouling and consequent misfiring. A spark plug that absorbs too much heat will have no deposits, but the electrodes will burn away quickly and, in some cases, preignition may result. Preignition occurs when the spark plug tips get so hot that they ignite the fuel/air mixture before the actual spark fires. This premature ignition will usually cause a pinging sound under conditions of low speed and heavy load. In severe cases, the heat may become high enough to start the fuel/air mixture burning throughout the combustion chamber rather than just to the front of the plug. In this case, the resultant explosion (detonation) will be strong enough to damage pistons, rings, and valves.

In most cases the factory recommended heat range is correct; it is chosen to perform well under a wide range of operating conditions. However, if most of your driving is long distance, high speed travel, you may want to install a spark plug one step colder than standard. If most of your driving is of the short trip variety, when the engine may not always reach operating temperature, a hotter plug may help burn off the deposits normally accumulated under those conditions.

REMOVAL

1. Number the wires with pieces of adhesive tape so that you won't cross them when you replace them.

2. The spark plug boots have large grips to aid in removal. Grasp the wire by the rubber boot and twist the boot ½ turn in either direction to break the tight seal between the boot and the plug. Then twist and pull on the boot to remove the wire from the spark plug. Do not pull on the wire itself or you will damage the carbon cord conductor.

3. Use a ⅝ inch spark plug socket to loosen all of the plugs about two turns. You will need an extension to reach the rear spark plugs if your car has the V6 engine. A universal joint installed at the socket end of the extension will ease the process.

If removal of the plugs is difficult, apply a few drops of penetrating oil or silicone spray to the area around the base of the plug, and allow it a few minutes to work.

4. If compressed air is available, apply it to the area around the spark plug holes. Otherwise, use a rag or a brush to clean the area. Be careful not to allow any foreign material to drop into the spark plug holes.

5. Remove the plugs by unscrewing them the rest of the way.

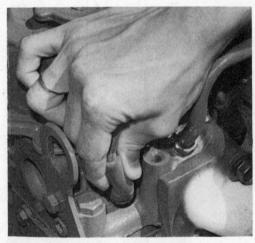

Twist and pull on the rubber boot to remove the spark plug wires

INSPECTION

Check the plugs for deposits and wear. If they are not going to be replaced, clean the plugs thoroughly. Remember that any kind of de-

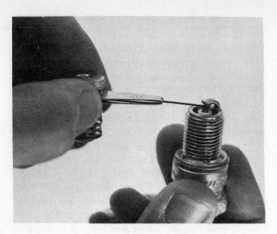

Check the electrode gap with a wire gauge

posit will decrease the efficiency of the plug. Plugs can be cleaned on a spark plug cleaning machine, which can sometimes be found in service stations, or you can do an acceptable job of cleaning with a stiff brush. If the plugs are cleaned, the electrodes must be filed flat. Use an ignition points file, not an emery board or the like, which will leave deposits. The electrodes must be filed perfectly flat with sharp edges; rounded edges reduce the spark plug voltage by as much as 50%.

Check the spark plug gap before installation. The ground electrode must be parallel to the center electrode and the specified size wire gauge should pass through the gap with a slight drag. Always check the gap on new plugs, too; they are not always correctly set at the factory. Do not use a flat feeler gauge when measuring the gap, because the reading will be inaccurate. Wire gapping tools usually have a bending tool attached. Use that to adjust the side electrode until the proper distance is obtained. Absolutely never bend the center electrode. Also, be careful not to bend the side electrode too far or too often; it may weaken and break off within the engine, requiring removal of the cylinder head to retrieve it.

Bend the side electrode to adjust the gap

INSTALLATION

1. Lubricate the threads of the spark plugs with a drop of oil or a shot of silicone spray. Install the plugs and tighten them handtight. Take care not to cross-thread them.

2. Tighten the spark plugs with the socket. Do not apply the same amount of force you would use for a bolt; just snug them in. These spark plugs do not use gaskets, and over-tightening will make future removal difficult. If a torque wrench is available, tighten to 7–15 ft. lbs.

NOTE: *While over-tightening the spark plug is to be avoided, under-tightening is just as bad. If combustion gases leak past the threads, the spark plug will overheat and rapid electrode wear will result.*

3. Install the wires on their respective plugs. Make sure the wires are firmly connected. You will be able to feel them click into place. Spark plug wiring diagrams are in this chapter if you get into trouble.

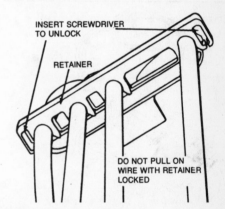

INSERT SCREWDRIVER TO UNLOCK

RETAINER

DO NOT PULL ON WIRE WITH RETAINER LOCKED

Unlock the plastic retainers to replace the plug wires

CHECKING AND REPLACING SPARK PLUG WIRES

Every 15,000 miles, inspect the spark plug wires for burns, cuts, or breaks in the insulation. Check the boots and the nipples on the distributor cap. Replace any damaged wiring.

Every 45,000 miles or so, the resistance of the wires should be checked with an ohmmeter. Wires with excessive resistance will cause misfiring, and may make the engine difficult to start in damp weather. Generally, the useful life of the cables is 45,000–60,000 miles.

To check resistance, remove the distributor cap, leaving the wires in place. Connect one lead of an ohmmeter to an electrode within the cap; connect the other lead to the corresponding spark plug terminal (remove it from the spark plug for this test). Replace any wire

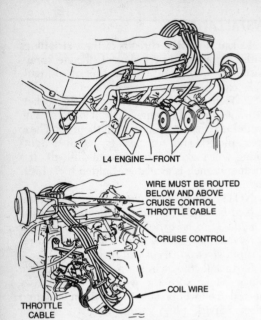

L4 ENGINE—FRONT

WIRE MUST BE ROUTED
BELOW AND ABOVE
CRUISE CONTROL
THROTTLE CABLE

CRUISE CONTROL

COIL WIRE

THROTTLE
CABLE

L4 ENGINE—REAR

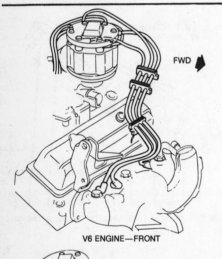

FWD

V6 ENGINE—FRONT

FWD

V6 ENGINE—REAR

Spark plug wire routing

which shows a resistance over 30,000 ohms. The following chart gives resistance values as a function of length. Generally speaking, however, resistance should not be considered the outer limit of acceptability.

- 0–15 inches—3000–10,000 Ω;

- 15–25 inches—4000–15,000 Ω;
- 25–35 inches—6000–20,000 Ω;
- Over 35 inches—25,000 Ω.

It should be remembered that resistance is also a function of length; the longer the wire, the greater the resistance. Thus, if the wires on your car are longer than the factory originals, resistance will be higher, quite possibly outside these limits.

When installing new wires, replace them one at a time to avoid mixups. Start by replacing the longest one first. Install the boot firmly over the spark plug. Route the wire over the same path as the original. Insert the nipple firmly onto the tower on the distributor cap, then install the cap cover and latches to secure the wires.

FIRING ORDER

To avoid confusion, replace spark plug wires one at a time.

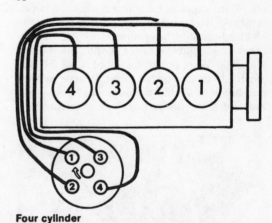

V6

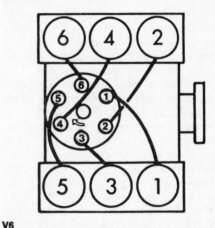

Four cylinder

High Energy Ignition (HEI) System

The General Motors, HEI system for 1980 is a pulse-triggered, transistor-controlled, inductive discharge ignition system. It is a completely self-contained unit—all parts are contained within the distributor.

The distributor, in addition to housing the mechanical and vacuum advance mechanisms, contains the ignition coil, the electronic control module, and the magnetic triggering device. The magnetic pick-up assembly contains a permanent magnet, a pole piece with internal "teeth", and a pick-up coil (not to be confused with the ignition coil).

For 1981 and later, an HEI distributor with Electronic Spark Timing is used (for more information on EST, refer to Chapter 4). The V6 engine uses a one piece distributor with the ignition coil mounted in the distributor cap, similar to 1980. The L4 engine uses a smaller distributor with an externally mounted coil. The coil on the one piece distributor connects to the rotor through a resistance brush, while the external coil is connected by means of a high tension wire.

All spark timing changes in the 1981 and later distributors are done electronically by the

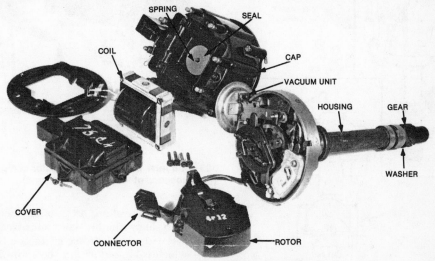

HEI distributor components (1980)

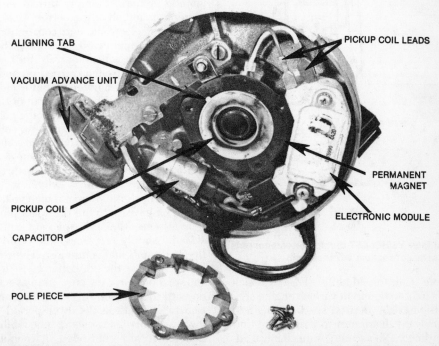

All HEI distributor circuitry is contained within the distributor body (1980 shown)

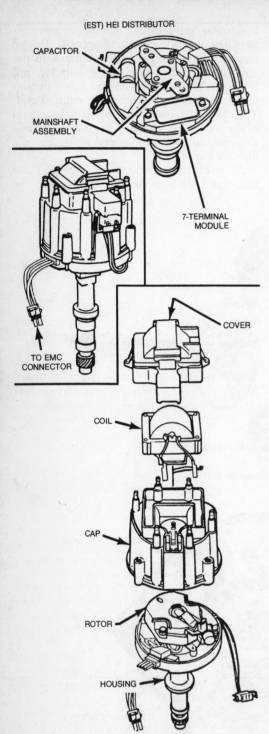

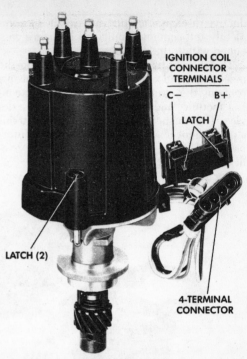

1981 and later L4 HEI EST distributor components (note absence of vacuum advance unit)

1981 and later V6 HEI EST distributor components (note absence of vacuum advance unit)

Electronic Control Module (ECM) which monitors information from various engine sensors, computes the desired spark timing and then signals the distributor to change the timing accordingly. No vacuum or mechanical advance systems are used whatsoever.

In the HEI system, as in other electronic ignition systems, the breaker points have been replaced with an electronic switch—a transistor—which is located *within* the control module. This switching transistor performs the same function the points did in a conventional ignition system; it simply turns coil primary current on and off at the correct time. Essentially then, electronic and conventional ignition systems operate on the same principle.

The module which houses the switching transistor is controlled (turned on and off) by a magnetically generated impulse induced in the pick-up coil. When the teeth of the rotating timer align with the teeth of the pole piece, the induced voltage in the pick-up coil signals the electronic module to open the coil primary circuit. The primary current then decreases, and a high voltage is induced in the ignition coil secondary windings which is then directed through the rotor and high voltage leads (spark plug wires) to fire the spark plugs.

In essence then, the pick-up coil module system simply replaces the conventional breaker points and condenser. The condenser found within the distributor is for radio suppression purposes only and has nothing to do with the ignition process. The module automatically controls the dwell period, increasing it with increasing engine speed. Since dwell is automatically controlled, it cannot be adjusted. The module itself is non-adjustable and non-repairable and must be replaced if found defective.

HEI SYSTEM PRECAUTIONS

Before going on to troubleshooting, it might be a good idea to take note of the following precautions:

Timing Light Use

Inductive pick-up timing lights are the best kind to use with HEI. Timing lights which connect between the spark plug and the spark plug wire occasionally (not always) give false readings.

Spark Plug Wires

The plug wires used with HEI systems are of a different construction than conventional wires. When replacing them, make sure you get the correct wires, since conventional wires won't carry the voltage. Also, handle them carefully to avoid cracking or splitting them and *never* pierce them.

Tachometer Use

Not all tachometers will operate or indicate correctly when used on a HEI system. While some tachometers may give a reading, this does not necessarily mean the reading is correct. In addition, some tachometers hook up differently from others. If you can't figure out whether or not your tachometer will work on your car, check with the tachometer manufacturer. Dwell readings, of course, have no significance at all.

HEI System Testers

Instruments designed specifically for testing HEI systems are available from several tool manufacturers. Some of these will even test the module itself. However, the tests given in the following section will require only an ohmmeter and a voltmeter.

TROUBLESHOOTING THE HEI SYSTEM

The symptoms of a defective component within the HEI system are exactly the same as those you would encounter in a conventional system. Some of these symptoms are:

• Hard or no Starting
• Rough Idle
• Poor Fuel Economy
• Engine misses under load or while accelerating

If you suspect a problem in your ignition system, there are certain preliminary checks which you should carry out before you begin to check the electronic portions of the system. First, it is extremely important to make sure the vehicle battery is in a good state of charge.

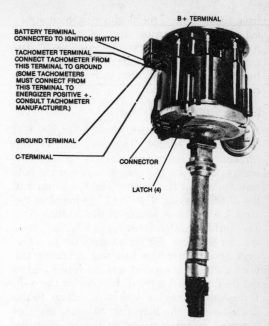

Tachometer connections to the HEI distributor

A defective or poorly charged battery will cause the various components of the ignition system to read incorrectly when they are being tested. Second, make sure all wiring connections are clean and tight, not only at the battery, but also at the distributor cap, ignition coil, and at the electronic control module.

Since the only change between electronic and conventional ignition systems is in the distributor component area, it is imperative to check the secondary ignition circuit first. If the secondary circuit checks out properly, then the engine condition is probably not the fault of the ignition system. To check the secondary ignition system, perform a simple spark test. Remove one of the plug wires and insert some sort of extension in the plug socket. An old spark plug with the ground electrode removed makes a good extension. Hold the wire and extension about ¼ in. away from the clock and crank the engine. If a normal spark occurs, then the problem is most likely *not* in the ignition system. Check for fuel system problems, or fouled spark plugs.

If, however, there is no spark or a weak spark, then further ignition system testing will

HEI Plug Wire Resistance Chart

Wire Length	Minimum	Maximum
0–15 inches	3000 ohms	10,000 ohms
15–25 inches	4000 ohms	15,000 ohms
25–35 inches	6000 ohms	20,000 ohms
Over 35 inches		25,000 ohms

have to be done. Troubleshooting techniques fall into two categories, depending on the nature of the problem. The categories are (1) Engine cranks, but won't start or (2) Engine runs, but runs rough or cuts out. To begin with, let's consider the first case.

Engine Fails to Start

If the engine won't start, perform a spark test as described earlier. This will narrow the problem area down considerably. If no spark occurs, check for the presence of normal battery voltage at the battery (BAT) terminal in the distributor cap. The "BAT" terminal on the 1981 L4 engine is found on the ignition coil. The ignition switch must be in the "on" position for this test. Either a voltmeter or a test light may be used for this test. Connect the test light wire to ground and the probe end to the BAT terminal at the distributor (or the coil). If the light comes on, you have voltage to the distributor. If the light fails to come on, this indicates an open circuit in the ignition primary wiring leading to the distributor. In this case, you will have to check wiring continuity back to the ignition switch using a test light. If there is battery voltage at the BAT terminal, but no spark at the plugs, then the problem lies within the distributor assembly. Go on to the distributor components test section.

Engine Runs, But Runs Rough or Cuts Out

1. Make sure the plug wires are in good shape first. There should be no obvious cracks or breaks. You can check the plug wires with an ohmmeter, but *do not* pierce the wires with a probe. Check the chart for the correct plug wire resistance.

2. If the plug wires are OK, remove the cap assembly and check for moisture, cracks, chips, or carbon tracks, or any other high voltage leaks or failures. Replace the cap if any defects are found. Make sure the timer wheel rotates when the engine is cranked. If everything is all right so far, go on to the distributor components test section following.

DISTRIBUTOR COMPONENTS TESTING

If the trouble has been narrowed down to the units within the distributor, the following tests can help pinpoint the defective component. An ohmmeter with both high and low ranges should be used. These tests are made with the cap assembly removed and the battery wire disconnected. If a tachometer is connected to the TACH terminal, disconnect it before making these tests.

1. Connect an ohmmeter between the TACH and BAT terminals in the distributor

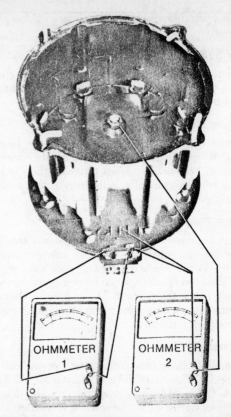

Ohmmeter 1 shows the primary coil resistance connections. Ohmmeter 2 shows the secondary resistance connections—1980 (all), 1981 and later V6

cap (at the coil on the L4). The primary coil resistance should be less than one ohm.

2. To check the coil secondary resistance, connect an ohmmeter between the rotor button and the BAT terminal. Note the reading. Connect the ohmmeter between the rotor button and the TACH terminal. Note the reading. The resistance in both cases should be between 6,000 and 30,000 ohms. Be sure to test between the rotor button and both the BAT and TACH terminals.

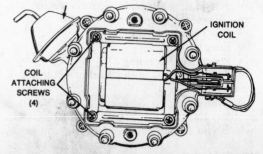

The coil on all but the 1981 and later L4 is accessible by removing the four attaching screws (1980 shown)

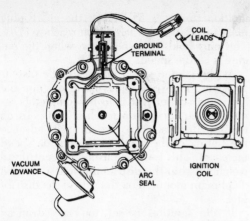

Check the condition of the arc seal under the coil

3. Replace the coil *only* if the readings in Step 1 and Step 2 are infinite.

NOTE: *These resistance checks will not disclose shorted coil windings. This condition can only be detected with scope analysis or a suitably designed coil tester. If these instruments are unavailable, replace the coil with a known good coil as a final coil test.*

4. To test the pick-up coil, first disconnect the white and green module leads. Set the ohmmeter on the high scale and connect it between a ground and either the white or green lead. Any resistance measurement *less* than infinity requires replacement of the pick-up coil.

5. Pick-up coil continuity is tested by connecting the ohmmeter (on low range) between the white and green leads. Normal resistance is between 650 and 850 ohms. Move the vacuum advance arm while performing this test. This will detect any break in coil continuity. Such a condition can cause intermittent misfiring. Replace the pick-up coil if the reading is outside the specified limits.

6. If no defects have been found at this time, and you still have a problem, then the module will have to be checked. If you do not have access to a module tester, the only possible alternative is a substitution test. If the module fails the substitution test, replace it.

HEI SYSTEM MAINTENANCE

Except for periodic checks of the spark plug wires, and an occasional check of the distributor cap for cracks (see Steps 1 and 2 under

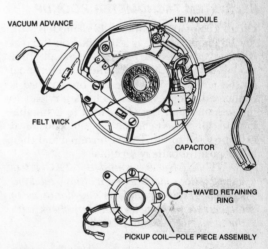

1980 pick-up coil removal; 1981 and later similar

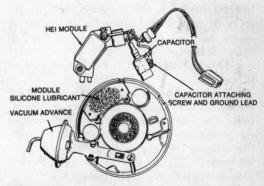

1980 module replacement; be sure to coat the mating surfaces with silicone lubricant (1981 and later similar)

Ohmmeter 1 shows connections for testing the pick-up coil. Ohmmeter 2 shows connections for testing the pick-up coil continuity

"Engine Runs, But Runs Rough or Cuts Out" for details), no maintenance is required on the HEI System. No periodic lubrication is necessary; engine oil lubricates the lower bushing, and an oil-filled reservoir lubricates the upper bushing.

DISTRIBUTOR CAP REMOVAL AND INSTALLATION

1. Disconnect the ignition switch wire from the distributor cap. Also disconnect the tachometer wire, if so equipped.

2. Release the coil connectors from the cap.

3. Remove the distributor cap by turning the four latches (the 1981 L4 distributor has 2 latches) counterclockwise. You will need a stubby screwdriver to get at the latches if your car has the four cylinder engine, because clearances are very tight between the distributor and the firewall.

4. Remove the cap. Installation is the reverse of removal. Be sure you get the ignition and tachometer wires connected to the correct terminals.

HEI SYSTEM TACHOMETER HOOKUP

On all 1980 models and all 1981 models with the V6 engine, there is a terminal on the distributor cap marked TACH. On all 1981 models with the L4 engine, there is a terminal on the ignition coil where the brown wire is connected. Connect one tachometer lead to this terminal and the other lead to a suitable ground. On some tachometers, the leads must be connected to the TACH terminal and then to the positive battery terminal.

CAUTION: *Never ground the TACH terminal; serious module and ignition coil damage will result. If there is any doubt as to the correct tachometer hookup, check with the tachometer manufacturer.*

Ignition Timing

Ignition timing is the measurement, in degrees of crankshaft rotation, of the point at which the spark plugs fire in each of the cylinders. It is measured in degrees before or after Top Dead Center (TDC) of the compression stroke.

Because it takes a fraction of a second for the spark plug to ignite the mixture in the cylinder, the spark plug must fire a little before the piston reaches TDC. Otherwise, the mixture will not be completely ignited as the piston passes TDC and the full power of the explosion will not be used by the engine.

The timing measurement is given in degrees of crankshaft rotation before the piston reaches TDC (BTDC). If the setting for the

ignition timing is 5° BTDC, the spark plug must fire 5° before each piston reaches TDC. This only holds true, however, when the engine is at idle speed.

As the engine speed increases, the pistons go faster. The spark plugs have to ignite the fuel even sooner if it is to be completely ignited when the piston reaches TDC. To do this, the distributor has two means to advance the timing of the spark as the engine speed increases. This is accomplished by centrifugal weights within the distributor, and a vacuum diaphragm mounted on the side of the distributor.

If the ignition is set too far advanced (BTDC), the ignition and expansion of the fuel in the cylinder will occur too soon and tend to force the piston down while it is still traveling up. This causes engine ping. If the ignition spark is set too far retarded, after TDC (ATDC), the piston will have already passed TDC and started on its way down when the fuel is ignited. This will cause the piston to be forced down for only a portion of its travel. This will result in poor engine performance and lack of power.

Timing marks consist of a notch on the rim of the crankshaft pulley and a scale of degrees attached to the front of the engine. The notch corresponds to the position of the piston in the number 1 cylinder. A stroboscopic (dynamic) timing light is used, which is hooked into the circuit of the No. 1 cylinder spark plug. Every time the spark plug fires, the timing light flashes. By aiming the timing light at the timing marks, the exact position of the piston within the cylinder can be read, since the stroboscopic flash makes the mark on the pulley appear to be standing still. Proper timing is indicated when the notch is aligned with the correct number on the scale.

There are three basic types of timing light available. The first is a simple neon bulb with two wire connections (one for the spark plug and one for the plug wire, connecting the light in series). This type of light is quite dim, and must be held closely to the marks to be seen, but it is quite inexpensive. The second type of light operates from the car's battery. Two alligator clips connect to the battery terminals, while a third wire connects to the spark plug with an adapter. This type of light is more expensive, but the xenon bulb provides a nice bright flash which can even be seen in sunlight. The third type replaces the battery source with 110 volt house current. Some timing lights have other functions built into them, such as dwell meters, tachometers, or remote starting switches. These are convenient, in that they reduce the tangle of wires under the hood, but may duplicate the functions of tools you already have.

Because your X-Body car has electronic ignition, you should use a timing light with an inductive pickup. This pickup simply clamps around the Number 1 spark plug wire, eliminating the adapter. It is not susceptible to crossfiring or flase triggering, which may occur with a conventional light due to the greater voltages produced by HEI.

ADJUSTMENT

1. Refer to the directions on the tune-up label inside the engine compartment. Follow all the instructions on the label.

2. Locate the timing marks on the crankshaft pulley and the front of the engine.

3. Clean off the timing marks so that you can see them. Use chalk or white paint to color the mark on the crankshaft pulley and the mark on the scale which will indicate the correct timing when aligned with the notch on the crankshaft pulley.

4. Attach a tachometer to the engine. See the preceding section, "HEI System Tachometer Hookup".

5. Attach a timing light to the engine, according to the manufacturer's instructions. If the timing light has three wires, one, usually green or blue, is attached to the No. 1 spark plug with an adapter, unless an inductive pickup is used, which simply clamps around the wire. The other wires are connected to the battery. The red wire goes to the positive side of the battery and the black wire is connected to the negative side of the battery. Do not pierce the No. 1 spark plug wire, or attempt to insert a wire between the boot and the wire. This will break the insulation and result in an ignition miss.

NOTE: *Number one spark plug is at the front of the four cylinder engine (right side*

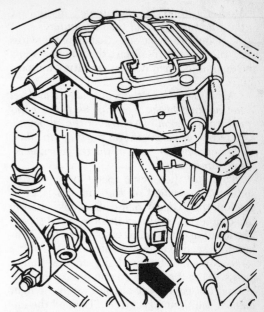

The V6 distributor lockbolt is at the base of the distributor shaft

of the car) and at the right front of the V6 engine (the left rear spark plug if you are facing the car). Firing order diagrams are in this chapter.

6. Disconnect and plug the vacuum hose at the distributor vacuum advance, if so directed by the tune-up label. This will be required in most cases to prevent vacuum advance to the distributor. The hose must be plugged to prevent a vacuum leak into the carburetor. A golf tee makes a good plug. Be careful not to split the hose.

NOTE: *1981 and later models with Electronic Spark Timing have no vacuum advance, therefore you may skip this step. On*

Four cylinder timing marks; V6 similar

The four cylinder distributor has two lockbolts. Loosen the outer one (lower arrow) to adjust timing

Models with (EST) distributor, disconnect the 4 terminal plug at the distributor.

7. Check to make sure that all of the wires clear the fan and then start the engine. Allow the engine to reach normal operating temperature.

CAUTION: *Block the front wheels and set the parking brake securely. Shift the manual transmission to Neutral or the automatic to Drive, as instructed on the tune-up label. Do not stand in front of the car when making adjustments!*

8. Adjust the engine speed to the correct setting (as specified on the tune-up label or given in the "Tune-Up Specifications" chart in this chapter) by means of the idle speed screw. The location of the screw is shown in the "Carburetor" section of this chapter.

9. Aim the timing light at the timing marks. If the marks which you put on the pulley and the engine are aligned when the light flashes, the timing is correct. Turn off the engine and disconnect the timing light and tachometer. If the marks not not in alignment, the timing will have to be adjusted.

10. Turn off the engine.

11. Loosen the distributor lockbolt so that the distributor can just be turned with a little effort. The V6 engine has a conventional lockbolt and clamp. The four cylinder engine has two lockbolts. One, at the outer edge, is the one you want. This loosens the distributor hold-down clamp but does not permit removal of the distributor itself. Loosen the outer lockbolt and slide the clamp away from the distributor slightly. This will allow the distributor to rotate.

12. Start the engine. Keep the wires of the timing light clear of the fan and pulleys. While observing the timing marks with the light, turn the distributor slightly until the timing marks are aligned.

13. Turn off the engine and tighten the distributor lockbolt. Start the engine and recheck the timing. Sometimes the distributor moves slightly during the tightening process. If the ignition timing is within 1° of the correct setting, that's close enough; a tolerance of 2° is permitted by the manufacturer.

14. Shut off the engine and disconnect the timing light and tachometer. Reconnect the distributor vacuum advance hose, if removed.

Valve Adjustment

Both the Pontiac-built four cylinder engine and the Chevrolet-built V6 have hydraulic valve lifters, which do not require periodic valve adjustments. The Chevrolet engine requires an initial valve adjustment anytime the lifters are removed or the valve train is disturbed. This procedure is covered in Chapter Three.

Idle Speed and Mixture Adjustment

This section contains only carburetor adjustments as they normally apply to engine tune-ups. Descriptions of the carburetors and complete adjustment procedures can be found in Chapter Four.

NOTE: *No idle speed or mixture adjustments are possible on 1982 and later fuel injected engines.*

When the engine in your car is running, air/fuel mixture from the carburetor is being drawn into the engine by a partial vacuum which is created by the downward movement of the pistons on the intake stroke of the four-stroke cycle of the engine. The amount of air/fuel mixture that enters the engine is controlled by throttle plates in the bottom of the carburetor. When the engine is not running, the throttle plates are closed, completely blocking off the bottom of the carburetor from the inside of the engine. The throttle plates are connected, through the throttle linkage, to the gas pedal. What you are actually doing when you depress the gas pedal is opening up the throttle plates in the carburetor to admit more of the fuel/air mixture to the engine. The further you open the throttle plates in the carburetor, the higher the engine speed becomes.

As previously stated, when the engine is not running, the throttle plates in the carburetor remain closed. When the engine is idling, it is necessary to open the throttle plates slightly. To prevent having to keep your foot on the gas pedal when the engine is idling, an idle speed adjusting screw was added to the carburetor. This screw has the same effect as keeping your foot slightly depressed on the gas pedal. The idle speed adjusting screw contacts a solenoid on the outside of the carburetor. When the screw is turned in, it opens the throttle plates

Carburetor solenoid electrical connector

on the carburetor, raising the idle speed of the engine. This screw is called the curb idle adjusting screw and the procedures in this section will tell you how to adjust it.

Since it is difficult for the engine to draw the air/fuel mixture from the carburetor with the small amount of throttle plate opening that is present when the engine is idling, an idle mixture passage is provided in the carburetor. This passage delivers air/fuel mixture to the engine from a hole which is located in the bottom of the carburetor below the throttle plates. This idle mixture passage contains an adjusting screw which restricts the amount of air/fuel mixture that enters the engine at idle.

On the X-Body cars, the idle mixture screws are concealed under staked-in plugs. Idle mixture is not considered to be a normal tune-up procedure, because of the sensitivity of emission control adjustments. Mixture adjustment requires not only special tools with which to remove the concealing plugs, but also the addition of an artificial enrichment substance (propane) which must be introduced into the carburetor by means of a finely calibrated metering valve. These tools are not generally available, and require a certain amount of expertise to use. Therefore, mixture adjustments are purposely not covered in this book. If you suspect that your car's carburetor requires a mixture adjustment, it is strongly recommended that the job be referred to your dealer or a qualified mechanic with specific training in making the adjustment.

IDLE SPEED ADJUSTMENTS
1980

There are actually two idle speed adjustments which must be made. One is an adjustment made with the idle speed screw, which is connected to the throttle plate linkage and contacts the idle speed solenoid. This is called "Curb" idle on cars with air conditioning, or "Basic" idle speed on cars without air conditioning. The second adjustment is made to the idle speed solenoid, which is mounted to the carburetor, and the plunger of which is contacted by the idle speed screw. This adjustment is called "Solenoid" rpm on cars with air conditioning, or "Curb" idle speed on cars without air conditioning. The illustrations given on these pages should help you sort out all this.

CARS WITHOUT AIR CONDITIONING

1. The first step is to prepare the engine for these adjustments. Follow the instructions given on the tune-up label inside the engine compartment. It will usually say to warm the engine to operating temperature, make sure the choke is fully open, and place the idle speed screw on the lowest step of the fast idle cam. The fast idle cam is normally marked "H", "2", and "1" on its three steps. Open the throttle by hand and place the idle speed screw on step "1". Connect a tachometer to the engine.

2. Place the automatic transaxle in Drive,

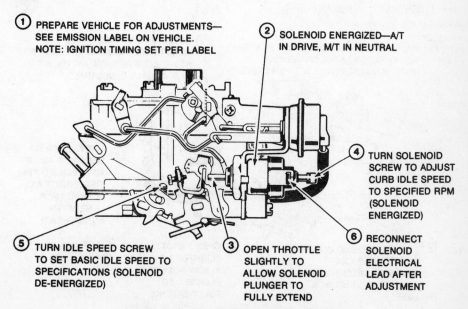

① PREPARE VEHICLE FOR ADJUSTMENTS—SEE EMISSION LABEL ON VEHICLE. NOTE: IGNITION TIMING SET PER LABEL

② SOLENOID ENERGIZED—A/T IN DRIVE, M/T IN NEUTRAL

④ TURN SOLENOID SCREW TO ADJUST CURB IDLE SPEED TO SPECIFIED RPM (SOLENOID ENERGIZED)

⑤ TURN IDLE SPEED SCREW TO SET BASIC IDLE SPEED TO SPECIFICATIONS (SOLENOID DE-ENERGIZED)

③ OPEN THROTTLE SLIGHTLY TO ALLOW SOLENOID PLUNGER TO FULLY EXTEND

⑥ RECONNECT SOLENOID ELECTRICAL LEAD AFTER ADJUSTMENT

Idle speed adjustment without air conditioning

or the manual transaxle in Neutral. Make sure the solenoid is energized (plunger extended).

3. Open the throttle slightly to allow the solenoid plunger to full extend.

4. Turn the solenoid screw to adjust the engine speed to the following "Curb" idle speed, according to carburetor number (the carburetor number is stamped on the flat vertical surface of the float bowl, adjacent to the vacuum tube):

Carb. No.	Curb rpm
• 17059614	650 (Drive)
• 17059615	1000 (Neutral)
• 17059714	650 (Drive)
• 17059715	1000 (Neutral)
• 17059650	700 (Drive)
• 17059651	750 (Neutral)
• 17059760	700 (Drive)
• 17059763	750 (Neutral)
• 17059618	860 (Drive)
• 17059619	1000 (Neutral)

NOTE: *If none of these carburetor numbers pertain to your particular carburetor, check the underhood specifications sticker for the proper curb idle setting.*

5. Disconnect the electrical connector from the solenoid. Turn the idle speed screw in or out to set the basic idle speed, according to carburetor number:

Carb No.	Basic rpm
• 17059614	500 (Drive)
• 17059615	500 (Neutral)
• 17059714	500 (Drive)
• 17059715	500 (Neutral)
• 17059650	800 (Drive)
• 17059651	1200 (Neutral)
• 17059760	800 (Drive)
• 17059763	800 (Neutral)
• 17059618	500 (Drive)
• 17059619	500 (Neutral)

NOTE: *If none of these carburetor numbers pertain to your particular carburetor, check the underhood specifications sticker for the proper basic idle setting.*

CARS WITH AIR CONDITIONING

1. Follow Step 1 given for "Cars Without Air Conditioning."

2. Disconnect the electrical lead from the air conditioning compressor. Turn the air conditioning "off" inside the car.

3. Turn the idle speed screw to set the curb idle to specifications, according to the carburetor number (the carburetor number is stamped on the flat vertical surface of the float

Carb. No.	Curb rpm
• 17059616	900 (Drive)
• 17059617	1300 (Neutral)
• 17059716	850 (Drive)
• 17059717	1200 (Neutral)
• 17059652	850 (Drive)
• 17059653	1200 (Neutral)
• 17059762	800 (Drive)
• 17059763	800 (Neutral)
• 17059620	900 (Drive)
• 17059621	1300 (Neutral)

NOTE: *If none of these carburetor numbers pertain to your particular carburetor, check the underhood specifications sticker for the proper curb idle setting.*

4. With the air conditioning lead still disconnected, turn the air conditioning "On", put the automatic transaxle in Drive, or the manual transaxle in Neutral, and open the throttle slightly to allow the solenoid plunger to extend.

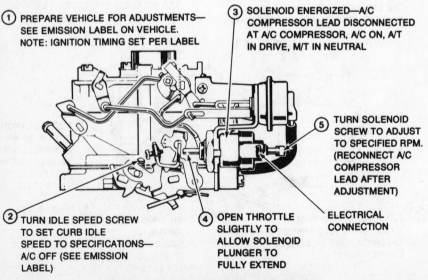

① PREPARE VEHICLE FOR ADJUSTMENTS—SEE EMISSION LABEL ON VEHICLE. NOTE: IGNITION TIMING SET PER LABEL

③ SOLENOID ENERGIZED—A/C COMPRESSOR LEAD DISCONNECTED AT A/C COMPRESSOR, A/C ON, A/T IN DRIVE, M/T IN NEUTRAL

⑤ TURN SOLENOID SCREW TO ADJUST TO SPECIFIED RPM. (RECONNECT A/C COMPRESSOR LEAD AFTER ADJUSTMENT)

② TURN IDLE SPEED SCREW TO SET CURB IDLE SPEED TO SPECIFICATIONS— A/C OFF (SEE EMISSION LABEL)

④ OPEN THROTTLE SLIGHTLY TO ALLOW SOLENOID PLUNGER TO FULLY EXTEND

ELECTRICAL CONNECTION

Idle speed adjustment with air conditioning

5. Turn the solenoid screw to adjust the engine speed to following figure, according to carburetor number:

Carb. No.	Solenoid rpm
• 17059616	650 (Drive)
• 17059617	1000 (Neutral)
• 17059716	650 (Drive)
• 17059717	1000 (Neutral)
• 17059652	700 (Drive)
• 17059653	750 (Neutral)
• 17059762	700 (Drive)
• 17059763	750 (Neutral)
• 17059620	650 (Drive)
• 17059621	1000 (Neutral)

NOTE: *If none of these carburetor numbers pertain to your particular carburetor, check the underhood specifications sticker for the proper solenoid setting.*

1981 and Later

There are three separate and individual means of controlling the idle speed on the 1981 and later X-Bodies. The first is basically the same as on the 1980 models and the adjustment procedures are as such. This system utilizes an

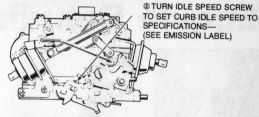

① PREPARE VEHICLE FOR ADJUSTMENTS—
SEE EMISSION LABEL ON VEHICLE.
NOTE: IGNITION TIMING SET PER LABEL.

② TURN IDLE SPEED SCREW TO SET CURB IDLE SPEED TO SPECIFICATIONS— (SEE EMISSION LABEL)

Idle speed adjustment without A/C and without an idle speed solenoid—1981

idle speed solenoid and is used primarily on the L4 engine WO/air conditioning and the V6 engine W/air conditioning or W/manual transmission. The second and third systems have Idle Speed Control (ISC) and are controlled by the Electronic Control Module.

For identification of the system that is used on your particular car and for the adjustment procedures and settings if your car is equipped with either of the last two systems, please refer to the underhood specifications sticker on your car.

Engine and Engine Rebuilding

3

ENGINE ELECTRICAL

Understanding the Engine Electrical System

The engine electrical system can be broken down into three separate and distinct systems—(1) the starting system; (2) the charging system (3) the ignition system.

BATTERY AND STARTING SYSTEM

The battery is the first link in the chain of mechanisms which work together to provide cranking of the automobile engine. In most modern cars, the battery is a lead-acid electrochemical device consisting of six two-volt (2 V) subsections connected in series so the unit is capable of producing approximately 12 V of electrical pressure. Each subsection, or cell, consists of a series of positive and negative plates held a short distance apart in a solution of sulfuric acid and water. The two types of plates are of dissimilar metals. This causes a chemical reaction to be set up, and it is this reaction which produces current flow from the battery when its positive and negative terminals are connected to an electrical appliance such as a lamp or motor. The continued transfer of electrons would eventually convert the sulfuric acid in the electrolyte to water, and make the two plates identical in chemical composition. As electrical energy is removed from the battery, its voltage output tends to drop. Thus, measuring battery voltage and battery electrolyte composition are two ways of checking the ability of the unit to supply power. During the starting of the engine, electrical energy is removed from the battery. However, if the charging circuit is in good condition and the operating conditions are normal, the power removed from the battery will be replaced by the generator (or alternator) which will force electrons back through the battery, reversing the normal flow, and restoring the battery to its original chemical state.

The battery and starting motor are linked by very heavy electrical cables designed to minimize resistance to the flow of current. Generally, the major power supply cable that leaves the battery goes directly to the starter, while other electrical system needs are supplied by a smaller cable. During starter operation, power flows from the battery to the starter and is grounded through the car's frame and the battery's negative ground strap.

The starting motor is a specially designed, direct current electric motor capable of producing a very great amount of power for its size. One thing that allows the motor to produce a great deal of power is its tremendous rotating speed. It drives the engine through a tiny pinion gear (attached to the starter's armature), which drives the very large fly-wheel ring gear at a greatly reduced speed. Another factor allowing it to produce so much power is that only intermittent operation is required of it. Thus, little allowance for air circulation is required, and the windings can be built into a very small space.

The starter solenoid is a magnetic device which employs the small current supplied by the starting switch circuit of the ignition switch. This magnetic action moves a plunger which mechanically engages the starter and electrically closes the heavy switch which connects it to the battery. The starting switch circuit consists of the starting switch contained within the ignition switch, a transmission neutral safety switch or clutch pedal switch, and the wiring necessary to connect these in series with the starter solenoid or relay.

A pinion, which is a small gear, is mounted to a one-way drive clutch. This clutch is splined to the starter armature shaft. When the ignition switch is moved to the "start" position, the solenoid plunger slides the pinion, toward the flywheel ring gear via a collar and spring.

If the teeth on the pinion and fly-wheel match properly, the pinion will engage the flywheel immediately. If the gear teeth butt one another, the spring will be compressed and will force the gears to mesh as soon as the starter turns far enough to allow them to do so. As the solenoid plunger reaches the end of its travel, it closes the contacts that connect the battery and starter and then the engine is cranked.

As soon as the engine starts, the flywheel ring gear begins turning fast enough to drive the pinion at an extremely high rate of speed. At this point, the one-way clutch begins allowing the pinion to spin faster than the starter shaft so that the starter will not operate at excessive speed. When the ignition switch is released from the starter position, the solenoid is de-energized, and a spring contained within the solenoid assembly pulls the gear out of mesh and interrupts the current flow to the starter.

Some starters employ a separate relay, mounted away from the starter, to switch the motor and solenoid current on and off. The relay thus replaces the solenoid electrical switch, but does not eliminate the need for a solenoid mounted on the starter used to mechanically engage the starter drive gears. The relay is used to reduce the amount of current the starting switch must carry.

THE CHARGING SYSTEM

The automobile charging system provides electrical power for operation of the vehicle's ignition and starting systems and all the electrical accessories. The battery serves as an electrical surge or storage tank, storing (in chemical form) the energy originally produced by the engine-driven generator. The system also provides a means of regulating generator output to protect the battery from being overcharged and to avoid excessive voltage to the accessories.

The storage battery is a chemical device incorporating parallel lead plates in a tank containing a sulfuric acid-water solution. Adjacent plates are slightly dissimilar, and the chemical reaction of the two dissimilar plates produces electrical energy when the battery is connected to a load such as the starter motor. The chemical reaction is reversible, so that when the generator is producing a voltage (electrical pressure) greater than that produced by the battery, electricity is forced into the battery, and the battery is returned to its fully charged state.

The vehicle's generator is driven mechanically, through V belts, by the engine crankshaft. It consists of two coils of fine wire, one stationary (the "stator"), and one movable (the "rotor"). The rotor may also be known as the "armature," and consists of fine wire wrapped around an iron core which is mounted on a shaft. The electricity which flows through the two coils of wire (provided initially by the battery in some cases) creates an intense magnetic field around both rotor and stator, and the interaction between the two fields creates voltage, allowing the generator to power the accessories and charge the battery.

There are two types of generators; the earlier is the direct current (DC) type. The current produced by the DC generator is generated in the armature and carried off the spinning armature by stationary brushes contacting the commutator. The commutator is a series of smooth metal contact plates on the end of the armature. The commutator plates, which are separated from one another by a very short gap, are connected to the armature circuits so that current will flow in one direction only in the wires carrying the generator output. The generator stator consists of two stationary coils of wire which draw some of the output current of the generator to form a powerful magnetic field and create the interaction of fields which generates the voltage. The generator field is wired in series with the regulator.

Newer automobiles use alternating current generators or "alternators," because they are more efficient, can be rotated at higher speeds, and have fewer brush problems. In an alternator, the field rotates while all the current produced passes only through the stator windings. The brushes bear against continuous slip rings rather than a commutator. This causes the current produced to periodically reverse the direction of its flow. Diodes (electrical one-way switches) block the flow of current from traveling in the wrong direction. A series of diodes is wired together to permit the alternating flow of the stator to be converted to a pulsating, but unidirectional flow at the alternator output. The alternator's field is wired in series with the voltage regulator.

The regulator consists of several circuits. Each circuit has a core, or magnetic coil of wire, which operates a switch. Each switch is connected to ground through one or more resistors. The coil of wire responds directly to system voltage. When the voltage reaches the required level, the magnetic field created by the winding of wire closes the switch and inserts a resistance into the generator field circuit, thus reducing the output. The contacts of the switch cycle open and closed many times each second to precisely control voltage.

While alternators are self-limiting as far as maximum current is concerned, DC generators employ a current regulating circuit which responds directly to the total amount of current flowing through the generator circuit rather than to the output voltage. The current regulator is similar to the voltage regulator except that all system current must flow through the energizing coil on its way to the various accessories.

SAFETY PRECAUTIONS

Observing these precautions will ensure safe handling of the electrical system components, and will avoid damage to the vehicle's electrical system:

A. Be *absolutely* sure of the polarity of a booster battery before making connections. Connect the cables positive to positive, and negative to negative. Connect positive cables first and then make the last connection to a ground on the body of the booster vehicle so that arcing cannot ignite hydrogen gas that may have accumulated near the battery. Even momentary connection of a booster battery with the polarity reversed will damage alternator diodes.

B. Disconnect both vehicle battery cables before attempting to charge a battery.

C. Never ground the alternator or generator output or battery terminal. Be cautious when using metal tools around a battery to avoid creating a short circuit between the terminals.

D. Never ground the field circuit between the alternator and regulator.

E. Never run an alternator or generator without load unless the field circuit is disconnected.

F. Never attempt to polarize an alternator.

G. Keep the regulator cover in place when taking voltage and current limiter readings.

H. Use insulated tools when adjusting the regulator.

I. Whenever DC generator-to-regulator wires have been disconnected, the generator *must* be repolarized. To do this with an externally grounded, light duty generator, momentarily place a jumper wire between the battery terminal and the generator terminal of the regulator. With an internally grounded heavy duty unit, disconnect the wire to the regulator field terminal and touch the regulator battery terminal with it.

High Energy Ignition (HEI) Distributor

The Delco-Remy High Energy Ignition (HEI) System is a breakerless, pulse triggered, transistor controlled, inductive discharge ignition system.

The ignition coil is located with the distributor cap (except on the 1981 and later L4 engines, where it is a separate unit), connecting directly to the rotor. The major difference between the HEI System and the Unit Ignition System is that the HEI System is a full 12 volt system, while the Unit Ignition System incorporates a resistance wire to limit the voltage to the coil except during periods of starter motor operation.

The magnetic pick-up assembly located inside the distributor contains a permanent magnet, a pole piece with internal teeth, and a pick-up coil. When the teeth of the rotating timer core and pole piece align, an induced voltage in the pick-up coil signals the electronic module to open the coil primary circuit. As the primary current decreases, a high voltage is induced in the secondary windings of the ignition coil, directing a spark through the rotor and high voltage leads to fire the spark plugs. The dwell period is automatically controlled by the electronic module and is increased with increasing engine rpm. The HEI System features a longer spark duration which is instrumental in firing lean and EGR diluted fuel/air mixtures. The condenser (capacitor) located within the HEI distributor is provided for noise (static) suppression purposes only and is not a regularly replaced ignition system component.

1981 and later models continue to use the HEI distributor although it now incorporates an Electronic Spark Timing system (for more information on the EST, please refer to Chapter 4). With the new EST system, all spark timing changes are performed electronically by the Electronic Control Module (ECM) which monitors information from various engine sensors, computes the desired spark timing and then signals the distributor to change the timing accordingly. Because all timing changes are controlled electronically, no vacuum or mechanical advance systems are used whatsoever.

The HEI distributor used on the 1981 and later V6 engine is, for the most part, identical to those used in 1980; the only discernible difference being the absence of a vacuum advance unit on its side. As noted previously, the distributor used on the L4 engine no longer utilizes an incorporated ignition coil and it too has no vacuum advance unit.

COMPONENT REPLACEMENT

Ignition Coil

1980 (ALL) 1981 AND LATER (V6)

1. Disconnect the feed and module wire terminal connectors from the distributor cap.
2. Remove the ignition set retainer.
3. Remove the 4 coil cover-to-distributor cap screws and the coil cover.
4. Remove the 4 coil-to-distributor cap screws.
5. Using a blunt drift, press the coil wire spade terminals up out of the distributor cap.
6. Lift the coil up out of the distributor cap.
7. Remove and clean the coil spring, rubber seal washer and coil cavity of the distributor cap.
8. Coat the rubber seal with a dielectric lubricant furnished in the replacement ignition coil package.
9. Reverse the above procedures to install.

1981 AND LATER (L4)

1. Disconnect the negative battery cable.
2. Remove the bolt securing the radio capacitor to the ignition coil and then remove the capacitor.
3. Disconnect the electrical connector and the coil high tension lead.
4. Unscrew the three remaining coil mounting bolts and remove the coil.
5. Installation is in the reverse order of removal.

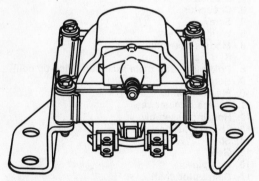

Ignition coil on the 1981 and later L4 engine

Distributor Cap

1980 (ALL), 1981 AND LATER (V6)

1. Remove the feed and module wire terminal connectors from the distributor cap.

NOTE: *It is a good idea to tag the connectors for proper reconnection.*

2. Remove the retainer and spark plug wires from the cap.
3. Depress and release the 4 distributor cap-to-housing retainers and lift off the cap assembly.
4. Remove the 4 coil cover screws and cover.
5. Using a finger or a blunt drift, push the spade terminals up out of the distributor cap.
6. Remove all 4 coil screws and lift the coil, coil spring and rubber seal washer out of the cap coil cavity.
7. Using a new distributor cap, reverse the above procedures to assemble being sure to clean and lubricate the rubber seal washer with dielectric lubricant.

1981 AND LATER (L4)

1. Disconnect the negative battery cable.
2. Tag and disconnect the two multi-terminal connectors leading from the distributor cap.
3. Depress and release the two distributor cap retaining latches and lift off the cap.
4. Installation is in the reverse order of removal.

Rotor

1. Disconnect the negative battery cable.
2. Remove the distributor cap as detailed previously.
3. Unscrew the two rotor attaching screws and then remove the rotor.
4. Installation is in the reverse order of removal.

Vacuum Advance Unit (1980 Only)

1. Remove the distributor cap and rotor as previously described.
2. Disconnect the vacuum hose from the vacuum advance unit.
3. Remove the two vacuum advance retaining screws, pull the advance unit outward, rotate and disengage the operating rod from its tang.
4. Reverse the above procedure to install.

Module

1. Disconnect the negative battery cable.
2. On V6 engines, remove the distributor cap and rotor. On L4 engines, remove the distributor cap, the rotor and the coil.
3. Remove the two module attaching screws and carefully lift the module up.
4. Disconnect the wire connectors from the module. Be sure to observe the color code on the leads as you are removing them because it is imperative that they not be interchanged.
5. Do not wipe the grease from the module

or from the distributor base if the module is to be reused. If a new module is to be installed; a package of silicone grease will be included with it. Spread the grease on the metal surface of the module and on the distributor base where the module will sit. DO NOT NEGLECT TO USE THIS GREASE.

DISTRIBUTOR REMOVAL AND INSTALLATION

CAUTION: *On Chevrolet V6 models the distributor body is involved in the engine lubricating system. The lubricating circuit to the right-bank valve train can be interrupted by misalignment of the distributor body. See Firing Order illustrations for correct distributor positioning.*

NOTE: *On 4-cylinder engines, it may be necessary to support the car with jack stands and remove the 2 rear cradle attaching bolts and lower the cradle enough to allow access to the distributor. If so, also disconnect the brake line support from the floor pan.*

1. Disconnect the negative battery cable.

2. Tag and disconnect all wires leading from the distributor cap.

3. Remove the ignition coil on the 1981 and later L4 engine.

4. Remove the distributor cap by turning the four latches counterclockwise. You will need a stubby screwdriver to get at the latches if your X-Body has the four cylinder engine, because there isn't much room between the distributor and the firewall. Remove the distributor cap and set it aside without disconnecting any of the wires.

5. Remove the vacuum hose from the vacuum advance unit. Mark the position of the vacuum advance unit in relation to the engine, so that the distributor goes back into the engine the same way (1980 only).

6. Remove the hold-down clamp and bolt at the base of the V6 distributor. The four cylinder engine has two bolts and a clamp. Remove the outer bolt first, then loosen, but do not remove, the inner bolt. Slide the clamp back and remove it.

7. Before removing the distributor, note the position of the rotor. Scribe a mark on the distributor body indicating the initial position of the rotor.

8. Remove the distributor from the engine. The drive gear on the distributor shaft is helical, and the shaft will rotate slightly as the distributor is removed. Note and mark the position of the rotor at this second position. Do not crank the engine with the distributor removed.

9. To install the distributor, rotate the distributor shaft until the rotor aligns with the

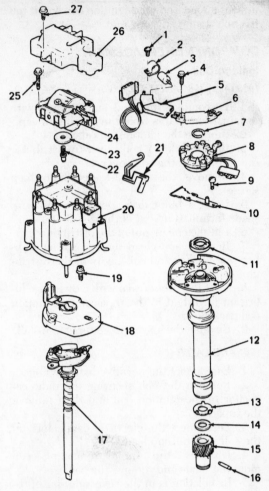

1. Screw
2. Bracket
3. Capacitor
4. Screw
5. Wiring harness
6. Module assembly
7. Retainer
8. Pole piece and plate assembly (Pick-up coil)
9. Screw
10. Plastic retainer
11. Grease retainer seal
12. Housing assembly
13. Thrust washer
14. Shim
15. Gear
16. Roll pin
17. Distributor shaft
18. Rotor
19. Screw
20. Distributor cap
21. Ground Wire
22. Resistor brush and spring
23. Seal
24. Coil
25. Screw
26. Cover
27. Screw

Exploded view of the HEI distributor

second mark you made (when the shaft stopped moving). Lubricate the drive gear with clean engine oil, then install the distributor into the engine, aligning the vacuum advance unit (1980 only) with the mark made before. As the distributor is installed, the rotor should move to the mark you made first, indicating rotor position before the distributor was removed. This will ensure proper timing. If the marks do not align properly remove the distributor and try again.

10. Install the clamp and hold-down bolt. Tighten them until the distributor can just be moved with a little effort.

11. Connect the ignition wire and tachometer wire, and install the distributor cap. Plug the vacuum advance hose (if so equipped). Set the ignition timing (see Chapter Two). Connect the vacuum hose.

INSTALLATION IF THE ENGINE WAS DISTURBED

If the engine was cranked while the distributor was removed, you will have to place the engine on TDC of the compression stroke to obtain proper ignition timing.

1. Remove the No. 1 spark plug.

2. Place your thumb over the spark plug hole. Crank the engine slowly until compression is felt. It will be easier if you have someone rotate the engine by hand, using a wrench on the crankshaft pulley.

3. Align the timing mark on the crankshaft pulley with the 0° mark on the timing scale attached to the front of the engine. This places the engine at TDC of the compression stroke.

4. Turn the distributor shaft until the rotor points between the No. 1 and No. 3 spark plug towers on the cap for the four cylinder engine, or between the No. 1 and No. 6 spark plug towers for the V6.

5. Install the distributor into the engine. For 1980 models, be sure to align the vacuum advance unit with the mark made earlier.

6. Perform Steps 9 and 10 of the preceding removal and installation procedure.

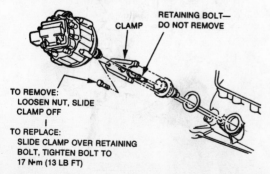

CLAMP

RETAINING BOLT—
DO NOT REMOVE

TO REMOVE:
LOOSEN NUT, SLIDE
CLAMP OFF

TO REPLACE:
SLIDE CLAMP OVER RETAINING
BOLT, TIGHTEN BOLT TO
17 N·m (13 LB FT)

The four cylinder distributor has two clamp bolts

Alternator

The alternating current generator (alternator) supplies a continuous output of electrical energy at all engine speeds. The alternator generates electrical energy for the engine and all electrical components, and recharges the battery by supplying it with current. This unit consists of four main assemblies: two end frame assemblies, a rotor assembly, and a stator assembly. The rotor is supported in the drive end frame by a ball bearing and at the other end by a roller bearing. These bearings are lubricated during manufacture and require no maintenance. There are six diodes in the end frame assembly. Diodes are electrical check valves that change the alternating current supplied from the stator windings to a direct current (DC), delivered to the output (BAT) terminal. Three diodes are negative and are mounted flush with the end frame; the other three are positive and are mounted into a strip called a heat sink. The positive diodes are easily identified as the ones within small cavities or depressions. A capacitor, or condenser, mounted on the end frame protects the rectifier bridge and diode trio from high voltages, and suppresses radio noise. This capacitor requires no maintenance.

Two models of the SI series alternator are used on X-Body cars. The 10 SI and 15 SI are of similar construction; the 15 SI is slightly larger, uses different stator windings, and produces more current. Several different output ratings are used in the X-Body cars.

ALTERNATOR PRECAUTIONS

1. When installing a battery, make sure that the positive and negative cables are not reversed.

2. When jump-starting the car, be sure that like terminals are connected. This also applies to using a battery charger. Reversed polarity will burn out the alternator and regulator in a matter of seconds.

3. Never operate the alternator with the battery disconnected or on an otherwise uncontrolled open circuit.

4. Do not short across or ground any alternator or regulator terminals.

5. Do not try to polarize the alternator.

6. Do not apply full battery voltage to the field (brown) connector.

7. Always disconnect the battery ground cable before disconnecting the alternator lead.

8. Always disconnect the battery (negative cable first) when charging it.

9. Never subject the alternator to excessive heat or dampness. If you are steamcleaning the engine, cover the alternator.

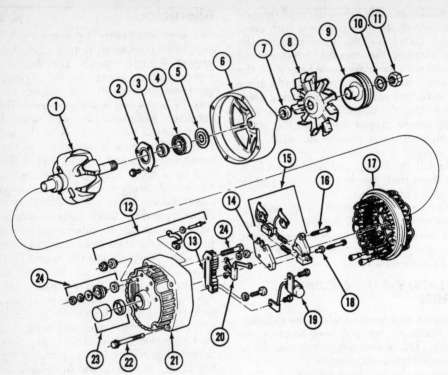

1. Rotor
2. Front bearing retainer
3. Inner collar
4. Bearing
5. Washer
6. Front housing
7. Outer collar
8. Fan
9. Pulley
10. Lockwasher
11. Pulley nut
12. Terminal assembly
13. Rectifier bridge
14. Regulator
15. Brush assembly
16. Screw
17. Stator
18. Insulating washer
19. Capacitor
20. Diode trio
21. Rear housing
22. Through bolt
23. Bearing and seal assembly
24. Terminal assembly

Exploded view of the 10-SI alternator

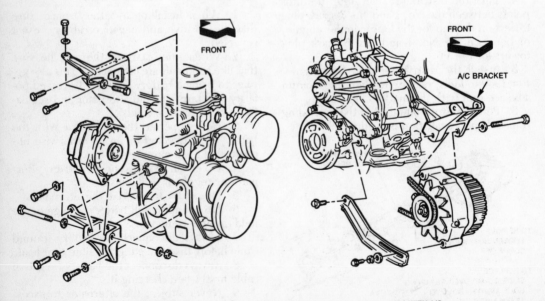

Alternator installation details; models without air conditioning similar

10. Never use arc-welding equipment on the car with the alternator connected.

REMOVAL AND INSTALLATION

1. Disconnect the negative battery cable at the battery.

CAUTION: *Failure to disconnect the negative cable may result in injury from the positive battery lead at the alternator, and may short the alternator and regulator during the removal process.*

2. Disconnect and label the two terminal plug and the battery leads from the rear of the alternator.

3. Loosen the mounting bolts. Push the alternator inwards and slip the drive belt off the pulley.

4. Remove the mounting bolts and remove the alternator.

5. To install, place the alternator in its brackets and install the mounting bolts. Do not tighten them yet.

6. Slip the belt back over the pully. Pull outwards on the unit and adjust the belt tension (see Chapter One). Tighten the mounting and adjusting bolts.

7. Install the electrical leads.

8. Install the negative battery cable.

Regulator

A solid state regulator is mounted within the alternator. All regulator components are enclosed in a solid mold. The regulator is now adjustable and requires no maintenance.

Starter

REMOVAL AND INSTALLATION

1. Disconnect the negative battery cable at the battery.

2. Remove the starter-to-engine brace. On the four cylinder engine, there are two nuts securing the brace to the end of the starter; on the V6, there is one nut.

3. Working under the car, remove the two starter-to-engine bolts, and allow the starter to drop down. Note the location and number of any shims.

4. Label and disconnect the solenoid wires and battery cable. Remove the starter.

5. Installation is the reverse. Tighten the mounting bolts to 25–35 ft. lbs.

STARTER OVERHAUL

Drive Replacement

1. Disconnect the field coil straps from the solenoid.

2. Remove the through bolts, and separate the commutator end frame, field frame assembly, drive housing, and armature assembly from each other.

3. Slide the two piece thrust collar off the end of the armature shaft.

4. Slide a suitably sized metal cylinder, such as a standard half-inch pipe coupling, or an old pinion, on the shaft so that the end of the coupling or pinion butts up against the edge of the pinion retainer.

5. Support the lower end of the armature

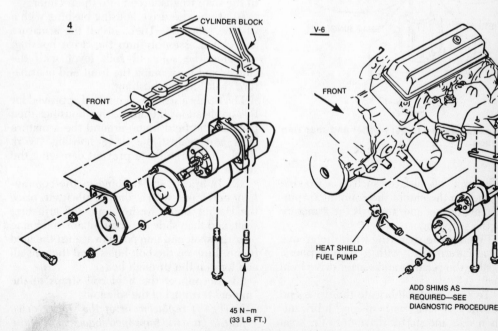

Starter installation details

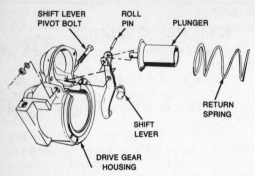

Starter shift lever and drive end housing disassembled

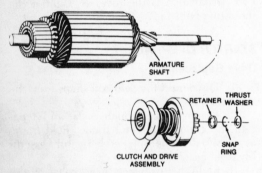

Starter drive assembly details

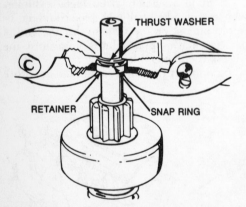

Starter drive retainer, thrust washer and snap ring installation

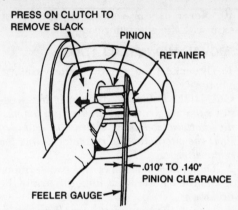

Pinion clearance measurement

securely on a soft surface, such as a wooden block, and tap the end of the coupling or pinion, driving the retainer towards the armature end of the snap ring.

6. Remove the snap ring from the groove in the armature shaft with a pair of pliers. Then, slide the retainer and starter drive from the shaft.

7. To reassemble, lubricate the drive end of the armature shaft with silicone lubricant, and then slide the starter drive onto the shaft with the pinion facing outward. Slide the re-

tainer onto the shaft with cupped surface facing outward.

8. Again support the armature on a soft surface, with the pinion at the upper end. Center the snap ring on the top of the shaft (use a new snap ring if the original was damaged during removal). Gently place a block of wood flat on top of the snap ring so as not to move it from a centered position. Tap the wooden block with a hammer in order to force the snap ring around the shaft. Then, slide the ring down into the snap ring groove.

9. Lay the armature down flat on the surface you're working on. Slide the retainer close up on to the shaft and position it and the thrust collar next to the snap ring. Using two pairs of pliers on opposite sides of the shaft, squeeze the thrust collar and the retainer together until the snap ring is forced into the retainer.

10. Lube the drive housing bushing with a silicone lubricant. Then, install the armature and clutch assembly into the drive housing, engaging the solenoid shift lever with the clutch, and positioning the front end of armature shaft into the bushing.

11. Apply a sealing compound approved for this application onto the drive housing; then position the field frame around the armature shaft and against the drive housing. Work slowly and carefully to prevent damaging the starter brushes.

12. Lubricate the bushing in the commutator end frame with a silicone lubricant, place the leather brake washer onto the armature shaft, and then slide the commutator end frame over the shaft and into position against the field frame. Line up the bolt holes, and then install and tighten the through bolts.

13. Reconnect the field coil straps to the "motor" terminal of the solenoid.

NOTE: *If replacement of the starter drive fails to cure the improper engagement of the starter pinion to the flywheel, there are*

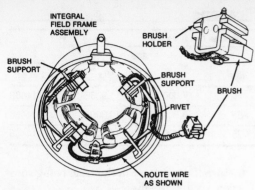

5-MT starter brush replacement detail

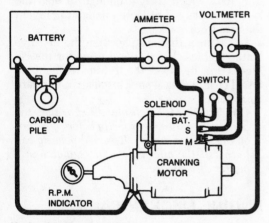

No-load test connections

probably defective parts in the solenoid and/or shift lever. The best procedure would probably be to take the assembly to a shop where a pinion clearance check can be made by energizing the solenoid on a test bench. If the pinion clearance is incorrect, disassemble the solenoid and the shift lever, inspect, and replace worn parts.

Brush Replacement

1. After removing the starter from the engine, disconnect the field coil from the motor solenoid terminal.

2. Remove the starter thru-bolts and remove the commutator end frame and washer.

3. Remove the field frame and the armature assembly from the drive housing.

4. Remove the brush holder pivot pin which positions one insulated and one grounded brush.

5. Remove the brush springs.

6. Remove the brushes.

7. Installation is in the reverse order of removal.

STARTER SOLENOID REMOVAL AND INSTALLATION

1. Remove the screw and washer from the motor connector strap terminal.

2. Remove the two screws which retain the solenoid housing to the end frame assembly.

3. Twist the solenoid clockwise to remove

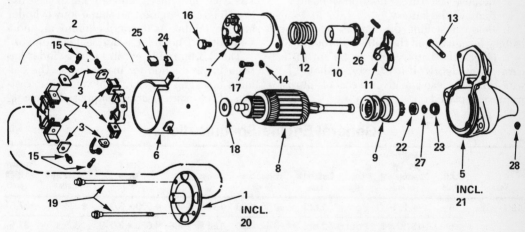

1. Commutator end frame	11. Shift lever	21. Drive end bushing
2. Brush and holder	12. Plunger return spring	22. Pinion stop collar
3. Brush	13. Shift lever shaft	23. Thrust collar
4. Brush holder	14. Lock washer	24. Grommet
5. Drive end housing	15. Brush attaching screw	25. Grommet
6. Frame and field assembly	16. Field lead to switch screw	26. Plunger pin
7. Solenoid switch	17. Switch attaching screw	27. Pinion stop retainer ring
8. Armature	18. Brake washer	28. Lever shaft retaining ring
9. Drive assembly	19. Through bolt	
10. Plunger	20. Commutator end bushing	

Exploded view of the 5-MT starter

Starter Specifications

Engine	Starter Part No.	Series	No-Load Test @ 9 Volts				Solenoid Part No.
			Amps		RPM		
			Min	Max	Min	Max	
'80–'81	1109526	5 MT	45	70	7,000	11,900	1114488
'82–'83	1109530	5 MT	—	85	6,800	10,300	1114488
'84–'85	1109564	5 MT	50	75	6,000	11,900	1114488

the flange key from the keyway slot in the housing.

4. Remove the solenoid assembly.

5. With the solenoid return spring installed on the plunger, position the solenoid body on the drive housing and turn it counterclockwise to engage the flange key in the keyway slot.

6. Install the two screws which retain the solenoid housing to the end frame.

Battery

Refer to Chapter One for details on battery maintenance.

REMOVAL AND INSTALLATION

1. Disconnect the negative (ground) cable first, then the positive cable. The side terminal cables are retained only by the center bolt.

CAUTION: *To avoid sparks, always disconnect the negative cable first, and connect it last.*

2. Remove the battery hold-down clamp.

3. Remove the battery.

4. Before installing the battery, clean the battery terminals and the cables thoroughly.

5. Check the battery tray to be sure it is clear of any debris. If it is rusty, it should be wire-brushed clean and given a coat of antirust paint, or replaced.

6. Install the battery in the tray, being sure it is centered in the lip.

7. Install the hold-down clamp. Tighten to 6 ft. lbs., which is tight enough to hold the battery in place, but loose enough to prevent the case from cracking.

8. Connect the positive, then the negative battery cables. Installation torque for the cables is 9 ft. lbs. Give the terminals a light external coat of grease after installation to retard corrosion.

CAUTION: *Make absolutely sure that the battery is connected properly before you turn on the ignition switch. Reversed polarity can burn out the alternator and regulator in a matter of seconds.*

ENGINE MECHANICAL

Design

The Citation, Omega, Phoenix and Skylark use two different engines, an inline four cylinder built by Pontiac as standard equipment, and a V6 built by Chevrolet as optional equipment.

The 2.5 liter (151 cu. in.) four cylinder has been in production for many years. The cylinder head and block are lightweight iron castings. Five main bearings support the crank-

General Engine Specifications

Year	V.I.N. Code	Engine No. Cyl Displacement (cu in.)	Eng. Mfg.	Carburetor Type	Horsepower @ rpm	Torque @ rpm (ft. lbs.)	Bore x Stroke (in.)	Compression Ratio	Oil Pressure @ 2000 rpm
1980–81	5	4-151	Pont.	2 bbl	90 @ 4000	134 @ 2400	4.000 x 3.000	8.2:1	37.5
	5	4-151 Calif.	Pont.	2 bbl	90 @ 4400	128 @ 2400	4.000 x 3.000	8.2:1	37.5
	X	6-173	Chev.	2 bbl	115 @ 4800	145 @ 2400	3.500 x 3.000	8.5:1	30–45
	X	6-173 Calif.	Chev.	2 bbl	110 @ 4800	140 @ 2400	3.500 x 3.000	8.5:1	30–45
	Z	6-173 HO①	Chev.	2 bbl	135 @ 4800	165 @ 2400	3.500 x 3.000	8.9:1	30–45
'82–'85	R	4-151	Pont.	T.B.I.	90 @ 4000	132 @ 2800	4.000 x 3.000	8.2:1	36–41
	5	4-151	Pont.	2-bbl.	90 @ 4000	132 @ 2800	4.000 x 3.000	8.2:1	36–41
	X	6-173	Chev.	2-bbl.	112 @ 4800	145 @ 3400	3.500 x 3.000	8.5:1	30–45
	Z	6-173 HO	Chev.	2-bbl.	135 @ 5400	145 @ 2400	3.500 x 3.000	8.9:1	30–45

① Available in Citation X-11 only

Torque Specifications
All readings in ft. lbs.

Year	Engine No. Cyl Displacement (cu in.)	Cylinder Head Bolts	Rod Bearing Bolts	Main Bearing Bolts	Crankshaft Bolt	Flywheel to Crankshaft Bolts	Manifold	
							Intake	Exhaust
1980–85	4-151	①	32	70	200	44	29	44
	6-173	70	37	68	75	50	22	25

① 1980–83: 75; 84–85: 92

Piston and Ring Specifications
(All measurements are given in inches. To convert inches to metric units, refer to the Metric Information section.)

Year	V.I.N. Code	Engine Type/ Disp. cu. in.	Eng. Mfg.	Piston-to-Bore Clearance	Ring Gap			Ring Side Clearance		
					Top Compression	Bottom Compression	Oil Control	Top Compression	Bottom Compression	Oil Control
'80–'85	R,5	4-151	Pont.	0.0025–0.0033	0.010–① 0.022	0.010–② 0.027	0.015–0.055	0.0015–0.0030	0.0015–0.0030	snug
	X,Z	6-173	Chev.	0.0017–0.0027	0.0098–0.0197	0.0098–0.0197	0.020–③ 0.055	0.0012–④ 0.0028	0.0016–④ 0.0037	0.008 max.

① 1980: 0.015–0.025   ③ 1980: 0.015–0.055
② 1980: 0.009–0.019   ④ 1980: 0.012–0.032

Valve Specifications

Year	Engine No. Cyl Displacement (cu in.)	Seat Angle (deg)	Face Angle (deg)	Spring Test Pressure (lbs. @ In.)	Spring Installed Height (in.)	Stem to Guide Clearance (in.)		Stem Diameter (in.)	
						Intake	Exhaust	Intake	Exhaust
1980–85	4-151	46	45	176 @ 1.25	1.66	.0010–.0027	.0010–.0027	.3421	.3421
	6-173	46	45	155 @ 1.16	1.61	.0010–.0027	.0010–.0027	.3413	.3413

Crankshaft and Connecting Rod Specifications
All measurements are given in inches

Year	Engine No. Cyl Displacement (cu in.)	Crankshaft				Connecting Rod		
		Main Brg Journal Dia	Main Brg Oil Clearance	Shaft End-Play	Thrust on No.	Journal Diameter	Oil Clearance	Side Clearance
1980–85	4-151	2.3000	.0005–.0022	.0035–.0085	5	2.0000	.0005–.0026	.006–.022
1980–83	6-173	2.4940	.0005–.0015	.0020–.0067 ①	3	2.0000	.0005–.0020	.006–.017
1984–85	6-173	2.4940	.0017–.0030	.0020–.0067 ①	3	1.9994	.0014–.0036	.006–.017

① 1980: 0.0020–0.0079

Camshaft Specifications
(All measurements in inches)

Year	Engine	Journal Diameter					Bearing Clearance	Lobe Lift		Camshaft End Play
		1	2	3	4	5		Intake	Exhaust	
'80–83	4-151	1.869	1.869	1.869	—	—	0.0007–0.0027	0.406 ①	0.406 ①	0.0015–0.0050
	6-173	1.871	1.871	1.871	1.871	—	0.0010–0.0039	0.231	0.263	—
'84–85	4-151	1.869	1.869	1.869	—	—	.0007–.0027	.398	.398	.0015–.0050
	6-173	1.869	1.869	1.869	1.869	—	.0010–.0040	.231	.263	—

① 1981: 0.398

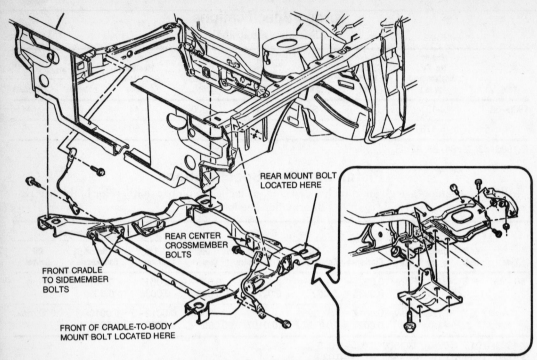

REAR MOUNT BOLT
LOCATED HERE

REAR CENTER
CROSSMEMBER
BOLTS

FRONT CRADLE
TO SIDEMEMBER
BOLTS

FRONT OF CRADLE-TO-BODY
MOUNT BOLT LOCATED HERE

Engine cradle attachment points

shaft, which is made from cast nodular iron. In 1979, Pontiac updated the cylinder head design to a crossflow configuration; in the X-Body cars, the intake manifold is at the rear of the car and the exhaust manifold is at the front. A crossflow design permits better scavenging of gases and more efficient combustion. The intake manifold is made from cast aluminum, and has an integral passage through which engine coolant circulates, providing faster warmup and lower exhaust emissions. An EGR port is cast into the manifold, receiving exhaust gases from an internal passage in the head. The cylinder head has integrally-cast straight valve guides. Ball-pivot rocker arms are operated by pushrods driven by the camshaft through hydraulic lifters. Zero lash is maintained by the lifters, which require no periodic adjustment. Three ring cast aluminum pistons are connected to the crankshaft by Armasteel connecting rods. Camshaft drive is taken from the crankshaft by a bakelite fabric composition gear; the crankshaft gear is cast iron. One feature of the engine appreciated by do-it-yourselfers is the inclusion of pushrod covers on the side of the engine, which permit lifter replacement without removal of the cylinder head.

The Chevrolet 2.8 liter (173 cu. in.) V6 is an entirely new design. Most striking is the 60° bank angle of the cylinders. This design creates a more compact engine layout than the conventional 90° V bank arrangement. A 60° layout is also inherently better balanced when used with six cylinders, since a 120° firing order results naturally, providing harmonic balancing without the need for special and less satisfactory crankshaft configurations. In other respects, the Chevrolet V6 follows the conventional design of the highly respected small-block Chevrolet V8. The cylinder block and head are cast from iron. The cast nodular iron crankshaft is supported by four main bearings; number three is the thrust bearing. Camshaft drive is taken from the crankshaft by a conventional ⅜ inch pitch chain and sintered iron sprockets. Ball-pivot rocker arms are used, mounted on individually-threaded studs. The rocker arms are driven by pushrods actuated by zero-lash hydraulic lifters. Push rods are located by a guide plate held under the rocker arm stud. The intake manifold is cast from aluminum, as are the water pump and pistons. Connecting rods are made from forged steel.

Engine Removal

Follow Steps 1–9 for all models.

1. Disconnect the battery cables at the battery, negative cable first.

2. Remove the air cleaner.

3. Drain the cooling system.

4. Disconnect and label the distributor starter and alternator wires, the engine-to-

ground strap, the oil pressure and engine temperature wires, and all other engine electrical connections.

5. Disconnect and label all vacuum hose connections.

6. Disconnect the throttle and transaxle linkage (automatic) at the carburetor.

7. Disconnect the radiator and heater hoses.

8. Remove the power steering pump and air conditioning compressor from their mounting brackets and set them aside, without disconnecting any hoses.

9. Remove the front engine strut assembly.

NOTE: *On 1982 and later 4 cyl. engines with electric fuel pumps, relieve the pressure in the fuel system as described under Electric Fuel Pump in Chapter Four.*

All Four Cylinder Models, and Six Cylinder with Automatic Transaxle

10. Remove the engine front mount-to-engine cradle nuts.

11. Remove the forward exhaust pipe or crossover pipe.

12. Disconnect and plug the fuel lines. Disconnect the battery cables from the starter and transaxle housing.

13. Remove the flywheel cover. Remove the starter on four cylinder models. Remove the torque converter-to-flywheel bolts on all automatic models.

14. On the four cylinder, remove the transaxle-to-engine bolts, leaving the upper two in place. Remove the two rear transaxle support bracket bolts. Place a block of wood under the transaxle and raise the engine and transaxle unit with a jack until the engine front mount studs clear the engine cradle. Support the engine with a lifting chain. Remove the two transaxle-to-engine bolts. Slide the engine forward and lift from the car.

15. On the six cylinder, remove the transaxle case-to-engine support bracket bolts. Place a support under the transaxle rear extension. Remove the transaxle-to-engine retaining bolts. Install a lifting chain on the engine and remove the engine from the car.

All Six Cylinder with Manual Transaxle

10. Disconnect the clutch cable, shift linkage cables, and speedometer cable from the transaxle.

11. Attach a lifting chain to the engine and raise it until the engine weight is off the mounts.

12. Remove all the transaxle-to-engine bolts except one.

13. Unlock the steering column. Raise the

car. Remove the stabilizer-to-lower control arm bolts. Remove the stabilizer bar plate on the left side, and loosen the plate bolts on the right side. Remove the left side crossmember assembly-to-side member bolts.

14. Remove the exhaust crossover pipe.

15. Remove all front, side and rear engine/transaxle-to-cradle nuts.

16. Remove the left wheel.

17. Remove the front crossmember-to-right side member bolts.

18. Pull the axle shafts from the transaxle using G.M. special tool J-28468 or equivalent.

19. Remove the engine cradle-to-body mount bolts on the left side.

20. Swing the side member and crossmember assembly to the left. Secure it outside the fender well.

21. Lower the left side of the engine/transaxle assembly. Place a block of wood under the transaxle and support the transaxle with a jack. Remove the last transaxle-to-engine bolt and separate and lower the transaxle out of the car. Lift the engine from the car.

Engine Installation
All Four Cylinder Models

1. Lower the engine into the cradle, aligning the transaxle and engine bellhousing.

2. With the engine still supported, install two upper transaxle-to-engine bolts. Do not lower the engine completely while the transaxle is still supported by the jack.

3. Remove the transaxle jack.

4. Lower the engine. Install the rest of the transaxle-to-engine bolts. Install the front mount-to-chassis nuts. The remainder of installation is the reverse of removal.

Six Cylinder with Automatic Transaxle

Lower the engine into the cradle. Check that the engine front mount studs are properly located. Line up the transaxle, install, and tighten the transaxle-to-engine bolts to 55 ft. lbs. The rest of installation is the reverse of removal.

Six Cylinder with Manual Transaxle

1. Lower the engine into place. Check that the engine front mount studs are properly located.

2. Support the engine with the lifting chain. Allow the left side to drop slightly.

3. Install the forward strut bracket to the radiator support.

4. Raise the car. Raise the transaxle into the car, align with the engine, and install at least one transaxle-to-engine bolt. Start the right

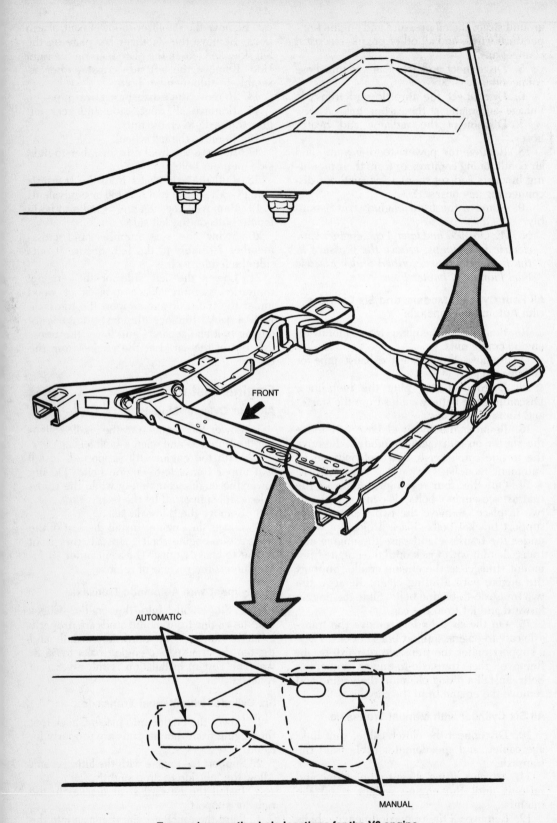

AUTOMATIC

MANUAL

FRONT

Transaxle mounting hole locations for the V6 engine

side axle shaft into the transaxle as the transaxle is installed.

5. Raise the left side of the engine/transaxle unit with the lifting chain.

6. Swing the side member and crossmember assembly into place, starting the left axle shaft into the transaxle as the assembly is installed. Assemble the cradle.

7. The rest of installation is the reverse of removal.

Rocker Arm (Valve) Cover
REMOVAL AND INSTALLATION
Four Cylinder

1. Remove the air cleaner.
2. Remove the PCV valve and hose from the rocker cover.
3. Remove the rocker cover bolts.
4. Remove the spark plug wires from the spark plugs and clips.
5. Rap the rocker cover with a rubber hammer to break the RTV gasket seal, then remove the cover.

NOTE: *Do not pry on the cover.*

6. Installation is the reverse of removal. Thoroughly clean the sealing surfaces then apply a continuous diameter bead of RTV to the rocker cover.

Six Cylinder
RIGHT SIDE

1. Disconnect the negative battery cable.
2. Remove the air cleaner.

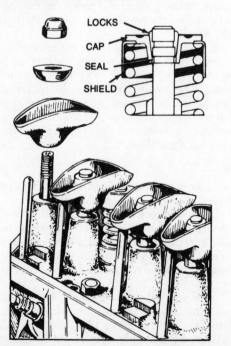

Rocker arm, pivot and nut, and valve lock details

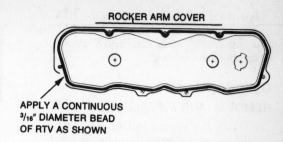

ROCKER ARM COVER

APPLY A CONTINUOUS
3/16" DIAMETER BEAD
OF RTV AS SHOWN

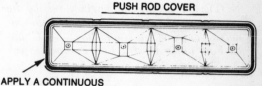

PUSH ROD COVER

APPLY A CONTINUOUS
3/16" DIAMETER BEAD
OF RTV AS SHOWN

Four cylinder rocker arm and pushrod cover sealer application

3. Disconnect the spark plug wires from the plugs and cover.

4. Remove the accelerator linkage and springs from the carburetor.

5. If equipped with automatic transaxle, disconnect the T.V. linkage from the carburetor.

6. If equipped with cruise control, remove the diaphragm actuator mounting bracket.

7. Remove the air management valve and necessary hoses.

8. Remove the cover retaining bolts and remove the cover.

9. Installation is the reverse of removal. Clean all sealing surfaces and apply a ⅛" bead of RTV sealant along sealing surfaces.

NOTE: *When sealing around the attaching bolt holes, always flow the RTV on the inboard side of the holes. Keep the RTV Sealant out of the bolt holes as this could cause a "hydraulic" condition which would damage the head casting.*

LEFT SIDE

1. Disconnect the negative battery cable.
2. Remove the air cleaner.
3. Remove the front engine strut, at the radiator support and engine bracket.
4. Disconnect the vacuum hoses and spark plug wires.
5. Remove the front engine strut bracket from the cylinder head.
6. Remove the cover to head retaining bolts and remove the cover.
7. Installation is the reverse of removal. Clean the sealing surfaces and apply a ⅛" bead of RTV sealant all around the sealing surfaces.

NOTE: *When sealing around the attaching bolt holes, always flow the RTV on the in-*

board side of the holes. Keep the RTV sealant out of the bolt holes as this could cause a "hydraulic" condition which would damage the head casting.

Cylinder Head

REMOVAL AND INSTALLATION

NOTE: *The engine should be "overnight" cold before removing the cylinder head.*
NOTE: *On fuel injected engines, relieve the pressure in the fuel system before disconnecting any fuel line connections. See Chapter Four under Electric Fuel Pump.*

Four Cylinder

1. Drain the cooling system into a clean container; the coolant can be reused if it is still good.
2. Remove the air cleaner.
3. Remove the intake and exhaust manifolds. Removal of these parts is covered later in this chapter.
4. Remove the alternator bracket bolts.
5. If the car has air conditioning, remove the A/C compressor bracket bolts and position the compressor to one side. *Do not disconnect any of the refrigerant lines.*
6. Disconnect and label all the vacuum and electrical connections from the cylinder head.
7. Disconnect the upper radiator hose.
8. Label and disconnect the spark plug wires. Remove the plugs.

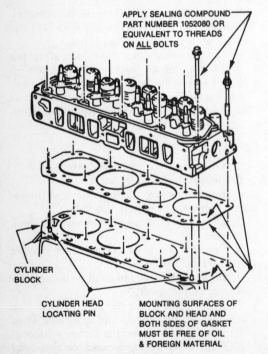

APPLY SEALING COMPOUND PART NUMBER 1052080 OR EQUIVALENT TO THREADS ON ALL BOLTS

CYLINDER BLOCK

CYLINDER HEAD LOCATING PIN

MOUNTING SURFACES OF BLOCK AND HEAD AND BOTH SIDES OF GASKET MUST BE FREE OF OIL & FOREIGN MATERIAL

Four cylinder head installation

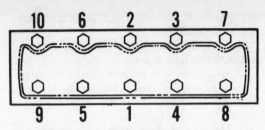

Four cylinder head torque sequence

9. Remove the rocker arm cover (valve cover), rocker arms and pushrods. Their removal is covered later in this chapter. Keep these parts in order; they must be returned to their original locations.
10. Remove the cylinder head bolts and carefully lift off the cylinder head.
11. Thoroughly clean the cylinder block and head mating surfaces. Check the block and head for flatness before installing the head. See the "Engine Rebuilding" section at the end of this chapter for details on how to do this. Clean out the bolt holes in the cylinder block; any dirt in them will affect the head bolt torque measurement.
12. Install a new gasket over the dowel pins on the cylinder block. The gasket, block and head must be absolutely free of any grease, oil, or other foreign matter.
13. Carefully lower the cylinder head into place on the block.
14. Coat the head bolt threads with sealer and install finger tight.
15. Tighten the bolts in the sequence shown, in three equal and progressive steps to the specified torque. Final torque is 90 ft. lbs. (120 Nm.).
16. The rest of installation is the reverse of removal. Be sure to use new gaskets on the manifolds. Lubricate all valve train parts with clean oil before assembly. See the rocker arm removal and installation procedure later in this chapter for rocker arm installation. It is not necessary to re-torque the cylinder head once it has been installed.

V6

1. Remove the intake manifold. This procedure is covered later in this chapter.
2. Disconnect the exhaust pipe from the exhaust manifold flange. You will need new bolts to reconnect these parts if you are working on the right cylinder head, see the exhaust manifold removal procedure later in this chapter.
3. If you are working on the left cylinder head, remove the alternator bracket and stud. Remove the heat stove pipe and the PULSAIR pipe (air supply pipe for 1981). Remove the oil dipstick tube bracket from the head.

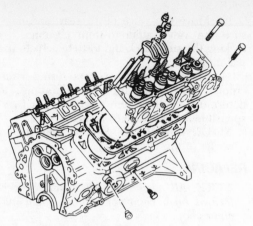

V6 cylinder head installation

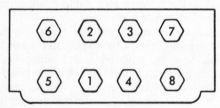

V6 cylinder head torque sequence

4. Remove the valve covers. Loosen the rocker arms until they can be pivoted aside, and remove the pushrods. Keep the pushrods in order; they must be returned to their original positions.

5. Remove the cylinder head bolts. Carefully lift off the cylinder head.

6. Thoroughly clean the cylinder block and head mating surfaces. Check the block and head for flatness before installing the head. See the "Engine Rebuilding" section at the end of this chapter for details on how to do this. Clean out the bolt holes in the cylinder block. Any dirt in them will affect the head bolt torque readings.

7. Place a new gasket in position over the dowel pins. The words "This Side Up" should be showing. Do not use sealer on the gasket.

8. Carefully lower the cylinder head into position.

9. Coat the head bolt threads with sealer and install them finger tight. Torque the cylinder head bolts in three progressive steps to the specified torque, using the pattern shown here. Final torque is 70 ft. lbs. (90 Nm.)

10. Install the pushrods into their original locations, pivot the rocker arms into place and tighten them just enough to hold the pushrods in place. Be sure the pushrods are correctly seated in the lifters.

11. Install the intake manifold.

12. Install the dipstick tube bracket, heat stove pipe, PULSAIR pipe (air supply pipe in 1981), and alternator bracket and stud to the left cylinder head.

13. Install the exhaust pipe to the manifold.

14. Adjust the valve lash to zero clearance, as described later in this chapter.

CLEANING AND INSPECTION

Chip carbon away from the valve heads, combustion chambers, and ports, using a chisel made of hardwood. Remove the remaining deposits with a stiff wire brush.

NOTE: *Be sure that the deposits are actually removed, rather than burnished.*

Have the cylinder head hot-tanked to remove grease, corrosion, and scale from the water passages. Clean the remaining cylinder head parts in an engine cleaning solvent. Do not remove the protective coating from the springs.

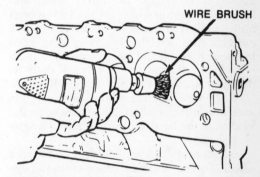

Remove the carbon from the cylinder head with a wire brush and electric drill

RESURFACING

NOTE: *All machine work should be performed by a competent, professional machine shop.*

Place a straight-edge across the gasket surface of the cylinder head. Using feeler gauges, determine the clearance at the center of the straight-edge. If warpage exceeds .003″ in a 6″ span, or .006″ over the total length, the cylinder head must be resurfaced.

NOTE: *If warpage exceeds the manufactur-*

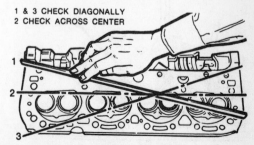

Check the cylinder head for warpage

er's maximum tolerance for material removal, the cylinder head must be replaced.

When milling the cylinder heads of V-type engines, the intake manifold mounting position is altered, and must be corrected by milling the manifold flange a proportionate amount.

Valves

REMOVAL AND INSPECTION

1. Remove the cylinder head(s) from the vehicle as previously outlined.

2. Using a suitable valve spring compressor, compress the valve spring and remove the valve keys using a magentic retrieval tool.

3. Slowly release the compressor and remove the valve spring caps (or rotators) and the valve springs.

4. Fabricate a valve arrangement board to use when you remove the valves, which will indicate the port in which each valve was originally installed (and which cylinder head on V6 models). Also note that the valve keys, rotators, caps, etc. should be arranged in a manner which will allow you to reinstall them on the valve on which they were originally used.

5. Remove and discard the valve seals. On models using the umbrella type seals, note the location of the large and small seals for assembly purposes.

6. Thoroughly clean the valves on the wire wheel of a bench grinder, then clean the cylinder head mating surface with a) a soft wire wheel, b) a soft wire brush, or c) a wooden scraper. Avoid using a metallic scraper, since this can cause damage to the cylinder head mating surface, especially on models with aluminum heads.

7. Using a valve guide cleaner chucked into a drill, clean all of the valve guides.

8. Reinstall each valve into its respective port (guide) of the cylinder head.

9. Mount a dial indicator so that the stem is at 90° to the valve stem, as close to the valve guide as possible.

10. Move the valve off its seat, and measure the valve guide-to-stem clearance by rocking the stem back and forth to actuate the dial indicator.

11. Measure the valve stems using a micrometer, and compare to specifications, to determine whether stem or guide wear is responsible for excessive clearance.

NOTE: *Consult the Specifications tables earlier in this chapter.*

REFACING

NOTE: *All machine work should be performed by a competent, professional machine shop.*

Using a valve grinder, resurface the valves according to specifications in this chapter.

CAUTION: *Valve face angle is not always identical to valve seat angle.*

A minimum margin of $1/32''$ should remain after grinding the valve. The valve stem top should also be squared and resurfaced, by placing the stem in the V-block of the grinder, and turning it while pressing lightly against the grinding wheel. Be sure to chamfer the edge of the tip so that the squared edges don't dig into the rocker arm.

LAPPING

This procedure should be performed after the valves and seats have been machined, to insure that each valve mates to each seat precisely.

1. Invert the cylinder head, lightly lubricate the valve stems, and install the valves in the head as numbered.

2. Coat valve seats with fine grinding compound, and attach the lapping tool suction cup to a valve head.

NOTE: *Moisten the suction cup.*

3. Rotate the tool between the palms,

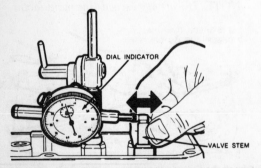

Checking the valve stem-to-guide clearance

Lapping the valves by hand

changing position and lifting the tool often to prevent grooving.

4. Lap the valve until a smooth, polished seat is evident.

5. Remove the valve and tool, and rinse away all traces of grinding compound.

VALVE GUIDE SERVICE

The valve guides used in any of the X-Car engines are integral with the cylinder head, that is, they cannot be replaced.

NOTE: *Refer to the previous "Valves—Removal and Installation" to check the valve guides for wear.*

Valve guides are most accurately repaired using the bronze wall rebuilding method. In this operation, "threads" are cut into the bore of the valve guide and bronze wire is turned into the threads. The bronze "wall" is then reamed to the proper diameter. This method is well received for a number of reasons: a) it is relatively inexpensive, b) offers better valve lubrication (the wire forms channels which retain oil), c) less valve friction, and d) preserves the original valve guide-to-seat relationship.

Another popular method of repairing valve guides is to have the guides "knurled". The knurling entails cutting into the bore of the valve guide with a special too. The cutting action "raises" metal off of the guide bore which actually narrows the inner diameter of the bore, thereby reducing the clearance between the valve guide bore and the valve stem. This method offers the same advantages as the bronze wall method, but will generally wear faster.

Either of the above services must be performed by a professional machine shop which has the specialized knowledge and tools necessary to perform the service.

VALVE SEAT SERVICE

The valve seats are integral with the cylinder head on all engines. On all engines the seats are machined into the cylinder head casting itself.

Machining of the valve seats should be referred to a professional machine shop.

VALVE SPRING TESTING

Place the spring on a flat surface next to a square. Measure the height of the spring, and rotate it against the edge of the square to measure distortion. If spring height varies (by comparison) by more than $^1/_{16}''$ or if distortion exceeds $^1/_{16}''$ replace the spring.

In addition to evaluating the spring as

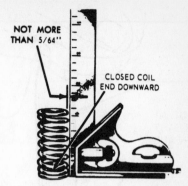

NOT MORE THAN 5/64"

CLOSED COIL END DOWNWARD

Checking the valve spring free length and squareness

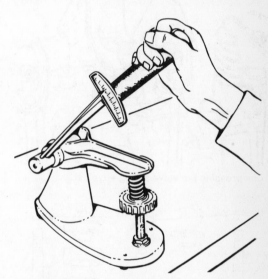

Checking the valve spring pressure

above, test the spring pressure at the installed and compressed (installed height minus valve lift) height using a valve spring tester. Spring pressure should be ± 1 lb of all other springs in either position.

VALVE AND SPRING INSTALLATION

NOTE: *Be sure that all traces of lapping compound have been cleaned off before the valves are installed.*

1. Lubricate all of the valve stems with a light coating of engine oil then install the valves into the proper ports/guides.

2. If umbrella-type valve seals are used, install them at this time. Be sure to use a seal protector to prevent damage to the seals as they are pushed over the valve keeper grooves.

If O-ring seals are used, don't install them yet.

3. Install the valve springs and the spring retainers (or rotators), and using the valve compressing tool, compress the springs.

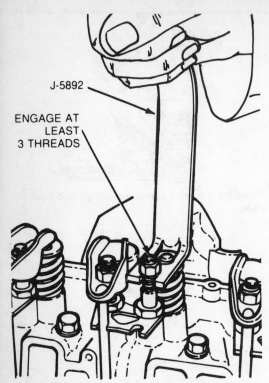

J-5892

ENGAGE AT
LEAST
3 THREADS

Compressing the valve spring—typical

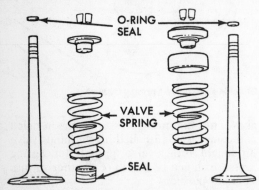

O-RING
SEAL

VALVE
SPRING

SEAL

Valves and parts—V6 engine (intake valve shown on the left)

4. If umbrella-type seals are used, just install the valve keepers (white grease may be used to hold them in place) and release the pressure on the compressing tool. If O-ring type seals are used, carefully work the seals into the second groove of the valve (closest to the head), install the valve keepers and release the pressure on the tool.

NOTE: *If the O-ring seals are installed BEFORE the springs and retainers are compressed, the seal will be destroyed.*

5. After all of the valves are installed and retained, tap each valve spring retainer with a rubber mallet to seat the keepers in the retainer.

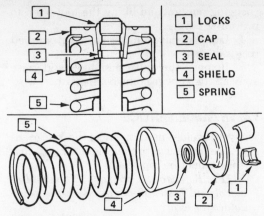

1	LOCKS
2	CAP
3	SEAL
4	SHIELD
5	SPRING

Valve spring installation—4 cylinder engine

Rocker Arms

REMOVAL AND INSTALLATION

1. Remove the valve (rocker arm) cover.
2. Remove the rocker arm nut and ball.
3. Lift the rocker arm off the stud. *Always keep the rocker arm assemblies together and install them on the same stud.*
4. Lubricate the parts with clean engine oil before installation. Install the rocker arm, then the ball and nut. On the four cylinder engine, tighten the rocker arm nut to 20 ft. lbs. with the lifter on the base circle of the camshaft: rotate the crankshaft with a wrench on the crankshaft pulley until the rocker arm is all the way down, then tighten the nut. On the V6, adjust the valve lash, as outlined in the following section.
5. Clean all the old sealant from the rocker arm cover. Apply a thin ($3/16''$) bead of RTV

NOTE: AT TIME OF INSTALLATION FLANGES MUST BE FREE OF OIL. A 2–3 MM BEAD OF SEALANT MUST BE APPLIED TO FLANGES & SEALANT MUST BE SET TO TOUCH WHEN BOLTS ARE TORQUED.

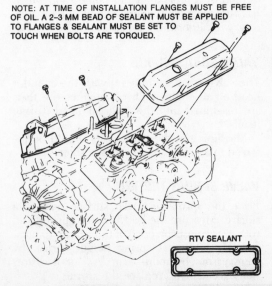

RTV SEALANT

V6 rocker arm cover sealer application

sealer to the rocker cover; run the bead to the inside of the bolt holes. Install the rocker cover, and tighten the retaining bolts to 8 ft. lbs. while the sealer is still wet.

Rocker Arm Studs

Rocker arm studs that have damaged threads or which are loose in the cylinder heads may be replaced with new studs. Studs are available in oversizes, or the bores may be tapped and replacement studs used, on the V6 engine. The standard studs in the V6 are a press fit. The studs in the four cylinder engine are threaded into the head. Old studs can be removed with a deep socket. New studs should be threaded in and tightened to 75 ft. lbs. (100 Nm.).

Valve Adjustment

No valve lash adjustment is required on the four cylinder engine. Tighten the rocker arm nuts to 20 ft. lbs., as outlined in the rocker arm removal and installation procedure given previously.

Anytime the V6 valve train is disturbed, the valve lash must be adjusted, as follows:

Crank the engine until the timing mark aligns with the "0" mark on the timing scale,

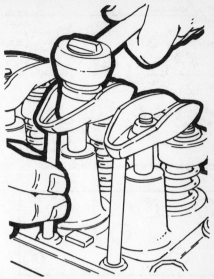

V6 valve adjustment; tighten the rocker arm nut until the pushrod cannot be rotated between your fingers

and both valves in the No. 1 cylinder are closed. If the valves are moving as the timing marks align, the engine is in the No. 4 firing position. Turn the crankshaft one more revolution. With the engine in the No. 1 firing position, adjust the following valves:

- Exhaust—1,2,3
- Intake—1,5,6

Rotate the crankshaft one full revolution, until it is in the No. 4 firing position. Adjust the following valves:

- Exhaust—4,5,6
- Intake—2,3,4

Adjustment is made by backing off the rocker arm adjusting nut until there is play in the pushrod. Tighten the nut to remove the pushrod clearance (this can be determined by rotating the pushrod with your fingers while tightening the adjusting nut). When the pushrod cannot be freely turned, tighten the nut 1½ additional turns to place the hydraulic lifter in the center of its travel. No further adjustment is required.

Intake Manifold

REMOVAL AND INSTALLATION

Four Cylinder

NOTE: *Bleed pressure from the fuel system, if equipped with fuel injection, before servicing. See Chapter Four, "Electric Fuel Pump."*

1. Remove the air cleaner and the PCV valve.

2. Drain the cooling system into a clean container.

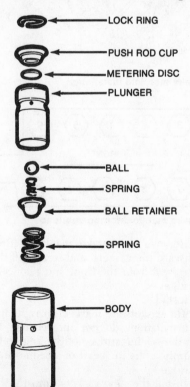

LOCK RING

PUSH ROD CUP

METERING DISC

PLUNGER

BALL

SPRING

BALL RETAINER

SPRING

BODY

Exploded view of a hydraulic lifter

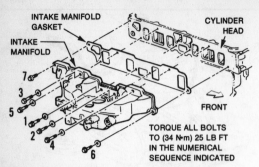

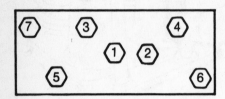

Four cylinder intake manifold installation

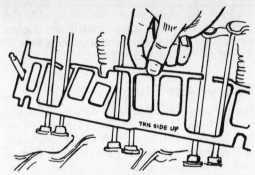

Cut the V6 intake manifold gasket as necessary to slip it past the inner pushrods

Four cylinder intake manifold torque sequence

3. Disconnect and label the fuel and vacuum lines and the electrical connections at the carburetor and the manifold.

4. Disconnect the throttle linkage and the transaxle downshift linkage at the carburetor or E.F.I Unit.

5. Remove the carburetor and the spacer.

6. Remove the bell crank and the throttle linkage. Position to the side for clearance.

7. Remove the heater hose at the intake manifold.

8. Remove the air system check valve bracket from the manifold.

9. Remove the manifold attaching bolts and remove the manifold.

10. To install, reverse the removal procedure. Always use a new gasket. Tighten all the bolts in two stages to 25 ft. lbs. in the proper sequence.

V6

1. Remove the rocker covers.

2. Drain the cooling system.

3. Remove the distributor cap. Mark the position of the ignition rotor in relation to the distributor body and remove the distributor. Do not crank the engine with the distributor removed.

4. Remove the heater and radiator hoses from the intake manifold.

5. Remove the power brake vacuum hose.

6. Disconnect and label the vacuum hoses. Remove the EFE pipe from the rear of the manifold.

7. Remove the carburetor linkage. Disconnect and plug the fuel line.

8. Remove the manifold retaining bolts and nuts.

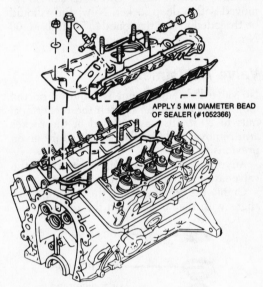

V6 intake manifold installation

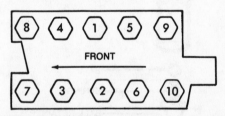

V6 intake manifold torque sequence

9. Remove the intake manifold. Remove and discard the gaskets, and scrape off the old silicone seal from the front and rear cylinder case ridges.

To install:

1. The gaskets are marked for right and left side installation; do not interchange them. Clean the sealing surface of the engine block, and apply a $^3/_{16}$ in. bead of silicone sealer to each ridge.

2. Install the new gaskets onto the heads. The gaskets will have to be cut slightly to fit past the center pushrods. Do not cut any more

material than necessary. Hold the gaskets in place by extending the ridge bead of sealer ¼ in. onto the gasket ends.

3. Install the intake manifold. The area between the ridges and the manifold should be completely sealed.

4. Install the retaining bolts and nuts, and tighten in sequence to 23 ft. lbs. Do not overtighten; the manifold is made from aluminum, and can be warped or cracked with excessive force.

5. The rest of installation is the reverse of removal. Adjust the ignition timing after installation, and check the coolant level after the engine has warmed up.

Exhaust Manifold

REMOVAL AND INSTALLATION

Four Cylinder

1. Remove the air cleaner and the carburetor or EFI pre-heat tube.

2. Remove the manifold strut bolts from the radiator support panel and the cylinder head.

3. If equipped with air conditioning, remove the A/C compressor bracket bolts and position the compressor to one side. *Do not disconnect any of the refrigerant lines.*

4. Remove the dipstick tube attaching bolt.

5. Raise the car and disconnect the exhaust pipe from the manifold.

6. Remove the manifold attaching bolts and remove the manifold.

7. To install, place a new gasket into position and install the exhaust manifold over it. Install the retaining bolts finger tight, then tighten in two stages to 44 ft. lbs. (60 Nm.) in the sequence shown. The remainder of installation is the reverse of removal.

V6

LEFT SIDE

1. Remove the air cleaner. Remove the carburetor heat stove pipe.

2. Remove the PULSAIR pipes from the exhaust manifold (on 1981 and later models, remove the air supply plumbing).

3. Raise and support the car. Unbolt and remove the exhaust pipe at the manifold.

4. Unbolt and remove the manifold.

To install:

1. Clean the mating surfaces of the cylinder head and manifold. Install the manifold onto the head, and install the retaining bolts finger tight.

2. Tighten the manifold bolts in a circular pattern, working from the center to the ends, to 25 ft. lbs. in two stages.

3. Connect the exhaust pipe to the manifold.

4. The remainder of installation is the reverse of removal.

RIGHT SIDE

1. Raise and support the car.

2. Tighten the exhaust pipe-to-manifold flange bolts until they break off. Remove the pipe from the manifold.

3. Lower the car. Remove the spark plug wires from the plugs. Number them first if they are not already labeled.

4. Remove the PULSAIR pipes from the manifold. Remove the PULSAIR bracket bolt from the rocker cover, then remove the pipe assembly (on 1981 and later models, remove the air supply plumbing).

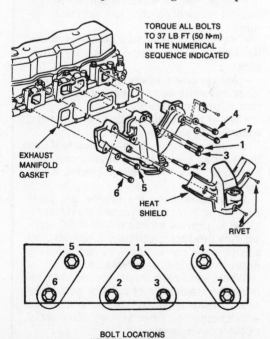

TORQUE ALL BOLTS TO 37 LB FT (50 N·m) IN THE NUMERICAL SEQUENCE INDICATED

EXHAUST MANIFOLD GASKET

HEAT SHIELD

RIVET

BOLT LOCATIONS

Four cylinder exhaust manifold installation

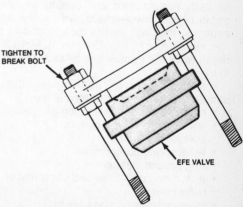

TIGHTEN TO BREAK BOLT

EFE VALVE

Tighten the right side exhaust flange bolts until they break on the V6

ENGINE OVERHAUL

Most engine overhaul procedures are fairly standard. In addition to specific parts replacement procedures and complete specifications for your individual engine, this chapter also is a guide to accepted rebuilding procedures. Examples of standard rebuilding practice are shown and should be used along with specific details concerning your particular engine.

Competent and accurate machine shop services will ensure maximum performance, reliability and engine life. Procedures marked with the symbol shown above should be performed by a competent machine shop, and are provided so that you will be familiar with the procedures necessary to a successful overhaul.

In most instances it is more profitable for the do-it-yourself mechanic to remove, clean and inspect the component, buy the necessary parts and deliver these to a shop for actual machine work.

On the other hand, much of the rebuilding work (crankshaft, block, bearings, pistons, rods, and other components) is well within the scope of the do-it-yourself mechanic.

Tools

The tools required for an engine overhaul or parts replacement will depend on the depth of your involvement. With a few exceptions, they will be the tools found in a mechanic's tool kit (see Chapter 1). More in-depth work will require any or all of the following:
- a dial indicator (reading in thousandths) mounted on a universal base
- micrometers and telescope gauges
- jaw and screw-type pullers
- scraper
- valve spring compressor
- ring groove cleaner
- piston ring expander and compressor
- ridge reamer
- cylinder hone or glaze breaker
- Plastigage®
- engine stand

Use of most of these tools is illustrated in this chapter. Many can be rented for a one-time use from a local parts jobber or tool supply house specializing in automotive work.

Occasionally, the use of special tools is called for. See the information on Special Tools and the Safety Notice in the front of this book before substituting another tool.

Inspection Techniques

Procedures and specifications are given in this chapter for inspecting, cleaning and assessing the wear limits of most major components. Other procedures such as Magnaflux and Zyglo can be used to locate material flaws and stress cracks. Magnaflux is a magnetic process applicable only to ferrous materials. The Zyglo process coats the material with a flourescent dye penetrant and can be used on any material. Check for suspected surface cracks can be more readily made using spot check dye. The dye is sprayed onto the suspected area, wiped off and the area sprayed with a developer. Cracks will show up brightly.

Overhaul Tips

Aluminum has become extremely popular for use in engines, due to its low weight. Observe the following precautions when handling aluminum parts:
- Never hot tank aluminum parts (the caustic hot-tank solution will eat the aluminum)
- Remove all aluminum parts (identification tag, etc.) from engine parts prior to hot-tanking.
- Always coat threads lightly with engine oil or anti-seize compounds before installation, to prevent seizure.
- Never over-torque bolts or spark plugs, especially in aluminum threads.

Stripped threads in any component can be repaired using any of several commercial repair kits (Heli-Coil, Microdot, Keen-serts, etc.)

When assembling the engine, any parts that will be in frictional contact must be pre-lubed to provide lubrication at initial start-up. Any product specifically formulated for this purpose can be used, but engine oil is not recommended as a pre-lube.

When semi-permanent (locked, but removable) installation of bolts or nuts is desired, threads should be cleaned and coated with Loctite® or other similar, commercial non-hardening sealant.

Repairing Damaged Threads

Several methods of repairing damaged threads are available. Heli-Coil® (shown here), Keenserts® and Microdot® are among the most widely used. All involve basically the same principle—drilling out stripped threads, tapping the hole and installing a prewound insert—making welding, plugging and oversize fasteners unnecessary.

Two types of thread repair inserts are usually supplied—a standard type for most Inch Coarse, Inch Fine, Metric Coarse and Metric Fine thread sizes and a spark plug type to fit most spark plug port sizes. Consult the individual manufacturer's catalog to determine exact applications. Typical thread repair kits will contain a selection of prewound threaded inserts, a tap (corresponding to the outside diameter threads of the insert) and an installation tool. Spark plug inserts usually differ because they require a tap equipped with pilot threads and a combined reamer/tap section. Most manufacturers also supply blister-packed thread repair inserts separately in addition to a master kit containing a variety of taps and inserts plus installation tools.

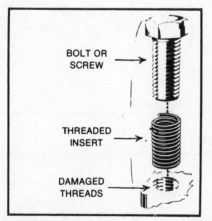

Damaged bolt holes can be repaired with thread repair inserts

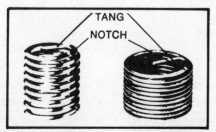

Standard thread repair insert (left) and spark plug thread insert (right)

Before effecting a repair to a threaded hole, remove any snapped, broken or damaged bolts or studs. Penetrating oil can be used to free frozen threads; the offending item can be removed with locking pliers or with a screw or stud extractor. After the hole is clear, the thread can be repaired, as follows:

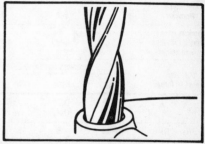

Drill out the damaged threads with specified drill. Drill completely through the hole or to the bottom of a blind hole

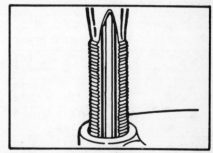

With the tap supplied, tap the hole to receive the thread insert. Keep the tap well oiled and back it out frequently to avoid clogging the threads

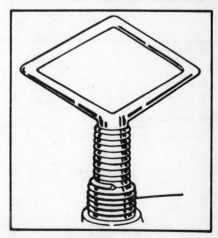

Screw the threaded insert onto the installation tool until the tang engages the slot. Screw the insert into the tapped hole until it is ¼–½ turn below the top surface, After installation break off the tang with a hammer and punch

Standard Torque Specifications and Fastener Markings

In the absence of specific torques, the following chart can be used as a guide to the maximum safe torque of a particular size/grade of fastener.

- There is no torque difference for fine or coarse threads.
- Torque values are based on clean, dry threads. Reduce the value by 10% if threads are oiled prior to assembly.
- The torque required for aluminum components or fasteners is considerably less.

U.S. Bolts

SAE Grade Number	1 or 2			5			6 or 7		
Number of lines always 2 less than the grade number.									
	Maximum Torque			Maximum Torque			Maximum Torque		
Bolt Size (Inches)—(Thread)	Ft./Lbs.	Kgm	Nm	Ft./Lbs.	Kgm	Nm	Ft./Lbs.	Kgm	Nm
¼ — 20	5	0.7	6.8	8	1.1	10.8	10	1.4	13.5
— 28	6	0.8	8.1	10	1.4	13.6			
5/16 — 18	11	1.5	14.9	17	2.3	23.0	19	2.6	25.8
— 24	13	1.8	17.6	19	2.6	25.7			
3/8 — 16	18	2.5	24.4	31	4.3	42.0	34	4.7	46.0
— 24	20	2.75	27.1	35	4.8	47.5			
7/16 — 14	28	3.8	37.0	49	6.8	66.4	55	7.6	74.5
— 20	30	4.2	40.7	55	7.6	74.5			
½ — 13	39	5.4	52.8	75	10.4	101.7	85	11.75	115.2
— 20	41	5.7	55.6	85	11.7	115.2			
9/16 — 12	51	7.0	69.2	110	15.2	149.1	120	16.6	162.7
— 18	55	7.6	74.5	120	16.6	162.7			
5/8 — 11	83	11.5	112.5	150	20.7	203.3	167	23.0	226.5
— 18	95	13.1	128.8	170	23.5	230.5			
¾ — 10	105	14.5	142.3	270	37.3	366.0	280	38.7	379.6
— 16	115	15.9	155.9	295	40.8	400.0			
7/8 — 9	160	22.1	216.9	395	54.6	535.5	440	60.9	596.5
— 14	175	24.2	237.2	435	60.1	589.7			
1 — 8	236	32.5	318.6	590	81.6	799.9	660	91.3	894.8
— 14	250	34.6	338.9	660	91.3	849.8			

Metric Bolts

Relative Strength Marking	4.6, 4.8			8.8		
Bolt Markings						
	Maximum Torque			Maximum Torque		
Bolt Size Thread Size x Pitch (mm)	Ft./Lbs.	Kgm	Nm	Ft./Lbs.	Kgm	Nm
6 x 1.0	2–3	.2–.4	3–4	3–6	.4–.8	5–8
8 x 1.25	6–8	.8–1	8–12	9–14	1.2–1.9	13–19
10 x 1.25	12–17	1.5–2.3	16–23	20–29	2.7–4.0	27–39
12 x 1.25	21–32	2.9–4.4	29–43	35–53	4.8–7.3	47–72
14 x 1.5	35–52	4.8–7.1	48–70	57–85	7.8–11.7	77–110
16 x 1.5	51–77	7.0–10.6	67–100	90–120	12.4–16.5	130–160
18 x 1.5	74–110	10.2–15.1	100–150	130–170	17.9–23.4	180–230
20 x 1.5	110–140	15.1–19.3	150–190	190–240	26.2–46.9	160–320
22 x 1.5	150–190	22.0–26.2	200–260	250–320	34.5–44.1	340–430
24 x 1.5	190–240	26.2–46.9	260–320	310–410	42.7–56.5	420–550

CHECKING ENGINE COMPRESSION

A noticeable lack of engine power, excessive oil consumption and/or poor fuel mileage measured over an extended period are all indicators of internal engine wear. Worn piston rings, scored or worn cylinder bores, blown head gaskets, sticking or burnt valves and worn valve seats are all possible culprits here. A check of each cylinder's compression will help you locate the problems.

As mentioned in the "Tools and Equipment" section of Chapter 1, a screw-in type compression gauge is more accurate than the type you simply hold against the spark plug hole, although it takes slightly longer to use. It's worth it to obtain a more accurate reading. Follow the procedures below for gasoline and diesel-engined cars.

Gasoline Engines

1. Warm up the engine to normal operating temperature.
2. Remove all spark plugs.

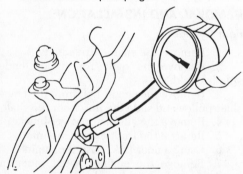

The screw-in type compression gauge is more accurate

3. Disconnect the high-tension lead from the ignition coil.
4. On carbureted cars, fully open the throttle either by operating the carburetor throttle linkage by hand or by having an assistant "floor" the accelerator pedal. On fuel-injected cars, disconnect the cold start valve and all injector connections.
5. Screw the compression gauge into the No. 1 spark plug hole until the fitting is snug.
NOTE: *Be careful not to crossthread the plug hole. On aluminum cylinder heads use extra care, as the threads in these heads are easily ruined.*
6. Ask an assistant to depress the accelerator pedal fully on both carbureted and fuel-injected cars. Then, while you read the compression gauge, ask the assistant to crank the engine two or three times in short bursts using the ignition switch.

7. Read the compression gauge at the end of each series of cranks, and record the highest of these readings. Repeat this procedure for each of the engine's cylinders. Compare the highest reading of each cylinder to the compression pressure specifications in the "Tune-Up Specifications" chart in Chapter 2. The specs in this chart are maximum values.

A cylinder's compression pressure is usually acceptable if it is not less than 80% of maximum. The difference between each cylinder should be no more than 12–14 pounds.

8. If a cylinder is unusually low, pour a tablespoon of clean engine oil into the cylinder through the spark plug hole and repeat the compression test. If the compression comes up after adding the oil, it appears that that cylinder's piston rings or bore are damaged or worn. If the pressure remains low, the valves may not be seating properly (a valve job is needed), or the head gasket may be blown near that cylinder. If compression in any two adjacent cylinders is low, and if the addition of oil doesn't help the compression, there is leakage past the head gasket. Oil and coolant water in the combustion chamber can result from this problem. There may be evidence of water droplets on the engine dipstick when a head gasket has blown.

Diesel Engines

Checking cylinder compression on diesel engines is basically the same procedure as on gasoline engines except for the following:
1. A special compression gauge adaptor suitable for diesel engines (because these engines have much greater compression pressures) must be used.
2. Remove the injector tubes and remove the injectors from each cylinder.
NOTE: *Don't forget to remove the washer underneath each injector; otherwise, it may get lost when the engine is cranked.*

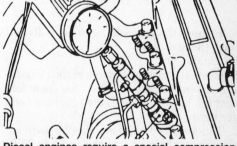

Diesel engines require a special compression gauge adaptor

3. When fitting the compression gauge adaptor to the cylinder head, make sure the bleeder of the gauge (if equipped) is closed.
4. When reinstalling the injector assemblies, install new washers underneath each injector.

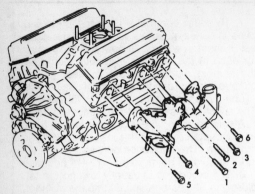

V6 exhaust manifold installation

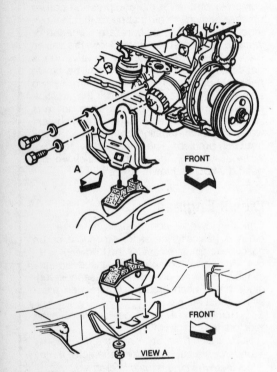

Four cylinder engine mount bracket

5. Remove the manifold retaining bolts and remove the manifold.

To install:

1. Clean the mating surfaces of the cylinder head and manifold. Position the manifold against the head and install the retaining bolts finger tight.

2. Tighten the bolts in a circular pattern, working from the center to the ends, to 25 ft. lbs. in two stages.

3. Install the PULSAIR system (air supply plumbing on 1981 and later models).

4. Install the spark plug wires.

5. Raise and support the car. Connect the exhaust pipe to the manifold and install new flange bolts.

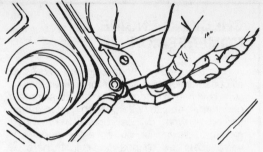

Cut the oil pan front seal flush with the front cover

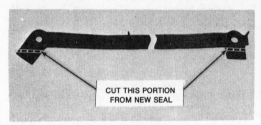

Cut the tabs from a new oil seal

Timing Cover

REMOVAL AND INSTALLATION

Four Cylinder

1. Remove the engine drive belts.

2. Remove the right front inner fender splash shield.

3. Remove the center bolt from the crankshaft pulley and slide the hub from the shaft.

4. Remove the alternator lower bracket.

5. Remove the front engine mounts.

6. Using a floor jack, raise the engine.

7. Remove the engine mount mounting bracket-to-cylinder block bolts. Remove the bracket and mount as an assembly.

8. Remove the oil pan-to-front cover bolts.

9. Remove the front cover-to-block bolts.

10. Pull the cover slightly forward, just enough to allow cutting of the oil pan front seal flush with the block on both sides.

11. Remove the front cover and attached portion of the oil pan seal.

12. Clean the gasket surfaces thoroughly.

13. Cut the tabs from the new oil pan front seal.

14. Install the seal on the front cover, pressing the tips onto the holes provided.

15. Coat the new gasket with sealer and position it on the front cover.

16. Apply a ⅛ in. bead of silicone sealer to the joint formed at the oil pan and block.

17. Align the front cover seal with a centering tool and install the front cover. Tighten the cover with the centering tool installed, then remove the tool.

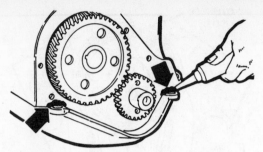

Apply sealer to the oil pan and block joint

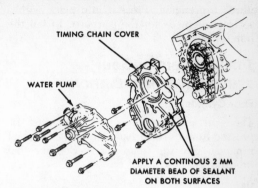

TIMING CHAIN COVER

WATER PUMP

APPLY A CONTINOUS 2 MM
DIAMETER BEAD OF SEALANT
ON BOTH SURFACES

V6 front cover installation

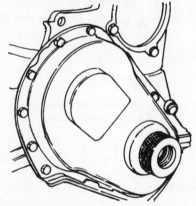

Install the front cover bolts with the centering tool installed

18. Install the front mount bracket assembly and lower alternator bracket. Lower the engine. Install the mount-to-engine cradle nuts.

19. Coat the front cover oil seal contact area on the hub with clean engine oil. Position the hub on the crankshaft and slide it on until it bottoms against the crankshaft gear. Install the hub retaining bolt and tighten to 160 ft. lbs. (212 Nm.). Install the belts and adjust their tension. Install the fender shield.

V6

1. Remove the water pump. The procedure for this is given later in this chapter.

2. If the car has air conditioning, remove the compressor from its brackets and move it aside. *Do not disconnect any of the hoses.*

3. Remove the torsional damper: remove the negative battery cable at the battery, remove the engine drive belts, raise the car, remove the right inner fender splash shield, remove the drive pulley, then remove the damper retaining bolt. Install a puller onto the damper and remove the damper.

NOTE: *The outer ring (weight) of the torsinal damper is bonded to the hub with rubber. The balancer must be removed with a puller which acts on the inner hub only.*

Pulling on the outer portion of the balancer will break the rubber bond or destroy the tuning of the damper.

4. Remove the front cover retaining bolts and remove the cover.

5. To install, clean the front cover mating surfaces of all old sealer. Apply a $3/32$ inch bead of silicone sealer to the front cover sealing surface.

6. Place the front cover on the engine, install the water pump, then install the retaining bolts and tighten the small bolts to 6–9 ft. lbs., the medium size bolts to 13–18 ft. lbs., and the large bolts to 20–30 ft. lbs. (8–12, 18–24, and 27–41 Nm., respectively).

7. Connect the lower radiator hose.

8. Install the torsional damper: coat the front cover seal contact area on the damper with clean engine oil. Place the damper on the crankshaft with the keyway aligned. Install the damper using a press which acts on the inner ring of the hub only. The press should thread into the crankshaft with at least ¼ inch of thread engagement.

9. Install the pulley onto the hub, and install both the pulley and the hub bolts. Tighten the pulley bolts to 20–30 ft. lbs. (27–41 Nm.) and the hub (damper) bolt to 66–84 ft. lbs. (90–115 Nm.).

10. Install the inner fender splash shield. Install the drive belts and adjust their tension. Install the air conditioning compressor, if removed, and its drive belt; adjust the tension. Connect the negative battery cable. Fill the cooling system as outlined in Chapter One.

TIMING COVER OIL SEAL

The oil seal on both engines can be replaced with the cover either on or off the engine. If the cover is on the engine, remove the crankshaft pulley and hub first. Pry out the seal using a large screwdriver, being careful not to distort the seal mating surface. Install the new seal so that the open side or helical side is towards the engine. Press it into place with a seal driver made for the purpose. Install the hub if removed.

Timing Chain or Gear

REMOVAL AND INSTALLATION

Four Cylinder

The four cylinder camshaft gear must be pressed from the camshaft, requiring camshaft removal. See the following section for that procedure.

V6

1. Remove the timing cover.
2. Place the No. 1 piston at TDC with the marks on the camshaft and crankshaft sprockets aligned as shown.
3. Remove the camshaft sprocket bolts and remove the sprocket and chain together. If the sprocket does not slide from the camshaft easily, a light blow with a soft mallet at the lower edge of the sprocket will dislodge it.
4. To install, hold the sprocket vertically with the chain hanging down. Align the marks

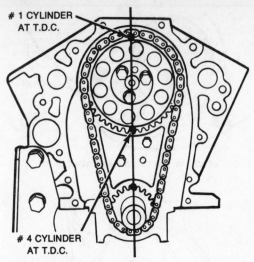

1 CYLINDER AT T.D.C.

4 CYLINDER AT T.D.C.

V6 timing mark alignment

as shown. Align the dowel in the camshaft with the hole in the sprocket, then install the sprocket and chain.

5. Install the camshaft sprocket bolts. Tighten to 15–20 ft. lbs. (20–27 Nm.). Lubricate the chain and sprocket with clean engine oil. Install the timing cover.

Camshaft

REMOVAL AND INSTALLATION

Four Cylinder

1. Remove the engine from the car.
2. Remove the valve cover, loosen the rocker arms and pivot them aside, and remove the pushrods. Keep them in order.
3. Remove the distributor and fuel pump.
4. Remove the pushrod cover from the side of the engine. Remove the lifters. Keep them in order.
5. Remove the alternator and its bracket, and remove the front engine mount bracket assembly.
6. Remove the oil pan. Remove the oil pump and gear assembly.
7. Remove the crankshaft hub and the front cover.
8. Remove the two camshaft thrust plate screws by working through the holes in the gear.
9. Remove the camshaft and gear assembly by pulling it through the front of the block. Be very careful not to damage the bearings.
10. If the timing gear must be removed, support the camshaft on a press, install press plates under the gear, and press off the gear.
CAUTION: *Position the thrust plate so that the woodruff key in the camshaft does not damage the plate when the gear is pressed off.*

The V6 timing chain rubber damper bolts to the front of the engine

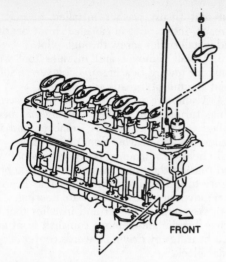

Four cylinder rocker arm, pushrod and valve lifter removal

Four cylinder camshaft thrust plate screw removal

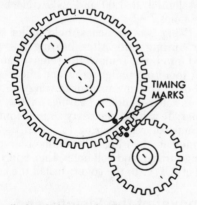

Four cylinder timing mark alignment

11. To press on the gear, support the camshaft behind the front journal with press plates. Place the gear spacer ring and thrust plate over the end of the camshaft, and install the woodruff key. Press the gear onto the camshaft until it bottoms against the gear spacer ring.

The end clearance of the thrust plate should be between 0.0015 and 0.0050 in. If more, the thrust plate should be replaced. If less, replace the spacer ring.

12. Coat the camshaft and gear with clean engine oil supplement. Install the camshaft into the block, being extremely careful not to contact the bearings with the cam lobes.

13. Align the timing marks. The engine should then be in the No. 4 firing position. Install the thrust plate-to-block bolts and tighten to 75 in. lbs. (10 Nm.).

14. Install the timing cover crankshaft pulley, valve lifters (in original position) pushrods (in original positions), and oil pump shaft and gear assembly and the oil pan and fuel pump. Install the pushrod side cover with a thin bead of silicone seal running to the inside of the bolt holes. Be sure all the old sealer is removed before applying the new sealer.

15. Install the distributor: rotate the crankshaft until No. 1 cylinder is in firing position. The number one valves will both be closed, and the timing marks will be at "0". Install the distributor in its original position, with the rotor pointing toward the No. 1 spark plug tower.

16. Pivot the rocker arms over the pushrods, and tighten the rocker arm nuts to 20 ft. lbs. (27 Nm.) with the lifters on the base circle of the cam lobe as described under rocker arm removal earlier in this chapter. The rest of installation is the reverse of removal.

V6

1. Remove the engine.
2. Remove the intake manifold.
3. Remove the rocker covers, pivot the rocker arms to the sides, and remove the pushrods, keeping them in order. Remove the valve lifters, keeping them in order. There are special tools which make lifter removal easier.
4. Remove the timing cover.
5. Remove the fuel pump and its pushrod.
6. Remove the timing chain and sprocket as described earlier in this chapter.
7. Carefully pull the camshaft from the block, being sure that the camshaft lobes do not contact the bearings.
8. To install, lubricate the camshaft journals with clean engine oil. Lubricate the lobes with "molykote" or the equivalent. Install the camshaft into the engine, being extremely careful not to contact the bearings with the cam lobes.
9. Install the timing chain and sprocket. Install the fuel pump and pushrod. Install the timing cover.
10. Install the valve lifters. If a new camshaft has been installed, new lifters should be used to ensure durability of the cam lobes.

11. Install the pushrods and rocker arms and the intake manifold. Adjust the valve lash after installing the engine. Install the valve covers.

Camshaft Bearings
REMOVAL AND INSTALLATION
4-151 Engine

1. Remove the engine from the vehicle as previously outlined.

2. Remove the camshaft from the engine as previnusly outlined.

3. Unbold and remove the engine fly-wheel.

4. Drive the rear camshaft expansion plug out of the engine block from the inside.

5. Using a camshaft bearing service tool, drive the front camshaft bearing towards the rear and the rear bearing towards the front.

6. Install the appropriate extension on the service tool and drive the center bearing out towards the rear.

7. Drive all of the new bearings into place in the opposite direction of which they were removed, making sure to align the oil holes of each bearing with each of the feed holes in the engine block bores.

NOTE: *The front camshaft bearing must be driven approximately ⅛" behind the front of the cylinder block to uncover the oil hole to the timing gear oiling nozzle.*

8. Install the camshaft into the engine, then reinstall the engine as previously outlined.

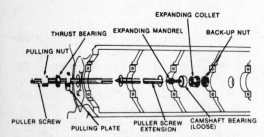

EXPANDING COLLET
THRUST BEARING   EXPANDING MANDREL   BACK-UP NUT
PULLING NUT
PULLER SCREW   PULLING PLATE   PULLER SCREW EXTENSION   CAMSHAFT BEARING (LOOSE)

Typical camshaft bearing removal tool

6-173 Engine

Camshaft bearings can be replaced with engine completely or partially disassembled. To replace bearings without complete disassembly remove the camshaft and crankshaft leaving cylinder heads attached and pistons in place. Before removing crankshaft, tape threads of connecting rod bolts to prevent damage to crankshaft. Fasten connecting rods against sides of engine so they will not be in the way while replacing camshaft bearings.

1. Remove the camshaft rear cover.

2. Using Tool J-6098 or its equivalent, with nut and thrust washer installed to end of threads, index pilot in camshaft front bearing and install puller screw through pilot.

3. Install remover and installer tool with shoulder toward bearing, making sure a sufficient amount of threads are engaged.

4. Using two wrenches, hold puller screw while turning nut. When bearing has been pulled from bore, remove remover and installer tool and bearing from puller screw.

5. Remove remaining bearings (except front and rear) in the same manner. It will be necessary to index pilot in camshaft rear bearing to remove the rear intermediate bearing.

6. Assemble remover and installer tool on driver handle and remove camshaft front and rear bearings by driving towards center of cylinder block.

The camshaft front and rear bearings should be installed first. These bearings will act as guides for the pilot and center the remaining bearings being pulled into place.

1. Assemble remover and installer tool on driver handle and install camshaft front and rear bearings by driving towards center of cylinder block.

2. Using Tool Set J-6098 or its equivalent, with nut then thrust washer installed to end of threads, index pilot in camshaft front bearing and install puller screw through pilot.

3. Index camshaft bearing in bore (with oil hole aligned as outlined below), then install remover and installer tool on puller screw with shoulder toward bearing.

- The rear and intermediate bearing oil holes must be aligned at 2:30 o'clock.
- The front bearing oil holes must be aligned at 1:00 and 2:30 o'clock (two holes).

4. Using two wrenches, hold puller screw while turning nut. After bearing has been pulled into bore, remove the remover and installer tool from puller screw and check alignment of oil hole in camshaft bearing.

5. Install remaining bearings in the same manner. It will be necessary to index pilot in the camshaft rear bearing to install the rear intermediate bearing. Clean the rear cover mating surfaces and bolt holes, then apply 2 ⅛" bead of R.T.V. to the cover. Install the cover.

Removal of the Pistons and Connecting Rod Assemblies

1. Remove the engine assembly from the car, see "Engine Removal and Installation".

2. Remove the intake manifold, cylinder head or heads.

3. Remove the oil pan.

4. Remove the oil pump assumbly.

5. Stamp the cylinder number on the machined surfaces of the bolt bosses of the connecting rod and cap for identification when reinstalling. If the pistons are to be removed from the connecting rod, mark the cylinder number on the piston with a silver pencil or quick drying paint for proper cylinder identification and cap to rod location. The 4-151 engine is numbered 1–4 from front to back; the V6-173 is numbered 1-3-5 on the right bank, 2-4-6 on the left bank.

6. Examine the cylinder bore above the ring travel. If a ridge exists, remove the ridge with a ridge reamer before attempting to remove the piston and rod assembly.

7. Remove the rod bearing cap and bearing.

8. Install a guide hose over threads of rod bolts. This is to prevent damage to bearing journal and rod bolt threads.

9. Remove the rod and piston assembly through the top of the cylinder bore.

10. Remove any other rod and piston assemblies in the same manner.

CLEANING AND INSPECTION

Connecting Rods

Wash connecting rods in cleaning solvent and dry with compressed air. Check for twisted or bent rods and inspect for nicks or cracks. Replace connecting rods that are damaged.

Pistons

Clean varnish from piston skirts and pins with a cleaning solvent. DO NOT WIRE BRUSH ANY PART OF THE PISTON. Clean the ring grooves with a groove cleaner and make sure oil ring holes and slots are clean.

Inspect the piston for cracked ring lands, skirts or pin bosses, wavy or worn ring lands, scuffed or damaged skirts, eroded areas at top of the piston. Replace pistons that are damaged or show signs of excessive wear.

Inspect the grooves for nicks or burrs that might cause the rings to hang up.

Measure piston skirt (across center line of piston pin) and check piston clearance.

PISTON PIN REMOVAL AND INSTALLATION

Use care at all times when handling and servicing connecting rods and pistons. To prevent possible damage to these units, do not clamp rod or piston in vise since they may become distorted. Do not allow pistons to strike against one another, against hard objects or bench surfaces, since distortion of piston contour or nicks in the soft aluminum material may result.

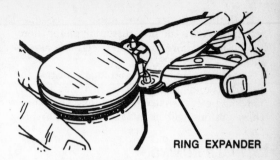

RING EXPANDER

Removing the piston rings

1. Remove piston rings using suitable piston ring remover.

2. Install guide bushing of piston pin removing and installing tool.

3. Install piston and connecting rod assembly on support and place assembly in an arbor press. Press pin out of connecting rod, using the appropriate piston pin tool.

MEASURING THE OLD PISTONS

Check used piston to cylinder bore clearance as follows:

1. Measure the cylinder bore diameter with a telescope gage or a dial gauge

2. Measure the piston diameter. When measuring piston for size or taper, measurement must be made with the piston pin removed.

3. Subtract piston diameter from cylinder bore diameter to determine piston-to-bore clearance.

4. Compare piston-to-bore clearance obtained with those clearances recommended. Determine if piston-to-bore clearance is in acceptable range.

5. When measuring taper, the largest reading must be at the bottom of the skirt.

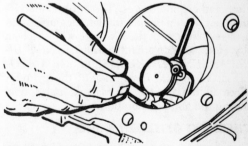

Measuring the cylinder bore with a dial gauge

SELECTING NEW PISTONS

1. If the used piston is not acceptable, check service piston sizes and determine if a new piston can be selected. (Service pistons are available in standard, high limit and standard .254 mm (.010″) oversize.)

2. If the cylinder bore must be reconditioned, measure the new piston diameter then hone cylinder bore to obtain preferable clearance.

3. Select new piston and mark piston to identify the cylinder for which it was fitted. (On some cars oversize pistons may be found. These pistons will be .254 mm (.010″) oversize).

CYLINDER HONING

1. When cylinders are being honed, follow the manufacturer's recommendations for the use of the hone.

2. Occasionally during the honing operation, the cylinder bore should be thoroughly cleaned and the selected piston checked for correct fit.

3. When finish honing a cylinder bore, the hone should be moved up and down at a sufficient speed to obtain very fine uniform surface finish marks in a cross hatch pattern of approximately 45 to 65 degrees included angle. The finish marks should be clean but not sharp, free from imbedded particles and torn or folded metal.

4. Permanently mark the piston for the cylinder to which it has been fitted and proceed to hone the remaining cylinders.

NOTE: *Handle pistons with care. Do not attempt to force pistons through cylinders until the cylinders have been honed to correct size. Pistons can be distorted through careless handling.*

5. Thoroughly clean the bores with hot water and detergent. Scrub well with a stiff bristle brush and rinse thoroughly with hot water. It is extremely essential that a good cleaning operation be performed. If any of the abrasive material is allowed to remain in the cylinder bores, it will rapidly wear the new rings and cylinder bores. The bores should be swabbed several times with light engine oil and a clean cloth and then wiped with a clean dry cloth. *CYLINDERS SHOULD NOT BE CLEANED WITH KEROSENE OR GASOLINE.* Clean the remainder of the cylinder block to remove the excess material spread during the honing operation.

CHECKING CYLINDER BORE

Cylinder bore size can be measured with inside micrometers or a cylinder gage. The most wear will occur at the top of the ring travel.

Reconditioned cylinder bores should be held to not more than .025 mm (.001″) out-of-round and .025 mm (.001″) taper.

If the cylinder bores are smooth, the cylinder walls should not be deglazed. If the cylinder walls are scored, the walls may have to be

honed before installing new rings. It is important that reconditioned cylinder bores be thoroughly washed with a soap and water solution to remove all traces of abrasive material to eliminate premature wear.

Piston Rings

The pistons have three rings (two compression rings and one oil ring). The oil ring consists of two rails and an expander. Pistons do not have oil drain holes behind the rings.

RING TOLERANCES

When installing new rings, ring gap and side clearance should be checked as follows:

PISTON RING AND RAIL GAP

Each ring and rail gap must be measured with the ring or rail positioned squarely and at the bottom of the ring-travel area of the bore.

SIDE CLEARANCE

Each ring must be checked for side clearance in its respective piston groove by inserting a feeler gage between the ring and its upper land. The piston grooves must be cleaned before checking ring for side clearance. See PISTON RING CLEARANCE specifications at

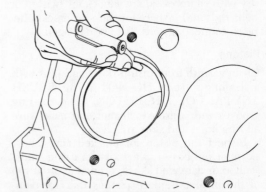

Check the ring end gap with the ring installed in its cylinder

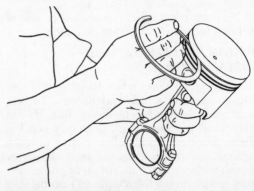

Check ring side clearance

the end of this section for ring side clearance specifications. To check oil ring side clearance, the oil rings must be installed on the piston.

RING INSTALLATION

For service ring specifications and detailed installation productions, refer to the instructions furnished with the parts package.

Connecting Rod Bearings

If you have already removed the connecting rod and piston assemblies from the engine, follow only steps 3–7 of the following procedure.

REMOVAL, INSPECTION, INSTALLATION

The connecting rod bearings are designed to have a slight projection above the rod and cap faces to insure a positive contact. The bearings can be replaced without removing the rod and piston assembly from the engine.

1. Remove the oil pan, see "Oil Pan". It may be necessary to remove the oil pump to provide access to rear connecting rod bearings.

2. With the connecting rod journal at the bottom, stamp the cylinder number on the machined surfaces of connecting rod and cap for identification when reinstalling, then remove caps.

3. Inspect journals for roughness and wear. Slight roughness may be removed with a fine grit polishing cloth saturated with engine oil. Burrs may be removed with a fine oil stone by moving the stone on the journal circumference. Do not move the stone back and forth across the journal. If the journals are scored or ridged, the crankshaft must be replaced.

4. The connecting rod journals should be checked for out-of-round and correct size with a micrometer.

NOTE: *Crankshaft rod journals will normally be standard size. If any undersized crankshafts are used, all will be .254 mm undersize and .254 mm will be stamped on the number 4 counterweight.*

If plastic gaging material is to be used:

5. Clean oil from the journal bearing cap, connecting rod and outer and inner surface of the bearing inserts. Position insert so that tang is properly aligned with notch in rod and cap.

6. Place a piece of plastic gaging material in the center of lower bearing shell.

7. Remove bearing cap and determine bearing clearances by comparing the width of the flattened plastic gaging material at its widest point with the graduation on the container. The number within the graduation on the envelope indicates the clearance in thousandths

of an inch or millimeters. If this clearance is excessive, replace the bearing and recheck clearance with plastic gaging material. Lubricate bearing with engine oil before installation. Repeat Steps 2 through 7 on remaining connecting rod bearings. All rods must be connected to their journals when rotating the crankshaft to prevent engine damage.

Installation of the Piston and Connecting Rod Assembly

1. Install connecting rod bolt guide hose over rod bolt threads.

2. Apply engine oil to the rings and piston, then install piston ring compressing tool on the piston.

3. Install the assembly in its respective cylinder bore.

4. Lubricate the crankshaft journal with engine oil and install connecting rod bearing and cap, with bearing index tang in rod and cap on same side.

NOTE: *When more than one rod and piston assembly is being installed, the connecting rod cap attaching nuts should only be tightened enough to keep each rod in position*

FRONT OF ENGINE

NOTCH

Install the pistons with the notch or notches facing the front of the engine

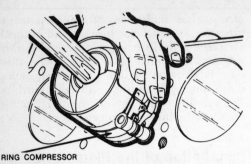

RING COMPRESSOR

Typical piston ring compressing tool

until all have been installed. This will aid installation of remaining piston assemblies.

5. Torque rod bolt nuts to specification.

6. Install all other removed parts.

7. Install the engine in the car, see "Engine Removal and Installation".

Crankshaft

REMOVAL

1. Remove the engine assembly as previously outlined.

2. Remove the engine front cover.

3. Remove the timing chain and sprockets.

4. Remove the oil pan.

5. Remove the oil pump.

6. Stamp the cylinder number on the machined surfaces of the bolt bosses of the connecting rods and caps for identification when reinstalling. If the pistons are to be removed from the connecting rod, mark cylinder number on piston with a silver pencil or quick drying paint for proper cylinder identification and cap to rod location.

7. Remove the connecting rod caps and install thread protectors.

8. Mark the main bearing caps so that they can be reinstalled in their original positions.

9. Remove all the main bearing caps.

10. Note position of keyway in crankshaft so it can be installed in the same position.

11. Lift crankshaft out of block. Rods will pivot to the center of the engine when the crankshaft is removed.

12. Remove both halves of the rear main oil seal.

INSTALLATION

1. Measure the crankshaft journals with a micrometer to determine the correct size rod and main bearings to be used. Whenever a new or reconditioned crankshaft is installed, new connecting rod bearings and main bearings should be installed. See "Main Bearings" and "Rod Bearings".

2. Clean all oil passages in the block (and crankshaft if it is being reused).

NOTE: *A new rear main seal should be installed anytime the crankshaft is removed or replaced.*

3. Install sufficient oil pan bolts in the block to align with the connecting rod bolts. Use rubber bands between the bolts to position the connecting rods as required. Connecting rod position can be adjusted by increasing the tension on the rubber bands with additional turns around the pan bolts or thread protectors.

4. Position the upper half of main bearings in the block and lubricate with engine oil.

5. Position crankshaft keyway in the same position as removed and lower into block. The connecting rods will follow the crank pins into the correct position as the crankshaft is lowered.

6. Lubricate the thrust flanges with 1050169 Lubricant or equivalent. Install caps with lower half of bearings lubricated with engine oil. Lubricate cap bolts with engine oil and install, but do not tighten.

7. With a block of wood, bump shaft in each direction to align thrust flanges of main bearing. After bumping shaft in each direction, wedge the shaft to the front and hold it while torquing the thrust bearing cap bolts.

NOTE: *In order to prevent the possibility of cylinder block and/or main bearing cap damage, the main bearing caps are to be tapped into their cylinder block cavity using a brass or leather mallet before attaching bolts are installed. Do not use attaching bolts to pull main bearing caps into their seats. Failure to observe this information may damage the cylinder block or a bearing cap.*

8. Torque all main bearing caps to specification.

9. Remove the connecting rod bolt thread protectors and lubricate the connecting rod bearings with engine oil.

10. Install the connecting rod bearing caps in their original position. Torque the nuts to specification.

11. Complete the installation by reversing the removal steps.

Main Bearings

CHECKING BEARING CLEARANCE

1. Remove bearing cap and wipe oil from crankshaft journal and outer and inner surfaces of bearing shell.

2. Place a piece of plastic gaging material in the center of bearing.

3. Use a floor jack or other means to hold crankshaft against upper bearing shell. This is

necessary to obtain accurate clearance readings when using plastic gaging material.

4. Reinstall bearing cap and bearing. Place engine oil on cap bolts and install. Torque bolts to specification.

5. Remove bearing cap and determine bearing clearance by comparing the width of the flattened plastic gaging material at its widest point with graduations on the gaging material container. The number within the graduation on the envelope indicates the clearance in millimeters or thousandths of an inch. If the clearance is greater than allowed, *REPLACE BOTH BEARING SHELLS AS A SET.* Recheck clearance after replacing shells. (Refer to Main Bearing Replacement.)

REPLACEMENT

Main bearing clearances must be corrected by the use of selective upper and lower shells. UNDER NO CIRCUMSTANCES should the use of shims behind the shells to compensate for wear be attempted. To install main bearing shells, proceed as follows:

1. Remove the oil pan as outlined elsewhere in this Chapter on some models, the oil pump may also have to be removed.

2. Loosen all main bearing caps.

3. Remove bearing cap and remove lower shell.

4. Insert a flattened cotter pin or roll out pin in the oil passage hole in the crankshaft, then rotate the crankshaft in the direction opposite to cranking rotation. The pin will contact the upper shell and roll it out.

5. The main bearing journals should be checked for roughness and wear. Slight roughness may be removed with a fine grit polishing cloth saturated with engine oil. Burrs may be removed with a fine oil stone. If the journals are scored or ridged, the crankshaft must be replaced. The journals can be measured for out-of-round with the crankshaft installed by using a crankshaft caliper and inside micrometer or a main bearing micrometer. The upper bearing shell must be removed when measuring the crankshaft journals. Maximum out-of-round of the crankshaft journals must not exceed .037 mm (.0015″).

6. Clean crankshaft journals and bearing caps thoroughly before installing new main bearings.

7. Apply special lubricant, No. 1050169 or equivalent, to the thrust flanges of bearing shells.

8. Place new upper shell on crankshaft journal with locating tang in correct position and rotate shaft to turn it into place using cotter pin or roll out pin as during removal.

9. Place new bearing shell in bearing cap.

10. Install a new oil seal in the rear main bearing cap and block.

11. Lubricate the removed or replaced main bearings with engine oil. Lubricate the thrust surface with lubricant 1050169 or equivalent.

12. Lubricate the main bearing cap bolts with engine oil.

NOTE: *In order to prevent the possibility of cylinder block and/or main bearing cap damage, the main bearing caps are to be tapped into their cylinder block cavity using a brass or leather mallet before attaching bolts are installed. Do not use attaching bolts to pull main bearing caps into their seats. Failure to observe this information may damage the cylinder block or a bearing cap.*

13. Torque the main bearing cap bolts to 145 N·m (107 ft. lbs.).

Oil Pan

REMOVAL AND INSTALLATION

Four Cylinder

1. Raise and support the car. Drain the oil.

2. Remove the engine cradle-to-front engine mounts.

3. Disconnect the exhaust pipe at both the exhaust manifold and at the rear transaxle mount.

4. Disconnect and remove the starter. Remove the flywheel housing or torque converter inspection cover.

5. Remove the alternator upper bracket.

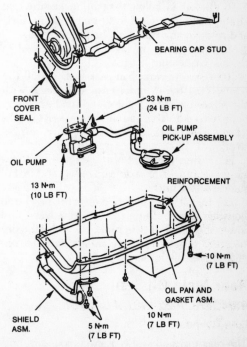

Four cylinder oil pan and pump installation details

6. Install an engine lifting chain and raise the engine.

7. Remove the lower alternator bracket. Remove the engine support bracket.

8. Remove the oil pan retaining bolts and remove the pan.

9. Reverse the procedure to install. Clean all gasket surfaces thoroughly. Install the rear oil pan gasket into the rear main bearing cap, then apply a thin bead of silicone sealer to the pan gasket depressions. Install the front pan gasket into the timing cover. Install the side gaskets onto the block, not the oil pan. They can be retained in place with grease. Apply a thin bead of silicone seal to the mating joints of the gaskets. Install the oil pan; install the timing gear bolts last, after the other bolts have been snugged down.

V6

1. Drain the oil. Disconnect the negative battery cable.

2. Remove the oil dipstick and tube.

3. Raise and support the car.

4. Remove the exhaust crossover pipe.

5. On cars with an automatic transaxle, remove the converter housing underpan. On X-Cars with a manual transaxle, remove the clutch housing cover, then remove the engine mounting bracket-to-engine mount nuts and raise the front of the engine ¾ in.

6. Remove the starter.

7. Remove the oil pan and discard the gaskets and seals.

8. Before installing the pan, make sure that all the mating surfaces are free of oil and dirt, and remove any traces of old silicone seal.

9. Apply a ⅛ in. bead of silicone seal to the oil pan sealing flange.

10. Use a new oil pan rear seal. Install the pan against the cylinder case and attach with the retaining bolts. Tighten the smaller oil pan bolts to 6–9 ft. lbs., and the larger bolts to 14–22 ft. lbs. (8–12 and 19–30 Nm., respectively).

11. Lower the front of the engine, if it was raised (manual transaxle cars only), and install the retaining nuts.

12. Install the starter, converter or clutch housing cover, the exhaust crossover, and lower the car. Fill the crankcase with oil, connect the negative battery cable, start the engine and check for leaks.

Rear Main Oil Seal

REMOVAL AND INSTALLATION

Four Cylinder

The rear main oil seal is a one piece unit, and is removed or installed without removal of the oil pan or crankshaft.

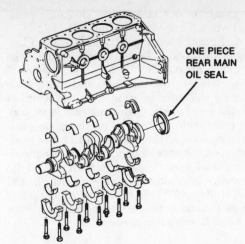

The four cylinder has a one piece ring type rear main seal

1. Remove the transaxle, the flywheel or torque converter bellhousing, and the flywheel or flexplate.

2. Remove the rear main oil seal with a screwdriver. Be extremely careful not to scratch the crankshaft.

3. Oil the lips of the new seal with clean engine oil. Install the new seal by hand onto the rear crankshaft flange. The helical lip of the seal should face the engine. Make sure that the seal is firmly and evenly installed.

4. Replace the flywheel or flexplate, bellhousing and transaxle.

V6

1. Remove the oil pan and pump.

2. Remove the rear main bearing cap.

3. Gently pack the upper seal into the groove approximately ¼ inch on each side.

4. Measure the amount the seal was driven

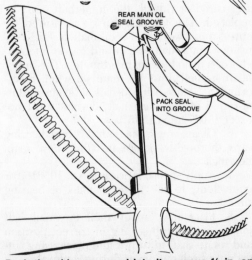

Pack the old upper seal into its groove ¼ in. on each side

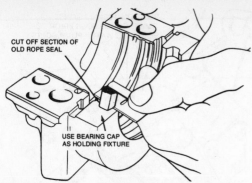

CUT OFF SECTION OF
OLD ROPE SEAL

USE BEARING CAP
AS HOLDING FIXTURE

Use the bearing cap to hold the old lower seal while you cut it

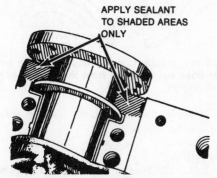

APPLY SEALANT
TO SHADED AREAS
ONLY

Sealer application on the V6 block

in on one side and add 1/16 in. Cut this length from the old lower cap seal. Be sure to get a sharp cut. Repeat for the other side.

5. Place the piece of cut seal into the groove and pack the seal into the block. Do this for each side.

6. Install a new lower seal in the rear main cap.

7. Install a piece of Plastigage or the equivalent on the bearing journal. Install the rear cap and tighten to 75 ft. lbs. Remove the cap and check the gauge for bearing clearance. If out of specification, the ends of the seal may be frayed or not flush, preventing the cap from proper seating. Correct as required.

8. Clean the journal, and apply a thin film of sealer to the mating surfaces of the cap and block. Do not allow any sealer to get onto the journal or bearing. Install the bearing cap and tighten to 70 ft. lbs. Install the pan and pump.

Oil Pump

REMOVAL AND INSTALLATION

All Engines

1. Remove the engine oil pan.

2. Remove the pump attaching bolts and carefully lower the pump.

3. Install in reverse order. To ensure immediate oil pressure on start-up, the oil pump gear cavity should be packed with petroleum jelly. Installation torque is 22 ft. lbs. (30 Nm.) for the four cylinder, 26–35 ft. lbs. (35–47 Nm.) for the V6.

Radiator

REMOVAL AND INSTALLATION

All Models

1. Disconnect the negative battery cable.

2. Drain the cooling system.

3. Remove the forward strut brace for the engine at the radiator. Loosen the bolt to prevent shearing the rubber bushing, then swing the strut rearward.

4. Disconnect the headlamp wiring harness from the fan frame. Unplug the fan electrical connector.

5. Remove the attaching bolts for the fan.

6. Scribe the hood latch location on the radiator support, then remove the latch.

7. Disconnect the coolant hoses from the radiator. Remove the coolant recovery tank hose from the radiator neck. Disconnect and plug the automatic transaxle fluid cooler lines from the radiator, if so equipped.

8. Remove the radiator attaching bolts and remove the radiator. If the car has air condi-

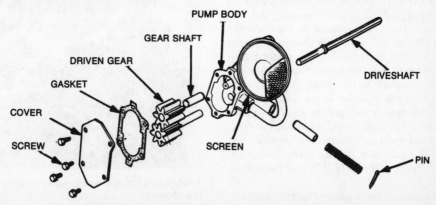

PUMP BODY

GEAR SHAFT

DRIVEN GEAR

GASKET

COVER

SCREW

SCREEN

DRIVESHAFT

PIN

Exploded view of the V6 oil pump; four cylinder similar

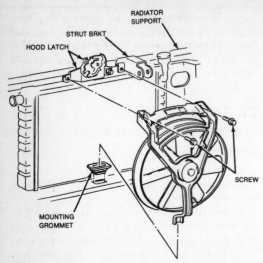

Coolant fan installation details. Heavy-duty units are similar; the only real difference is the presence of a shroud

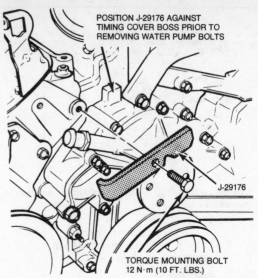

Install the special tool to insure that the front cover does not separate from the crankcase on the V6 engine

tioning, it first may be necessary to raise the left side of the radiator so that the radiator neck will clear the compressor.

To install:

1. Install the radiator in the car, tightening the mounting bolts to 7 in. lbs. Connect the transaxle cooler lines and hoses. Install the coolant recovery hose.

2. Install the hood latch. Tighten to 6 ft. lbs.

3. Install the fan, making sure the bottom leg of the frame fits into the rubber grommet at the lower support. Install the fan wires and the headlamp wiring harness. Swing the strut and brace forward, tightening to 11 ft. lbs. Connect the engine ground strap to the strut brace. Install the negative battery cable, fill the cooling system, and check for leaks.

Water Pump

REMOVAL AND INSTALLATION

All Models

NOTE: *When replacing the water pump on a car equipped with the V-6 engine, the timing cover must be clamped to the cylinder block PRIOR TO removing the water pump bolts. Certain bolts holding the water pump pass through the front cover and when removed, may allow the front cover to pull away from the cylinder block, breaking the seal. This may or may not be readily apparent and if left undetected, could allow coolant to enter the crankcase. To prevent this possible separation during water pump removal, Special Tool #J29176 will have to be installed.*

1. Disconnect the negative battery cable.

2. Remove the drive belts for the water pump and accessories.

3. Disconnect the coolant hoses from the water pump.

4. Install the Special Tool #J29176 as shown in the illustration (V-6 engines only).

5. Remove the water pump mounting bolts and then remove the pump.

6. No gasket is used. Clean the mating surfaces thoroughly, then apply a $3/32''$ bead of

Apply sealer to the water pump mating surfaces (V6 shown)

RTV sealant to the water pump sealing surface.

7. While the sealer is still wet, install the pump onto the engine. Tighten the bolts to 25 ft. lbs. (30 Nm.) on the four cylinder engine. On the V-6, tighten the small bolts to 8 ft. lbs. (10 Nm.), the medium bolts to 16 ft. lbs. (21 Nm.) and the large bolts to 25 ft. lbs. (30 Nm.).

8. Remove the Special Tool from the V-6 engines.

9. The remainder of installation is the reverse of removal. Adjust the drive belt tension after installation.

Thermostat

The factory-installed thermostat is designed to open at 195°F (91°C).

REMOVAL AND INSTALLATION

All Models

The thermostat is located inside a housing on the front of the cylinder head on the four cylinder engine, and inside the front of the intake manifold casting on the V6. It is not necessary to remove the radiator hose from the thermostat housing when removing the thermostat.

1. Remove the two retaining bolts from the thermostat housing and lift up the housing with the hose attached. Remove the thermostat.

2. Insert the new thermostat, spring end down. Apply a thin bead of silicone sealer to the housing mating surface and install the housing while the sealer is still wet. Tighten the housing retaining bolts to 6 ft. lbs. (8 Nm.).

NOTE: *Poor heater output and slow warmup is often caused by a thermostat stuck in the open position; occasionally one sticks shut causing immediate overheating. Do not attempt to correct a chronic overheating condition by permanently removing the thermostat. Thermostat flow restriction is designed into the system; without it, localized overheating (due to coolant turbulence) may occur, causing expensive troubles.*

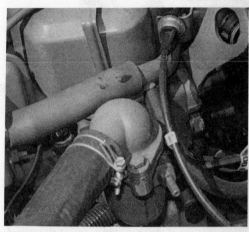

Four cylinder thermostat housing

V6 thermostat housing bolt locations

Emission Controls and Fuel System

EMISSION CONTROLS

There are three sources of automotive pollutants: crankcase fumes, exhaust gases, and gasoline evaporation. The pollutants formed from these substances fall into three categories: unburnt hydrocarbons (HC), carbon monoxide (CO), and oxides of nitrogen (NO_x). The equipment that is used to limit these pollutants is commonly called emission control equipment.

Crankcase Emission Controls

POSITIVE CRANKCASE VENTILATION SYSTEM

All X-Body cars are equipped with a positive crankcase ventilation (PCV) system to control crankcase blow-by vapors. The system functions as follows:

When the engine is running, a small portion of the gases which are formed in the combustion chamber leak by the piston rings and enter the crankcase. Since these gases are under pressure, they tend to escape from the crankcase and enter the atmosphere. If these gases are allowed to remain in the crankcase for any period of time, they contaminate the engine oil and cause sludge to build up in the crankcase. If the gases are allowed to escape into the atmosphere, they pollute the air with unburned hydrocarbons. The job of the crankcase emission control equipment is to recycle these gases back into the engine combustion chamber where they are reburned.

The crankcase (blow-by) gases are recycled

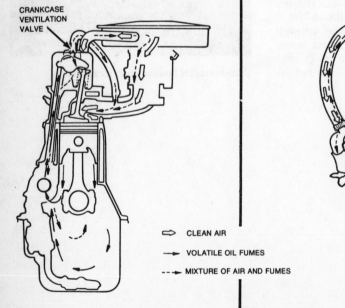

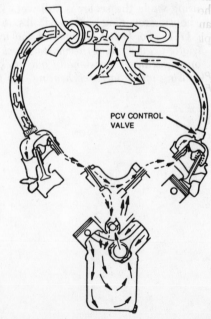

CRANKCASE
VENTILATION
VALVE

PCV CONTROL
VALVE

⇨ CLEAN AIR

→ VOLATILE OIL FUMES

- - → MIXTURE OF AIR AND FUMES

Cross-section schematics of the four cylinder (left) and V6 (right) PCV systems

in the following way: as the engine is running, clean, filtered air is drawn through the air filter and into the crankcase. As the air passes through the crankcase, it picks up the combustion gases and carries them out of the crankcase, through the oil separator, through the PCV valve, and into the induction system. As they enter the intake manifold, they are drawn into the combustion chamber where they are reburned.

The most critical component in the system is the PCV valve. This valve controls the amount of gases which are recycled into the combustion chamber. At low engine speeds, the valve is partially closed, limiting the flow of gases into the intake manifold. As engine speed increases, the valve opens to admit greater quantities of gases into the intake manifold. If the valve should become blocked or plugged, the gases will be prevented from escaping from the crankcase by the normal route. Since these gases are under pressure, they will find their own way out of the crankcase. This alternate route is usually a weak oil seal or gasket in the engine. As the gas escapes by the gasket, it also creates an oil leak. Besides causing oil leaks, a clogged PCV valve also allows these gases to remain in the crankcase for an extended period of time, promoting the formation of sludge in the engine.

Service

Inspect the PCV system hose and connections at each tune-up and replace any deteriorated hoses. Check the PCV valve at every tune-up and replace it at 30,000 mile intervals. Replacement procedures are in Chapter One.

PCV FILTER REMOVAL AND INSTALLATION—FOUR CYLINDER ONLY

1. Slide the rubber coupling that joins the tube coming from the valve cover to the filter off the filter nipple. Remove the air cleaner case lid. Side the spring clamp off the filter, and remove the filter.

2. Inspect the rubber grommet in the valve cover and the rubber coupling for brittleness or cracking. Replace parts as necessary.

3. Insert the new PCV filter through the hole in the air cleaner case, with the open portion of the filter upward. Make sure the square portion of the filter behind the nipple fits into the square hole in the air cleaner case.

4. Install a new spring clamp onto the nipple. Make sure that the clamp goes under the ridge on the filter nipple all the way around. Reconnect the rubber coupling and install the cover.

Evaporative Emission Control System

The basic Evaporative Emission Control System (EECS) used on all X-Body cars is the carbon canister storage method. This method transfers fuel vapors to an activated carbon storage device which absorbs and stores the vapor that is emitted from the engine's induction system while the engine is not running. When the engine is running, the stored vapor is purged from the carbon storage device by the intake air flow and then consumed in the normal combustion process. As manifold vacuum reaches a certain point, it opens a purge control valve atop the charcoal storage canister. This allows air to be drawn into the canister, thus forcing the existing fuel vapors back into the engine to be burned normally.

In 1981, the purge function on the V6 engine is electrically controlled by a purge solenoid in the line which is itself controlled by the Electronic Control Module. When the system is in the "Open Loop" mode, the solenoid valve is energized and blocks all vacuum to the purge valve. When the system is in the "Closed Loop" mode, the solenoid is de-energized and vacuum is then supplied to operate the purge valve. This releases the fuel vapors and it is forced into the induction system.

Most of the carbon canisters used are of the "Open" design, meaning that air is drawn in through the bottom (filter) of the cannister. Some (1981 and later V6) cannisters are of the

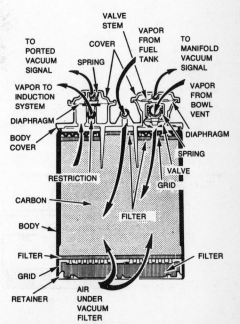

Cross-sectional diagram of the charcoal canister

"Closed" design, which means that the incoming air is drawn directly from the air cleaner.

SERVICE

The only service required is the periodic replacement of the cannister filter (if so equipped). This procedure is covered in Chapter 1. If the fuel tank cap on your X-Body ever requires replacement, make sure that it is of the same type as the original.

Exhaust Emission Controls

Exhaust emission control systems constitute the largest body of emission control devices installed on your X-car. Included in this category are: Catalytic Converter, Early Fuel Evaporation System (EFE), Exhaust Gas Recirculation system (EGR), Thermostatic Air Cleaner (THERMAC), Pulse Air Injection (PULSAIR; 1980), Air Management (AIR; 1981), Deceleration Valve, Computer Controlled Catalytic Converter system (C-4; 1980 Calif. only) and the Computer Command Control system (CCC; 1981 and later). A brief description of each system and any applicable service procedures follows.

Catalytic Converter

The catalytic converter is a muffler-like container built into the exhaust system to aid in the reduction of exhaust emissions. The cata-

lyst element consists of individual pellets or a honeycomb monolithic substrate coated with a noble metal such as platinum, palladium, rhodium or a combination. When the exhaust gases come into contact with the catalyst, a chemical reaction occurs which will reduce the pollutants into harmless substances like water and carbon dioxide.

There are essentially two types of catalytic converters: an oxidizing type and a three-way type. The oxidizing type is used on all 1980 models with the exception of those built for Calif. It requires the addition of oxygen to spur the catalyst into reducing the engine's HC and CO emissions into H_2O and CO_2. Because of this need for oxygen, the PULSAIR system is used with all these models.

The oxidizing catalytic converter, while effectively reducing HC and CO emissions, does little, if anything in the way of reducing NO_x emissions. Thus, the three-way catalytic converter.

The three-way converter, unlike the oxidizing type, is capable of reducing HC, CO and NO_x emissions; all at the same time. In theory, it seems impossible to reduce all three pollutants in one system since the reduction of HC and CO requires the addition of oxygen, while the reduction of NO_x calls for the removal of oxygen. In actuality, the three-way system really can reduce all three pollutants, but only if the amount of oxygen in the exhaust system is precisely controlled. Due to

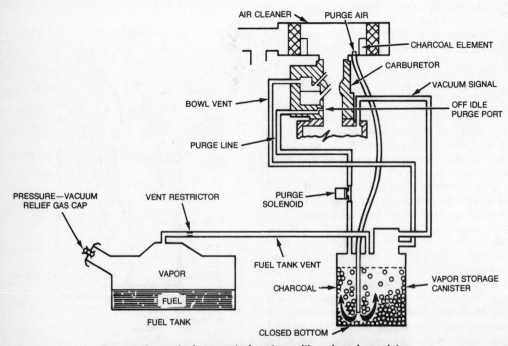

Evaporative emissions control system with a closed cannister

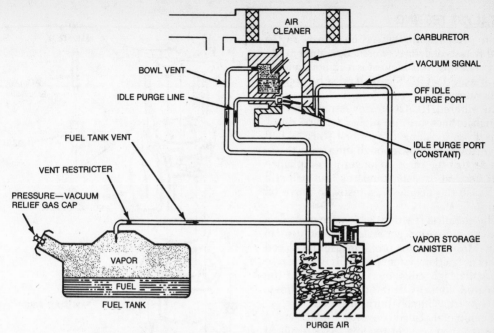

Evaporative emissions control system with an open cannister

this precise oxygen control requirement, the three-way converter system is used only in cars equipped with an oxygen sensor system (1980 Calif. cars and all 1981 and later models).

There are no service procedures required for the catalytic converter, although the converter body should be inspected occasionally for damage.

Some models with the V-6 engine require a catalyst change at 30,000 mile intervals. The first such replacement is covered under an extended emissions warranty by General Motors and is performed at no charge by your dealer. Subsequent replacement is the responsibility of the owner.

PRECAUTIONS

1. Use only unleaded fuel.
2. Avoid prolonged idling; the engine

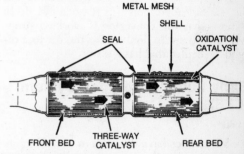

Cutaway view of the three-way catalytic converter

should run no longer than 20 min. at curb idle and no longer than 10 min. at fast idle.

3. Do not disconnect any of the spark plug leads while the engine is running.

4. Make engine compression checks as quickly as possible.

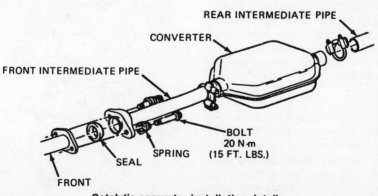

Catalytic converter installation details

CATALYST TESTING

At the present time there is no known way to reliably test catalytic convertor operation in the field. The only reliable test is a 12 hour and 40 min. "soak" test (CVS) which must be done in a laboratory.

An infrared HC/CO tester is not sensitive enough to measure the higher tailpipe emissions from a failing convertor. Thus, a bad convertor may allow enough emissions to escape so that the car is no longer in compliance with Federal or state standards, but will still not cause the needle on a tester to move off zero.

The chemical reactions which occur inside a catalytic convertor generate a great deal of heat. Most convertor problems can be traced to fuel or ignition system problems which cause unusually high emissions. As a result of the increased intensity of the chemical reactions, the convertor literally burns itself up.

A completely failed convertor might cause a tester to show a slight reading. As a result, it is occasionally possible to detect one of these.

As long as you avoid severe overheating and the use of leaded fuels it is reasonably safe to assume that the convertor is working properly. If you are in doubt, take the car to a diagnostic center that has a tester.

Early Fuel Evaporation System (EFE)

1980

All V6 engines have this system to reduce engine warm-up time, improve driveability, and reduce emissions. On start-up, a vacuum motor acts to close a heat valve in the exhaust manifold which causes exhaust gases to enter the intake manifold heat riser passages. The incoming fuel mixture is thus heated, resulting in more complete fuel evaporation. When the engine warms up, the valve opens. Vacuum to the EFE valve is controlled by a thermal vacuum switch (TVS) installed in the intake manifold, which monitors engine coolant temperatures and permits or restricts manifold vacuum to the valve accordingly.

Service procedures for this system are covered in Chapter One.

1981 and later

As in 1980, only V6 engines utilize this system. Although the function of the 1981 EFE system remains the same—to reduce engine warm-up time, improve driveability and to reduce emissions—the operation is entirely different. The new system is electric and uses a ceramic heater grid located underneath the

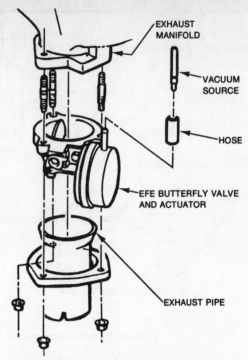

1980 EFE valve installation details (V6 only)

primary bore of the carburetor as part of the carburetor insulator/gasket. When the engine coolant is below the specified calibration level, electrical current is supplied to the heater through an ECM controlled relay.

REMOVAL AND INSTALLATION

1. Remove the air cleaner.
2. Disconnect all electrical, vacuum and fuel connections from the carburetor.
3. Disconnect the EFE heater electrical connection.

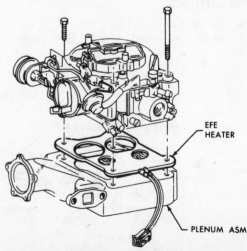

1981 and later EFE heater grid (V6 only)

CHILTON'S
FUEL ECONOMY
& TUNE-UP TIPS

Tune-up • Spark Plug Diagnosis • Emission Controls

Fuel System • Cooling System • Tires and Wheels

General Maintenance

CHILTON'S FUEL ECONOMY & TUNE-UP TIPS

Fuel economy is important to everyone, no matter what kind of vehicle you drive. The maintenance-minded motorist can save both money and fuel using these tips and the periodic maintenance and tune-up procedures in this Repair and Tune-Up Guide.

There are more than 130,000,000 cars and trucks registered for private use in the United States. Each travels an average of 10-12,000 miles per year, and, and in total they consume close to 70 billion gallons of fuel each year. This represents nearly ⅔ of the oil imported by the United States each year. The Federal government's goal is to reduce consumption 10% by 1985. A variety of methods are either already in use or under serious consideration, and they all affect you driving and the cars you will drive. In addition to "down-sizing", the auto industry is using or investigating the use of electronic fuel delivery, electronic engine controls and alternative engines for use in smaller and lighter vehicles, among other alternatives to meet the federally mandated Corporate Average Fuel Economy (CAFE) of 27.5 mpg by 1985. The government, for its part, is considering rationing, mandatory driving curtailments and tax increases on motor vehicle fuel in an effort to reduce consumption. The government's goal of a 10% reduction could be realized — and further government regulation avoided — if every private vehicle could use just 1 less gallon of fuel per week.

How Much Can You Save?

Tests have proven that almost anyone can make at least a 10% reduction in fuel consumption through regular maintenance and tune-ups. When a major manufacturer of spark plugs sur-

TUNE-UP

1. Check the cylinder compression to be sure the engine will really benefit from a tune-up and that it is capable of producing good fuel economy. A tune-up will be wasted on an engine in poor mechanical condition.

2. Replace spark plugs regularly. New spark plugs alone can increase fuel economy 3%.

3. Be sure the spark plugs are the correct type (heat range) for your vehicle. See the Tune-Up Specifications.

Heat range refers to the spark plug's ability to conduct heat away from the firing end. It must conduct the heat away in an even pattern to avoid becoming a source of pre-ignition, yet it must also operate hot enough to burn off conductive deposits that could cause misfiring.

The heat range is usually indicated by a number on the spark plug, part of the manufacturer's designation for each individual spark plug. The numbers in bold-face indicate the heat range in each manufacturer's identification system.

Periodically, check the spark plugs to be sure they are firing efficiently. They are excellent indicators of the internal condition of your engine.

Manufacturer	Typical Designation
AC	R **45** TS
Bosch (old)	WA **145** T30
Bosch (new)	HR **8** Y
Champion	RBL **15** Y
Fram/Autolite	4**15**
Mopar	P-**62** PR
Motorcraft	BRF-**42**
NGK	BP **5** ES-15
Nippondenso	W **16** EP
Prestolite	14GR **5** 2A

On AC, Bosch (new), Champion, Fram/Autolite, Mopar, Motorcraft and Prestolite, a higher number indicates a hotter plug. On Bosch (old), NGK and Nippondenso, a higher number indicates a colder plug.

4. Make sure the spark plugs are properly gapped. See the Tune-Up Specifications in this book.

5. Be sure the spark plugs are firing efficiently. The illustrations on the next 2 pages show you how to "read" the firing end of the spark plug.

6. Check the ignition timing and set it to specifications. Tests show that almost all cars have incorrect ignition timing by more than 2°.

veyed over 6,000 cars nationwide, they found that a tune-up, on cars that needed one, increased fuel economy over 11%. Replacing worn plugs alone, accounted for a 3% increase. The same test also revealed that 8 out of every 10 vehicles will have some maintenance deficiency that will directly affect fuel economy, emissions or performance. Most of this mileage-robbing neglect could be prevented with regular maintenance.

Modern engines require that all of the functioning systems operate properly for maximum efficiency. A malfunction anywhere wastes fuel. You can keep your vehicle running as efficiently and economically as possible, by being aware of your vehicle's operating and performance characteristics. If your vehicle suddenly develops performance or fuel economy problems it could be due to one or more of the following:

PROBLEM	POSSIBLE CAUSE
Engine Idles Rough	Ignition timing, idle mixture, vacuum leak or something amiss in the emission control system.
Hesitates on Acceleration	Dirty carburetor or fuel filter, improper accelerator pump setting, ignition timing or fouled spark plugs.
Starts Hard or Fails to Start	Worn spark plugs, improperly set automatic choke, ice (or water) in fuel system.
Stalls Frequently	Automatic choke improperly adjusted and possible dirty air filter or fuel filter.
Performs Sluggishly	Worn spark plugs, dirty fuel or air filter, ignition timing or automatic choke out of adjustment.

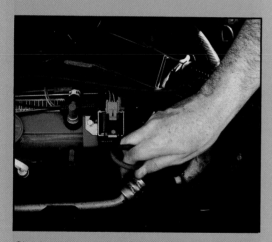

Check spark plug wires on conventional point type ignition for cracks by bending them in a loop around your finger.

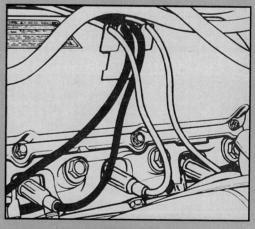

Be sure that spark plug wires leading to adjacent cylinders do not run too close together. (Photo courtesy Champion Spark Plug Co.)

7. If your vehicle does not have electronic ignition, check the points, rotor and cap as specified.

8. Check the spark plug wires (used with conventional point-type ignitions) for cracks and burned or broken insulation by bending them in a loop around your finger. Cracked wires decrease fuel efficiency by failing to deliver full voltage to the spark plugs. One misfiring spark plug can cost you as much as 2 mpg.

9. Check the routing of the plug wires. Misfiring can be the result of spark plug leads to adjacent cylinders running parallel to each other and too close together. One wire tends to

pick up voltage from the other causing it to fire "out of time".

10. Check all electrical and ignition circuits for voltage drop and resistance.

11. Check the distributor mechanical and/or vacuum advance mechanisms for proper functioning. The vacuum advance can be checked by twisting the distributor plate in the opposite direction of rotation. It should spring back when released.

12. Check and adjust the valve clearance on engines with mechanical lifters. The clearance should be slightly loose rather than too tight.

SPARK PLUG DIAGNOSIS

Normal

APPEARANCE: This plug is typical of one operating normally. The insulator nose varies from a light tan to grayish color with slight electrode wear. The presence of slight deposits is normal on used plugs and will have no adverse effect on engine performance. The spark plug heat range is correct for the engine and the engine is running normally.

CAUSE: Properly running engine.

RECOMMENDATION: Before reinstalling this plug, the electrodes should be cleaned and filed square. Set the gap to specifications. If the plug has been in service for more than 10-12,000 miles, the entire set should probably be replaced with a fresh set of the same heat range.

Oil Deposits

APPEARANCE: The firing end of the plug is covered with a wet, oily coating.

CAUSE: The problem is poor oil control. On high mileage engines, oil is leaking past the rings or valve guides into the combustion chamber. A common cause is also a plugged PCV valve, and a ruptured fuel pump diaphragm can also cause this condition. Oil fouled plugs such as these are often found in new or recently overhauled engines, before normal oil control is achieved, and can be cleaned and reinstalled.

RECOMMENDATION: A hotter spark plug may temporarily relieve the problem, but the engine is probably in need of work.

Incorrect Heat Range

APPEARANCE: The effects of high temperature on a spark plug are indicated by clean white, often blistered insulator. This can also be accompanied by excessive wear of the electrode, and the absence of deposits.

CAUSE: Check for the correct spark plug heat range. A plug which is too hot for the engine can result in overheating. A car operated mostly at high speeds can require a colder plug. Also check ignition timing, cooling system level, fuel mixture and leaking intake manifold.

RECOMMENDATION: If all ignition and engine adjustments are known to be correct, and no other malfunction exists, install spark plugs one heat range colder.

Photos Courtesy Fram Corporation

Carbon Deposits

APPEARANCE: Carbon fouling is easily identified by the presence of dry, soft, black, sooty deposits.

CAUSE: Changing the heat range can often lead to carbon fouling, as can prolonged slow, stop-and-start driving. If the heat range is correct, carbon fouling can be attributed to a rich fuel mixture, sticking choke, clogged air cleaner, worn breaker points, retarded timing or low compression. If only one or two plugs are carbon fouled, check for corroded or cracked wires on the affected plugs. Also look for cracks in the distributor cap between the towers of affected cylinders.

RECOMMENDATION: After the problem is corrected, these plugs can be cleaned and reinstalled if not worn severely.

MMT Fouled

APPEARANCE: Spark plugs fouled by MMT (Methycyclopentadienyl Maganese Tricarbonyl) have reddish, rusty appearance on the insulator and side electrode.

CAUSE: MMT is an anti-knock additive in gasoline used to replace lead. During the combustion process, the MMT leaves a reddish deposit on the insulator and side electrode.

RECOMMENDATION: No engine malfunction is indicated and the deposits will not affect plug performance any more than lead deposits (see Ash Deposits). MMT fouled plugs can be cleaned, regapped and reinstalled.

High Speed Glazing

APPEARANCE: Glazing appears as shiny coating on the plug, either yellow or tan in color.

CAUSE: During hard, fast acceleration, plug temperatures rise suddenly. Deposits from normal combustion have no chance to fluff-off; instead, they melt on the insulator forming an electrically conductive coating which causes misfiring.

RECOMMENDATION: Glazed plugs are not easily cleaned. They should be replaced with a fresh set of plugs of the correct heat range. If the condition recurs, using plugs with a heat range one step colder may cure the problem.

Ash (Lead) Deposits

APPEARANCE: Ash deposits are characterized by light brown or white colored deposits crusted on the side or center electrodes. In some cases it may give the plug a rusty appearance.

CAUSE: Ash deposits are normally derived from oil or fuel additives burned during normal combustion. Normally they are harmless, though excessive amounts can cause misfiring. If deposits are excessive in short mileage, the valve guides may be worn.

RECOMMENDATION: Ash-fouled plugs can be cleaned, gapped and reinstalled.

Detonation

APPEARANCE: Detonation is usually characterized by a broken plug insulator.

CAUSE: A portion of the fuel charge will begin to burn spontaneously, from the increased heat following ignition. The explosion that results applies extreme pressure to engine components, frequently damaging spark plugs and pistons.

Detonation can result by over-advanced ignition timing, inferior gasoline (low octane) lean air/fuel mixture, poor carburetion, engine lugging or an increase in compression ratio due to combustion chamber deposits or engine modification.

RECOMMENDATION: Replace the plugs after correcting the problem.

EMISSION CONTROLS

13. Be aware of the general condition of the emission control system. It contributes to reduced pollution and should be serviced regularly to maintain efficient engine operation.

14. Check all vacuum lines for dried, cracked or brittle conditions. Something as simple as a leaking vacuum hose can cause poor performance and loss of economy.

15. Avoid tampering with the emission control system. Attempting to improve fuel econ-

FUEL SYSTEM

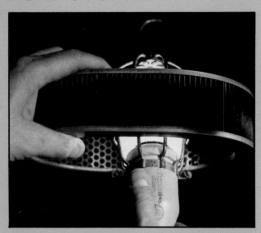

Check the air filter with a light behind it. If you can see light through the filter it can be reused.

Extremely clogged filters should be discarded and replaced with a new one.

18. Replace the air filter regularly. A dirty air filter richens the air/fuel mixture and can increase fuel consumption as much as 10%. Tests show that ⅓ of all vehicles have air filters in need of replacement.

19. Replace the fuel filter at least as often as recommended.

20. Set the idle speed and carburetor mixture to specifications.

21. Check the automatic choke. A sticking or malfunctioning choke wastes gas.

22. During the summer months, adjust the automatic choke for a leaner mixture which will produce faster engine warm-ups.

COOLING SYSTEM

29. Be sure all accessory drive belts are in good condition. Check for cracks or wear.

30. Adjust all accessory drive belts to proper tension.

31. Check all hoses for swollen areas, worn spots, or loose clamps.

32. Check coolant level in the radiator or ex-

pansion tank.

33. Be sure the thermostat is operating properly. A stuck thermostat delays engine warm-up and a cold engine uses nearly twice as much fuel as a warm engine.

34. Drain and replace the engine coolant at least as often as recommended. Rust and scale

TIRES & WHEELS

38. Check the tire pressure often with a pencil type gauge. Tests by a major tire manufacturer show that 90% of all vehicles have at least 1 tire improperly inflated. Better mileage can be achieved by over-inflating tires, but never exceed the maximum inflation pressure on the side of the tire.

39. If possible, install radial tires. Radial tires

deliver as much as ½ mpg more than bias belted tires.

40. Avoid installing super-wide tires. They only create extra rolling resistance and decrease fuel mileage. Stick to the manufacturer's recommendations.

41. Have the wheels properly balanced.

omy by tampering with emission controls is more likely to worsen fuel economy than improve it. Emission control changes on modern engines are not readily reversible.

16. Clean (or replace) the EGR valve and lines as recommended.

17. Be sure that all vacuum lines and hoses are reconnected properly after working under the hood. An unconnected or misrouted vacuum line can wreak havoc with engine performance.

23. Check for fuel leaks at the carburetor, fuel pump, fuel lines and fuel tank. Be sure all lines and connections are tight.

24. Periodically check the tightness of the carburetor and intake manifold attaching nuts and bolts. These are a common place for vacuum leaks to occur.

25. Clean the carburetor periodically and lubricate the linkage.

26. The condition of the tailpipe can be an excellent indicator of proper engine combustion. After a long drive at highway speeds, the inside of the tailpipe should be a light grey in color. Black or soot on the insides indicates an overly rich mixture.

27. Check the fuel pump pressure. The fuel pump may be supplying more fuel than the engine needs.

28. Use the proper grade of gasoline for your engine. Don't try to compensate for knocking or "pinging" by advancing the ignition timing. This practice will only increase plug temperature and the chances of detonation or pre-ignition with relatively little performance gain.

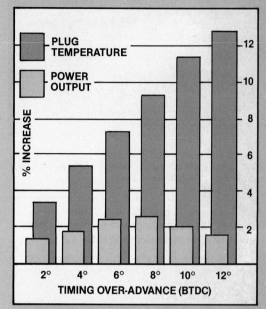

Increasing ignition timing past the specified setting results in a drastic increase in spark plug temperature with increased chance of detonation or preignition. Performance increase is considerably less. (Photo courtesy Champion Spark Plug Co.)

that form in the engine should be flushed out to allow the engine to operate at peak efficiency.

35. Clean the radiator of debris that can decrease cooling efficiency.

36. Install a flex-type or electric cooling fan, if you don't have a clutch type fan. Flex fans use curved plastic blades to push more air at low speeds when more cooling is needed; at high speeds the blades flatten out for less resistance. Electric fans only run when the engine temperature reaches a predetermined level.

37. Check the radiator cap for a worn or cracked gasket. If the cap does not seal properly, the cooling system will not function properly.

42. Be sure the front end is correctly aligned. A misaligned front end actually has wheels going in differed directions. The increased drag can reduce fuel economy by .3 mpg.

43. Correctly adjust the wheel bearings. Wheel bearings that are adjusted too tight increase rolling resistance.

Check tire pressures regularly with a reliable pocket type gauge. Be sure to check the pressure on a cold tire.

GENERAL MAINTENANCE

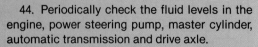

Check the fluid levels (particularly engine oil) on a regular basis. Be sure to check the oil for grit, water or other contamination.

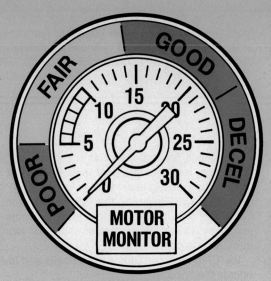

A vacuum gauge is another excellent indicator of internal engine condition and can also be installed in the dash as a mileage indicator.

44. Periodically check the fluid levels in the engine, power steering pump, master cylinder, automatic transmission and drive axle.

45. Change the oil at the recommended interval and change the filter at every oil change. Dirty oil is thick and causes extra friction between moving parts, cutting efficiency and increasing wear. A worn engine requires more frequent tune-ups and gets progressively worse fuel economy. In general, use the lightest viscosity oil for the driving conditions you will encounter.

46. Use the recommended viscosity fluids in the transmission and axle.

47. Be sure the battery is fully charged for fast starts. A slow starting engine wastes fuel.

48. Be sure battery terminals are clean and tight.

49. Check the battery electrolyte level and add distilled water if necessary.

50. Check the exhaust system for crushed pipes, blockages and leaks.

51. Adjust the brakes. Dragging brakes or brakes that are not releasing create increased drag on the engine.

52. Install a vacuum gauge or miles-per-gallon gauge. These gauges visually indicate engine vacuum in the intake manifold. High vacuum = good mileage and low vacuum = poorer mileage. The gauge can also be an excellent indicator of internal engine conditions.

53. Be sure the clutch is properly adjusted. A slipping clutch wastes fuel.

54. Check and periodically lubricate the heat control valve in the exhaust manifold. A sticking or inoperative valve prevents engine warm-up and wastes gas.

55. Keep accurate records to check fuel economy over a period of time. A sudden drop in fuel economy may signal a need for tune-up or other maintenance.

4. Remove the carburetor as detailed later in this chapter.

5. Lift off the EFE heater.

6. Installation is in the reverse order of removal.

7. Start the engine and check for any fuel leaks.

EFE HEATER RELAY REPLACEMENT

1. Disconnect the negative battery cable.

2. Tag and disconnect all electrical connections.

3. Unscrew the retaining bolts and remove the relay.

4. Installation is in the reverse order of removal.

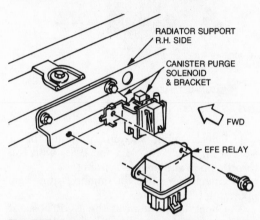

RADIATOR SUPPORT
R.H. SIDE

CANISTER PURGE
SOLENOID
& BRACKET

FWD

EFE RELAY

The EFE heater relay can be found on the right side radiator support

Exhaust Gas Recirculation (EGR)

All engines are equipped with this system, which consists of a metering valve, a vacuum line to the carburetor or intake manifold, and cast-in exhaust passages in the intake manifold. The EGR valve is controlled by vacuum, and opens and closes in response to the vacuum signals to admit exhaust gases into the air/fuel mixture. The exhaust gases lower peak combustion temperatures, reducing the formation of NO_x. The valve is closed at idle and wide open throttle, but is open between the two extreme positions.

There are actually two types of EGR systems: Vacuum Modulated and Exhaust Back Pressure Modulated. The principle of both systems is the same; the only difference is in the method used to control how far the EGR valve opens.

In the Vacuum Modulated system, the amount of exhaust gas admitted into the intake manifold depends on a ported vacuum signal. A ported vacuum signal is one taken from the carburetor above the throttle plates; thus, the vacuum signal (amount of vacuum) is dependent on how far the throttle plates are opened. When the throttle is closed (idle or deceleration) there is no vacuum signal. Thus, the EGR valve is closed, and no exhaust gas enters the intake manifold. As the throttle is opened, a vacuum is produced, which opens the EGR valve, admitting exhaust gas into the intake manifold.

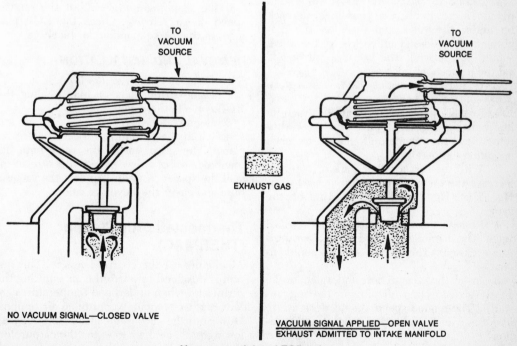

TO
VACUUM
SOURCE

TO
VACUUM
SOURCE

EXHAUST GAS

NO VACUUM SIGNAL—CLOSED VALVE

VACUUM SIGNAL APPLIED—OPEN VALVE
EXHAUST ADMITTED TO INTAKE MANIFOLD

Vacuum modulated EGR valve

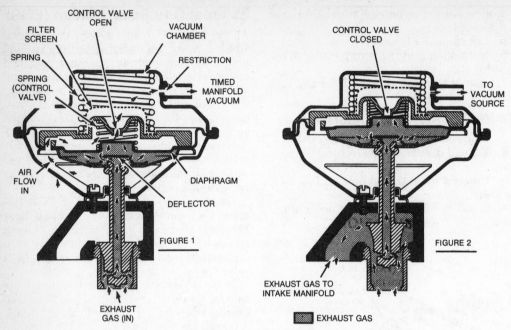

Exhaust gas modulated EGR valve

In the Exhaust Back Pressure Modulated system, a transducer is installed in the EGR valve body. The vacuum is still ported vacuum, but the transducer uses exhaust gas pressure to control an air bleed within the valve to modify this vacuum signal.

SYSTEM CHECKS

1. Check to see if the EGR valve diaphragm moves freely. Use your finger to reach up under the valve and push on the diaphragm. If it doesn't move freely, the valve should be replaced. The use of a mirror will aid the inspection process.

CAUTION: *If the engine is hot, wear a glove to protect your hand.*

2. Install a vacuum gauge into the vacuum line between the EGR valve and the carburetor. Start the engine and allow it to reach operating temperature.

3. With the car in either Park or Neutral, increase the engine speed until at least 5 in. Hg. (7 in. Hg. for 1981) is showing on the gauge.

4. Remove the vacuum hose from the EGR valve. The diaphragm should move downward (valve closed). The engine speed should increase.

5. Install the vacuum hose and watch for the EGR valve to open (diaphragm moving upward). The engine speed should decrease to its former level, indicating exhaust recirculation.

If the diaphragm doesn't move:

1. Check engine vacuum; it should be at least 5 in. Hg. (7 in. Hg. for 1981) with the throttle open and engine running.

2. Check to see that the engine is at normal operating temperature.

3. Check for vacuum at the EGR hose. If no vacuum is present, check the hose for leaks, breaks, kinks, improper connections, etc., and replace as necessary.

If the diaphragm moves, but the engine speed doesn't change, check the EGR passages in the intake manifold for blockage.

REMOVAL AND INSTALLATION

1. Disconnect the vacuum hose.

2. Remove the bolts or nuts holding the EGR valve to the engine.

3. Remove the valve.

4. Clean the mounting surfaces before replacing the valve. Install the valve onto the manifold, using a new gasket. Be sure to install the spacer, if used. Connect the vacuum hose and check the valve operation.

Thermostatic Air Cleaner (THERMAC)

All engines use the Thermac system. This system is designed to warm the air entering the carburetor when underhood temperatures are low, and to maintain a controlled air temperature into the carburetor at all times. By allowing preheated air to enter the carburetor, the amount of time the choke is on is reduced,

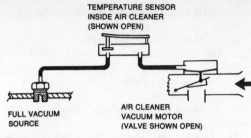

Thermac schematic

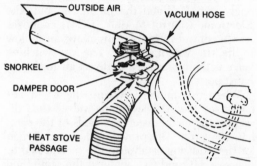

The thermac system can be tested by applying vacuum to the unit when cold

resulting in better fuel economy and lower emissions. Engine warm-up time is also reduced.

The Thermac system is composed of the air cleaner body, a filter, sensor unit, vacuum diaphragm, damper door, and associated hoses and connections. Heat radiating from the exhaust manifold is trapped by a heat stove and is ducted to the air cleaner to supply heated air to the carburetor. A movable door in the air cleaner case snorkel allows air to be drawn in from the heat stove (cold operation) or from underhood air (warm operation). The door position is controlled by the vacuum motor, which receives intake manifold vacuum as modulated by the temperature sensor.

SYSTEM CHECKS

1. Check the vacuum hoses for leaks, kinks, breaks, or improper connections and correct any defects.

2. With the engine off, check the position of the damper door within the snorkel. A mirror can be used to make this job easier. The damper door should be open to admit outside air.

3. Apply at least 7 in. Hg. of vacuum to the damper diaphragm unit. The door should close. If it doesn't, check the diaphragm linkage for binding and correct hookup.

4. With vacuum still applied and the door closed, clamp the tube to trap the vacuum. If

the door doesn't remain closed, there is a leak in the diaphragm assembly.

Pulse Air Injection (PULSAIR)
1980

All engines use the Pulsair air injection system, which uses exhaust system air pulses to siphon fresh air into the exhaust manifold. The injected air supports continued combustion of the hot exhaust gases in the exhaust manifold, reducing exhaust emissions. A secondary purpose of the Pulsair system is to introduce more oxygen into the exhaust system upstream of the catalytic converter, to supply the converter with the oxygen required for the oxidation reaction.

Air is drawn into the Pulsair valve through a hose connected to the air cleaner. The air passes through a check valve (there is one check valve for each cylinder; all check valves are installed in the Pulsair valve), then through a manifold pipe to the exhaust manifold. All manifold pipes are the same length, to prevent uneven pulsation. The check valves open during pulses of negative exhaust back pressure, admitting air into the manifold pipe and the exhaust manifold. During pulses of positive exhaust back pressure, the check valves close, preventing backfiring into the Pulsair valve and air cleaner.

The Pulsair check valves, hoses and pipes should be checked occasionally for leaks, cracks, or breaks.

REMOVAL AND INSTALLATION

1. Remove the air cleaner case. Disconnect the rubber hose(s) from the Pulsair valve(s).

2. Disconnect the support bracket, if present. Some V6 engines have a Pulsair solenoid and bracket, which must be removed.

3. Unscrew the attaching nuts and remove the Pulsair tubes from the exhaust manifold(s).

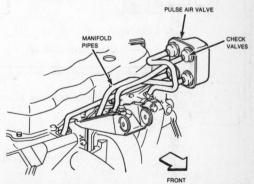

Pulsair installed on the four cylinder engine; V6 similar

4. To install, first apply a light coat of clean oil to the ends of the Pulsair tubes.

5. Install the tubes to the exhaust manifold(s), tightening the nuts to 10–13 ft. lbs. (10 Nm.). Connect the support bracket and solenoid and bracket, if used. Connect the rubber hose(s) and install the air cleaner.

Air Injection Reaction (AIR)

1981 and later

The AIR management system is used to provide additional oxygen to continue the combustion process after the exhaust gases leave the combustion chamber. Air is injected into either the exhaust port(s), the exhaust manifold(s) or the catalytic converter by an engine driven air pump. The system is in operation at all times and will bypass air only momentarily during deceleration and at high speeds. The bypass function is performed by the Air Management Valve, while the check valve protects the air pump by preventing any backflow of exhaust gases.

The AIR system helps reduce HC and CO content in the exhaust gases by injecting air into the exhaust ports during cold engine operation. This air injection also helps the catalytic converter to reach the proper temperature quicker during warm-up. When the engine is warm (Closed Loop), the AIR system injects air into the beds of a three-way converter to lower the HC and the CO content in the exhaust.

The AIR system utilizes the following components:

1. An engine driven AIR pump.
2. AIR management valves (Air Control, Air Switching).
3. Air flow and control hoses.
4. Check valves.
5. A dual-bed, three-way catalytic converter.

The belt driven, vane type air pump is located at the front of the engine and supplies clean air to the AIR system for purposes already stated. When the engine is cold, the Electronic Control Module (ECM) energizes an AIR control solenoid. This allows air to flow to the AIR switching valve. The AIR switching valve is then energized to direct air to the exhaust ports.

When the engine is warm, the ECM de-energizes the AIR switching valve, thus directing the air between the beds of the catalytic converter. This provides additional oxygen for the oxidizing catalyst in the second bed to decrease HC and CO, while at the same time keeping oxygen levels low in the first bed, enabling the reducing catalyst to effectively decrease the levels of NO_x.

If the AIR control valve detects a rapid increase in manifold vacuum (deceleration), certain operating modes (wide open throttle, etc.) or the ECM self-diagnostic system detects any problem in the system, air is diverted to the air cleaner or directly into the atmosphere.

The primary purpose of the ECM's divert mode is to prevent backfiring. Throttle clo-

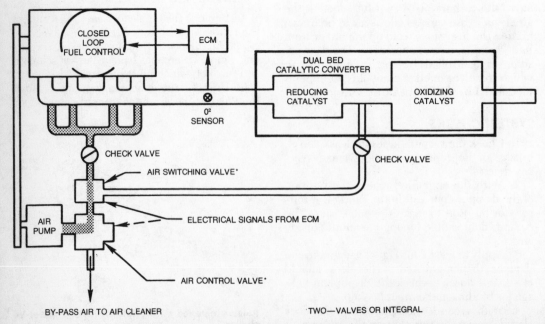

BY-PASS AIR TO AIR CLEANER   TWO—VALVES OR INTEGRAL

AIR management system operation—cold engine (1981 and later)

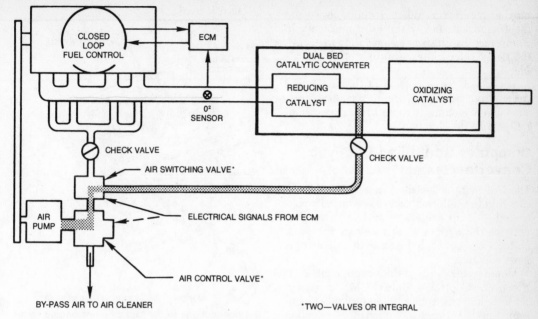

AIR management system operation—warm engine (1981 and later)

sure at the beginning of deceleration will temporarily create air/fuel mixtures which are too rich to burn completely. These mixtures become burnable when they reach the exhaust if combined with the injection air. The next firing of the engine will ignite this mixture causing an exhaust backfire. Momentary diverting of the injection air from the exhaust prevents this.

The AIR management system check valves and hoses should be checked periodically for any leaks, cracks or deterioration.

REMOVAL AND INSTALLATION

1. Remove the AIR management valves and/or adapter at the pump.

2. Loosen the air pump adjustment bolt and remove the drive belt.

3. Unscrew the three mounting bolts and then remove the pump pulley.

4. Unscrew the pump mounting bolts and then remove the pump.

5. Installation is the reverse order of removal. Be sure to adjust the drive belt tension after installing it.

Deceleration Valve

All 1980 models and all 1981 and later models with the V6 engine utilize the deceleration valve. Its purpose is to prevent backfiring in the exhaust system during engine deceleration. The valve is normally closed. When the throttle is suddenly closed, vacuum increases in the signal line (hose) to the valve. This opens

the valve, which bleeds air into the intake manifold, leaning out the rich deceleration mixture.

Air trapped in a chamber above the vacuum diaphragm bleeds at a predetermined rate through the delay valve portion of a check and delay valve, located centrally in the diaphragm. The air bleed reduces vacuum acting

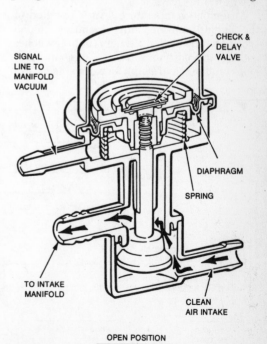

Cross-section of the deceleration valve in the open position

on the diaphragm. When vacuum above the diaphragm falls below the level necessary to counteract diaphragm-closing spring pressure, the delay valve closes, shutting off intake air bleed.

The check valve portion of the check and delay valve balances vacuum chamber pressure when vacuum is caused by acceleration, rather than deceleration.

Computer Controlled Catalytic Converter System

The C-4 System, installed on all 1980 X-Body cars sold in California, is an electronically controlled exhaust emissions system. The purpose of the system is to maintain the ideal air/fuel ratio at which the catalytic converter is most effective.

Major components of the system include an Electronic Control Module (ECM), an oxygen sensor, an electronically controlled carburetor, and a three-way oxidation-reduction catalytic converter. The system also includes a maintenance reminder flag connected to the odometer which becomes visible in the instrument cluster at regular intervals, signaling the need for oxygen sensor replacement.

The oxygen sensor, installed in the exhaust manifold, generates a voltage which varies with exhaust gas oxygen content. Lean mixtures (more oxygen) reduce voltage; rich mixtures (less oxygen) increase voltage. Voltage output is sent to the ECM.

An engine temperature sensor installed in the engine coolant outlet monitors engine coolant temperatures. Vacuum control switches and throttle position sensors also monitor engine conditions and supply signals to the ECM.

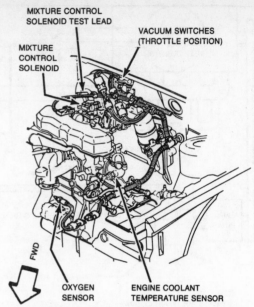

C-4 connections in the four cylinder engine compartment

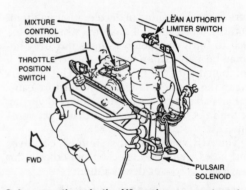

C-4 connections in the V6 engine compartment

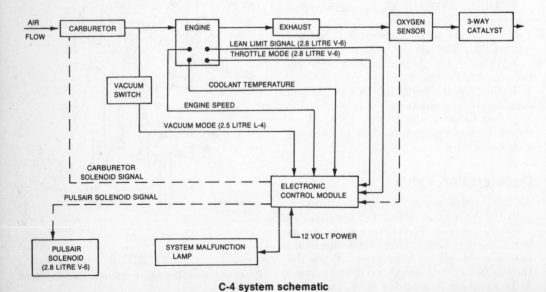

C-4 system schematic

The Electronic Control Module receives input signals from all sensors. It processes these signals and generates a control signal sent to the carburetor. The control signal cycles between on (lean command) and off (rich command). The amount of on and off time is a function of the input voltage sent to the ECM by the oxygen sensor.

A Rochester Dualjet E2SE carburetor is used with the C-4 System. Basically, an electrically operated mixture control solenoid is installed in the carburetor float bowl. The solenoid controls the air/fuel mixture metered to the idle and main metering systems. Air metering to the idle system is controlled by an idle air bleed valve. It follows the movement of the mixture solenoid to control the amount of air bled into the idle system, enrichening or leaning out the mixture as appropriate. Air/fule mixture enrichment occurs when the fuel valve is open and the air bleed valve is closed. All cycling of this system, which occurs ten times per second, is controlled by the ECM. A throttle position switch informs the ECM of open or closed throttle operation. A number of different switches are used, varying with application. The 1980 Citation, Omega, Phoenix and Skylark use two vacuum switches on the four cylinder engine, and a throttle position sensor on the V6. When the ECM receives a signal from the throttle switch, indicating a change of position, it immediately searches its memory for the last set of operating conditions that resulted in an ideal air/fule ratio, and shifts to that set of conditions. The memory is continually updated during normal operation.

A "Check-Engine" light is included in the C-4 System installation. When a fault develops, the light comes on, and a trouble code is set into the ECM memory. However, if the fault is intermittent, the light will go out, but the trouble code will remain in the ECM memory as long as the engine is running. The trouble codes are used as a diagnostic aid, and are pre-programmed.

Unless the required tools are available, troubleshooting the C-4 System should be confined to mechanical checks of electrical connectors, vacuum hoses and the like. All diagnosis and repair should be performed by a qualified mechanic.

Computer Command Control System

The Computer Command Control System, installed on all 1981 and later X-Body cars, is basically a modified version of the C-4 system. Its main advantage over its predecessor is that it can monitor and control a larger number of interrelated emission control systems.

This new system can monitor up to 15 various engine/vehicle operating conditions and then use this information to control as many as 9 engine related systems. The "System" is thereby making constant adjustments to maintain good vehicle performance under all normal driving conditions while at the same time allowing the catalytic converter to effectively control the emissions of NO_x, HC and CO.

In addition, the "System" has a built-in diagnostic system that recognizes and identifies possible operational problems and alerts the driver through a "Check Engine" light in the instrument panel. The light will remain "ON" until the problem is corrected. The "System" also has built-in back-up systems that in most cases of an operational problem will allow for the continued operation of the vehicle in a near normal manner until the repairs can be made.

The CCC system has some components in common with the C-4 system, although they are not interchangeable. These components include the Electronic Control Module (ECM), which, as previously stated, controls many more functions than does its predecessor, an oxygen sensor system, an electronically controlled variable-mixture carburetor, a three-way catalytic converter, throttle position and coolant sensors, a Barometric Pressure Sensor (BARO), a Manifold Absolute Pressure Sensor (MAP) and a "Check Engine" light in the instrument panel.

Components unique to the CCC system include the Air Injection Reaction (AIR) management system, a charcoal cannister purge solenoid, EGR valve controls, a vehicle speed sensor (in the instrument panel), a transmission converter clutch solenoid (Only on models with automatic transmission), idle speed control and Electronic Spark Control (ESC).

The ECM, in addition to monitoring sensors and sending out a control signal to the carburetor, also controls the following components or sub-systems: charcoal cannister purge control, the AIR system, idle speed, automatic transmission converter lock-up, distributor ignition timing, the EGR valve, and the air conditioner converter clutch.

The EGR valve control solenoid is activated by the ECM in a fashion similar to that of the charcoal connister purge solenoid described earlier in this chapter. When the engine is cold, the ECM energizes the solenoid, which blocks the vacuum signal to the EGR valve. When the engine is warm, the ECM de-energizes the solenoid and the vacuum signal is allowed to reach and then activate the EGR valve.

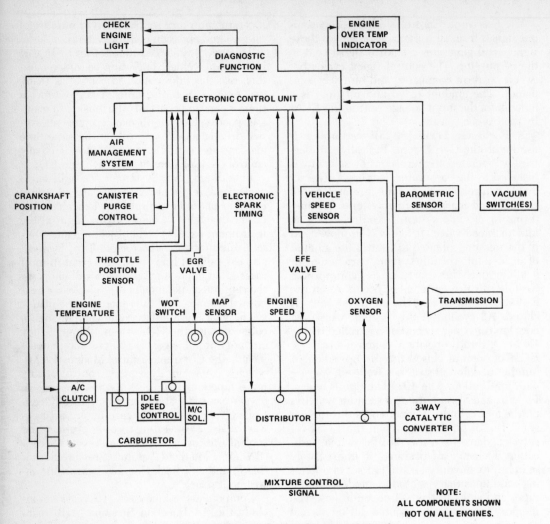

Computer Command Control System schematic

The Transmission Converter Clutch (TCC) lock is controlled by the ECM through an electrical solenoid in the automatic transmission. When the vehicle speed sensor in the dash signals the ECM that the car has attained the pre-determined speed, the ECM energizes the solenoid which then allows the torque converter to mechanically couple the engine to the transmission. When the brake pedal is pushed, or during deceleration or passing, etc., the ECM returns the transmission to fluid drive.

The idle speed control adjusts the idle speed to all particular engine load conditions and will lower the idle under no-load or low-load conditions in order to conserve fuel.

BASIC TROUBLESHOOTING

NOTE: *The following explains how to activate the Trouble Code signal light in the instrument cluster. This is not a full-fledged*

C-4 or CCC System troubleshooting and isolation procedure.

Before suspecting the C-4 or CCC System or any of its components as faulty, check the ignition system including distributor, timing, spark plugs, and wires. Check the engine compression, air cleaner, and emission control components not controlled by the ECM. Also check the intake manifold, vacuum hoses and hose connectors for leaks and the carburetor bolts for tightness.

The following symptoms could indicate a possible problem with the C-4 or CCC System.

1. Detonation
2. Stalls or rough idle—cold
3. Stalls or rough idle—hot
4. Missing
5. Hesitation
6. Surges
7. Poor gasoline mileage

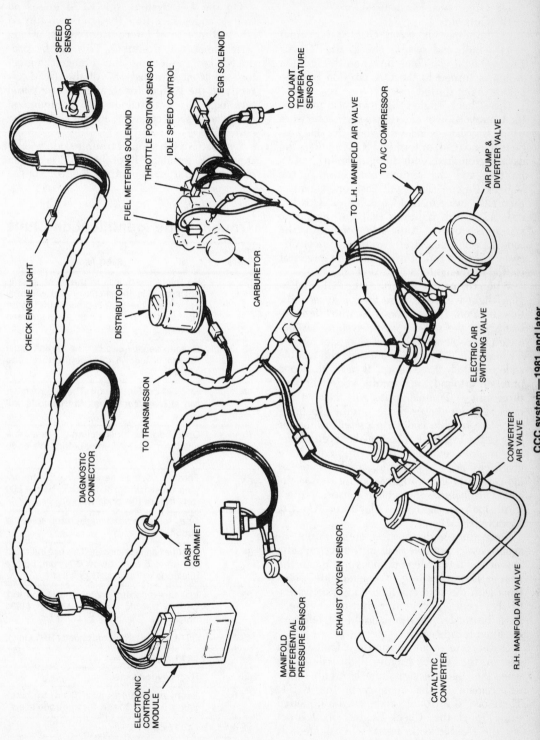

SPEED SENSOR

THROTTLE POSITION SENSOR

IDLE SPEED CONTROL

EGR SOLENOID

COOLANT TEMPERATURE SENSOR

FUEL METERING SOLENOID

TO L.H. MANIFOLD AIR VALVE

TO A/C COMPRESSOR

AIR PUMP & DIVERTER VALVE

CHECK ENGINE LIGHT

CARBURETOR

DISTRIBUTOR

ELECTRIC AIR SWITCHING VALVE

TO TRANSMISSION

DIAGNOSTIC CONNECTOR

CONVERTER AIR VALVE

DASH GROMMET

EXHAUST OXYGEN SENSOR

ELECTRONIC CONTROL MODULE

MANIFOLD DIFFERENTIAL PRESSURE SENSOR

CATALYTIC CONVERTER

R.H. MANIFOLD AIR VALVE

CCC system—1981 and later

8. Sluggish or spongy performance
9. Hard starting—cold
10. Hard starting—hot
11. Objectionable exhaust odors
12. Cuts out
13. Improper idle speed (CCC System only)

As a bulb and system check, the "Check Engine" light will come on when the ignition switch is turned to the ON position but the engine is not started.

The "Check Engine" light will also produce the trouble code or codes by a series of flashes which translate as follows. When the diagnostic test lead (C-4) or terminal (CCC) under the dash is grounded, with the ignition in the ON position and the engine not running, the "Check Engine" light will flash once, pause, then flash twice in rapid succession. This is a code 12, which indicates that the diagnostic system is working. After a longer pause, the code 12 will repeat itself two more times. The cycle will then repeat itself until the engine is started or the ignition is turned off.

When the engine is started, the "Check Engine" light will remain on for a few seconds, then turn off. If the "Check Engine" light remains on, the self-diagnostic system has detected a problem. If the test lead (C-4) or test terminal (CCC) is then grounded, the trouble code will flash three times. If more than one problem is found, each trouble code will flash three times. Trouble codes will flash in numerical order (lowest code number to highest). The trouble codes series will repeat as long as the test lead or terminal is grounded.

A trouble code indicates a problem with a given circuit. For example, trouble code 14 indicates a problem in the cooling sensor circuit. This includes the coolant sensor, its electrical harness, and the Electronic Control Module (ECM).

Since the self-diagnostic system cannot diagnose every possible fault in the system, the absence of a trouble code does not mean the system is trouble-free. To determine problems with the system which do not activate a trouble code, a system performance check must be made. This job should be left to a qualified technician.

In the case of an intermittent fault in the system, the "Check Engine" light will go out when the fault goes away, but the trouble code will remain in the memory of the ECM. Therefore, if a trouble code can be obtained even though the "Check Engine" light is not on, the trouble code must be evaluated. It must be determined if the fault is intermittent or if the engine must be at certain operating conditions (under load, etc.) before the "Check Engine" light will come on. Some trouble codes will not be recorded in the ECM until the engine has been operated at part throttle for about 5 to 18 minutes.

On the C-4 System, the ECM erases all trouble codes everytime the ignition is turned off. In the case of intermittent faults, a long term memory is desirable. This can be produced by connecting the orange connector/load from terminal "S" of the ECM directly to the battery (or to a "hot" fuse panel terminal). This terminal must be disconnected after diagnosis is complete or it will drain the battery.

On the CCC System, a trouble code will be stored until terminal "R" of the ECM had been disconnected from the battery for 10 seconds.

Trouble Code Identification Chart

Trouble Code	Refers To:
12	No reference pulses to the ECM. This is not stored in the memory and will only flash when the fault is present (not to be confused with the Code 12 discussed earlier).
13	Oxygen sensor circuit. The engine must run for at least 5 min. before this code will set.
14	Shorted coolant circuit. The engine must run at least 2 min. before this code will set.
15	Open coolant sensor circuit. The engine must run at least 5 min. before this code will set.
21	Throttle position sensor circuit. The engine must run up to 25 sec., below 800 rpm, before this code will set.
23	Open or grounded carburetor solenoid circuit.
34	Vacuum sensor circuit. The engine must run up to 5 min., below 800 rpm, before this code will set (1981 only).
35	Idle speed control switch circuit shorted. Over ½ throttle for at least 2 sec. (1981 only).
42	EST by-pass circuit grounded (1981 Only).
44	Lean oxygen sensor
45	Rich oxygen sensor
51	Faulty calibration unit (PROM) or installation. It takes 30 sec. for this code to set.
52 & 53	Faulty ECM
54	Shorted carburetor solenoid
55	Faulty oxygen sensor or ECM

NOTE: *Not all codes will apply to every model.*

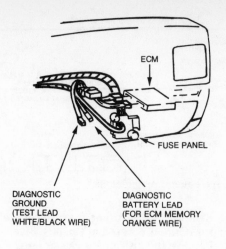

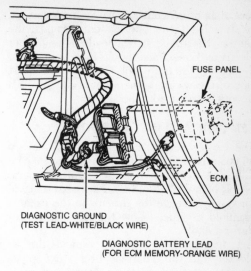

2.8L-V6

2.5L-L4

Test lead locations for the 1980 models with the C-4 system

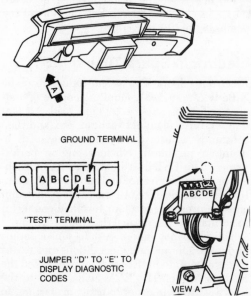

Test terminal locations on the 1981 and later models (CCC)

ACTIVATING THE TROUBLE CODE

On the C-4 System, activate the trouble code by grounding the trouble code test lead. Use the illustrations to locate the test lead under the instrument panel (usually a white and black wire with a green connector). Run a jumper wire from the lead to ground.

On the CCC System, locate the test terminal under the instrument panel. Ground only the test lead. Use a jumper wire.

NOTE: *Ground the test lead or terminal according to the instructions given in "Basic Troubleshooting", above.*

Oxygen Sensor

An oxygen sensor is used on all 1980 models built for Calif. and on all 1981 and later models. The sensor protrudes into the exhaust stream and monitors the oxygen content of the exhaust gases. The difference between the oxygen content of the exhaust gases and that of the outside air generates a voltage signal to the ECM. The ECM monitors this voltage and, depending upon the value of the signal received, issues a command to adjust for a rich or a lean condition.

No attempt should ever be made to measure the voltage output of the sensor. The cur-

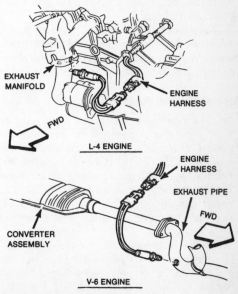

Oxygen sensor installation details

rent drain of any conventional voltmeter would be such that it would permanently damage the sensor. No jumpers, test leads or any other electrical connections should ever be made to the sensor. Use these tools ONLY on the ECM side of the wiring harness connector AFTER disconnecting it from the sensor.

REMOVAL AND INSTALLATION

The oxygen sensor must be replaced every 30,000 miles (48,000 km.). The sensor may be difficult to remove when the engine temperature is below 120°F (48°C). Excessive removal force may damage the threads in the exhaust manifold or pipe; follow the removal procedure carefully.

1. On the four cylinder, remove the air cleaner and the Thermac heat stove pipe, which is attached to the air cleaner case snorkel with a sheet metal screw. With the V6, raise the car to make access to the sensor easier.

2. Disconnect the electrical connector from the oxygen sensor.

3. Spray a commercial heat riser solvent onto the sensor threads and allow it to soak in for at least five minutes.

4. Carefully unscrew and remove the sensor.

5. To install, first coat the new sensor's threads with G.M. anti-seize compound no. 5613695 or the equivalent. This is *not* a conventional anti-seize paste. The use of a regular compound may electrically insulate the sensor, rendering it inoperative. You must coat the threads with an electrically conductive anti-seize compound.

6. Installation torque is 30 ft. lbs. (42 Nm.). Do not overtighten.

7. Reconnect the electrical connector. Be careful not to damage the electrical pigtail. Check the sensor boot for proper fit and installation. Install the air cleaner, if removed.

Mileage Counter Reset

NOTE: *The mileage counter must only be reset after the oxygen sensor has been replaced. If the sensor is not changed at regular intervals, it will cease to monitor the exhaust gas content, resulting in incorrect interpretation of its signal by the ECM. The result will be an overly rich fuel mixture, causing stumbling, stalling, and poor fuel economy.*

At 30,000 mile intervals, the word "Sensor" will appear in the speedometer face, indicating the need for oxygen sensor replacement. After the sensor has been replaced, the mileage counter may be reset as follows:

Mileage counter reset details

1. Remove the instrument cluster bezel. This procedure is covered in Chapter Five.

2. Remove the instrument cluster lens.

3. Using an awl, punch, or other pointed tool, apply a light downward force on the detent on the outer rim of the reminder flag, until it "clicks" into place.

4. Install the lens and bezel.

Do *not* reset the reminder flag until the sensor has been replaced. See the note at the beginning of this procedure.

Electronic Spark Timing (EST)

Electronic Spark Timing, introduced on the X-Body cars in 1981, monitors engine operating conditions such as engine load, coolant temperature, manifold vacuum, etc. and then constantly adjusts the spark timing so as to maintain maximum efficient engine performance. The EST distributor uses no mechanical or vacuum advance and can be easily identified by the absence of a vacuum advance unit and the presence of a four terminal connector in addition to the normal distributor wiring.

The EST may ignore certain sensor inputs under certain operating conditions and revert to a programmed HEI spark control called the By-Pass Mode. The ECM will switch to the By-Pass Mode in order to assist in starting, in the event of most EST operational problems, the distributor will almost always switch to the By-Pass Mode with its programmed spark advance. This allows the car to be driven in a near normal manner until the problem can be solved.

FUEL SYSTEM

Mechanical Fuel Pump

The fuel pump on the 1980–81 4-151 and on the V6 is the single action AC diaphragm type.

The pump is actuated by an eccentric located on the engine camshaft. On the V6 a pushrod between the camshaft eccentric and the fuel pump actuates the pump rocker arm.

TESTING THE FUEL PUMP

To determine if the pump is in good condition, tests for both volume and pressure should be performed. The tests are made with the pump installed, and the engine at normal operating temperature and idle speed. Never replace a fuel pump without first performing these simple tests.

Be sure that the fuel filter has been changed at the specified interval. If in doubt, install a new filter first.

Pressure Test

1. Disconnect the fuel line at the carburetor and connect a fuel pump pressure gauge. Fill the carburetor float bowl with gasoline.

2. Start the engine and check the pressure with the engine at idle. If the pump has a vapor return hose, squeeze it off so that an accurate reading can be obtained. Pressure for the four cylinder engine should be 6.5–8.0 psi; for the V6, it should measure 6.0–7.5 psi.

3. If the pressure is incorrect, replace the pump. If it is ok, go on to the volume test.

Volume Test

4. Disconnect the pressure gauge. Run the fuel line into a graduated container.

5. Run the engine at idle until one pint of gasoline has been pumped. One pint should be delivered in 30 seconds or less. There is normally enough fuel in the carburetor float bowl to perform this test, but refill it if necessary.

6. If the delivery rate is below the minimum, check the lines for restrictions or leaks, then replace the pump.

REMOVAL AND INSTALLATION

All Models

The fuel pump is located at the center rear of the four cylinder engine, and at the right front of the V6.

1. Disconnect the negative cable at the battery. Raise and support the car.

2. On X-Bodies with the V6 engine, remove the pump shields and the oil filter.

3. Disconnect the inlet hose from the pump. Disconnect the vapor return hose, if equipped.

4. Loosen the fuel line at the carburetor, then disconnect the outlet pipe from the pump.

5. Remove the two mounting bolts and remove the pump from the engine.

6. To install, place a new gasket on the pump and install the pump on the engine.

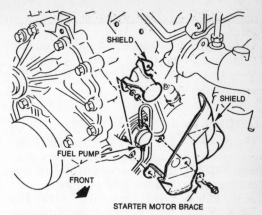

V6 fuel pump installation; four cylinder similar

Tighten the two mounting bolts alternately and evenly.

7. Install the pump outlet pipe. This is easier if the pipe is disconnected from the carburetor. Tighten the fitting while backing up the pump nut with another wrench. Install the pipe at the carburetor.

8. Install the inlet and vapor hoses. Install the shields and oil filter on the V6 engine. Lower the car, connect the negative battery cable, start the engine, and check for leaks.

Electric Fuel Pump

1982 and later 4-cylinder engines with the TBI (Throttle Body Injection) system use an electric fuel pump located in the fuel tank. The pump is activated by signals from the ECM (Electronic Control Module) through a fuel pump relay.

REMOVAL AND INSTALLATION

NOTE: *Before opening any part of the fuel system, the pressure must be relieved. Follow the procedure below to relieve the pressure:*

1. Remove the fuel pump fuse from the fuse panel.

2. Start the engine and let it run until all fuel in the line is used.

3. Crank the starter an additional three seconds to relieve any residual pressure.

4. With the ignition OFF, replace the fuse.

5. Drain the fuel tank.

6. Disconnect wiring from the tank.

7. Remove the ground wire retaining screw from under the body.

8. Disconnect all hoses from the tank.

9. Support the tank on a jack and remove the retaining strap nuts.

10. Lower the tank and remove it.

11. Remove the fuel gauge/pump retaining

ring using a spanner wrench such as tool J-24187.

12. Remove the gauge unit and the pump.

13. Installation is the reverse of removal. Always replace the O-ring under the gauge/pump retaining ring.

Carburetors

The Rochester 2SE and E2SE Varajet II carburetors are two barrel, two stage down-draft units. Most carburetor components are aluminum, although a zinc choke housing is used on the four cylinder engine installations. The E2SE is used both in conventional installations and in the Computer Controlled Catalytic Converter System. In that installation, the E2SE is equipped with an electrically operated mixture control solenoid, controlled by the Electronic Control Module. In 1981 and later, the 2SE carburetor is no longer used. The E2SE equipped with the electronically operated mixture control solenoid is used exclusively in conjunction with the Computer Command Control System.

REMOVAL AND INSTALLATION

1. Remove the air cleaner and gasket.

2. Disconnect the fuel line. Disconnect and label the vapor hoses and electrical connectors from the carburetor.

3. Disconnect the accelerator linkage.

4. Remove the mounting bolts and remove the carburetor and gasket.

5. Before installing the carburetor, fill the float bowl with gasoline to reduce battery strain and the possibility of backfiring when the engine is started.

6. Check the mating surfaces on the carburetor and intake manifold for cleanliness. Install a new gasket.

7. Place the carburetor on the gasket and loosely install the attaching bolts.

8. Install the vacuum lines and loosely install the fuel line.

9. Tighten the carburetor mounting nuts evenly to 145 in. lbs. (16 Nm.).

10. Tighten the fuel line. Connect the accelerator linkage and electrical connectors.

11. Adjust the idle speed and install the air cleaner.

FLOAT ADJUSTMENT

1. Remove the air horn from the throttle body.

2. Use your fingers to hold the retainer in place, and to push the float down into light contact with the needle.

3. Measure the distance from the toe of the float (furthest from the hinge) to the top of the carburetor (gasket removed).

4. To adjust, remove the float and gently bend the arm to specification. After adjustment, check the float alignment in the chamber.

PUMP ADJUSTMENT

NOTE: *1981 and Later E2SE carburetors have a non-adjustable pump lever. Therefore no adjustments are necessary or possible.*

1. With the throttle closed and the fast idle screw off the steps of the fast idle cam, measure the distance from the air horn casting to the top of the pump stem.

2. To adjust, remove the retaining screw and washer and remove the pump lever. Bend the end of the lever to correct the stem height. Do not twist the lever or bend it sideways.

3. Install the lever, washer and screw and check the adjustment. When correct, open and close the throttle a few times to check the linkage movement and alignment.

FAST IDLE ADJUSTMENT

1. Set the ignition timing and curb idle speed, and disconnect and plug hoses as directed on the emission control decal.

2. Place the fast idle screw on the highest step of the cam.

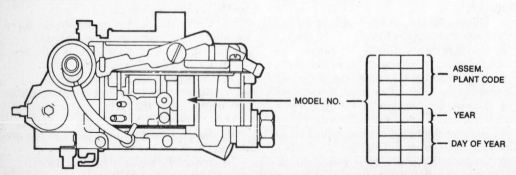

The carburetor identification number is stamped on the float bowl

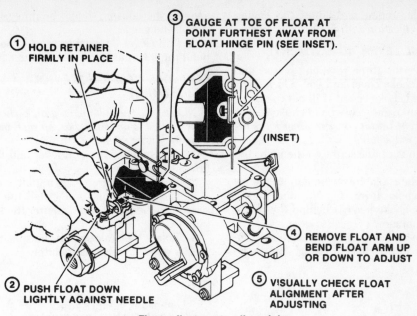

③ GAUGE AT TOE OF FLOAT AT POINT FURTHEST AWAY FROM FLOAT HINGE PIN (SEE INSET).

① HOLD RETAINER FIRMLY IN PLACE

(INSET)

④ REMOVE FLOAT AND BEND FLOAT ARM UP OR DOWN TO ADJUST

② PUSH FLOAT DOWN LIGHTLY AGAINST NEEDLE

⑤ VISUALLY CHECK FLOAT ALIGNMENT AFTER ADJUSTING

Float adjustment—all models

NOTE: ON MODELS USING A CLIP TO RETAIN PUMP ROD IN PUMP LEVER, NO PUMP ADJUSTMENT IS REQUIRED. ON MODELS USING THE "CLIPLESS" PUMP ROD, THE PUMP ADJUSTMENT SHOULD NOT BE CHANGED FROM ORIGINAL FACTORY SETTING UNLESS GAUGING SHOWS OUT OF SPECIFICATION. THE PUMP LEVER IS MADE FROM HEAVY DUTY, HARDENED STEEL MAKING BENDING DIFFICULT. DO NOT REMOVE PUMP LEVER FOR BENDING UNLESS ABSOLUTELY NECESSARY.

② GAUGE FROM AIR HORN CASTING SURFACE TO TOP OF PUMP STEM. DIMENSION SHOULD BE AS SPECIFIED.

① THROTTLE VALVES COMPLETELY CLOSED. MAKE SURE FAST IDLE SCREW IS OFF STEPS OF FAST IDLE CAM.

③ IF NECESSARY TO ADJUST, REMOVE PUMP LEVER RETAINING SCREW AND WASHER AND REMOVE PUMP LEVER BY ROTATING LEVER TO REMOVE FROM PUMP ROD. PLACE LEVER IN A VISE, PROTECTING LEVER FROM DAMAGE, AND BEND END OF LEVER (NEAREST NECKED DOWN SECTION).

⑤ OPEN AND CLOSE THROTTLE VALVES CHECKING LINKAGE FOR FREEDOM OF MOVEMENT AND OBSERVING PUMP LEVER ALIGNMENT.

④ REINSTALL PUMP LEVER, WASHER AND RETAINING SCREW. RECHECK PUMP ADJUSTMENT ① AND ②. TIGHTEN RETAINING SCREW SECURELY AFTER THE PUMP ADJUSTMENT IS CORRECT.

NOTE: DO NOT BEND LEVER IN A SIDEWAYS OR TWISTING MOTION.

1980 pump adjustment—all models

3. Start the engine and adjust the engine speed to specification with the fast idle screw.

CHOKE COIL LEVER ADJUSTMENT

1. Remove the three retaining screws and remove the choke cover and coil. On models with a riveted choke cover, drill out the three rivets and remove the cover and choke coil.

NOTE: *A choke stat cover retainer kit is required for reassembly.*

2. Place the fast idle screw on the high step of the cam.

3. Close the choke by pushing in on the intermediate choke lever. On V6 models, the intermediate choke lever is behind the choke vacuum diaphragm.

4. Insert a drill or gauge of the specified size into the hole in the choke housing. The choke lever in the housing should be up against the side of the gauge.

5. If the lever does not just touch the gauge, bend the intermediate choke rod to adjust.

FAST IDLE CAM (CHOKE ROD) ADJUSTMENT

NOTE: *A special angle gauge should be used. If it is not available, an inch measurement can be made.*

1. Adjust the choke coil lever and fast idle first.

2. Rotate the degree scale until it is zeroed.

3. Close the choke and install the degree scale onto the choke plate. Center the leveling bubble.

4. Rotate the scale so that the specified degree is opposite the scale pointer.

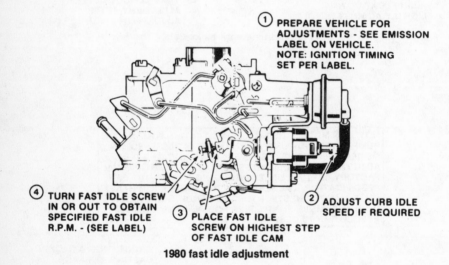

① PREPARE VEHICLE FOR ADJUSTMENTS - SEE EMISSION LABEL ON VEHICLE. NOTE: IGNITION TIMING SET PER LABEL.

④ TURN FAST IDLE SCREW IN OR OUT TO OBTAIN SPECIFIED FAST IDLE R.P.M. - (SEE LABEL)

③ PLACE FAST IDLE SCREW ON HIGHEST STEP OF FAST IDLE CAM

② ADJUST CURB IDLE SPEED IF REQUIRED

1980 fast idle adjustment

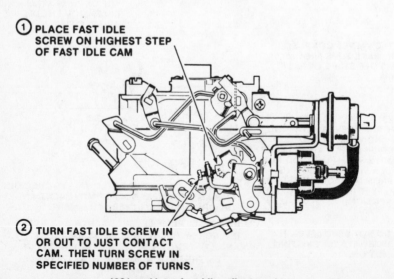

① PLACE FAST IDLE SCREW ON HIGHEST STEP OF FAST IDLE CAM

② TURN FAST IDLE SCREW IN OR OUT TO JUST CONTACT CAM. THEN TURN SCREW IN SPECIFIED NUMBER OF TURNS.

1981 and later fast idle adjustment

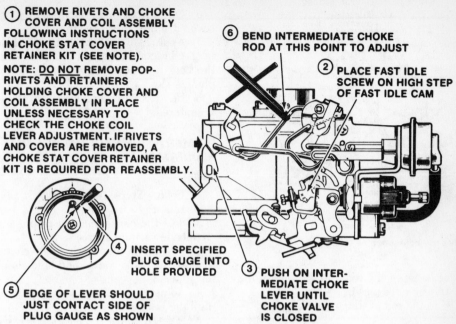

① REMOVE RIVETS AND CHOKE COVER AND COIL ASSEMBLY FOLLOWING INSTRUCTIONS IN CHOKE STAT COVER RETAINER KIT (SEE NOTE).
NOTE: <u>DO NOT</u> REMOVE POP-RIVETS AND RETAINERS HOLDING CHOKE COVER AND COIL ASSEMBLY IN PLACE UNLESS NECESSARY TO CHECK THE CHOKE COIL LEVER ADJUSTMENT. IF RIVETS AND COVER ARE REMOVED, A CHOKE STAT COVER RETAINER KIT IS REQUIRED FOR REASSEMBLY.

⑥ BEND INTERMEDIATE CHOKE ROD AT THIS POINT TO ADJUST

② PLACE FAST IDLE SCREW ON HIGH STEP OF FAST IDLE CAM

④ INSERT SPECIFIED PLUG GAUGE INTO HOLE PROVIDED

③ PUSH ON INTERMEDIATE CHOKE LEVER UNTIL CHOKE VALVE IS CLOSED

⑤ EDGE OF LEVER SHOULD JUST CONTACT SIDE OF PLUG GAUGE AS SHOWN

Four cylinder choke coil lever adjustment

5. Place the fast idle screw on the second step of the cam (against the high step). Close the choke by pushing in the intermediate lever.

6. Push on the vacuum break lever in the direction of opening choke until the lever is against the rear tang on the choke lever.

7. Bend the fast idle cam rod at the U to adjust the angle to specifications.

AIR VALVE ROD ADJUSTMENT

1980

1. Seat the vacuum diaphragm with an outside vacuum source. Tape over the purge bleed hole if present.

2. Close the air valve.

3. Insert the specified gauge between the rod and the end of the slot in the plunger on

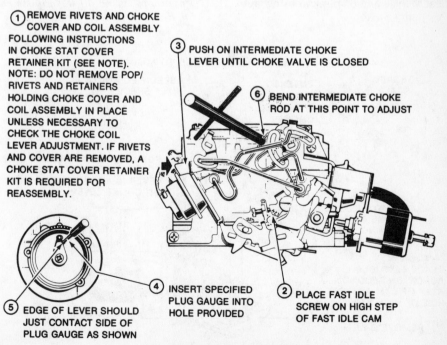

① REMOVE RIVETS AND CHOKE COVER AND COIL ASSEMBLY FOLLOWING INSTRUCTIONS IN CHOKE STAT COVER RETAINER KIT (SEE NOTE).
NOTE: DO NOT REMOVE POP/RIVETS AND RETAINERS HOLDING CHOKE COVER AND COIL ASSEMBLY IN PLACE UNLESS NECESSARY TO CHECK THE CHOKE COIL LEVER ADJUSTMENT. IF RIVETS AND COVER ARE REMOVED, A CHOKE STAT COVER RETAINER KIT IS REQUIRED FOR REASSEMBLY.

③ PUSH ON INTERMEDIATE CHOKE LEVER UNTIL CHOKE VALVE IS CLOSED

⑥ BEND INTERMEDIATE CHOKE ROD AT THIS POINT TO ADJUST

④ INSERT SPECIFIED PLUG GAUGE INTO HOLE PROVIDED

② PLACE FAST IDLE SCREW ON HIGH STEP OF FAST IDLE CAM

⑤ EDGE OF LEVER SHOULD JUST CONTACT SIDE OF PLUG GAUGE AS SHOWN

V6 choke coil lever adjustment

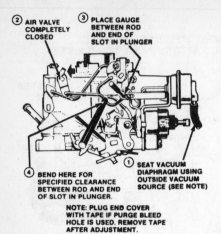

Air valve rod adjustment—1980

fours, or between the rod and the end of the slot in the air valve on V6s.

4. Bend the rod to adjust the clearance.

1981 and Later

NOTE: *A special angle gauge should be used. If it is not available, an inch measurement can be made.*

1. Align the zero degree mark with the pointer on an angle gauge.

2. Close the air valve and place a magnet on top of it.

3. Rotate the bubble until it is centered.

4. Rotate the degree scale until the specified degree mark is aligned with the pointer.

5. Seat the vacuum diaphragm using an external vacuum source.

6. On four cylinder models plug the end cover. Unplug after adjustment.

7. Apply light pressure to the air valve shaft in the direction to open the air valve until all the slack is removed between the air link and plunger slot.

8. Bend the air valve link until the bubble is centered.

PRIMARY SIDE VACUUM BREAK ADJUSTMENT

1980

1. Follow Steps 1–4 of the Fast Idle Cam Adjustment.

2. Seat the choke vacuum diaphragm with an outside vacuum source.

3. Push in on the intermediate choke lever to close the choke valve, and hold closed during adjustment.

4. Adjust by bending the vacuum break rod until the bubble is centered.

NOTE: *To adjust the vacuum break on the 1981 engines, use a ⅛ in. Hex wrench and turn the screw in the rear cover until the bubble is centered.*

1981 and Later

NOTE: *A special angle gauge should be used. If it is not available, an inch measurement can be made.*

NOTE: *Prior to adjustment, remove the vacuum break from the carburetor. Place the bracket in a vise and using the proper safety precautions, grind off the adjustment screw cap then reinstall the vacuum break.*

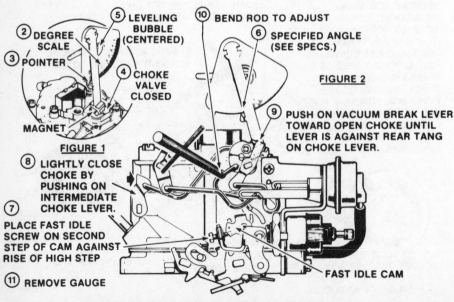

Four cylinder fast idle cam (choke rod) adjustment

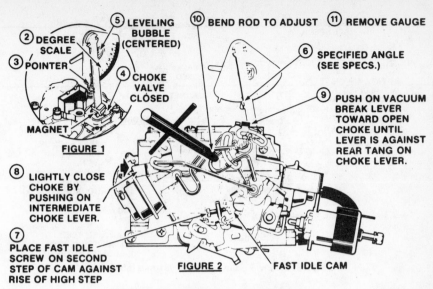

V6 fast idle cam (choke rod) adjustment

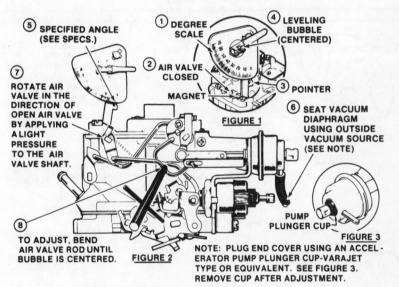

Four cylinder air valve rod adjustment—1981 and later

1. Rotate the degree scale on the measuring gauge until the zero is opposite the pointer.

2. Seat the choke vacuum diaphragm by applying an external vacuum source of over 5″ vacuum to the vacuum break.

NOTE: *If the air valve rod is restricting the vacuum diaphragm from seating it may be necessary to bend the air valve rod slightly to gain clearance. Make an air valve rod adjustment after the vacuum break adjustment.*

3. Read the angle gauge while lightly pushing on the intermediate choke lever so that the choke valve is toward the close position.

4. Use a ⅛″ hex wrench and turn the screw in the rear cover until the bubble is centered. Apply a silicone sealant over the screw head to seal the setting.

ELECTRIC CHOKE SETTING

This procedure is only for those carburetors with choke covers retained by screws. Riveted choke covers are preset and nonadjustable.

1. Loosen the three retaining screws.

2. Place the fast idle screw on the high step of the cam.

3. Rotate the choke cover to align the cover mark with the specified housing mark.

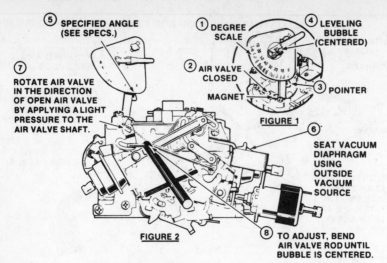

V6 air valve rod adjustment—1981 and later

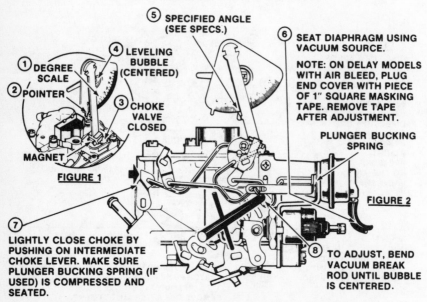

1980 four cylinder primary side vacuum break adjustment

SECONDARY VACUUM BREAK ADJUSTMENT

1980

This procedure is for V6 installations only.

1. Follow Steps 1–4 of the Fast Idle Cam Adjustment.

2. Seat the choke vacuum diaphragm with an outside vacuum source.

3. Push in on the intermediate choke lever to close the choke valve, and hold closed during adjustment. Make sure the plunger spring is compressed and seated, if present.

4. Bend the vacuum break rod at the U next to the diaphragm until the bubble is centered.

1981 and Later

NOTE: *A special angle gauge should be used. If it is not available, an inch measurement can be made.*

NOTE: *Prior to adjustment, remove the vacuum break from the carburetor. Place the bracket in the vise and using the proper safety precautions, grind off the adjustment screw cap then reinstall the vacuum break.*

NOTE: *Plug the end cover using an accelerator pump plunger cup or equivalent. Remove the cup after the adjustment.*

1. Rotate the degree scale on the measuring gauge until the zero is opposite the pointer.

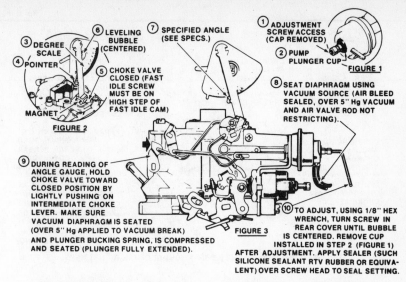

1981 and later four cylinder primary side vacuum break adjustment

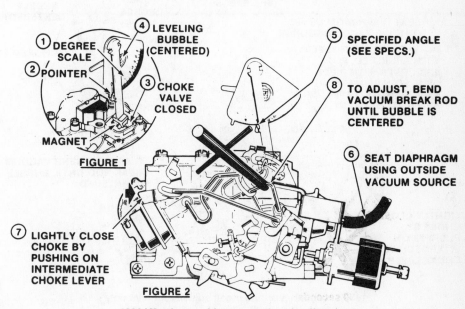

1980 V6 primary side vacuum break adjustment

2. Seat the choke vacuum diaphragm by applying an external vacuum source of over 5″ vacuum to the vacuum break.

NOTE: *If the air valve rod is restricting the vacuum diaphragm from seating it may be necessary to bend the air valve rod slightly to gain clearance. Make an air valve rod adjustment after the vacuum break adjustment.*

3. Read the angle gauge while lightly pushing on the intermediate choke lever so that the choke valve is toward the close position.

4. Use a ⅛″ hex wrench and turn the screw in the rear cover until the bubble is centered.

Apply a silicone sealant over the screw head to seal the setting.

CHOKE UNLOADER ADJUSTMENT

1. Follow Steps 1–4 of the Fast Idle Cam Adjustment.

2. Install the choke cover and coil, if removed, aligning the marks on the housing and cover as specified.

3. Hold the primary throttle wide open.

4. If the engine is warm, close the choke valve by pushing in on the intermediate choke lever.

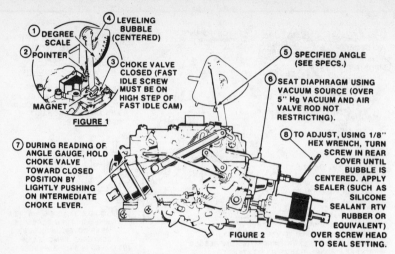

1981 and later V6 primary side vacuum break adjustment

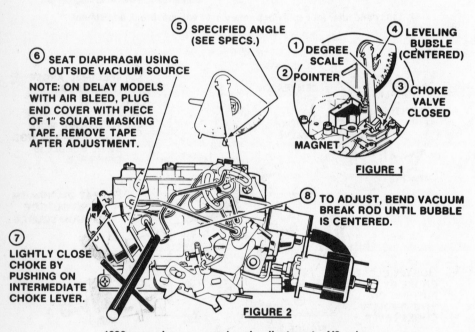

1980 secondary vacuum break adjustment—V6 only

5. Bend the unloader tang until the bubble is centered.

SECONDARY LOCKOUT ADJUSTMENT

1. Pull the choke wide open by pushing out on the intermediate choke lever.

2. Open the throttle until the end of the secondary actuating lever is opposite the toe of the lockout lever.

3. Gauge clearance between the lockout lever and secondary lever should be as specified.

4. To adjust, bend the lockout lever where it contacts the fast idle cam.

OVERHAUL

Efficient carburetion depends greatly on careful cleaning and inspection during overhaul, since dirt, gum, water, or varnish in or on the carburetor parts are often responsible for poor performance.

Overhaul your carburetor in a clean, dust-free area. Carefully disassemble the carburetor, referring often to the exploded view supplied in the rebuilding kit. Keep all similar and look-alike parts segregated during disassembly and cleaning to avoid accidental interchange during assembly. Make a note of all jet sizes.

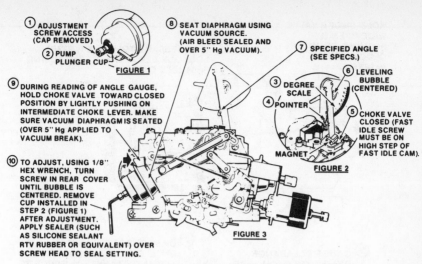

① ADJUSTMENT SCREW ACCESS (CAP REMOVED)

② PUMP PLUNGER CUP

FIGURE 1

⑨ DURING READING OF ANGLE GAUGE, HOLD CHOKE VALVE TOWARD CLOSED POSITION BY LIGHTLY PUSHING ON INTERMEDIATE CHOKE LEVER. MAKE SURE VACUUM DIAPHRAGM IS SEATED (OVER 5" Hg APPLIED TO VACUUM BREAK).

⑩ TO ADJUST, USING 1/8" HEX WRENCH, TURN SCREW IN REAR COVER UNTIL BUBBLE IS CENTERED. REMOVE CUP INSTALLED IN STEP 2 (FIGURE 1) AFTER ADJUSTMENT. APPLY SEALER (SUCH AS SILICONE SEALANT RTV RUBBER OR EQUIVALENT) OVER SCREW HEAD TO SEAL SETTING.

⑧ SEAT DIAPHRAGM USING VACUUM SOURCE. (AIR BLEED SEALED AND OVER 5" Hg VACUUM).

⑦ SPECIFIED ANGLE (SEE SPECS.)

⑥ LEVELING BUBBLE (CENTERED)

③ DEGREE SCALE

④ POINTER

⑤ CHOKE VALVE CLOSED (FAST IDLE SCREW MUST BE ON HIGH STEP OF FAST IDLE CAM).

MAGNET

FIGURE 2

FIGURE 3

1981 and later secondary vacuum break adjustment—V6 only

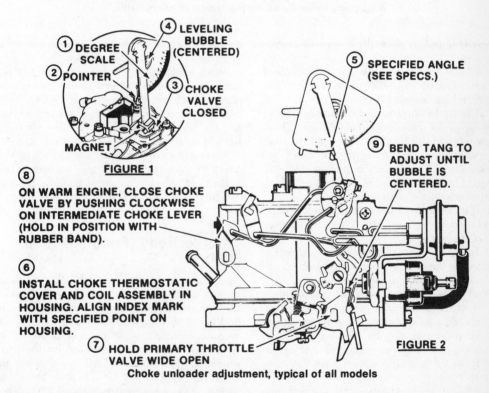

① DEGREE SCALE

② POINTER

④ LEVELING BUBBLE (CENTERED)

③ CHOKE VALVE CLOSED

MAGNET

FIGURE 1

⑧ ON WARM ENGINE, CLOSE CHOKE VALVE BY PUSHING CLOCKWISE ON INTERMEDIATE CHOKE LEVER (HOLD IN POSITION WITH RUBBER BAND).

⑥ INSTALL CHOKE THERMOSTATIC COVER AND COIL ASSEMBLY IN HOUSING. ALIGN INDEX MARK WITH SPECIFIED POINT ON HOUSING.

⑦ HOLD PRIMARY THROTTLE VALVE WIDE OPEN

⑤ SPECIFIED ANGLE (SEE SPECS.)

⑨ BEND TANG TO ADJUST UNTIL BUBBLE IS CENTERED.

FIGURE 2

Choke unloader adjustment, typical of all models

When the carburetor is disassembled, wash all parts (except diaphragms, electric choke units, pump plunger, and any other plastic, leather, fiber, or rubber parts) in clean carburetor solvent. Do not leave parts in the solvent any longer than is necessary to sufficiently loosen the deposits. Excessive cleaning may remove the special finish from the float bowl and choke valve bodies, leaving these parts unfit for service. Rince all parts in clean solvent and blow them dry with compressed air or allow them to air dry. Wipe clean all cork, plastic, leather, and fiber parts with a clean, lint-free cloth.

Blow out all passages and jets with compressed air and be sure that there are no restrictions or blockages. Never use wire or similar tools to clean jets, fuel passages, or air bleeds. Clean all jets and valves separately to avoid accidental interchange.

Check all parts for wear or damage. If wear or damage is found, replace the defective parts. Especially check the following:

1. Check the float needle and seat for wear.

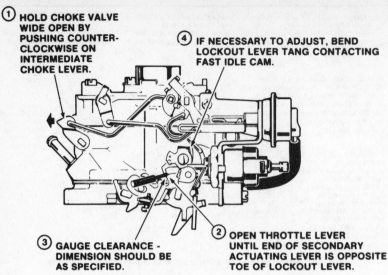

① HOLD CHOKE VALVE WIDE OPEN BY PUSHING COUNTER-CLOCKWISE ON INTERMEDIATE CHOKE LEVER.

④ IF NECESSARY TO ADJUST, BEND LOCKOUT LEVER TANG CONTACTING FAST IDLE CAM.

③ GAUGE CLEARANCE - DIMENSION SHOULD BE AS SPECIFIED.

② OPEN THROTTLE LEVER UNTIL END OF SECONDARY ACTUATING LEVER IS OPPOSITE TOE OF LOCKOUT LEVER.

Secondary lockout adjustment, typical of all models

If wear is found, replace the complete assembly.

2. Check the float hinge pin for wear and the float(s) for dents or distortion. Replace the float if fuel has leaked into it.

3. Check the throttle and choke shaft bores for wear or an out-of-round condition. Damage or wear to the throttle arm, shaft, or shaft bore will often require replacement of the throttle body. These parts require a close tolerance of fit; wear may allow air leakage, which could affect starting and idling.

NOTE: *Throttle shafts and bushings are not included in overhaul kits. They can be purchased separately.*

4. Inspect the idle mixture adjusting needles for burrs or grooves. Any such condition requires replacement of the needle, since you will not be able to obtain a satisfactory idle.

5. Test the accelerator pump check valves. They should pass air one way but not the other. Test for proper seating by blowing and sucking on the valve. Replace the valve if necessary. If the valve is satisfactory, wash the valve again to remove breath moisture.

6. Check the bowl cover for warped surfaces with a straightedge.

7. Closely inspect the valves and seats for wear and damage, replacing as necessary.

8. After the carburetor is assembled, check the choke valve for freedom of operation.

Carburetor overhaul kits are recommended for each overhaul. These kits contain all gaskets and new parts to replace those which deteriorate most rapidly. Failure to replace all parts supplied with the kit (especially gaskets) can result in poor performance later.

Some carburetor manufacturers supply overhaul kits of three basic types: minor repair; major repair; and gasket kits.

After cleaning and checking all components, reassemble the carburetor, using new parts and referring to the exploded view. When reassembling, make sure that all screws and jets are tight in their seats, but do not overtighten as the tips will be distorted. Tighten all screws gradually, in rotation. Do not tighten needle valves into their seats; uneven jetting will result. Always use new gaskets. Be sure to adjust the float level when reassembling.

Throttle Body (Fuel) Injection (TBI)

The TBI system, used on 1982–85 four cylinders is a completely electronic system which meters and delivers precise amounts of fuel and air to the engine, according to the exact engine operating requirements at any given time. The system is controlled by the same on-board computer (ECM) used with the emissions system (CCC). Through the monitoring of various sensors, the ECM determines the optimum air/fuel ratio and signals the TBI unit to adjust the ratio accordingly. TBI is designed to offer the owner trouble-free starting, immediate throttle response, and maximum fuel efficiency; regardless of weather conditions, engine rpm, temperature or load.

Trouble diagnosis of the injection system is nearly impossible for the novice mechanic to perform, because of the interaction between the injection, emissions, and ignition systems; all of which are controlled by the ECM. Should you encounter any type of engine perfor-

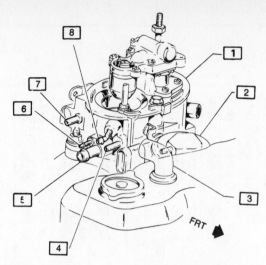

1 T.B.I. UNIT	**5** CRANKCASE VENT PORT
2 E.G.R. VALVE	**6** E.G.R. VALVE PORT
3 CRANKCASE VENT GROMMET	**7** M.A.P. SENSOR PORT
4 AIR CLEANER PORT	**8** CANISTER PURGE PORT

Vacuum port identification

mance problem, have a complete CCC system test performed by a qualified, professional technician.

REMOVAL AND INSTALLATION

NOTE: *Before attempting TBI removal, perform step 1 of the electric Fuel Pump Removal and Installation procedure to relieve fuel pressure.*

1. Remove the air cleaner.
2. Disconnect the harness electrical connectors to the idle air control, throttle position sensor and injector.
3. Disconnect the throttle linkage, return spring, and cruise control linkage, if so equipped.
4. Disconnect the vacuum hose from the throttle body. Note the hose routing for installation.
5. Disconnnct the fuel supply and return lines at the throttle body. (See note above.)
6. Remove the three throttle body retaining bolts and remove the throttle body.
7. Installation is the reverse of removal. Torque the throttle body retaining bolts to 120–168 in. lbs.

Fuel Tank

REMOVAL AND INSTALLATION

1. Disconnect the negative cable at the battery. Raise and support the car.
2. Drain the tank. There is no drain plug; remaining fuel in the tank must be siphoned through the fuel feed line (the line to the fuel pump), because of the restrictor in the filler neck.
3. Disconnect the hose and the vapor return hose from the level sending unit fittings.
4. Remove the ground wire screw.
5. Unplug the level sending unit electrical connector.
6. Disconnect the vent hose.
7. Unbolt the support straps, and lower and remove the tank. Installation is the reverse.

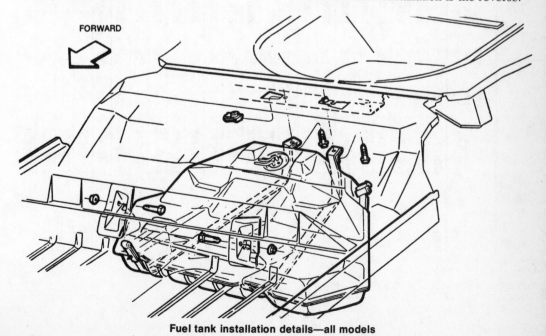

Fuel tank installation details—all models

Carburetor Specifications
Citation, Omega, Phoenix, Skylark

Year	Carburetor Identification	Float Level (in.)	Pump Rod (in.)	Fast Idle (rpm)	Choke Coil Lever (in.)	Fast Idle Cam (deg/in.)	Air Valve Rod (in.)	Primary Vacuum Break (deg/in.)	Choke Setting (notches)	Secondary Vacuum Break (deg/in.)	Choke Unloader (deg/in.)	Secondary Lockout (in.)
1980	17059614	3/16	1/2	2600	.085	18/.096	.025	17/.090	Fixed	—	36/.227	.120
	17059615	3/16	5/32	2600	.085	18/.096	.025	19/.103	Fixed	—	36/.227	.120
	17059616	3/16	1/2	2600	.085	18/.096	.025	17/.090	Fixed	—	36/.227	.120
	17059617	3/16	5/32	2600	.085	18/.096	.025	19/.103	Fixed	—	36/.227	.120
	17059650	3/16	3/32	2000	.085	27/.157	.025	30/.179	Fixed	38/.243	30/.179	.120
	17059651	3/16	3/32	1900	.085	27/.157	.025	22/.123	Fixed	23/.120	30/.179	.120
	17059652	3/16	3/32	2000	.085	27/.157	.025	30/.179	Fixed	38/.243	30/.179	.120
	17059653	3/16	3/32	1900	.085	27/.157	.025	22/.123	Fixed	23/.120	30/.179	.120
	17059714	11/16	5/32	2600	.085	18/.096	.025	23/.129	Fixed	—	32/.195	.120
	17059715	11/16	3/32	2200	.085	18/.096	.025	25/.142	Fixed	—	32/.195	.120
	17059716	11/16	5/32	2600	.085	18/.096	.025	23/.129	Fixed	—	32/.195	.120
	17059717	11/16	3/32	2200	.085	18/.096	.025	25/.142	Fixed	—	32/.195	.120
	17059760	1/8	5/64	2000	.085	17.5/.093	.025	20/.110	Fixed	33/.203	35/.220	.120
	17059762	1/8	5/64	2000	.085	17.5/.093	.025	20/.110	Fixed	33/.203	35/.220	.120
	17059763	1/8	5/64	2000	.085	17.5/.093	.025	20/.110	Fixed	33/.203	35/.220	.120
	17059618	3/16	1/2	2600	.085	18/.096	.025	17/.090	Fixed	—	36/.227	.120
	17059619	3/16	5/32	2600	.085	18/.096	.025	19/.103	Fixed	—	36/.227	.120
	17059620	3/16	1/2	2600	.085	18/.096	.025	17/.090	Fixed	—	36/.227	.120
	17059621	3/16	5/32	2600	.085	18/.096	.025	19/.103	Fixed	—	36/.227	.120
1981 Except Canada	17081650	1/4	①	②	.085	17/.090	1 ③	25/.142	②	34/.211	35/.220	.012
	17081651	1/4	①	②	.085	17/.090	1 ③	29/.168	②	35/.220	35/.220	.012
	17081652	1/4	①	②	.085	17/.090	1 ③	25/.142	②	34/.211	35/.220	.012
	17081653	1/4	①	②	.085	17/.090	1 ③	29/.168	②	35/.220	35/.220	.012

Part No.	Year/Notes										
17081670		5/32	①	②	.085	18/.096	1③	19/.103	②	—	32/.195	.012
17081671		5/32	①	②	.085	33.5/.201	1③	21/.111	②	—	32/.195	.012
17081672		5/32	①	②	.085	18/.096	1③	19/.103	②	—	32/.195	.012
17081673		5/32	①	②	.085	33.5/.201	1③	21/.111	②	—	32/.195	.012
17081740		1/4	①	②	.085	17/.090	1③	25/.142	②	34/.211	35/.220	.012
17081742		1/4	①	②	.085	17/.090	1③	25/.142	②	34/.211	35/.220	.012
17082196	1982 Except Canada	5/16	Fixed	①	.085	18/.096	1③	21/.117	Fixed	19/.103	27/157	.025
17082316		1/4	Fixed	2600	.085	17/.090	1③	26/.149	Fixed	34/.211	35/.220	.025
17082317		1/4	Fixed	2600	.085	17/.090	1③	29/.171	Fixed	35/.220	35/.220	.025
17082320		1/4	Fixed	2800	.085	25/.142	1③	30/.179	Fixed	35/.220	33/.203	.025
17082321		1/4	Fixed	2600	.085	25/.142	1③	29/.171	Fixed	35/.220	35/.220	.025
17082640		1/4	Fixed	2600	.085	17/.090	1③	26/.149	Fixed	34/.211	35/.220	.025
17082641		1/4	Fixed	2400	.085	17/.090	1③	29/.171	Fixed	35/.220	35/.220	.025
17082642		1/4	Fixed	2800	.085	25/.142	1③	30/.179	Fixed	35/.220	33/.203	.025
17083348	1983 Except Canada	7/16	Fixed	②	.085	22/.123	1③	30/.179	Fixed	32/.195	40/.260	.025
17083349		7/16	Fixed	②	.085	22/.123	1③	30/.179	Fixed	32/.195	40/.260	.025
17083350		7/16	Fixed	②	.085	22/.123	1③	30/.179	Fixed	32/.195	40/.260	.025
17083351		7/16	Fixed	②	.085	22/.123	1③	30/.179	Fixed	32/.195	40/.260	.025
17083352		7/16	Fixed	②	.085	22/.123	1③	30/.179	Fixed	35/.220	40/.260	.025
17083353		7/16	Fixed	②	.085	22/.123	1③	30/.179	Fixed	35/.220	40/.260	.025
17083354		7/16	Fixed	②	.085	22/.123	1③	30/.179	Fixed	35/.220	40/.260	.025
17083355		7/16	Fixed	②	.085	22/.123	1③	30/.179	Fixed	35/.220	40/.260	.025
17083360		7/16	Fixed	②	.085	22/.123	1③	30/.179	Fixed	32/.220	40/.260	.025
17083361		7/16	Fixed	②	.085	22/.123	1③	28/.164	Fixed	32/.220	40/.260	.025
17083362		7/16	Fixed	②	.085	22/.123	1③	30/.179	Fixed	32/.220	40/.260	.025
17083363		7/16	Fixed	②	.085	22/.123	1③	28/.164	Fixed	32/.220	40/.260	.025
17083364		7/16	Fixed	②	.085	22/.123	1③	30/.179	Fixed	35/.220	40/.260	.025
17083365		7/16	Fixed	②	.085	22/.123	1③	30/.179	Fixed	35/.220	40/.260	.025

Carburetor Specifications (continued)
Citation, Omega, Phoenix, Skylark

Year	Carburetor Identification	Float Level (in.)	Pump Rod (in.)	Fast Idle (rpm)	Choke Coil Lever (in.)	Fast Idle Cam (deg./in.)	Air Valve Rod (in.)	Primary Vacuum Break (deg./in.)	Choke Setting (notches)	Secondary Vacuum Break (deg./in.)	Choke Unloader (deg./in.)	Secondary Lockout (in.)
1983 Except Canada	17083366	7/16	Fixed	②	.085	22/.123	1 ③	30/.179	Fixed	35/.220	40/.260	.025
	17083367	7/16	Fixed	②	.085	22/.123	1 ③	30/.179	Fixed	35/.220	40/.260	.025
1984 Except Canada	17072683	9/32	Fixed	②	.085	28°	1 ③	25 ③	②	35 ③	45 ③	④
	17074812	9/32	Fixed	②	.085	28°	1 ③	25 ③	②	35 ③	45 ③	④
	17084356	9/32	Fixed	②	.085	22°	1 ③	25 ③	②	30 ③	30 ③	④
	17084357	9/32	Fixed	②	.085	22°	1 ③	25 ③	②	30 ③	30 ③	④
	17084358	9/32	④	②	.085	22°	1 ③	25 ③	②	30 ③	30 ③	④
	17084359	9/32	④	②	.085	22°	1 ③	25 ③	②	30 ③	30 ③	④
	17084368	1/8	④	②	.085	22°	1 ③	25 ③	②	30 ③	30 ③	④
	17084370	1/8	④	②	.085	22°	1 ③	25 ③	②	30 ③	30 ③	④
	17084430	11/32	④	②	.085	15°	1 ③	26 ③	②	38 ③	42 ③	④
	17084431	11/32	④	②	.085	15°	1 ③	26 ③	②	38 ③	42 ③	④
	17084434	11/32	④	②	.085	15°	1 ③	26 ③	②	38 ③	42 ③	④
	17084435	11/32	④	②	.085	15°	1 ③	26 ③	②	38 ③	42 ③	④
	17084452	5/32	④	②	.085	28°	1 ③	25 ③	②	35 ③	45 ③	④
	17084453	5/32	④	②	.085	28°	1 ③	25 ③	②	35 ③	45 ③	④
	17084455	5/32	④	②	.085	28°	1 ③	25 ③	②	35 ③	45 ③	④
	17084456	5/32	④	②	.085	28°	1 ③	25 ③	②	35 ③	45 ③	④
	17084458	5/32	④	②	.085	28°	1 ③	25 ③	②	35 ③	45 ③	④
	17084532	5/32	④	②	.085	28°	1 ③	25 ③	②	35 ③	45 ③	④
	17084534	5/32	④	②	.085	28°	1 ③	25 ③	②	35 ③	45 ③	④
	17084535	5/32	④	②	.085	28°	1 ③	25 ③	②	35 ③	45 ③	④
	17084537	5/32	④	②	.085	28°	1 ③	25 ③	②	35 ③	45 ③	④

Part No.										
17084538	5/32	④	②	.085	28°	1③	25③	②	35③	45③	④
17084540	5/32	④	②	.085	28°	1③	25③	②	35③	45③	④
17084542	1/8	④	②	.085	28°	1③	25③	②	35③	45③	④
17084632	9/32	④	②	.085	28°	1③	25③	②	35③	45③	④
17084633	9/32	④	②	.085	28°	1③	25③	②	35③	45③	④
17084635	9/32	④	②	.085	28°	1③	25③	②	35③	45③	④
17084636	9/32	④	②	.085	28°	1③	25③	②	35③	45③	④
1985 Except Canada										
17085190	10/32	④	②	.120G	④	④	28③	②	24③	32③	④
17085192	11/32	④	②	.120G	④	④	27③	②	25③	35③	④
17085194	11/32	④	②	.120G	④	④	27③	②	25③	35③	④

CANADIAN SPECIFICATIONS

Part No.										
1981										
17059660	1/4	17/32	②	.085	24/.136	1③	30/.179	Fixed	32/.195	30/.179	④
17059662	1/4	17/32	②	.085	24/.136	1③	30/.179	Fixed	37/.195	30/.179	④
17059651	1/4	17/32	②	.085	24/.136	1③	30/.179	Fixed	32/.195	30/.179	④
17059666	1/4	17/32	②	.085	24/.136	1③	26/.149	Fixed	32/.195	30/.179	④
17059667	1/4	17/32	②	.085	24/.136	1③	26/.149	Fixed	32/.195	30/.179	④
17059622	5/32	17/32	②	.085	18/.096	1③	17/.090	Fixed	—	36/.227	④
17059623	5/32	17/32	②	.085	18/.096	1③	19/.103	Fixed	—	36/.227	④
17059624	5/32	17/32	②	.085	18/.096	1③	17/.090	Fixed	—	36/.227	④
1982										
17082440	1/4	19/32	②	.085	24/.136	1②	26/.149	Fixed	32/.195	30/.179	①
17082441	1/4	19/32	②	.085	24/.136	1②	26/.149	Fixed	32/.195	30/.179	①
17082443	1/4	19/32	②	.085	24/.136	1②	26/.149	Fixed	32/.195	30/.179	①
17082460	1/4	19/32	②	.085	18/.096	1②	21/.117	Fixed	—	36/.227	①
17082461	1/4	19/32	②	.085	18/.096	1②	21/.117	Fixed	—	36/.227	①
17082462	1/4	19/32	②	.085	18/.096	1②	21/.117	Fixed	—	36/.227	①
17082464	1/8	19/32	②	.085	18/.096	1②	21/.117	Fixed	—	36/.227	①
17082465	1/8	19/32	②	.085	18/.096	1②	21/.117	Fixed	—	36/.227	①

Carburetor Specifications (continued)
Citation, Omega, Phoenix, Skylark

Year	Carburetor Identification	Float Level (in.)	Pump Rod (in.)	Fast Idle (rpm)	Choke Coil Lever (in.)	Fast Idle Cam (deg/in.)	Air Valve Rod (in.)	Primary Vacuum Break (deg/in.)	Choke Setting (notches)	Secondary Vacuum Break (deg/in.)	Choke Unloader (deg/in.)	Secondary Lockout (in.)
	17082466	1/8	19/32	②	.085	18/.096	1 ②	21/.117	Fixed	—	36/.227	①
	17082620	7/16	19/32	②	.085	24/.136	1 ②	26/.149	Fixed	32/.195	30/.179	①
	17082621	7/16	19/32	②	.085	24/.136	1 ②	26/.149	Fixed	32/.195	30/.179	①
	17082622	7/16	19/32	②	.085	24/.136	1 ②	26/.149	Fixed	32/.195	30/.179	①
	17082623	7/16	19/32	②	.085	24/.136	1 ②	26/.149	Fixed	32/.195	30/.179	①
1983	17083311	5/16	Fixed	②	.085	24/.136	1 ③	18/.096	Fixed	20/.110	35/.220	.025
	17083401	5/16	Fixed	②	.085	24/.136	1 ③	18/.096	Fixed	20/.110	35/.220	.025
	17083440	1/4	19/32	②	.085	24/.136	1 ③	28/.164	Fixed	32/.195	40/.260	.025
	17083441	1/4	19/32	②	.085	24/.136	1 ③	28/.164	Fixed	32/.195	40/.260	.025
	17083442	1/4	19/32	②	.085	24/.136	1 ③	28/.164	Fixed	32/.195	40/.260	.025
	17083443	1/4	19/32	②	.085	24/.136	1 ③	28/.164	Fixed	32/.195	40/.260	.025
	17083444	1/4	19/32	②	.085	24/.136	1 ③	28/.164	Fixed	32/.195	40/.260	.025
	17083445	1/4	19/32	②	.085	24/.136	1 ③	28/.164	Fixed	32/.195	40/.260	.025
	17083460	1/4	19/32	②	.085	18/.096	1 ③	19/.103	Fixed	—	36/.227	.025
	17083461	1/4	19/32	②	.085	18/.096	1 ③	18/.096	Fixed	—	36/.227	.025
	17083462	1/4	19/32	②	.085	18/.096	1 ③	19/.103	Fixed	—	36/.227	.025
	17083464	1/8	19/32	②	.085	18/.096	1 ③	19/.103	Fixed	—	36/.227	.025
	17083465	1/8	19/32	②	.085	18/.096	1 ③	20/.110	Fixed	—	36/.227	.025

Part No.											
17083466	1/8	19/32	②	.085	18/.096	① ③	19/.103	Fixed	—	36/.227	.025
17083620	7/16	19/32	②	.085	24/.136	① ③	28/.164	Fixed	32/.195	40/.260	.025
17083621	7/16	19/32	②	.085	24/.136	① ③	28/.164	Fixed	32/.195	40/.260	.025
17083622	7/16	19/32	②	.085	24/.136	① ③	28/.164	Fixed	32/.195	40/.260	.025
17083623	7/16	19/32	②	.085	24/.136	① ③	28/.164	Fixed	32/.195	40/.260	.025
1984											
17084312	5/16	Fixed	②	.085	24/.136	① ③	18/.096	Fixed	20/.110	35/.220	.025
17084314	5/16	Fixed	②	.085	29/.171	① ③	16/.083	Fixed	20/.110	30/.179	.025
17084480	1/4	Fixed	②	.085	24/.136	① ③	28/.164	Fixed	32/.195	45/.304	.025
17084481	1/4	Fixed	②	.085	24/.136	① ③	28/.164	Fixed	32/.195	45/.304	.025
17084482	1/4	Fixed	②	.085	24/.136	① ③	28/.164	Fixed	32/.195	45/.304	.025
17084483	1/4	Fixed	②	.085	24/.136	① ③	28/.164	Fixed	32/.195	45/.304	.025
17084484	1/4	Fixed	②	.085	24/.136	① ③	28/.164	Fixed	32/.195	45/.304	.025
17084485	1/4	Fixed	②	.085	24/.136	① ③	28/.164	Fixed	32/.195	45/.304	.025
17084486	1/4	Fixed	②	.085	24/.136	① ③	28/.164	Fixed	32/.195	45/.304	.025
17084487	1/4	Fixed	②	.085	24/.136	① ③	28/.164	Fixed	32/.195	45/.304	.025
17084620	7/16	Fixed	②	.085	24/.136	① ③	26/.149	Fixed	32/.195	45/.304	.025
17084621	7/16	Fixed	②	.085	24/.136	① ③	26/.149	Fixed	32/.195	45/.304	.025
17084622	7/16	Fixed	②	.085	24/.136	① ③	26/.149	Fixed	32/.195	45/.304	.025
17084623	7/16	Fixed	②	.085	24/.136	① ③	26/.149	Fixed	32/.195	45/.304	.025

① —Pump lever is pre-set and non-adjustable
② —See underhood emissions sticker
③ —Measurement in degrees, not inches
④ —Not available
G—Gauge

Chassis Electrical

5

HEATER

Blower

REMOVAL AND INSTALLATION

This procedure is for all cars, with or without air conditioning.

1. Disconnect the negative cable at the battery.
2. Working inside the engine compartment, disconnect the blower motor electrical leads.
3. Remove the motor retaining screws, and remove the blower motor.
4. Reverse to install.

Heater Core

REMOVAL AND INSTALLATION

Cars Without Air Conditioning

1. Drain the cooling system.
2. Remove the heater inlet and outlet hoses

The blower is accessible through the engine compartment

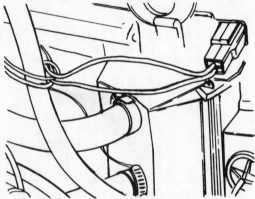

The heater inlet and outlet hoses connect to the core tubes at the firewall, below the windshield wiper motor

at the firewall, inside the engine compartment.

3. Remove the radio noise suppression strap.
4. Remove the heater core cover retaining screws. Remove the cover.
5. Remove the core. Reverse to install.

Cars With Air Conditioning

1. Drain the cooling system.
2. Remove the heater hoses from the core tubes at the firewall.
3. Remove the heater duct and heater case side cover from under the instrument panel.
4. Remove the core retaining clamps. Remove the inlet and outlet tube support clamps.
5. Remove the core. Reverse to install.

RADIO

REMOVAL AND INSTALLATION

NOTE: *Do not operate the radio with the speaker leads disconnected. Operating the radio without an electrical load will damage the output transistors.*

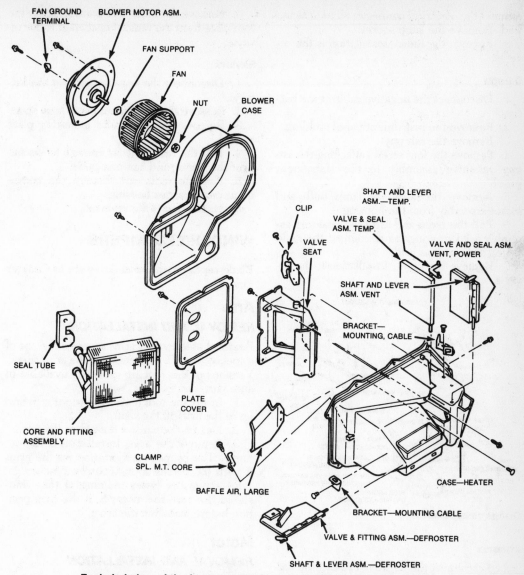

Exploded view of the heater assembly; air conditioned models similar

Citation

1. Disconnect the negative cable at the battery.

2. Remove the radio knobs (pull off), the radio shaft nuts, and the clock knob if your Citation has one.

3. Remove the instrument cluster trim bezel attaching screws and pull the bezel rearward.

4. Remove the headlamp switch and knob.

5. Disconnect the wiring and remove the bezel.

6. Remove the two screws attaching the radio bracket to the instrument panel.

7. Pull the radio rearward while, at the same time, twisting it slightly to the left, and dis-

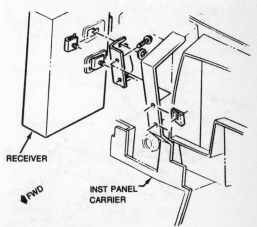

Citation radio removal

connect the electrical connectors and antenna lead. Remove the lamp socket.

8. Remove the radio. Installation is the reverse.

Omega

1. Disconnect the negative cable at the battery.

2. Remove the instrument panel molding.

3. Remove the ash tray.

4. Remove the four screws attaching the ash tray retaining assembly to the instrument panel.

5. Remove the ash tray lamp bulb and socket assembly from the housing.

6. Pull the radio and ash tray retaining assembly out far enough to disconnect the radio wiring and antenna lead.

7. Remove the radio. Installation is the reverse.

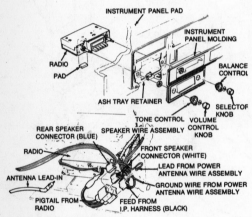

Omega radio removal

Phoenix

1. Disconnect the negative cable at the battery.

2. Remove the trim plate from the center of the instrument panel.

3. Remove the two attaching screws, and pull the radio out far enough to disconnect the wiring and antenna lead.

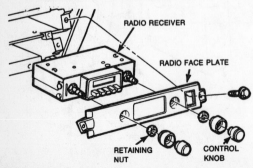

Phoenix radio removal

4. Remove the radio knobs and separate the face plate from the radio. Installation is the reverse.

Skylark

1. Disconnect the negative cable at the battery.

2. Remove the instrument panel trim plate.

3. Remove the four radio mounting plate screws.

4. Pull the radio out far enough to disconnect the wiring and antenna cable.

5. Pull the radio out through the instrument panel carrier housing.

6. Installation is the reverse.

WINDSHIELD WIPERS

Blade replacement procedures are in Chapter One.

Arm

REMOVAL AND INSTALLATION

Removal of the wiper arms requires the use of a special tool, G.M. J-8966, or the equivalent. Versions of this tool are generally available in auto parts stores.

1. Insert the tool under the wiper arm and lever the arm off the shaft.

2. Detach the washer hose from the arm.

3. Remove the arm. Installation is the reverse. The proper park position for the arms is with the blades approximately 2 inches (50 mm) above the lower molding of the windshield. Be sure the motor is in the park position before installing the arms.

Motor

REMOVAL AND INSTALLATION

1. Remove the wiper arms.

2. Remove the lower windshield reveal

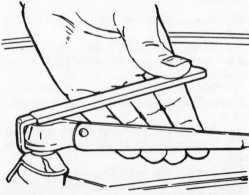

The wiper arms can be removed with the aid of this special tool

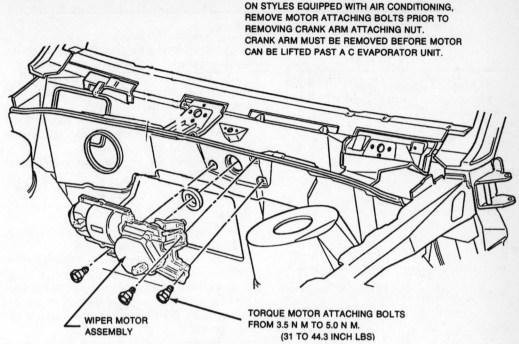

ON STYLES EQUIPPED WITH AIR CONDITIONING,
REMOVE MOTOR ATTACHING BOLTS PRIOR TO
REMOVING CRANK ARM ATTACHING NUT.
CRANK ARM MUST BE REMOVED BEFORE MOTOR
CAN BE LIFTED PAST A C EVAPORATOR UNIT.

WIPER MOTOR
ASSEMBLY

TORQUE MOTOR ATTACHING BOLTS
FROM 3.5 N M TO 5.0 N M.
(31 TO 44.3 INCH LBS)

Windshield wiper motor removal

molding, the front cowl panel and the cowl
screen. Disconnect the washer hose under the
screen.

3. Disconnect the motor electrical leads.

4. Loosen, but do not remove, the transmission drive link attaching nuts to the motor
crank arm.

5. Disconnect the drive link from the motor crank arm.

6. Remove the three motor attaching bolts.
On models with air conditioning, remove the
bolts and while supporting the motor, remove
the motor crank arm nut using lock-ring type
pliers and a closed end wrench. The motor attaching bolts must be removed first to avoid
damage to the nylon gear inside the motor.
On all models, rotate the motor up and out to
remove.

7. Reverse the procedure to install.

Linkage

REMOVAL AND INSTALLATION

1. Remove the lower windshield reveal
molding, the wiper arms, and the cowl panel.

2. Loosen but do not remove the drive link
to crank arm attaching nuts.

3. Remove the linkage to cowl panel attaching bolts.

4. Installation is the reverse. Tighten the
attaching bolts to 27–36 in. lbs. (3–4 Nm.).

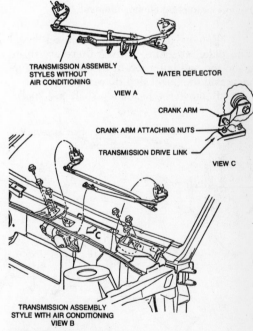

TRANSMISSION ASSEMBLY
STYLES WITHOUT
AIR CONDITIONING

WATER DEFLECTOR

VIEW A

CRANK ARM

CRANK ARM ATTACHING NUTS

TRANSMISSION DRIVE LINK

VIEW C

TRANSMISSION ASSEMBLY
STYLE WITH AIR CONDITIONING
VIEW B

Windshield wiper linkage

INSTRUMENT CLUSTER

REMOVAL AND INSTALLATION

Citation

1. Disconnect the negative battery cable.

2. Remove the radio knobs (pull off), the
shaft nuts, and the clock knob.

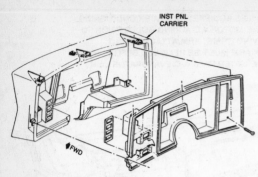

Citation trim plate removal

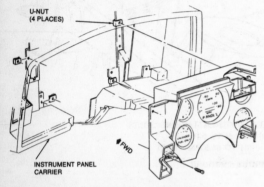

Citation instrument cluster removal

3. Remove the instrument cluster bezel (trim plate) attaching screws; there are three at the top and one each in the two lower corners. Pull the bezel slightly rearward.

4. Remove the headlamp shaft and knob.

5. Disconnect the accessory switch wiring.

6. Remove the bezel.

7. Remove the four screws holding the instrument cluster to the instrument panel.

8. Disconnect the shift indicator cable from the steering column shift bowl on models with automatic transaxle.

9. Pull the cluster towards you and disconnect the speedometer cable and instrument electrical connections.

10. Remove the instrument cluster. Installation is the reverse.

Omega

1. Remove the steering column trim cover.

2. Lower the steering column.

3. Remove the four screws holding the instrument panel trim cover to the panel.

4. Pull the trim cover rearward and disconnect the switch wiring, and the remote control mirror cable if your car has one. Remove the trim panel.

5. Remove the four screws holding the instrument cluster to the panel.

6. Disconnect the shift indicator cable from the steering column shift bowl, if your Omega has an automatic transaxle.

7. Pull the cluster towards you and disconnect the speedometer cable and electrical wiring.

8. Remove the instrument cluster. Installation is the reverse.

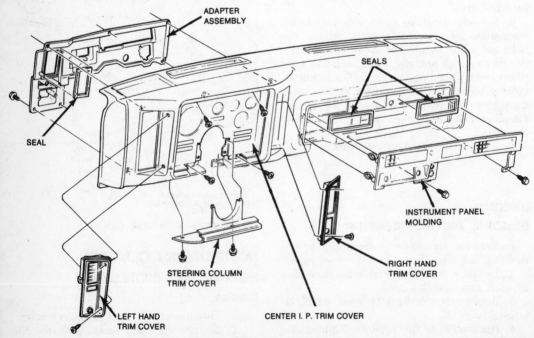

Omega trim panel removal

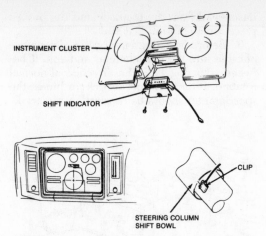

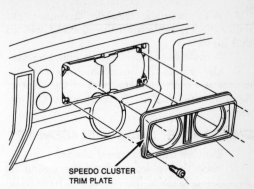

Phoenix speedometer cluster trim plate

Omega shift indicator attachment; other models similar

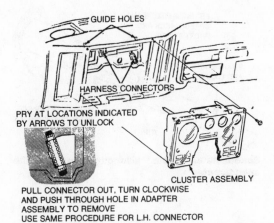

PRY AT LOCATIONS INDICATED BY ARROWS TO UNLOCK

PULL CONNECTOR OUT, TURN CLOCKWISE AND PUSH THROUGH HOLE IN ADAPTER ASSEMBLY TO REMOVE
USE SAME PROCEDURE FOR L.H. CONNECTOR

Omega instrument cluster removal

Phoenix

1. Disconnect the negative battery cable.
2. Remove the speedometer cluster trim plate. There is one screw in each corner.
3. Remove the screws attaching the steering column trim cover to the instrument panel and remove the trim cover.
4. Remove the four cluster attaching screws.
5. With automatic transaxle, disconnect the shift indicator cable, marking the cable location on the steering column shift bowl prior to disconnecting.
6. Disconnect the speedometer cable and pull the cluster towards you. Disconnect the electrical wiring from the back of the cluster and remove the cluster. Installation is the reverse.

Skylark

1. Disconnect the negative battery cable.
2. Remove the radio and accessory switch knobs.
3. Remove the instrument panel trim plate.

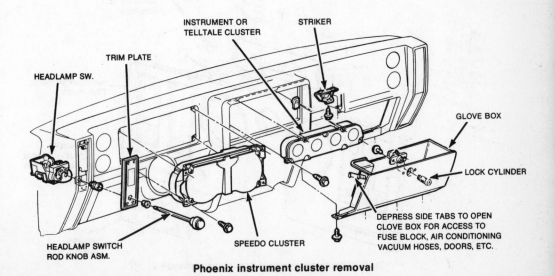

Phoenix instrument cluster removal

4. With automatic transaxle, disconnect the shift indicator cable from the steering column shift bowl.

5. Remove the four cluster attaching screws.

6. Disconnect the speedometer cable and electrical wiring from the back of the cluster. Remove the cluster. Installation is the reverse.

SPEEDOMETER CABLE REPLACEMENT

1. Remove the instrument cluster.
2. Slide the cable out from the casing. If the cable is broken, the casing will have to be unscrewed from the transaxle and the broken piece removed from that end.

3. Before installing a new cable, slip a piece of cable into the speedometer and spin it between your fingers in the direction of normal rotation. If the mechanism sticks or binds, the speedometer should be repaired or replaced.

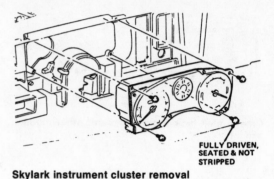

Skylark instrument cluster removal

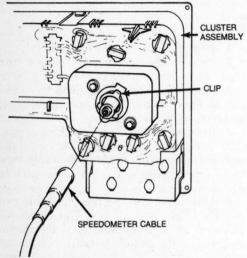

The speedometer cable connects to the back of the instrument cluster assembly

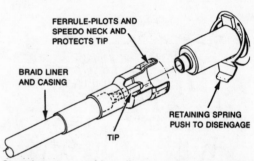

Speedometer cable disengagement at the speedometer

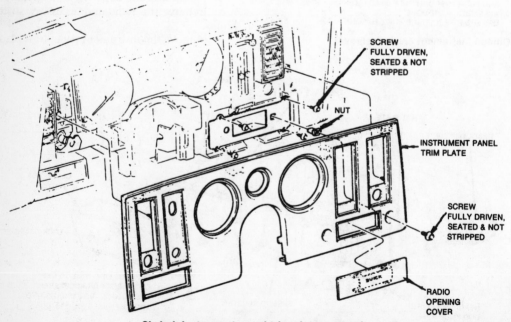

Skylark instrument panel trim plate removal

4. Inspect the casing; if it is cracked, kinked, or broken, the casing should be replaced.

5. Slide a new cable into the casing, engaging the transaxle end securely. Sometimes it is easier to unscrew the casing at the transaxle end, install the cable into the transaxle fitting, and screw the casing back into place. Install the instrument cluster.

Ignition Switch

The ignition switch removal and installation procedure is given in Chapter Seven, under "Steering," because the steering wheel must be removed for access to the ignition switch.

LIGHTING

Headlights

REMOVAL AND INSTALLATION

1. Remove the headlamp trim panel (grille panel) attaching screws.

2. Remove the four headlamp bulb retaining screws. These are the screws which hold the retaining ring for the bulb to the front of the car. Do not touch the two headlamp aiming screws, at the top and side of the retaining ring, or the headlamp aim will have to be readjusted.

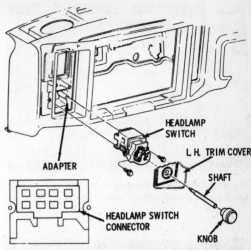

The headlamp switch is removed on all models by pulling the knob out, depressing the retaining button on the switch assembly, removing the knob and shaft, and removing the switch

Light Bulb Chart

Application	Candle Power	Type
Headlamp	55/65W	6052
High Intensity (Opt.)	55/65W	H6052
Front Park and Turn Signal	24/2.2	1157NA
Front Side Marker	2	194
Rear Side Marker	2	194
Tail Light, Stop Light and Turn Signal—		
Base Model	32/3	1157
License Plate Light	2	194
Back-Up Lights	32	1156
Courtesy Light	6	906
Dome Light	12	561
Instrument Illumination Lights	1	161
	2	194
	3	168
Indicator Lights ①		
High Beam	2	194
Generator (GEN)	2	194
Oil/Choke	2	194
Temperature System (TEMP)	2	194
Brake Warning (BRAKE)	2	194
Turn Signal	2	194
Seat Belt Warning (FASTEN SEAT BELTS)	2	194
Heater or A/C Control Panel Light ①	2	194
Glove Box Light ①	2	194
Underhood Light	15	93
Luggage Compartment Light	15	1003
Rear Light Assy. Turn Signal	32	1156
Tail and Stop Light Assy.	32/3	1157
Hazard Warning Flasher	6	Lamp Type
Turn Signal Flasher	2	Lamp Type

NOTE: *Do not use bulbs of higher candlepower than indicated above.*
①—Certain models may differ, check with owner's manual first.

The arrows point to the headlight aiming screws; don't touch these when replacing the headlamp

Remove the trim panel attaching bolts

Remove the four retaining screws

Unplug the old bulb, plug in the new one, and reverse the removal process

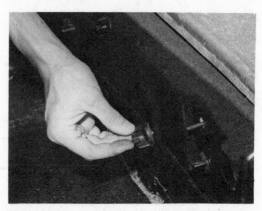

The taillight assemblies are retained by four wing-nuts

CIRCUIT PROTECTION

Fusible Links

A fusible link is a protective device used in an electrical circuit. When the current increases beyond a certain amperage, the fusible metal of the wire link melts, thus breaking the electrical circuit and preventing further damage to other components and wiring. Whenever a fusible link is melted because of a short circuit, correct the cause before installing a new one.

The X-Body cars have three fusible links. Two of them are located at the front center of the engine, at the starter solenoid. One protects the lighting circuit and the other protects the starting and charging circuit. The third fusible link is in the wiring harness at the right-hand side of the car, at the cowl; it protects the engine cooling fan.

To replace a fusible link, cut off the burned link beyond the original splice. Replace the link

3. Pull the bulb and ring forward and separate them. Unplug the electrical connector from the rear of the bulb.

4. Plug the new bulb into the electrical connector. Install the bulb into the retaining ring and install the ring and bulb. Install the trim panel.

with a new one of the same rating. If the splice has two wires, two repair links are required, one for each wire. Connect the new fusible link to the wires, then crimp securely.

CAUTION: *Use only replacements of the same electrical capacity as the original, available from your dealer. Replacements of a different electrical value will not provide adequate system protection.*

Fuses

Fuses protect all the major electrical systems in the car. In case of an electrical overload, the fuse melts, breaking the circuit and stopping the flow of electricity.

If a fuse blows, the cause should be investigated and corrected before the installation of a new fuse. This, however, is easier to say than to do. Because each fuse protects a limited number of components, your job is narrowed down somewhat. Begin your investigation by looking for obvious fraying, loose connections, breaks in insulation, etc. Use the techniques outlined at the beginning of this chapter. Electrical problems are almost always a real headache to solve, but if you are patient and persistent, and approach the problem logically (that is, don't start replacing electrical components randomly), you will eventually find the solution.

The amperage of each fuse and the circuit it protects are marked on the fusebox, which is located under the left side (driver's side) of the instrument panel.

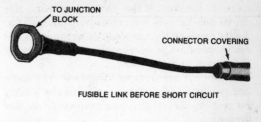

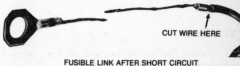

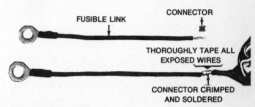

Fusible links before and after a short circuit

New fusible links are spliced to the wire

Circuit Breakers

The headlights are protected by a circuit breaker in the headlamp switch. If the circuit breaker trips, the headlights will either flash on and off, or stay off altogether. The circuit breaker resets automatically after the overload is removed.

The windshield wipers are also protected by

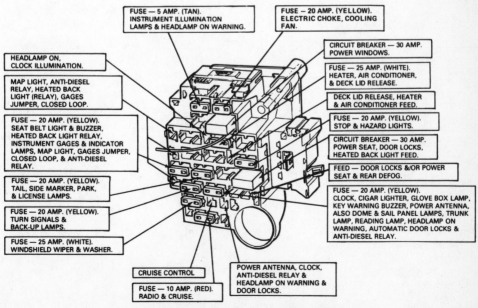

Fuse block on the Skylark; others similar

a circuit breaker. If the motor overheats, the circuit breaker will trip, remaining off until the motor cools or the overload is removed. One common cause of overheating is operation of the wipers in heavy snow.

The circuit breakers for the power door locks and power windows are located in the wiring harness in the engine compartment, on the firewall.

Flashers

The hazard flasher is located at the top left corner of the fusebox. The turn signal flasher is installed in a clamp attached to the base of the steering column support inside the car. In both cases, replacement is made by unplugging the old flasher and plugging in a new one.

WIRING DIAGRAMS

Wiring diagrams have been omitted from this book. As cars have become more complex, wiring diagrams have grown in size and complexity as well. It has become impossible to provide a readable reproduction in a reasonable number of pages. Information on ordering wiring diagrams from the vehicle manufacturer can be found in the owner's manual.

MANUAL TRANSAXLE

"Transaxle" is the term used to identify a unit which combines the transmission and drive axle into one component. The X-Body cars use a model MT-125 manual transaxle as standard equipment. This is an all-new design, sharing no parts with any other G.M. transmission or differential. All forward gears in this design are in constant mesh. Final drive from the transmission is taken from the output gear, which is an integral part of the output shaft; the output gear transfers power to the differential ring gear and differential assembly. The differential is of conventional design.

Because of the complexity of the transaxle, no overhaul procedures are given in this book. However, removal and installation, adjustment, and halfshaft removal, installation and overhaul are covered.

REMOVAL AND INSTALLATION

1. Disconnect the negative battery cable from the transaxle case.
2. Remove the two transaxle strut bracket bolts on the left side of the engine compartment, if so equipped.
3. Remove the top four engine-to-transaxle bolts, and the one at the rear near the firewall. The one at the rear is installed from the engine side.
4. Loosen the engine-to-transaxle bolt near the starter, but do not remove.
5. Disconnect the speedometer cable at the transaxle, or at the speed control transducer on cars so equipped.
6. Remove the retaining clip and washer from the shift linkage at the transaxle. Remove the clips holding the cables to the mounting bosses on the case.
7. Support the engine with a lifting chain.
8. Unlock the steering column and raise and support the car. Drain the transaxle. Re-

move the two nuts attaching the stabilizer bar to the left lower control arm. Remove the four bolts which attach the left retaining plate to the engine cradle. The retaining plate covers and holds the stabilizer bar.

9. Loosen the four bolts holding the right stabilizer bracket.
10. Disconnect and remove the exhaust pipe if necessary.
11. Pull the stabilizer bar down on the left side.
12. Remove the four nuts and disconnect the front and rear transaxle mounts from the engine cradle. Remove the two rear center crossmember bolts.
13. Remove the three right side front cradle attaching bolts. They are accessible under the splash shield.
14. Remove the top bolt from the lower front transaxle shock absorber if equipped.
15. Remove the left front wheel. Remove the front cradle-to-body bolts on the left side, and the rear cradle-to-body bolts.
16. Pull the left side drive shaft from the transaxle using G.M. special tool J-28468 or the equivalent. The right side axle shaft will simply disconnect from the case. When the

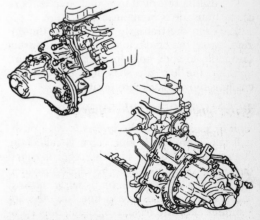

Engine-to-transaxle bolts

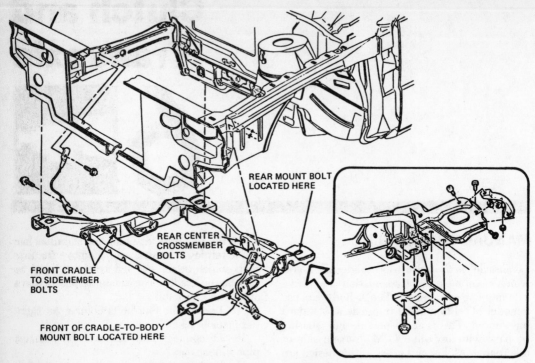

REAR MOUNT BOLT LOCATED HERE

REAR CENTER CROSSMEMBER BOLTS

FRONT CRADLE TO SIDEMEMBER BOLTS

FRONT OF CRADLE-TO-BODY MOUNT BOLT LOCATED HERE

Transaxle and engine cradle assembly

transaxle is removed, the right shaft can be swung out of the way. A boot protector should be used when disconnecting the driveshafts.

17. Swing the cradle to the left side. Secure out of the way, outboard of the fender well.

18. Remove the flywheel and starter shield bolts, and remove the shields.

19. Remove the two transaxle extension bolts from the engine-to-transaxle bracket, if equipped.

20. Place a jack under the transaxle case. Remove the last engine-to-transaxle bolt. Pull the transaxle to the left, away from the engine, then down and out from under the car.

Installation is the reverse.

1. Position the right axle shaft into its bore as the transaxle is being installed.

2. When the transaxle is bolted to the engine, swing the cradle into position and install the cradle-to-body bolts immediately. Be sure to guide the left axle shaft into place as the cradle is moved back into position.

SHIFT LINKAGE ADJUSTMENT

Shift linkage in the X-Body cars is via a push-pull two cable affair. One cable is called the "trans-selector" cable, and the other is called the "trans-shifter" cable. The range provided for shift linkage adjustments is fairly narrow, and it may be necessary to fine tune the adjustment after the factory-recommended procedure is completed.

1. Remove the shifter boot and retainer inside the car. Shift into first gear.

2. Install two No. 22 drill bits, or two $^5/_{32}$ in. rods, into the two alignment holes in the shifter assembly to hold it in first gear.

3. Place the transaxle into first gear by pushing the rail selector shaft down just to the point of feeling the resistance of the inhibitor spring. Then rotate the shift lever all the way counterclockwise.

4. Install the stud, with the cable attached, into the slotted area of the shift lever.

5. Install the stud, with the cable attached, into the slotted area of the select lever, while gently pulling on the lever to remove all lash.

Remove the two drill bits or pins from the shifter.

Check the shifter for proper operation. It may be necessary to fine tune the adjustment after road testing.

Halfshafts

The X-Body cars use unequal-length half-shafts, with specific applications for automatic and manual transaxle use. All halfshafts except the left-hand inboard joint of the automatic transaxle incorporate a male spline; the shafts interlock with the transaxle gears through the use of barrel-type snap rings. The left-hand inboard shaft on the automatic transaxle uses a female spline which installs over a stub shaft

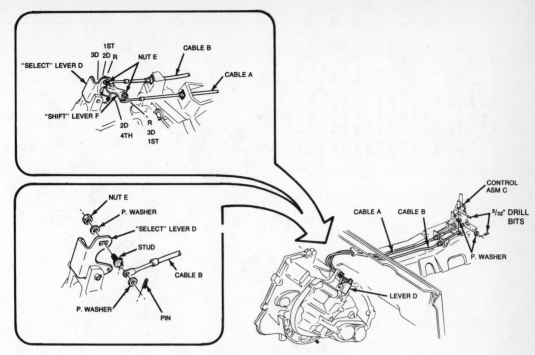

Shift cable adjustments

protruding from the transaxle. Four constant velocity joints are used, two on each shaft. The inner joints are of the double offset design; the outer joints are Rzeppa-type.

REMOVAL AND INSTALLATION

1. Remove the hub nut.
2. Raise the front of the car. Remove the wheel and tire.
3. Install an axle shaft boot seal protector, G.M. special tool no. J-28712 or the equivalent, onto the seal.
4. Disconnect the brake hose clip from the MacPherson strut, but do not disconnect the hose from the caliper. Remove the brake caliper from the spindle, and hang the caliper out of the way by a length of wire. *Do not allow the caliper to hang by the brake hose.*
5. Mark the camber alignment cam bolt for reassembly. Remove the cam bolt and the upper attaching bolt from the strut and spindle.
6. Pull the steering knuckle assembly from the strut bracket.
7. Using G.M. special tool J-28468 or the equivalent, remove the axle shaft from the transaxle.
8. Using G.M. special tool J-28733 or the equivalent spindle remover, remove the axle shaft from the hub and bearing assembly.

To install:

1. If a new drive axle is to be installed, a new knuckle seal should be installed first.

2. Loosely install the drive axle into the transaxle and steering knuckle.
3. Loosely attach the steering knuckle to the suspension strut.
4. Install the brake caliper. Tighten the bolts to 30 ft. lbs. (40 Nm.).
5. The drive axle is an interference fit in the steering knuckle. Press the axle into place, then install the hub nut. When the shaft begins to turn with the hub, insert a drift through the caliper into one of the cooling slots in the rotor to keep it from turning. Tighten the hub nut to 70 ft. lbs. (100 Nm.) to completely seat the shaft.
6. Load the hub assembly by lowering it onto a jackstand. Align the camber cam bolt marks made during removal, install the bolt and tighten to 140 ft. lbs. (190 Nm.). Tighten the upper nut to the same value.
7. Install the axle shaft all the way into the transaxle using a screwdriver inserted into the groove provided on the inner retainer. Tap the screwdriver until the shaft seats in the transaxle.
8. Connect the brake hose clip to the strut. Install the tire and wheel, lower the car, and tighten the hub nut to 225 ft. lbs. (305 Nm.).

CONSTANT VELOCITY JOINT OVERHAUL

Outer Joint

1. Remove the axle shaft.
2. Cut off the seal retaining clamp. Using a

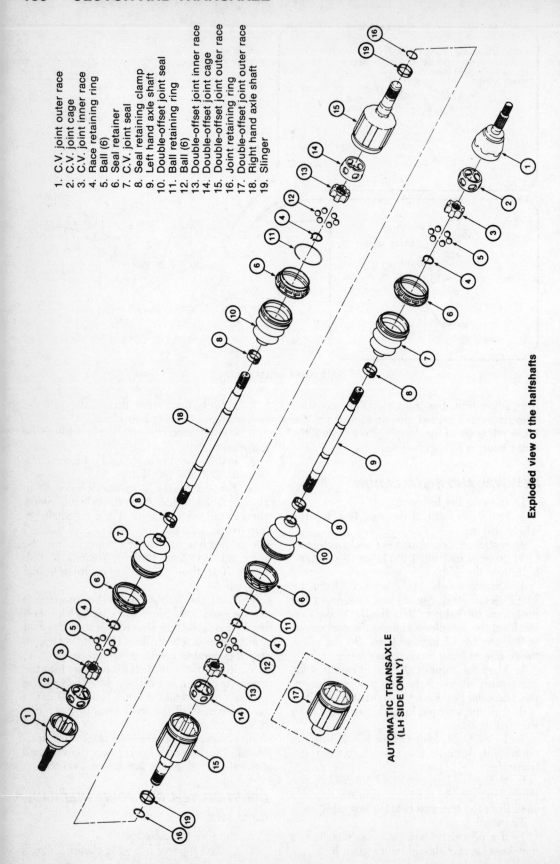

1. C.V. joint outer race
2. C.V. joint cage
3. C.V. joint inner race
4. Race retaining ring
5. Ball (6)
6. Seal retainer
7. C.V. joint seal
8. Seal retaining clamp
9. Left hand axle shaft
10. Double-offset joint seal
11. Ball retaining ring
12. Ball (6)
13. Double-offset joint inner race
14. Double-offset joint cage
15. Double-offset joint outer race
16. Joint retaining ring
17. Double-offset joint outer race
18. Right hand axle shaft
19. Slinger

Exploded view of the halfshafts

AUTOMATIC TRANSAXLE (LH SIDE ONLY)

J-28712

BOOT PROTECTOR

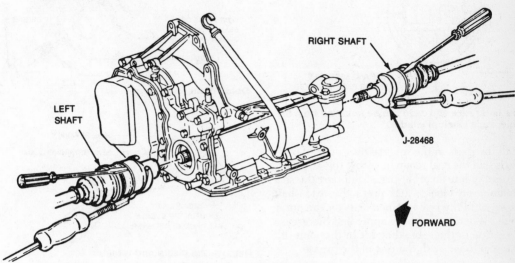

RIGHT SHAFT

LEFT SHAFT

J-28468

FORWARD

Halfshaft removal; the special tools are attached to slide hammers in this diagram

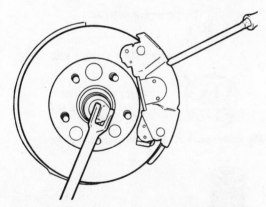

Insert a drift into the caliper when tightening the hub nut

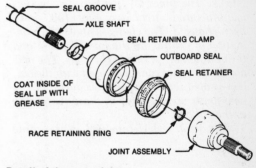

SEAL GROOVE

AXLE SHAFT

SEAL RETAINING CLAMP

OUTBOARD SEAL

SEAL RETAINER

COAT INSIDE OF SEAL LIP WITH GREASE

RACE RETAINING RING

JOINT ASSEMBLY

Detail of the outer joint

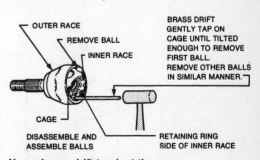

OUTER RACE

REMOVE BALL

INNER RACE

BRASS DRIFT GENTLY TAP ON CAGE UNTIL TILTED ENOUGH TO REMOVE FIRST BALL. REMOVE OTHER BALLS IN SIMILAR MANNER.

CAGE

DISASSEMBLE AND ASSEMBLE BALLS

RETAINING RING SIDE OF INNER RACE

Use a brass drift to pivot the cage

brass drift and a hammer, lightly tap the seal retainer from the outside toward the inside of the shaft to remove from the joint.

3. Use a pair of snap ring pliers to spread the retaining ring apart. Pull the axle shaft from the joint.

4. Using a brass drift and a hammer, lightly tap on the inner race cage until it has tilted sufficiently to remove one of the balls. Remove the other balls in the same manner.

5. Pivot the cage 90° and, with the cage ball windows aligned with the outer joint windows, lift out the cage and the inner race.

6. The inner race can be removed from the cage by pivoting it 90° and lifting out. Clean all parts thoroughly and inspect for wear.

7. To install, put a light coat of the grease provided in the rebuilding kit onto the ball grooves of the inner race and outer joint. In-

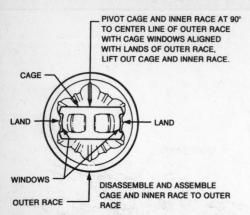

PIVOT CAGE AND INNER RACE AT 90°
TO CENTER LINE OF OUTER RACE
WITH CAGE WINDOWS ALIGNED
WITH LANDS OF OUTER RACE,
LIFT OUT CAGE AND INNER RACE.

CAGE

LAND — LAND

WINDOWS

OUTER RACE

DISASSEMBLE AND ASSEMBLE
CAGE AND INNER RACE TO OUTER
RACE

The inner race and cage can be removed from the outer race when pivoted 90°

stall the parts in the reverse order of removal. To install the seal retainer, install the axle shaft assembly into an arbor press. Support the seal retainer on blocks, and press the axle shaft down until the seal retainer seats on the outer joint. When assembling, apply half the grease provided in the rebuilding kit to the joint; fill the seal (boot) with the rest of the grease.

Inner Joint

NOTE: *The inner CV joints on all models manufactured after August of 1980 have been changed. The change entails the elimination of venting on the joint housing and the addition of venting in the seals. The new non-vented joint cannot be used with the old, non-vented seal. Service procedures for the new joints are identical to those pertaining to the old one.*

1. The joint seal is removed in the same

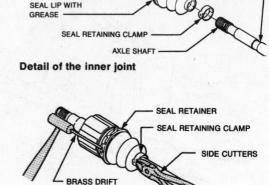

RETAINING RING

JOINT ASSEMBLY

RACE RETAINING RING

SEAL RETAINER

SEAL

SEAL GROOVE

COAT INSIDE OF
SEAL LIP WITH
GREASE

SEAL RETAINING CLAMP

AXLE SHAFT

Detail of the inner joint

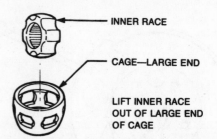

SEAL RETAINER

SEAL RETAINING CLAMP

SIDE CUTTERS

BRASS DRIFT
LIGHTLY TAP EVENLY
ALL AROUND RETAINER

Remove the clamp and retainer

INNER RACE

CAGE—LARGE END

LIFT INNER RACE
OUT OF LARGE END
OF CAGE

The inner race exits from the large end of the cage

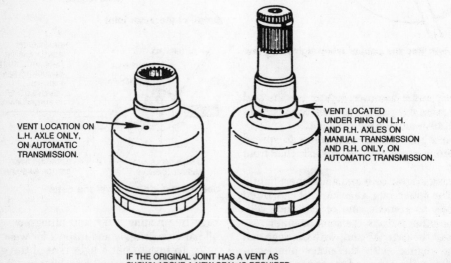

VENT LOCATION ON
L.H. AXLE ONLY,
ON AUTOMATIC
TRANSMISSION.

VENT LOCATED
UNDER RING ON L.H.
AND R.H. AXLES ON
MANUAL TRANSMISSION
AND R.H. ONLY, ON
AUTOMATIC TRANSMISSION.

IF THE ORIGINAL JOINT HAS A VENT AS
SHOWN ABOVE A NEW SEAL IS REQUIRED

A comparison of the old and new inner CV joints

SMALL END OF CAGE

RETAINING RING ON INNER RACE FACES
SMALL END OF CAGE BEFORE
INSTALLING ANY BALLS

Inner race installed in the cage

manner as the outer joint seal. Follow Steps
1–3 of the outer joint procedure.

2. To disassemble the inner joint, remove
the ball retaining ring from the joint. Pull the
cage and inner race from the joint. The balls
will come out with the race.

3. Center the inner race lobes in the cage
windows, pivot the race 90°, and lift the race
from the cage.

4. Assembly of the joint is the reverse. The
inner joint seal retainer must be pressed onto
the joint. See Step 7 of the outer joint procedure.

CLUTCH

ADJUSTMENT

The X-Body cars have a self-adjusting clutch
mechanism located on the clutch pedal, eliminating the need for periodic free play adjustments. The self-adjusting mechanism should
be inspected periodically as follows:

1. Depress the clutch pedal and look for the
pawl on the self-adjusting mechanism to firmly
engage the teeth on the ratchet.

2. Release the clutch. The pawl should be
lifted off of the teeth by the metal stop on the
bracket.

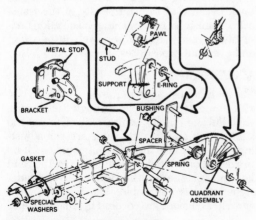

Clutch pedal installation details

NEUTRAL START SWITCH

A neutral start switch is located on the clutch
pedal assembly; the switch prevents the engine from starting unless the clutch is depressed. If the switch is faulty, it can be un-
bolted and replaced without removing the

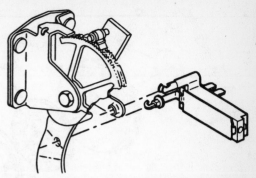

**The neutral start switch is attached to the clutch
pedal**

pedal assembly from the car. No adjustments
for the switch are provided.

CLUTCH REMOVAL AND INSTALLATION

1. Remove the transaxle.

2. Mark the pressure plate assembly and the
flywheel so that they can be assembled in the
same position. They were balanced as an assembly at the factory.

3. Loosen the attaching bolts one turn at a
time until spring tension is relieved.

4. Support the pressure plate and remove
the bolts. Remove the pressure plate and
clutch disc. Do not disassemble the pressure
plate assembly; replace it if defective.

5. Inspect the flywheel, clutch disc, pressure plate, throwout bearing and the clutch
fork and pivot shaft assembly for wear. Replace the parts as required. If the flywheel
shows any signs of overheating, or if it is badly
grooved or scored, it should be refaced or replaced.

6. Clean the pressure plate and flywheel
mating surfaces thoroughly. Position the clutch
disc and pressure plate into the installed position, and support with a dummy shaft or
clutch aligning tool. The clutch plate is assembled with the damper springs offset toward the
transaxle. One side of the factory-supplied
clutch disc is stamped "Flywheel side."

7. Install the pressure plate-to-flywheel
bolts. Tighten them gradually in a criss-cross
pattern.

8. Lubricate the outside groove and the inside recess of the release bearing with high
temperature grease. Wipe off any excess. Install the release bearing.

9. Install the transaxle.

CLUTCH CABLE REPLACEMENT

1. Disconnect the end of the cable from the
clutch release lever at the transaxle. Do not
allow the cable to snap rapidly toward the rear
of the car; doing so will damage the quadrant
in the self-adjusting mechanism.

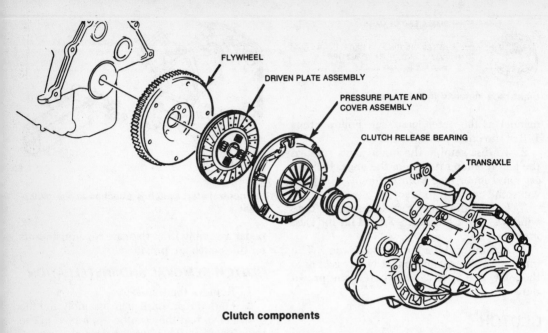

FLYWHEEL

DRIVEN PLATE ASSEMBLY

PRESSURE PLATE AND
COVER ASSEMBLY

CLUTCH RELEASE BEARING

TRANSAXLE

Clutch components

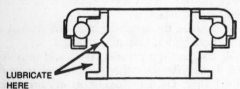

LUBRICATE
HERE

Release bearing lubrication

2. Disconnect the clutch cable from the self-adjusting quadrant. Lift the locking pawl away from the quadrant, then slide the cable out to the right.

3. Unbolt the two nuts holding the cable retainer to the upper studs on the engine side of the firewall. Disconnect the cable from the retaining bracket bolted to the transaxle. Remove the cable.

4. To install a new cable, place the gasket in position on the two upper studs on the firewall. Place a new cable into position with the retaining flange against the bracket.

5. Attach the end of the cable to the self-adjusting mechanism quadrant. Be sure to route the cable underneath the pawl.

6. Install the two nuts to the firewall cable retainer. Tighten to 30 ft. lbs. (38 Nm.).

7. Attach the cable to the transaxle bracket.

8. Attach the end of the cable to the clutch release lever. Don't yank too hard on the cable, which will damage the stop on the quadrant.

AUTOMATIC TRANSAXLE

All of the X-Body cars use the Turbo Hydra-Matic 125 automatic transaxle as optional equipment. This is a fully automatic unit of conventional design, incorporating a three element hydraulic torque converter, a compound planetary gear set, and a dual sprocket and drive link assembly. The sprockets and drive link (Hy-Vo® chain) connect the torque converter assembly to the transmission gears. The transaxle also incorporates the differential assembly, which is of conventional design. Power is transmitted from the transmission to the final drive and differential assembly through helical cut gears.

No overhaul procedures are given in this book because of the complexity of the transaxle. Transaxle removal and installation, adjustment, and halfshaft removal, installation, and overhaul procedures are covered.

ADJUSTMENTS

The only adjustment required on the TH-M 125 transaxle on models through 1981 is the shift linkage (cable) adjustment. The neutral start switch and throttle valve are self-adjusting. The transaxle has only one band, with no provision for periodic adjustment. On 1982 and later models the throttle valve cable was redesigned and is adjustable. Pan removal, fluid and filter changes are covered in Chapter One.

SHIFT LINKAGE ADJUSTMENT

1980 and Later

1. Place the shift lever inside the car into Neutral.

2. Disconnect the shift cable from the transaxle lever. Place the transaxle lever in Neutral, by moving the lever clockwise to the

Low (L) detent, then counterclockwise through the Second (S) and Drive (D) detents to the Neutral detent.

3. Attach the shift cable to the pin on the transaxle lever. Check the shift operation.

THROTTLE VALVE OR DETENT CABLE ADJUSTMENT

1982 and Later

1. Depress and hold the metal lock tab on the TV cable.

2. Move the slider back through the fitting in the direction away from the throttle body until the slider stops against fitting.

3. Release the metal lock tab.

4. Open the throttle lever to "full throttle stop" position. This will automatically adjust the slider on the cable to the correct setting.

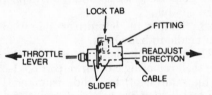

Throttle valve or detent cable adjustment—1982 and later

NEUTRAL SAFETY AND BACK-UP SWITCH ADJUSTMENT

1. Position the transmission control shifter assembly in the neutral notch in the detent plate.

2. Loosen the switch attaching screws.

3. Rotate the switch on the shifter assembly to align the service adjustment hole with the carrier tang hole. Insert a 2.34 dia. gauge pin to a depth of 15 mm.

4. Tighten the attaching screws to the recommended torque of 1.5 ft. lb.

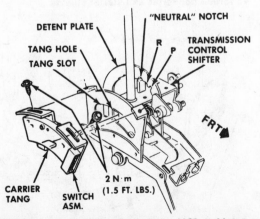

Neutral safety switch adjustment—1982 and later

REMOVAL AND INSTALLATION

1. Disconnect the negative battery cable from the transaxle. Tape the wire to the upper radiator hose to keep it out of the way.

2. Slide the detent cable in the opposite direction of the cable to remove it from the carburetor.

3. Unbolt the detent cable attaching bracket at the transaxle.

4. Pull up on the detent cable cover at the transaxle until the cable is exposed. Disconnect the cable from the rod.

5. Remove the two transaxle strut bracket bolts at the transaxle, if equipped.

6. Remove all the engine-to-transaxle bolts except the one near the starter. The one nearest the firewall is installed from the engine side; you will need a short handled box wrench or ratchet to reach it.

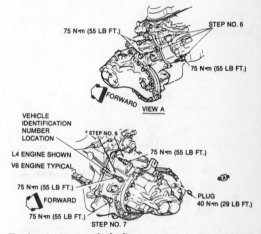

Engine-to-transaxle bolts

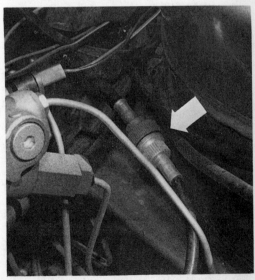

The speedometer coupling is next to the left strut tower and the brake master cylinder

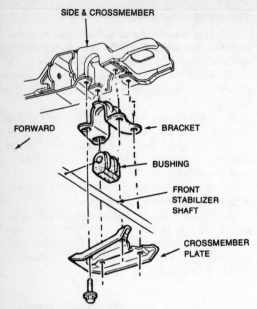

Stabilizer bar attachment

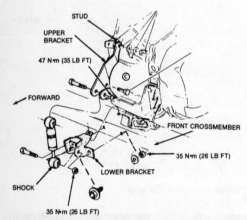

V6 transaxle shock absorber

7. Loosen, but do not remove the engine-to-transaxle bolt near the starter.

8. Disconnect the speedometer cable at the upper and lower coupling. On cars with cruise control, remove the speedometer cable at the transducer.

9. Remove the retaining clip and washer from the shift linkage at the transaxle. Remove the two shift linkage at the transaxle. Remove the two shift linkage bracket bolts.

10. Disconnect and plug the two fluid cooler lines at the transaxle. These are inch-size fittings ($\frac{1}{2}$ and $^{11}/_{16}$); use a back-up wrench to avoid twisting the lines.

11. Install an engine holding chain or hoist. Raise the engine enough to take its weight off the mounts.

12. Unlock the steering column and raise the car.

13. Remove the two nuts holding the anti sway (stabilizer) bar to the left lower control arm (driver's side).

14. Remove the four bolts attaching the covering plate over the stabilizer bar to the engine cradle on the left side (driver's side).

15. Loosen but do not remove the four bolts holding the stabilizer bar bracket to the right side (passenger's side) of the engine cradle. Pull the bar down on the driver's side.

16. Disconnect the front and rear transaxle mounts at the engine cradle.

17. Remove the two rear center crossmember bolts.

18. Remove the three right (passenger) side front engine cradle attaching bolts. The nuts are accessible under the splash shield next to the frame rail.

19. Remove the top bolt from the lower front transaxle shock absorber, if equipped (V6 engine only).

20. Remove the left (driver) side front and rear cradle-to-body bolts.

21. Remove the left front wheel. Attach an axle shaft removing tool (G.M. part no. J-28468 or the equivalent) to a slide hammer. Place the tool behind the axle shaft cones and pull the cones out away from the transaxle. Remove the right shaft in the same manner. Set the shafts out of the way. Plug the openings in the transaxle to prevent fluid leakage and the entry of dirt.

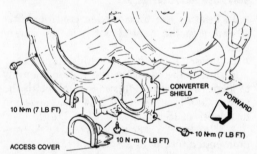

V6 torque converter and starter shields

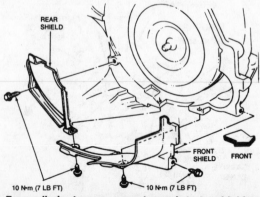

Four cylinder torque converter and starter shields

22. Swing the partial engine cradle to the left (driver) side and wire it out of the way outboard of the fender well.

23. Remove the four torque converter and starter shield bolts. Remove the two transaxle extension bolts from the engine-to-transaxle bracket.

24. Attach a transaxle jack to the case.

25. Use a felt pen to matchmark the torque converter and flywheel. Remove the three torque converter-to-flywheel bolts.

26. Remove the transaxle-to-engine bolt near the starter. Remove the transaxle by sliding it to the left, away from the engine.

Installation is the reverse. As the transaxle is installed, slide the right axle shaft into the case. Install the cradle-to-body bolts before the stabilizer bar is installed. To aid in stabilizer bar installation, a pry hole has been provided in the engine cradle.

HALFSHAFT REMOVAL, INSTALLATION AND OVERHAUL

The procedures for the automatic transaxle halfshafts are the same as those outlined earlier for the manual transaxle.

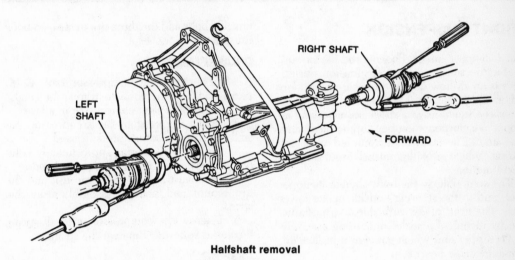

RIGHT SHAFT

LEFT SHAFT

FORWARD

Halfshaft removal

Suspension and Steering

FRONT SUSPENSION

The Citation, Omega, Phoenix and Skylark use a MacPherson strut front suspension design. This is an all-new design, not shared with any other G.M. car. A MacPherson strut combines the functions of a shock absorber and an upper suspension member (upper arm) into one unit. The strut is surrounded by a coil spring, which provides normal front suspension functions.

The strut bolts to the body shell at its upper end, and to the steering knuckle at the lower end. The strut pivots with the steering knuckle by means of a sealed mounting assembly at the upper end which contains a preloaded, non-adjustable bearing.

The steering knuckle is connected to the chassis at the lower end by a conventional lower arm, and pivots in the arm in a preloaded ball joint of standard design. The knuckle clamps to the ball joint stud.

Advantages of the MacPherson strut design, aside from its relative simplicity, include reduced weight and friction, minimal intrusion into the engine and passenger compartments, and ease of service.

MacPherson Strut

The MacPherson strut is a combination coil spring and shock absorber (damper) unit. The strut is removed as an assembly from the car. A special strut compressor must be used to disassemble the strut and coil spring.

REMOVAL

1. Loosen the wheel nuts, raise the car, and remove the wheel and tire.
2. Remove the brake hose clip-to-strut bolt. Do not disconnect the hose from the caliper.
3. Mark the camber cam eccentric adjuster for assembly.
4. Remove the two lower strut-to-steering knuckle bolts and the three upper strut-to-body nuts. Remove the strut.

DISASSEMBLY

A MacPherson strut compressor tool, G.M. part J-26584 or the equivalent must be used.
1. Clamp the strut compressor in a vise.
2. Install the strut in the compressor. Install the compressor adapters, if used.
3. Compress the spring approximately ½ in. *Do not bottom the spring or the strut rod.*
4. Remove the strut shaft top nut and the top mount and bearing assembly from the strut.
5. Uncrew the compressor until all spring tension is relieved. Remove the spring.

ASSEMBLY

1. Place the strut into the compressor. Rotate the strut until the spindle mounting flange is facing out, away from the compressor.
2. Place the spring on the strut. Make sure it is properly seated on the strut bottom plate.
3. Install the strut spring assembly on the spring. Install the compressor adapters, if used.
4. Tighten the strut compressor until it just contacts the spring seat, or the adapters if a tool with adapters is being used.
5. Thread an alignment rod, G.M. tool J-26584-27 or the equivalent, onto the strut damper shaft, hand tight.
6. Compress the spring until approximately 1½ in. of the damper rod can be pulled up through the top spring seat. *Do not compress the spring until it bottoms.*
7. Remove the alignment rod and install the top mount and nut. Tighten the nut to 68 ft. lbs. (90 nm.).
8. Unscrew the compressor and remove the strut.

INSTALLATION

1. Install the strut to the body. Tighten the upper nuts hand tight.

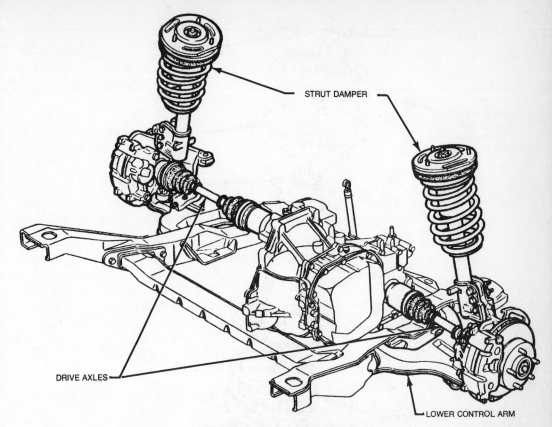

Front suspension components

2. Place a jack under the lower arm. Raise the arm and install the lower strut-to-knuckle bolts. Align the camber eccentric cam with the marks made during removal. Tighten the strut-to-knuckle bolts to 140 ft. lbs. (190 Nm.), and the strut-to-body nuts to 18 ft. lbs. (24 Nm.).

3. Install the brake hose clip on the strut.

4. Install the wheel and lower the car.

NOTE: *If a new strut damper has been installed, the front end will have to be realigned.*

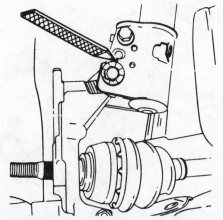

Mark the camber eccentric before removal

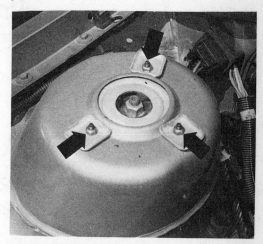

The upper strut-to-body nuts are in the engine compartment

Ball Joints

INSPECTION

The ball joints have built-in wear indicators. As long as the wear indicator (part of the grease nipple) extends below the ball joint seat, the ball joint is OK. When the indicator recedes beneath the seat, replacement is necessary.

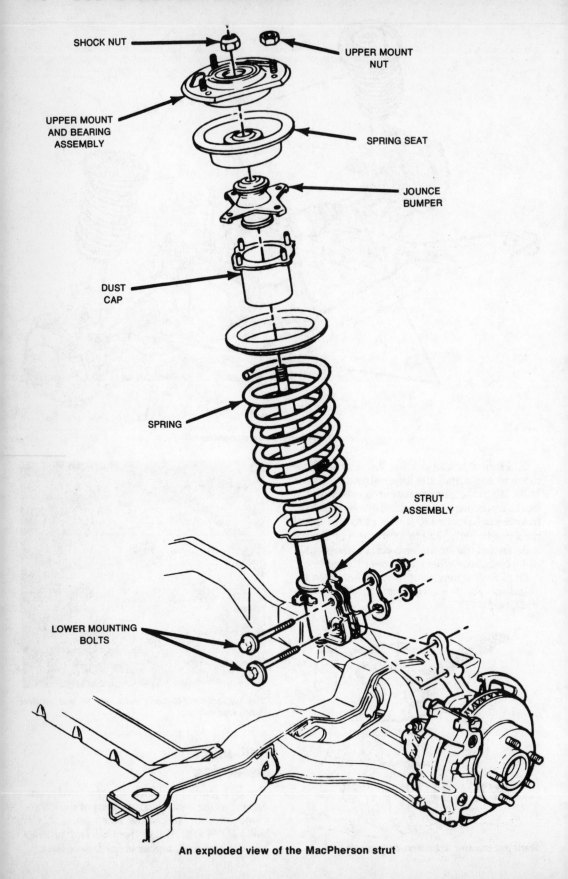

SHOCK NUT

UPPER MOUNT NUT

UPPER MOUNT AND BEARING ASSEMBLY

SPRING SEAT

JOUNCE BUMPER

DUST CAP

SPRING

STRUT ASSEMBLY

LOWER MOUNTING BOLTS

An exploded view of the MacPherson strut

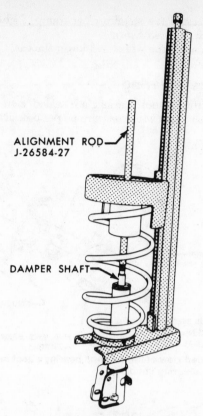

ALIGNMENT ROD
J-26584-27

DAMPER SHAFT

ASSEMBLE STRUT

Use an alignment rod when assembling the strut

Drill out the ball joint rivets

REPLACEMENT

Only one ball joint is used in each lower arm. The MacPherson strut design does not use an upper ball joint.

1. Loosen the wheel nuts, raise the car, and remove the wheel.

2. Use a ⅛ in. drill bit to drill a hole approximately ¼ in. deep in the center of each of the three ball joint rivets.

3. Use a 4 in. drill bit to drill off the rivet heads. Drill only enough to remove the rivet head.

4. Use a hammer and punch to remove the rivets. Drive them out from the bottom.

5. Loosen the ball joint pinch bolt in the steering knuckle.

6. Remove the ball joint.

7. Install the new ball joint in the control arm. Tighten the bolts supplied with the replacement joint to 8 ft. lbs.

8. Install the ball stud into the knuckle pinch bolt fitting. It should go in easily; if not, check the stud alignment. Install the pinch bolt from the rear to the front. Tighten to 45 ft. lbs. (60 Nm.).

9. Install the wheel and lower the car.

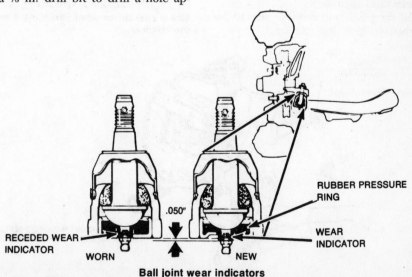

RUBBER PRESSURE RING

WEAR INDICATOR

RECEDED WEAR INDICATOR

.050"

WORN　NEW

Ball joint wear indicators

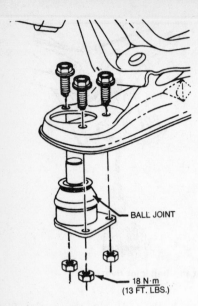

Ball joint installation

Control Arm

REMOVAL AND INSTALLATION

1. Loosen the wheel nuts, raise the car, and remove the wheel.

2. Remove the stabilizer bar from the control arm.

3. Remove the ball joint pinch bolt in the steering knuckle.

4. Remove the control arm pivot bolts and the control arm.

5. To install, insert the control arm into its fittings. Install the pivot bolts from the rear to the front. Tighten the bolts to 48 ft. lbs. (68 Nm.).

6. Insert the ball stud into the knuckle pinch bolt fitting. It should go in easily; if not, check the ball joint stud alignment.

7. Install the pinch bolt from the rear to the front. Tighten to 45 ft. lbs. (60 Nm.).

8. Install the stabilizer bar clamp. Tighten to 35 ft. lbs. (45 Nm.).

9. Install the wheel and lower the car.

Wheel Bearing

The front wheel bearings are sealed, non-adjustable units which require no periodic atten-

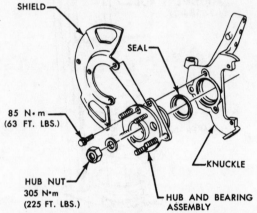

Exploded view of the hub and bearing attachment to the steering knuckle

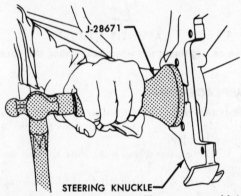

Use a seal driver when installing a new seal into the knuckle

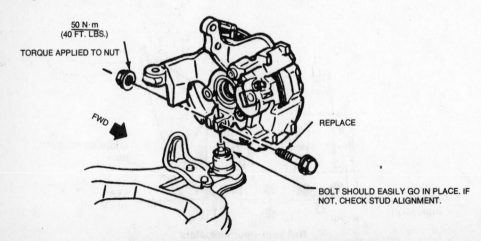

The ball joint stud should slip into the knuckle fitting

Front Suspension Torque Specifications

	'80–'81	'82	'83	'84	'85
Hub Nut	225	214	192	192	192
Ball Joint Clamp Bolt	40	40	40	40	33
Strut-to-Steering Knuckle	140	140	140	140	140
Hub/Bearing Assy-to-Steering Knuckle	63	63	63	63	77
Control Arm-to-Frame	48	66	66	66	66
Stabilizer Bar-to-Control Arm	35	33	33	33	33
Tie Rod-to-Steering Knuckle	40	40	40	40	30

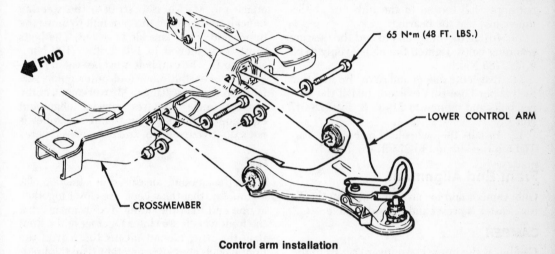

Control arm installation

tion. They are bolted to the steering knuckle by means of an integral flange.

REPLACEMENT

You will need a special tool to pull the bearing free of the halfshaft, G.M. tool no. J-28733 or the equivalent. You should also use a halfshaft boot protector, G.M. tool no. J-28712 or the equivalent to protect the parts from damage.

1. Remove the wheel cover, loosen the hub nut, and raise and support the car. Remove the front wheel.

2. Install the boot cover, G.M. part no. J-28712 or the equivalent.

3. Remove and discard the hub nut. Be sure to use a new one on assembly, not the old one.

4. Remove the brake caliper and rotor:

   a. Remove the allen head caliper mounting bolts;

   b. Remove the caliper from the knuckle and suspend from a length of wire. Do not allow the caliper to hang from the brake hose. Pull the rotor from the knuckle.

5. Remove the three hub and bearing attaching bolts. If the old bearing is to be reused, match mark the bolts and holes for installation. The brake rotor splash shield will have to come off, too.

6. Attach a puller, G.M. part no. J-28733 or the equivalent, and remove the bearing. If corrosion is present, make sure the bearing is loose in the knuckle before using the puller.

7. Clean the mating surfaces of all dirt and corrosion. Check the knuckle bore and knuckle seal for damage. If a new bearing is to be installed, remove the old knuckle seal and install a new one. Grease the lips of the new seal before installation; install with a seal driver made for the purpose, G.M. tool no. J-28671 or the equivalent.

8. Push the bearing onto the halfshaft. Install a new washer and hub nut.

9. Tighten the new hub nut on the halfshaft until the bearing is seated. If the rotor and hub start to rotate as the hub nut is tightened, insert a drift through the caliper and into

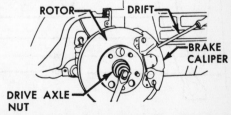

Insert a drift into the rotor when installing the hub nut

Wheel Alignment Specifications

Year	Model	Caster* Range (deg)	Caster* Pref Setting (deg)	Camber Range (deg)	Camber Pref Setting (deg)	Toe-In (in.)	Steering Axis (deg) Inclination
'80–'81	All	2N–2P	0	0–1P	½P	0–³⁄₁₆	14.5
'82–'83	All	0–4P	2P	½N–½P	0	¹⁄₁₆ out–¹⁄₁₆ in	14.5
'84–'85	All	0–4P	2P	½N–½P	0	¹³⁄₆₄ out–¹³⁄₆₄ in	14.5

*Caster is not adjustable

the rotor cooling fins to prevent rotation. Do not apply full torque to the hub nut at this time—just seat the bearing.

10. Install the brake shield and the bearing retaining bolts. Tighten the bolts evenly to 63 ft. lbs. (85 Nm.).

11. Install the caliper and rotor. Be sure that the caliper hose isn't twisted. Install the caliper bolts and tighten to 21–35 ft. lbs. (28–47 Nm.).

12. Install the wheel. Lower the car. Tighten the hub nut to 225 ft. lbs. (305 Nm.).

Front End Alignment

Only camber and toe are adjustable on the X-cars; caster is preset and non-adjustable.

CAMBER

Camber is the inward or outward tilt from the vertical, measured in degrees, of the front wheels at the top. An outward tilt gives the wheel positive camber; an inward tilt is called negative camber. Proper camber is critical to assure even tire wear.

Camber angle is adjusted on the X-Bodies by loosening the cam and through bolts which attach the MacPherson strut to the steering knuckle and rotating the cam bolt to move the upper end of the knuckle in or out. The bolts must be tightened to 140 ft. lbs. (190 Nm.) afterwards. The cam bolt must be seated properly between the inner and outer guide surfaces on the strut flange. Measurement of the camber angle requires special alignment equipment; thus the adjustment of camber is not a do-it-yourself job, and not covered here.

TOE

Toe is the amount, measured in a fraction of a millimeter, that the wheels are closer together at one end than the other. Toe-in means that the front wheels are closer together at the front than the rear; toe-out means the rear of the front wheels are closer together than the front. X-Body cars are designed to have a slight amount of toe-in.

Toe is adjusted by turning the tie rods. It must be checked after camber has been adjusted, but it can be adjusted without disturbing the camber setting. You can make this ad-

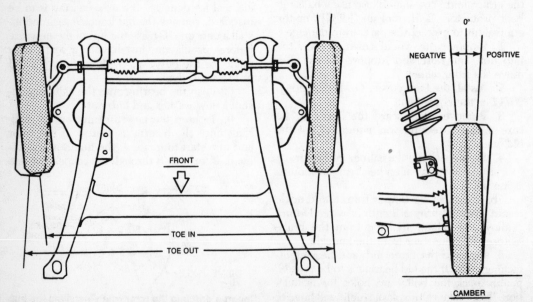

Wheel alignment: toe (left) and camber (right)

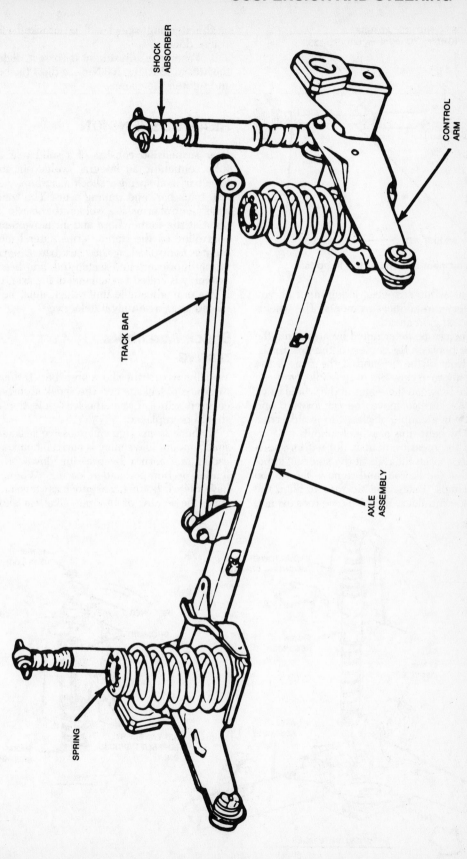

SHOCK
ABSORBER

CONTROL
ARM

TRACK BAR

AXLE
ASSEMBLY

SPRING

Rear axle and suspension components

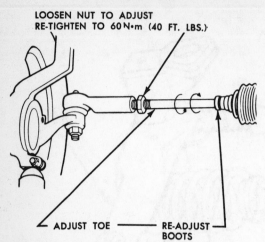

LOOSEN NUT TO ADJUST
RE-TIGHTEN TO 60 N•m (40 FT. LBS.)

ADJUST TOE ———— RE-ADJUST
BOOTS

Toe adjustment is made at the tie rods

justment without special equipment if you make very careful measurements. The wheels must be straight ahead.

1. Toe can be determined by measuring the distance between the centers of the tire treads, at the front of the tire and at the rear. If the tread pattern makes this impossible, you can measure between the edges of the wheel rims, but make sure to move the car forward and measure in a couple of places to avoid errors caused by bent rims or wheel runout.

2. If the measurement is not within specifications, loosen the nuts at the steering knuckle end of the tie rod, and remove the tie rod boot clamps. Rotate the tie rods to align the toe to specifications. Rotate the tie rods evenly,

or the steering wheel will be crooked when you're done.

3. When the adjustment is correct, tighten the nuts to 45 ft. lbs. (60 Nm.). Adjust the boots and tighten the clamps.

REAR SUSPENSION

Rear suspension consists of a solid rear axle tube containing an integral, welded-in stabilizer bar, coil springs, shock absorbers, a lateral track bar, and trailing arms. The trailing arms (control arms) are welded to the axle, and pivot at the frame. Fore and aft movement is controlled by the trailing arms; lateral movement is controlled by the track bar. A permanently lubricated and sealed hub and bearing assembly is bolted to each end of the axle tube; it is a non-adjustable unit which must be replaced as an assembly if defective.

Shock Absorbers
TESTING

Visually inspect the shock absorber. If there is evidence of leakage and the shock absorber is covered with oil, the shock is defective and should be replaced.

If there is no sign of excessive leakage (a small amount of weeping is normal) bounce the car at one corner by pressing down on the fender or bumper and releasing. When you have the car bouncing as much as you can, release the fender or bumper. The car should

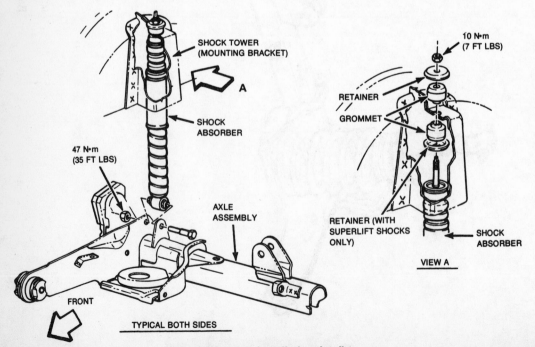

Shock absorber installation details

The upper shock absorber mounts are accessible in the trunk

stop bouncing after the first rebound. If the bouncing continues past the center point of the bounce more than once, the shock absorbers are worn and should be replaced.

REMOVAL AND INSTALLATION

1. Open the hatch or trunk lid, remove the trim cover if present, and remove the upper shock absorber nut.

2. Raise and support the car at a convenient working height if you desire. It is not necessary to remove the weight of the car from the shock absorbers, however, so you can leave the car on the ground if you prefer.

3. If the car is equipped with superlift shock absorbers, disconnect the air line.

4. Remove the lower attaching bolt and remove the shock.

5. If new shock absorbers are being installed, repeatedly compress them while inverted and extend them in their normal upright position. This will purge them of air.

6. Install the shocks in the reverse order of removal. Tighten the lower mount nut and bolt to 35 ft. lbs. (47 Nm.), the upper to 7 ft. lbs. (10 Nm.).

Springs

REMOVAL AND INSTALLATION

CAUTION: *The coil springs are under a considerable amount of tension. Be very careful when removing or installing them; they can exert enough force to cause very serious injuries.*

1. Raise and support the car on a hoist. Do not use twin-post hoist. The swing arc of the axle may cause it to slip from the hoist when the bolts are removed. If a suitable hoist is not available, raise and support the car on jackstands, and use a jack under the axle.

2. Support the axle with a jack that can be raised and lowered.

3. Remove the brake hose attaching brackets (right and left), allowing the hoses to hang freely. Do not disconnect the hoses.

4. Remove the track bar attaching bolts from the rear axle.

5. Remove both shock absorber lower attaching bolts from the axle.

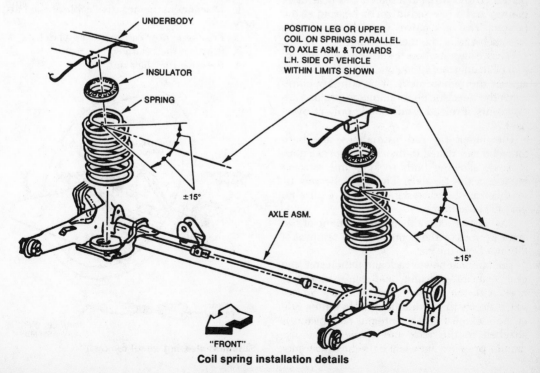

Coil spring installation details

6. Lower the axle. Remove the coil spring and insulator.

7. To install, position the spring and insulator on the axle. The leg on the upper coil of the spring must be parallel to the axle, facing the lefthand side of the car.

8. Install the shock absorber bolts. Tighten to 34 ft. lbs. (47 Nm.). Install the track bar, tightening to 33 ft. lbs. (45 Nm.). Install the brake line brackets. Tighten to 8 ft. lbs. (11 Nm.).

Rear Hub and Bearing
REMOVAL AND INSTALLATION

1. Loosen the wheel lug nuts. Raise and support the car and remove the wheel.

2. Remove the brake drum. Removal procedures are covered in the next chapter, if needed.

NOTE: *Do not hammer on the brake drum to remove; damage to the bearing will result.*

3. Remove the four hub and bearing retaining bolts and remove the assembly from the axle.

4. Installation is the reverse. Hub and bearing bolt torque is 35 ft. lbs. (55 Nm.).

STEERING

The X-Body cars use an aluminum-housed Saginaw manual rack and pinion steering gear as standard equipment. The pinion is supported by and turns in a sealed ball bearing at the top and a pressed-in roller bearing at the bottom. The rack moves in bushings pressed into each end of the rock housing.

Wear compensation occurs through the action of an adjuster spring which forces the rack against the pinion teeth. This adjuster eliminates the need for periodic pinion preload adjustments. Preload is adjustable only at overhaul.

The inner tie rod assemblies are both threaded and staked to the rack. A special joint is used, allowing both rocking and rotating motion of the tie rods. The inner tie rod assemblies are lubricated for life and require no periodic attention.

Any service other than replacement of the outer tie rods or the boots requires removal of the unit from the car.

The optional power rack and pinion steering gear is an integral unit, and shares most features with the manual gear. A rotary control valve directs the hydraulic fluid to either side of the rack piston. The integral rack piston is attached to the rack and converts the hydraulic pressure into left or right linear motion. A vane-type constant displacement pump with integral reservoir provides hydraulic pressure. No in-car adjustments are necessary or possible on the system, except for periodic belt tension checks and adjustments for the pump. See Chapter One for belt tension adjustments.

Steering Wheel
REMOVAL AND INSTALLATION
Standard Wheel

1. Disconnect the negative cable at the battery.

2. Pull the pad from the wheel. The horn lead is attached to the pad at one end; the other end of the pad has a wire with a spade connector. The horn lead is disconnected by pushing and turning; the spade connector is simply unplugged.

3. Remove the retainer under the pad.

4. Remove the steering shaft nut.

5. There should be alignment marks already present on the wheel and shaft. If not, matchmark the parts.

6. Remove the wheel with a puller.

7. Install the wheel on the shaft, aligning the matchmarks. Install the shaft nut and tighten to 30 ft. lbs. (40 Nm.).

8. Install the retainer.

9. Plug in the spade connector, and push and turn the horn lead to connect. Install the pad. Connect the negative battery cable.

Sport Wheel

1. Disconnect the negative cable at the battery.

2. Pry the center cap from the wheel.

3. Remove the retainer.

4. Remove the shaft nut.

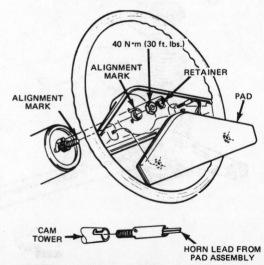

Standard steering wheel removal

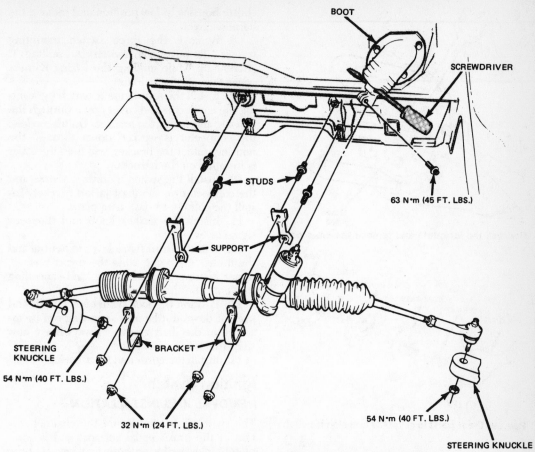

BOOT

SCREWDRIVER

STUDS

63 N·m (45 FT. LBS.)

SUPPORT

STEERING
KNUCKLE

54 N·m (40 FT. LBS.)

BRACKET

32 N·m (24 FT. LBS.)

54 N·m (40 FT. LBS.)

STEERING KNUCKLE

Manual steering gear installation details; power steering similar

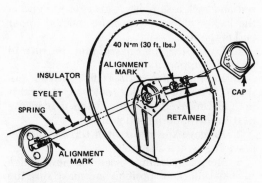

40 N·m (30 ft. lbs.)

ALIGNMENT
MARK

INSULATOR

EYELET

CAP

SPRING

RETAINER

ALIGNMENT
MARK

Sport steering wheel removal

5. If the wheel and shaft do not have factory-installed alignment marks, matchmark the parts before removal of the wheel.

6. Install a puller and remove the wheel. A horn spring, eyelet and insulator are underneath; don't lose the parts.

7. Install the spring, eyelet and insulator into the tower on the column.

8. Align the matchmarks and install the wheel onto the shaft. Install the retaining nut and tighten to 30 ft. lbs. (40 Nm.).

9. Install the retainer. Install the center cap. Connect the negative battery cable.

Turn Signal Switch

NOTE: *All 1981 and later models utilize a combination switch in place of the previous turn signal switch. The combination switch, in addition to operating the turn signals, will also control the windshield wiper/washer functions and the cruise control if so equipped. Removal and installation procedures for the new combination switch are basically the same as those given for the turn signal switch.*

REMOVAL AND INSTALLATION

1. Remove the steering wheel. Remove the trim cover.

2. Pry the cover from the steering column.

3. Position a U-shaped lockplate compressing tool on the end of the steering shaft and compress the lock plate by turning the shaft nut clockwise. Pry the wire snap-ring out of the shaft groove.

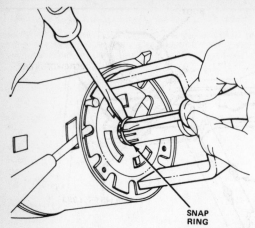

Depress the lockplate and remove the snap ring

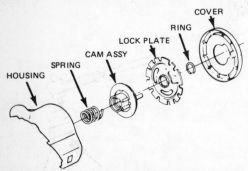

Remove these parts to get at the turn signal switch

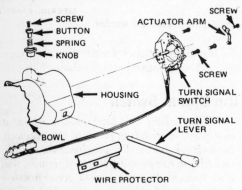

Turn signal switch installation details

4. Remove the tool and lift the lockplate off the shaft.

5. Slip the cancelling cam, upper bearing preload spring, and thrust washer off the shaft.

6. Remove the turn signal lever. Remove the hazard flasher button retaining screw and remove the button, spring and knob.

7. Pull the switch connector out of the mast jacket and tape the upper part to facilitate switch removal. Attach a long piece of wire to the turn signal switch connector. When installing the turn signal switch, feed this wire through the column first, and then use this wire to pull the switch connector into position. On tilt wheels, place the turn signal and

shifter housing in low position and remove the harness cover.

8. Remove the three switch mounting screws. Remove the switch by pulling it straight up while guiding the wiring harness cover through the column.

9. Install the replacement switch by working the connector and cover down through the housing and under the bracket. On tilt models, the connector is worked down through the housing, under the bracket, and then the cover is installed on the harness.

10. Install the switch mounting screws and the connector on the mast jacket bracket. Install the column-to-dash trim plate.

11. Install the flasher knob and the turn signal lever.

12. With the turn signal lever in neutral and the flasher knob out, slide the thrust washer, upper bearing preload spring, and cancelling cam onto the shaft.

13. Position the lock plate on the shaft and press it down until a new snap-ring can be inserted in the shaft groove. Always use a new snap-ring when assembling.

14. Install the cover and the steering wheel.

Ignition Switch

REMOVAL AND INSTALLATION

The switch is located inside the channel section of the brake pedal support and is completely inaccessible without first lowering the steering column. The switch is actuated by a rod and rack assembly. A gear on the end of the lock cylinder engages the toothed upper end of the rod.

1. Lower the steering column; be sure to properly support it.

2. Put the switch in the "Off-Unlocked" position. With the cylinder removed, the rod is in "Off-Unlocked" position when it is in the next to the uppermost detent.

3. Remove the two switch screws and remove the switch assembly.

4. Before installing, place the new switch in "Off-Unlocked" position and make sure the lock cylinder and actuating rod are in "Off-Unlocked" position (second detent from the top).

5. Install the activating rod into the switch and assemble the switch on the column. Tighten the mounting screws. Use only the specified screws, since overlength screws could impair the collapsibility of the column.

6. Reinstall the steering column.

Ignition Lock Cylinder

REMOVAL AND INSTALLATION

1. Remove the steering wheel.

2. Turn the lock to the Run position.

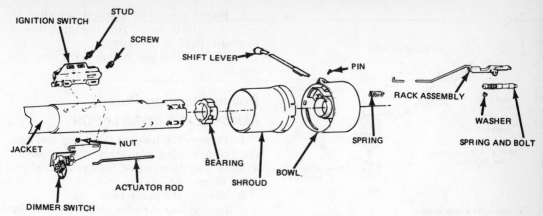

Ignition switch installation details

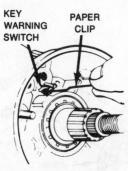

Remove the key warning buzzer switch with a paper clip

TO ASSEMBLE, ROTATE TO STOP WHILE HOLDING CYLINDER

LOCK CYLINDER

LOCK RETAINING SCREW

CLIP

KEY WARNING SWITCH

HOUSING

Lock cylinder installation

3. Remove the lock plate, turn signal switch or combination switch, and the key warning buzzer switch. The warning buzzer switch can be fished out with a bent paper clip.

4. Remove the lock cylinder retaining screw and lock cylinder.

CAUTION: *If the screw is dropped on removal, it could fall into the column, requiring complete disassembly to retrieve the screw.*

5. Rotate the cylinder clockwise to align the cylinder key with the keyway in the housing.

6. Push the lock all the way in.

7. Install the screw. Tighten to 15 in. lbs.

8. The rest of installation is the reverse of removal. Turn the lock to Run to install the key warning buzzer switch, which is simply pushed down into place.

Tie-Rod Ends

REMOVAL AND INSTALLATION

1. Loosen the jam nut on the steering rack (inner tie-rod).

2. Remove the tie-rod and end nut. Separate the tie-rod end from the steering knuckle using a puller.

3. Unscrew the tie rod end, counting the number of turns.

4. To install, screw the tie-rod end onto the steering rack (inner tie-rod) the same number of turns as counted for removal. This will give approximately correct toe.

5. Install the tie-rod end into the knuckle. Install the nut and tighten to 40 ft. lbs. (54 Nm.).

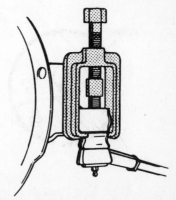

Separate the tie-rod end from the knuckle with a puller

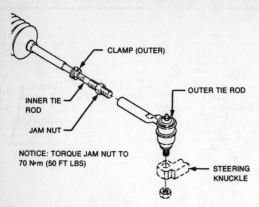

Tie-rod end installation

6. If the toe must be adjusted, use pliers to expand the boot clamp. Turn the inner tie-rod to adjust. Replace the clamp.

7. Tighten the jam nut to 50 ft. lbs. (70 Nm.).

Power Steering Pump
REMOVAL AND INSTALLATION

1. Remove the hoses at the pump and tape the openings shut to prevent contamination. Position the disconnected lines in a raised position to prevent leakage.

2. Remove the pump belt.

3. On the four cylinder, remove the radia-

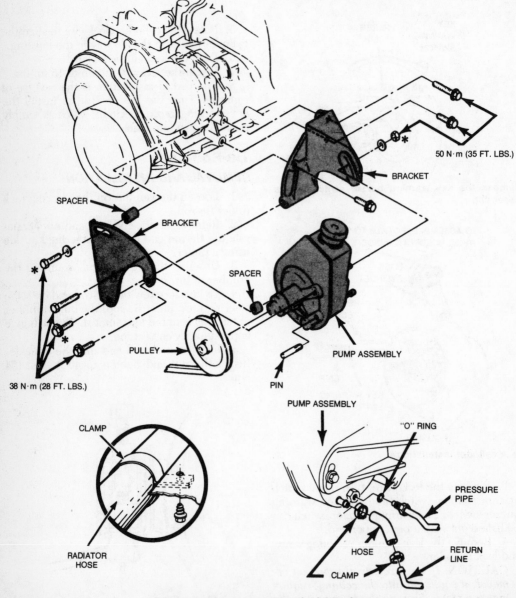

Power steering pump removal—L4 engine

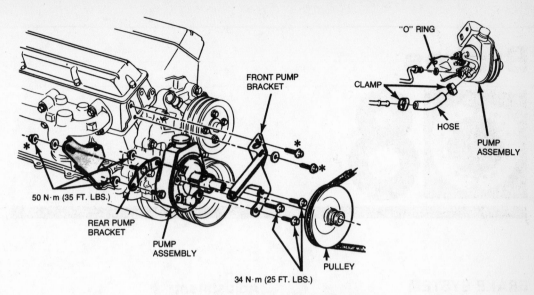

Power steering pump removal—V6 engine

tor hose clamp bolt. On the V6, disconnect the negative battery cable, disconnect the electrical connector at the blower motor, drain the cooling system, and remove the heater hose at the water pump.

4. Loosen the retaining bolts and any braces, and remove the pump.

5. Install the pump on the engine with the retaining bolts handtight.

6. Connect and tighten the hose fittings.

7. Refill the pump with fluid and bleed by turning the pulley counterclockwise (viewed from the front). Stop the bleeding when air bubbles no longer appear.

8. Install the pump belt on the pulley and adjust the tension. Bleed the system.

9. Replace the four cylinder radiator hose clamp bolt. On the V6, install the heater hose.

Install the blower and electrical connector. Refill the cooling system. Connect the negative battery cable.

BLEEDING THE POWER STEERING SYSTEM

1. Fill the reservoir.

2. Let the fluid stand undisturbed for two minutes, then crank the engine for about two seconds. Refill the reservoir if necessary.

3. Repeat Steps 1 and 2 until the fluid level remains constant after cranking the engine.

4. Raise the front of the car until the wheels are off the ground, then start the engine. Increase the engine speed to about 1,500 rpm.

5. Turn the wheels lightly against the stops to the left and right, checking the fluid level and refilling if necessary.

Brakes

BRAKE SYSTEM

The X-Body cars have a diagonally-split hydraulic system. This differs from conventional practice in that the left front and right rear brakes are on one hydraulic circuit, and the right front and left rear are on the other.

A diagonally-split system necessitates the use of a special master cylinder design. The X-Body master cylinder incorporates the functions of a standard tandem master cylinder, plus a warning light switch and proportioning valves. Additionally, the master cylinder is designed with a quick take-up feature which provides a large volume of fluid to the brakes at low pressure when the brakes are initially applied. The low pressure fluid acts to quickly fill the large displacement requirements of the system.

The front disc brakes are single piston sliding caliper units. Fluid pressure acts equally against the piston and the bottom of the piston bore in the caliper. This forces the piston outward until the pad contacts the rotor. The force on the caliper bore forces the caliper to slide over, carrying the outher pad into contact with the other side of the rotor. The disc brakes are self-adjusting.

Rear drum brakes are conventional duo-servo units. A dual piston wheel cylinder, mounted to the top of the backing plate, actuates both brake shoes. Wheel cylinder force to the shoes is supplemented by the tendency of the shoes to wrap into the drum (servo action). An actuating link, pivot and lever serve to automatically engage the adjuster as the brakers are applied when the car is moving in reverse. Provisions for manual adjustment are also provided. The rear brakes also serve as the parking brakes; linkage is mechanical.

Vacuum boost is an option. The booster is a conventional tandem vacuum unit.

Adjustment

DISC BRAKES

The front disc brakes are inherently self-adjusting. No adjustments are either necessary or possible.

DRUM BRAKES

The drum brakes are designed to self-adjust when applied with the car moving in reverse. However, they can also be adjusted manually. This manual adjustment should also be performed whenever the linings are replaced.

1. Use a punch to knock out the stamped area on the brake drum. If this is done with the drum installed on the car, the drum must then be removed to clean out all metal pieces. After adjustments are complete, obtain a hole cover from your dealer (Part no. 4874119 or the equivalent) to prevent entry of dirt and water into the brakes.

2. Use an awl, a screwdriver, or an adjusting tool especially made for the purpose to turn the brake adjusting screw star wheel. Expand the shoes until the drum can just barely be turned by hand.

3. Back off the adjusting screw 30 notches. If the shoes still are dragging lightly, back off the adjusting screw one or two additional notches. If the brakes still drag, the parking brake adjustment is incorrect or the parking brake is applied. Fix and start over.

4. Install the hole cover into the drum.

5. Check the parking brake adjustment.

On some models, no marked area or stamped area is present on the drum. In this case, a hole must be drilled in the backing plate:

1. All backing plates have two round flat areas in the lower half through which the parking brake cable is installed. Drill a ½ in.

hole into the round flat area on the backing plate opposite the parking brake cable. This will allow access to the star wheel.

2. After drilling the hole, remove the drum and remove all metal particles. Install a hole plug (Part no. 4874119 or the equivalent) to prevent the entry of water or dirt.

HYDRAULIC SYSTEM

Master Cylinder

REMOVAL AND INSTALLATION

1. If your car does not have power brakes, disconnect the master cylinder pushrod at the brake pedal inside the car. The pushrod is retained to the brake pedal by a clip; there is a washer under the clip, and a spring washer on the other side of the pushrod.

2. Unplug the electrical connector from the master cylinder.

3. Place a number of cloths or a container under the master cylinder to catch the brake fluid. Disconnect the brake tubes from the

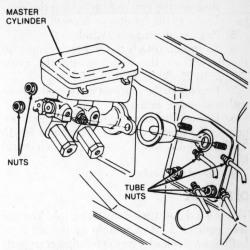

Master cylinder removal; power brakes similar

master cylinder; use a flare nut wrench if one is available. Tape over the open ends of the tubes.

NOTE: *Brake fluid eats paint. Wipe up any spilled fluid immediately, then flush the area with clear water.*

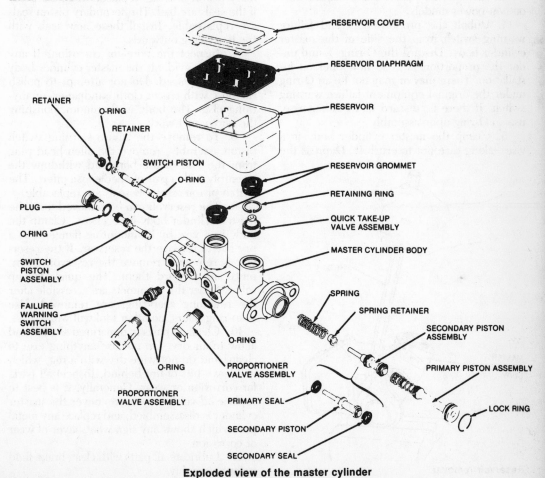

Exploded view of the master cylinder

4. Remove the two nuts attaching the master cylinder to the booster or firewall.

5. Remove the master cylinder.

6. To install, attach the master cylinder to the firewall or the booster with the nuts. Torque to 22–30 ft. lbs. (30–45 Nm.).

7. Reconnect the pushrod to the brake pedal with non-power brakes.

8. Remove the tape from the lines and connect to the master cylinder. Torque to 10–15 ft. lbs. (13–20 Nm.). Connect the electrical lead.

9. Bleed the brakes.

OVERHAUL

This is a tedious, time-consuming job. You can save yourself a lot of trouble by buying a rebuilt master cylinder from your dealer or parts supply house. The small difference in price between a rebuilding kit and a rebuilt part usually makes it more economical, in terms of time and work, to buy the rebuilt part.

1. Remove the master cylinder.

2. Remove the reservoir cover and drain the fluid.

3. Remove the pushrod and rubber boot on non-power models.

4. Unbolt the proportioners and failure warning switch from the side of the master cylinder body. Discard the O-rings found under the proportioners. Use new ones on installation. There may or may not be an O-ring under the original equipment failure warning switch. If there is, discard it. In either case, use an O-ring upon assembly.

5. Clamp the master cylinder body in a vise, taking care not to crush it. Depress the

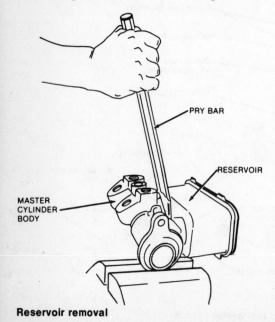

Reservoir removal

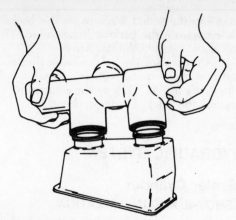

Install the master cylinder body to the reservoir with a rocking motion

primary piston with a wooden dowel and remove the lock ring with a pair of snap-ring pliers.

6. The primary and secondary pistons can be removed by applying compressed air into one of the outlets at the end of the cylinder and plugging the other three outlets. The primary piston must be replaced as an assembly if the seals are bad. The secondary piston seals are replaceable. Install these new seals with the lips facing outwards.

7. Inspect the bore for corrosion. If any corrosion is evident, the master cylinder body must be replaced. Do not attempt to polish the bore with crocus cloth, sandpaper, or anything else. The body is aluminum; polishing the bore won't work.

8. To remove the failure warning switch piston assembly, remove the allen head plug from the end of the bore and withdraw the assembly with a pair of needlenose pliers. The switch piston assembly seals are replacable.

9. The reservoir can be removed from the master cylinder body if necessary. Clamp the body in a vise by its mounting flange. Use a pry bar to remove the reservoir. If the reservoir is removed, remove the reservoir grommets and discard them. The quick takeup valves under the grommets are accessible after the retaining snap-rings are removed. Use snap-ring pliers; no other tool will work.

10. Clean all parts in denatured alcohol and allow to air dry. Do not use anything else to clean, and do not wipe dry with a rag, which will leave bits of lint behind. Inspect all parts for corrosion or wear. Generally, it is best to replace *all* rubber parts whenever the master cylinder is disassembled, and replace any metal part which shows any sign whatsoever of wear or corrosion.

11. Lubricate all parts with clean brake fluid before assembly.

12. Install the quick take-up valves into the master cylinder body and secure with the snap-rings. Make sure the snap-rings are properly seated in their grooves. Lubricate the new reservoir grommets with clean brake fluid and press them into the master cylinder.

13. Install the reservoir into the grommets by placing the reservoir on its lid and pressing the master cylinder body down onto it with a rocking motion.

14. Lubricate the switch piston assembly with clean brake fluid. Install new O-rings and retainers on the piston. Install the piston assembly into the master cylinder and secure with the plug, using a new O-ring on the plug. Torque is 40–140 in. lbs. (5–16 Nm.).

15. Assemble the new secondary piston seals onto the piston. Lubricate the parts with clean brake fluid, then install the spring, spring retainer and secondary piston into the cylinder. Install the primary piston, depress, and install the lock ring.

16. Install new O-rings on the proportioners and the failure warning switch. Install the proportioners and torque to 18–30 ft. lbs. (25–40 Nm.). Install the failure warning switch and torque to 15–50 in. lbs. (2–6 Nm.).

17. Clamp the master cylinder body upright into a vise by one of the mounting flanges. Fill the reservoir with fresh brake fluid. Pump the piston with a dowel until fluid squirts from the outlet ports. Continue pumping until the expelled fluid is free of air bubbles.

18. Install the master cylinder, and bleed the brakes. Check the brake system for proper operation. Do not move the car until a "hard" brake pedal is obtained and the brake system has been thoroughly checked for soundness.

Proportioning Valves and Failure Warning Switch

These parts are installed in the master cylinder body. No separate proportioning or metering valve is used. Replacement of these parts requires disassembly of the master cylinder. See the preceding master cylinder overhaul for replacement instructions.

Bleeding

The purpose of bleeding the brakes is to expel air trapped in the hydraulic system. The system must be bled whenever the pedal feels spongy, indicating that compressible air has entered the system. It must also be bled whenever the system has been opened or repaired. You will need a helper for this job.

CAUTION: *Never reuse brake fluid which has been bled from the brake system.*

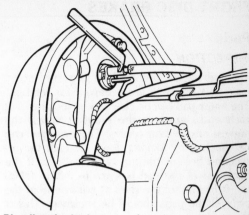

Bleeding the brakes

1. The sequence for bleeding is right rear, left front, left rear and right front. If the car has power brakes, remove the vacuum by applying the brakes several times. Do not run the engine while bleeding the brakes.

2. Clean all the bleeder screws. You may want to give each one a shot of penetrating solvent to loosen it up; seizure is a common problem with bleeder screws, which then break off, sometimes requiring replacement of the part to which they are attached.

3. Fill the master cylinder with DOT 3 brake fluid.

NOTE: *Brake fluid absorbs moisture from the air. Don't leave the master cylinder or the fluid container uncovered any longer than necessary. Be careful handling the fluid—it eats paint.*

Check the level of the fluid often when bleeding, and refill the reservoirs as necessary. Don't let them run dry, or you will have to repeat the process.

4. Attach a length of clear vinyl tubing to the bleeder screw on the wheel cylinder. Insert the other end of the tube into a clear, clean jar half filled with brake fluid.

5. Have your assistant slowly depress the brake pedal. As this is done, open the bleeder screw ⅓–½ of a turn, and allow the fluid to run through the tube. Then close the bleeder screw before the pedal reaches the end of its travel. Have your assistant slowly release the pedal. Repeat this process until no air bubbles appear in the expelled fluid.

6. Repeat the procedure on the other three brakes, checking the level of fluid in the master cylinder reservoir often.

After you're done, there should be no sponginess in the brake pedal feel. If there is, either there is still air in the line, in which case the process should be repeated, or there is a leak somewhere, which of course must be corrected before the car is moved.

FRONT DISC BRAKES

Pads

INSPECTION

The pad thickness should be inspected every time that the tires are removed for rotation. The outer pad can be checked by looking in at each end, which is the point at which the highest rate of wear occurs. The inner pad can be checked by looking down through the inspection hole in the top of the caliper. If the thickness of the pad is worn to within 0.030 in. (0.76 mm) of the rivet at either end of the pad, all the pads should be replaced. This is the factory-recommended measurement; your state's automobile inspection laws may not agree with this.

NOTE: *Always replace all pads on both front wheels at the same time. Failure to do so will result in uneven braking action and premature wear.*

REMOVAL AND INSTALLATION

1. Siphon ⅔ of the brake fluid from the master cylinder reservoir. Loosen the wheel lug nuts and raise the car. Remove the wheel.

2. Position a C-clamp across the caliper so that it presses on the pads and tighten it until the caliper piston bottoms in its bore.

NOTE: *If you haven't removed some brake fluid from the master cylinder, it will overflow when the piston is retracted.*

3. Remove the C-clamp.

4. Remove the allen head caliper mounting bolts. Inspect the bolts for corrosion, and replace as necessary.

5. Remove the caliper from the steering

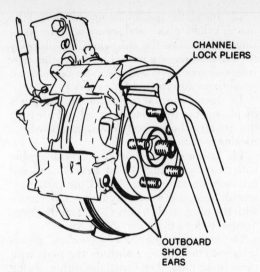

Bend the outboard pad ears into place with a large pair of slip joint pliers

knuckle and suspend it from the body of the car with a length of wire. Do not allow the caliper to hang by its hose.

6. Remove the pad retaining springs and remove the pads from the caliper.

7. Remove the plastic sleeves and the rubber bushings from the mounting bolt holes.

8. Install new sleeves and bushings. Lubricate the sleeves with a light coating of silicone grease before installation. These parts must always be replaced when the pads are replaced. The parts are usually included in the pad replacement kits.

9. Install the outboard pad into the caliper.

10. Install the retainer spring on the inboard pad. A new spring should be included in the pad replacement kit.

11. Install the new inboard pad into the caliper. The retention lugs fit into the piston.

12. Use a large pair of slip joint pliers to bend the outer pad ears down over the caliper.

13. Install the caliper onto the steering knuckle. Tighten the mounting bolts to 21–35 ft. lbs. (28–47 Nm.). Install the wheel and lower the car. Fill the master cylinder to its proper level with fresh brake fluid meeting DOT 3 specifications. Since the brake hose wasn't disconnected, it isn't really necessary to bleed the brakes, although most mechanics do this as a matter of course.

Caliper

REMOVAL AND INSTALLATION

1. Follow Steps 1, 2 and 3 of the pad replacement procedure.

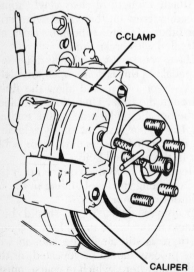

Install a C-clamp to retract the disc brake pads

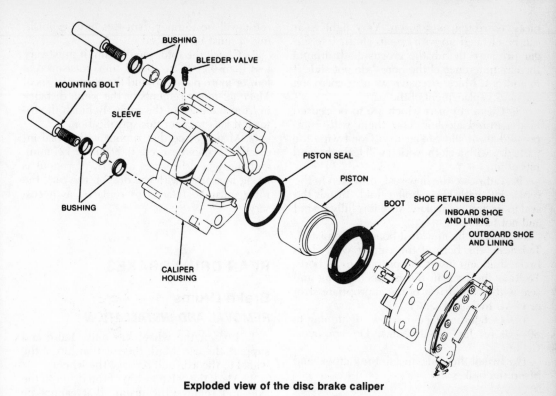

Exploded view of the disc brake caliper

2. Before removing the caliper mounting bolts, remove the bolt holding the brake hose to the caliper.

3. Remove the allen head caliper mounting bolts. Inspect them for corrosion and replace them if necessary.

4. Installation is the reverse. Mounting bolt torque is 21–35 ft. lbs. (28–47 Nm.) for the caliper. The brake hose fitting should be tightened to 18–30 ft. lbs. (24–40 Nm.).

OVERHAUL

1. Remove the caliper.
2. Remove the pads.
3. Place some cloths or a slat of wood in front of the piston. Remove the piston by applying compressed air to the fluid inlet fitting. Use just enough air pressure to ease the piston from the bore.

CAUTION: *Do not try to catch the piston with your fingers, which can result in serious injury.*

4. Remove the piston boot with a screwdriver, working carefully so that the piston bore is not scratched.

5. Remove the bleeder screw.

6. Inspect the piston for scoring, nicks, corrosion, wear, etc., and damaged or worn chrome plating. Replace the piston if any defects are found.

7. Remove the piston seal from the caliper bore groove using a piece of pointed wood or plastic. Do not use a screwdriver, which will damage the bore. Inspect the caliper bore for

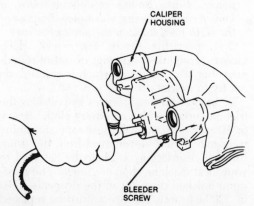

Use air pressure to remove the piston from the bore

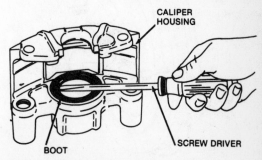

Remove the piston boot with a screwdriver

nicks, corrosion, and so on. Very light wear can be cleaned up with crocus cloth. Use finger pressure to rub the crocus cloth around the circumference of the bore—do not slide it in and out. More extensive wear or corrosion warrants replacement of the part.

8. Clean any part which are to be reused in denatured alcohol. Dry them with compressed air or allow to air dry. Don't wipe the parts dry with a cloth, which will leave behind bits of lint.

9. Lubricate the new seal, provided in the repair kit, with clean brake fluid. Install the seal in its groove, making sure it is fully seated and not twisted.

10. Install the new dust boot on the piston. Lubricate the bore of the caliper with clean brake fluid and insert the piston into its bore. Position the boot in the caliper housing and seat with a seal driver of the appropriate size, or G.M. tool no. J-29077.

11. Install the bleeder screw, tightening to 80–140 in. lbs. (9–16 Nm.). Do not overtighten.

12. Install the pads, install the caliper, and bleed the brakes.

Disc (Rotor)
REMOVAL AND INSTALLATION

1. Remove the caliper.
2. Remove the rotor.
3. Installation is the reverse.

INSPECTION

1. Check the rotor surface for wear or scoring. Deep scoring, grooves or rust pitting can be removed by refacing, a job to be referred to your local machine shop or garage. Minimum thickness is stamped on the rotor. If the rotor will be thinner than this after refinishing, it must be replaced.

2. Check the rotor parallelism; it must vary less than 0.0005 in. (0.013 mm) measured at four or more points around the circumference. Make all measurements at the same distance in from the edge of the rotor. Refinish the rotor if it fails to meet this specification.

3. Measure the disc runout with a dial indicator. If runout exceeds 0.005 in. (0.127 mm), and the wheel bearings are OK (if runout is being measured with the disc on the car), the rotor must be refaced or replaced as necessary.

REAR DRUM BRAKES

Brake Drums
REMOVAL AND INSTALLATION

1. Loosen the wheel lug nuts. Raise and support the car. Mark the relationship of the wheel to the axle and remove the wheel.

2. Mark the relationship of the drum to the axle and remove the drum. If it cannot be slipped off easily, check to see that the parking brake is fully released. If so, the brake shoes are probably locked against the drum. See the "Adjustment" section earlier in this chapter for details on how to back off the adjuster.

3. Installation is the reverse. Be sure to align the matchmarks made during removal. Lug nut torque is 102 ft. lbs. (140 Nm.).

INSPECTION

1. After removing the brake drum, wipe out the accumulated dust with a damp cloth.

WARNING: *Do not blow the brake dust out of the drums with compressed air or lung-power. Brake linings contain asbestos, a known cancer causing substance. Dispose of the cloth used to clean the parts after use.*

2. Inspect the drums for cracks, deep grooves, roughness, scoring, or out-of-roundness. Replace any drum which is cracked; do not try to weld it up.

3. Smooth any slight scores by polishing the friction surface with fine emery cloth. Heavy or extensive scoring will cause excessive lining wear and should be removed from the drum through resurfacing, a job to be referred to your local machine shop or garage. The maximum finished diameter of the drums is 7.894 in. (200.64 mm). The drum must be replaced if the diameter is 7.924 in. (201.40 mm) or greater.

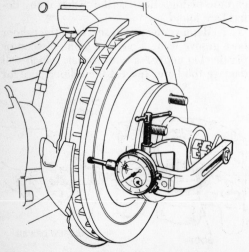

Check the rotor runout with a dial indicator

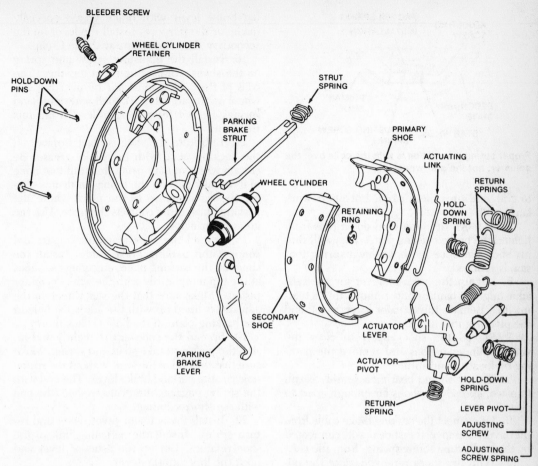

Exploded view of the drum brake

Brake Shoes

INSPECTION

After removing the brake drum, inspect the brake shoes. If the lining is worn down to within $1/32$ in. (0.76 mm) of a rivet, the shoes must be replaced.

NOTE: *This figure may disagree with your state's automobile inspection laws.*

If the brake lining is soaked with brake fluid or grease, it must be replaced. If this is the case, the brake drum should be sanded with crocus cloth to remove all traces of brake fluid, and the wheel cylinders should be rebuilt. Clean all grit from the friction surface of the drum before replacing it.

If the lining is chipped, cracked, or otherwise damaged, it must be replaced with a new lining.

NOTE: *Always replace the brake linings in sets of two on both ends of the axle. Never replace just one shoe, or both shoes on one side.*

Check the condition of the shoes, retracting springs, and hold-down springs for signs of ov-

erheating. If the shoes or springs have a slight blue color, this indicates overheating and replacement of the shoes and springs is recommended. The wheel cylinders should be rebuilt as a precaution against future problems.

REMOVAL AND INSTALLATION

1. Loosen the lug nuts on the wheel to be serviced, raise and support the car, and remove the wheel and brake drum.

NOTE: *It is not really necessary to remove the hub and wheel bearing assembly from the axle, but it does make the job easier. If you can work with the hub and bearing assembly in place, skip down to Step 3.*

2. Remove the four hub and bearing assembly retaining bolts and remove the assembly from the axle.

3. Remove the return springs from the shoes with a pair of needle nose pliers. There are also special brake spring pliers for this job.

4. Remove the hold down springs by gripping them with a pair of pliers, then pressing down and turning 90°. There are special tools

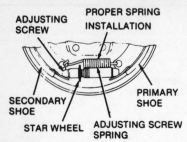

Proper spring installation is with the coils over the adjuster, not the star wheel

to grab and turn these parts, but pliers work fairly well.

5. Remove the shoe hold-down pins from behind the brake backing plate. They will simply slide out once the hold-down spring tension is relieved.

6. Lift up the actuator lever for the self-adjusting mechanism and remove the actuating link. Remove the actuator lever, pivot, and the pivot return spring.

7. Spread the shoes apart to clear the wheel cylinder pistons and remove the parking brake strut and spring.

8. If the hub and bearing assembly is still in place, spread the shoes far enough apart to clear it.

9. Disconnect the parking brake cable from the lever. Remove the shoes, still connected by their adjusting screw spring, from the car.

10. With the shoes removed, note the position of the adjusting spring and remove the spring and adjusting screw.

11. Remove the C-clip from the parking brake lever and remove the lever from the secondary shoe.

12. Use a damp cloth to remove all dirt and dust from the backing plate and brake parts. See the warning about brake dust in the drum removal procedure.

13. Check the wheel cylinders by carefully pulling the lower edges of the wheel cylinder boots away from the cylinders. If there is excessive leakage, the inside of the cylinder will be moist with fluid. If leakage exists, a wheel cylinder overhaul is in order. Do not delay, because brake failure could result.

NOTE: *A small amount of fluid will be present to act as a lubricant for the wheel cylinder pistons. Fluid spilling from the boot center hole, after the piston is removed, indicates cup leakage and the necessity for cylinder overhaul.*

14. Check the backing plate attaching bolts to make sure that they are tight. Use fine emery cloth to clean all rust and dirt from the shoe contact surfaces on the plate.

15. Lubricate the fulcrum end of the park-

ing brake lever with brake grease specially made for the purpose. Install the lever on the secondary shoe and secure with the C-clip.

16. Install the adjusting screw and spring on the shoes, connecting them together. The coils of the spring must *not* be over the star wheel on the adjuster. The left and right hand springs are *not* interchangeable. Do not mix them up.

17. Lubricate the shoe contact surfaces on the backing plate with the brake grease. Be certain when you are using this stuff that none of it actually gets on the linings or drums. Apply the same grease to the point where the parking brake cable contacts the plate. Use the grease sparingly.

18. Spread the shoe assemblies apart and connect the parking brake cable. Install the shoes on the backing plate, engaging the shoes at the top temporarily with the wheel cylinder pistons. Make sure that the star wheel on the adjuster is lined up with the adjusting hole in the backing plate, if the hole is back there.

19. Spread the shoes apart slightly and install the parking brake strut and spring. Make sure that the end of the strut without the spring engages the parking brake lever. The end with the spring engages the primary shoe (the one with the shorter lining).

20. Install the actuator pivot, lever and return spring. Install the actuating link in the shoe retainer. Lift up the actuator lever and hook the link into the lever.

21. Install the hold-down pins through the back of the plate, install the lever pivots and hold-down springs. Install the shoe return springs with a pair of pliers. Be very careful not to stretch or otherwise distort these springs.

22. Take a look at everything. Make sure the linings are in the right place, the self-adjusting mechanism is correctly installed, and the parking brake parts are all hooked up. If in doubt, remove the other wheel and take a look at that one for comparison.

23. Measure the width of the linings, then measure the inside width of the drum. Adjust the linings by means of the adjuster so that the drum will fit onto the linings.

24. Install the hub and bearing assembly onto the axle if removed. Tighten the retaining bolts to 35 ft. lbs. (55 Nm.).

25. Install the drum and wheel. Adjust the brakes using the procedure given earlier in this chapter. Be sure to install a rubber hole cover in the knock-out hole after the adjustment is complete. Adjust the parking brake.

26. Lower the car and check the pedal for any sponginess or lack of a "hard" feel. Check the braking action and the parking brake. The

brakes must not be applied severely immediately after installation. They should be used moderately for the first 200 miles of city driving or 100 miles of highway driving, to allow the linings to conform to the shape of the drum.

Wheel Cylinders
REMOVAL AND INSTALLATION

1. Loosen the wheel lug nuts, raise and support the car, and remove the wheel. Remove the drum and brake shoes. Leave the hub and wheel bearing assembly in place.

2. Remove any dirt from around the brake line fitting. Disconnect the brake line.

3. Remove the wheel cylinder retainer by using two awls or punches with a tip diameter of ⅛ in. or less. Insert the awls or punches into the access slots between the wheel cylinder pilot and retainer locking tabs. Bend both tabs away simultaneously. Remove the wheel cylinder from the backing plate.

4. To install, position the wheel cylinder against the backing plate and hold it in place with a wooden block between the wheel cylinder and the hub and bearing assembly.

5. Install a new retainer over the wheel cylinder abutment on the rear of the backing plate by pressing it into place with a 1⅛ in. 12-point socket and an extension.

6. Install a new bleeder screw into the wheel cylinder. Install the brake line and tighten to 10–15 ft. lbs. (13–20 Nm.).

7. The rest of installation is the reverse of removal. After the drum is installed, bleed the brakes using the procedure outlined earlier in this chapter.

OVERHAUL

As is the case with master cylinders, overhaul kits are available for the wheel cylinders. And, as is the case with master cylinders, it is usu-

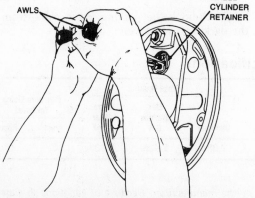

Remove the wheel cylinder retainer from the backing plate with a pair of awls or punches

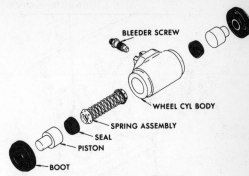

Exploded view of the wheel cylinder

ally more profitable to simply buy new or rebuilt wheel cylinders rather than rebuilding them. When rebuilding wheel cylinders, avoid getting any contaminants in the system. Always install new high-quality brake fluid; the use of improper fluid will swell and deteriorate the rubber parts.

1. Remove the wheel cylinders.

2. Remove the rubber boots from the cylinder ends. Discard the boots.

3. Remove and discard the pistons and cups.

4. Wash the cylinder and metal parts in denatured alcohol.

CAUTION: *Never use mineral-based solvents to clean the brake parts.*

5. Allow the parts to air dry and inspect the cylinder bore for corrosion or wear. Light corrosion can be cleaned up with crocus cloth; use finger pressure and rotate the cloth around the circumference of the bore. Do not move the cloth in and out. Any deep corrosion or pitting or wear warrants replacement of the parts.

6. Rinse the parts and allow to dry. Do not dry with a rag, which will leave bits of lint behind.

7. Lubricate the cylinder bore with clean brake fluid. Insert the spring assembly.

8. Install new cups. Do not lubricate prior to assembly.

9. Install the new pistons.

10. Press the new boots onto the cylinders by hand. Do not lubricate prior to assembly.

11. Install the wheel cylinders. Bleed the brakes after installation of the drum.

Vacuum Booster
REMOVAL AND INSTALLATION

1. Remove the master cylinder from the booster. It is not necessary to disconnect the lines from the master cylinder. Just move the cylinder aside.

2. Disconnect the vacuum booster pushrod

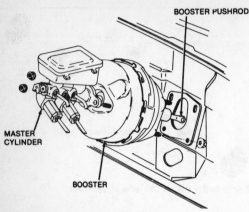

Vacuum booster mounting

from the brake pedal inside the car. It is retained by a bolt. A spring washer lives under the bolt head, and a flat washer goes on the other side of the pushrod eye, next to the pedal arm.

3. Remove the four attaching nuts from inside the car. Remove the booster.

4. Install the booster on the firewall. Tighten the mounting nuts to 22–33 ft. lbs. (30–45 Nm.).

5. Connect the pushrod to the brake pedal.

6. Install the master cylinder. Mounting torque is 25 ft. lbs. (40 Nm.).

OVERHAUL

This job is not difficult, but requires a number of special tools which are expensive, expecially if they're to be used only once. Generally, it's better to leave this job to your dealer, or buy a rebuilt vacuum booster and install it yourself.

PARKING BRAKE

ADJUSTMENT

1. Raise and support the car with both rear wheels off the ground.

2. Depress the parking brake pedal exactly two ratchet clicks.

3. Loosen the equalizer locknut, then tighten the adjusting nut until the left rear wheel can just be turned backward using two hands, but is locked in forward rotation.

4. Tighten the locknut.

5. Release the parking brake. Rotate the rear wheels—there should be no drag.

6. Lower the car.

Cable

REMOVAL AND INSTALLATION

Front Cable

1. Depress the parking brake pedal.

2. Clamp a pair of locking pliers on the upper cable where it enters the casing.

3. Pull the brake release, and remove the cable from the control assembly.

4. Release the locking tabs on the casing and remove the casing from the control assembly.

5. Push the grommet and the cable through the firewall into the engine compartment.

6. Remove the cable from its guide bracket on the firewall.

7. Remove the cable from the rear cable guide. Unhook the cable from the equalizer lever.

8. Installation is the reverse. Coat all areas in sliding contact with white waterproof grease. Adjust the parking brake after cable installation.

Right Rear Cable

1. Raise and support the car. Remove the wheel and the brake drum.

2. Insert a screwdriver between the brake shoe and the top part of the adjuster bracket. Push the bracket to the front and release the top adjuster bracket rod.

3. Remove the rear hold-down spring and remove the actuator lever and return spring.

4. Remove the adjuster screw spring.

5. Remove the top rear brake shoe return spring.

6. Unhook the parking brake cable from the parking brake lever.

Brake Specifications

Model	Lug Not Torque (ft./lb.)	Master Cylinder Bore	Brake Disc		Brake Drum			Minimum Lining Thickness	
			Minimum Thickness	Maximum Run-Out	Diameter	Max Machine O/S	Max Wear Limit	Front	Rear
All	103	0.874	0.965 ②	0.005	7.884	7.905	7.935	①	①

① Minimum lining thickness is to 1/32 of rivet
② 1981 and later: .830
NOTE: *Minimum lining thickness is as recommended by the manufacturer. Because of variations in state inspection regulations, the minimum allowable thickness may be different than recommended by the manufacturer.*

7. Pull the cable casing from the backing plate after the retaining legs have been released.

8. Remove the equalizer retaining bolt. Remove the nut attaching the cable to the pivot. Remove the cable casing from the cable guide bracket behind the equalizer by releasing the retaining legs.

9. Unhook the cable from the connector that attaches to the left cable.

10. Installation is the reverse. Apply white grease to all parts in sliding contact. Adjust the parking brake after installation.

Left Rear Cable

1. Perform Steps 1–7 of the right rear cable procedure.

2. Remove the cable casing from the rear axle.

3. Disconnect the cable at the connector at the center of the axle.

4. Installation is the reverse. Lubricate all parts in sliding contact with white waterproof grease, and adjust the parking brake after installation.

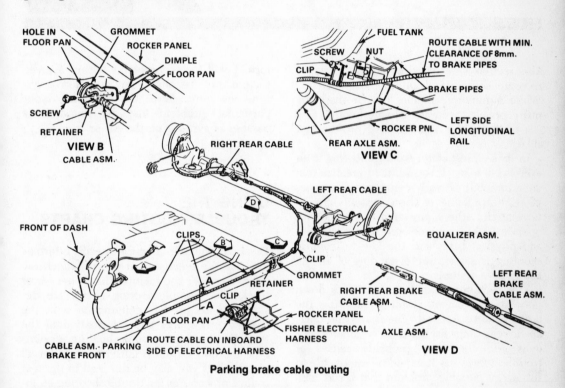

Parking brake cable routing

Troubleshooting

9

This section is designed to aid in the quick, accurate diagnosis of automotive problems. While automotive repairs can be made by many people, accurate troubleshooting is a rare skill for the amateur and professional alike.

In its simplest state, troubleshooting is an exercise in logic. It is essential to realize that an automobile is really composed of a series of systems. Some of these systems are interrelated; others are not. Automobiles operate within a framework of logical rules and physical laws, and the key to troubleshooting is a good understanding of all the automotive systems.

This section breaks the car or truck down into its component systems, allowing the problem to be isolated. The charts and diagnostic road maps list the most common problems and the most probable causes of trouble. Obviously it would be impossible to list every possible problem that could happen along with every possible cause, but it will locate MOST problems and eliminate a lot of unnecessary guesswork. The systematic format will locate problems within a given system, but, because many automotive systems are interrelated, the solution to your particular problem may be found in a number of systems on the car or truck.

USING THE TROUBLESHOOTING CHARTS

This book contains all of the specific information that the average do-it-yourself mechanic needs to repair and maintain his or her car or truck. The troubleshooting charts are designed to be used in conjunction with the specific procedures and information in the text. For instance, troubleshooting a point-type ignition system is fairly standard for all models, but you may be directed to the text to find procedures for troubleshooting an individual type of electronic ignition. You will also have to refer to the specification charts throughout the book for specifications applicable to your car or truck.

TOOLS AND EQUIPMENT

The tools illustrated in Chapter 1 (plus two more diagnostic pieces) will be adequate to troubleshoot most problems. The two other tools needed are a voltmeter and an ohmmeter. These can be purchased separately or in combination, known as a VOM meter.

In the event that other tools are required, they will be noted in the procedures.

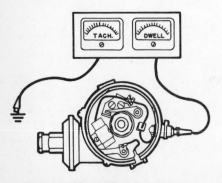

Tach-dwell hooked-up to distributor

Troubleshooting Engine Problems

See Chapters 2, 3, 4 for more information and service procedures.

Index to Systems

System	To Test	Group
Battery	Engine need not be running	1
Starting system	Engine need not be running	2
Primary electrical system	Engine need not be running	3
Secondary electrical system	Engine need not be running	4
Fuel system	Engine need not be running	5
Engine compression	Engine need not be running	6
Engine vacuum	Engine must be running	7
Secondary electrical system	Engine must be running	8
Valve train	Engine must be running	9
Exhaust system	Engine must be running	10
Cooling system	Engine must be running	11
Engine lubrication	Engine must be running	12

Index to Problems

Problem: Symptom	Begin at Specific Diagnosis, Number ___
Engine Won't Start:	
Starter doesn't turn	1.1, 2.1
Starter turns, engine doesn't	2.1
Starter turns engine very slowly	1.1, 2.4
Starter turns engine normally	3.1, 4.1
Starter turns engine very quickly	6.1
Engine fires intermittently	4.1
Engine fires consistently	5.1, 6.1
Engine Runs Poorly:	
Hard starting	3.1, 4.1, 5.1, 8.1
Rough idle	4.1, 5.1, 8.1
Stalling	3.1, 4.1, 5.1, 8.1
Engine dies at high speeds	4.1, 5.1
Hesitation (on acceleration from standing stop)	5.1, 8.1
Poor pickup	4.1, 5.1, 8.1
Lack of power	3.1, 4.1, 5.1, 8.1
Backfire through the carburetor	4.1, 8.1, 9.1
Backfire through the exhaust	4.1, 8.1, 9.1
Blue exhaust gases	6.1, 7.1
Black exhaust gases	5.1
Running on (after the ignition is shut off)	3.1, 8.1
Susceptible to moisture	4.1
Engine misfires under load	4.1, 7.1, 8.4, 9.1
Engine misfires at speed	4.1, 8.4
Engine misfires at idle	3.1, 4.1, 5.1, 7.1, 8.4

Sample Section

Test and Procedure	Results and Indications	Proceed to
4.1—Check for spark: Hold each spark plug wire approximately ¼″ from ground with gloves or a heavy, dry rag. Crank the engine and observe the spark.	If no spark is evident:	4.2
	If spark is good in some cases:	4.3
	If spark is good in all cases:	4.6

Specific Diagnosis

This section is arranged so that following each test, instructions are given to proceed to another, until a problem is diagnosed.

Section 1—Battery

Test and Procedure	Results and Indications	Proceed to
1.1—Inspect the battery visually for case condition (corrosion, cracks) and water level.	If case is cracked, replace battery:	**1.4**
	If the case is intact, remove corrosion with a solution of baking soda and water (**CAUTION**: *do not get the solution into the battery*), and fill with water:	**1.2**

DIRT ON TOP OF BATTERY

CORROSION

PLUGGED VENT

LOOSE CABLE OR POSTS

CRACKS

LOW WATER LEVEL

Inspect the battery case

1.2—Check the battery cable connections: Insert a screwdriver between the battery post and the cable clamp. Turn the headlights on high beam, and observe them as the screwdriver is gently twisted to ensure good metal to metal contact.	If the lights brighten, remove and clean the clamp and post; coat the post with petroleum jelly, install and tighten the clamp:	**1.4**
	If no improvement is noted:	**1.3**

TESTING BATTERY CABLE CONNECTIONS USING A SCREWDRIVER

1.3—Test the state of charge of the battery using an individual cell tester or hydrometer.	If indicated, charge the battery. **NOTE:** *If no obvious reason exists for the low state of charge (i.e., battery age, prolonged storage), proceed to:*	**1.4**

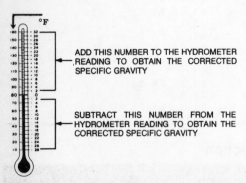

°F

ADD THIS NUMBER TO THE HYDROMETER READING TO OBTAIN THE CORRECTED SPECIFIC GRAVITY

SUBTRACT THIS NUMBER FROM THE HYDROMETER READING TO OBTAIN THE CORRECTED SPECIFIC GRAVITY

Specific Gravity (@ 80° F.)

Minimum	Battery Charge
1.260	100% Charged
1.230	75% Charged
1.200	50% Charged
1.170	25% Charged
1.140	Very Little Power Left
1.110	Completely Discharged

The effects of temperature on battery specific gravity (left) and amount of battery charge in relation to specific gravity (right)

1.4—Visually inspect battery cables for cracking, bad connection to ground, or bad connection to starter.	If necessary, tighten connections or replace the cables:	**2.1**

Section 2—Starting System

See Chapter 3 for service procedures

Test and Procedure	Results and Indications	Proceed to
Note: Tests in Group 2 are performed with coil high tension lead disconnected to prevent accidental starting.		
2.1—Test the starter motor and solenoid: Connect a jumper from the battery post of the solenoid (or relay) to the starter post of the solenoid (or relay).	If starter turns the engine normally:	2.2
	If the starter buzzes, or turns the engine very slowly:	2.4
	If no response, replace the solenoid (or relay).	3.1
	If the starter turns, but the engine doesn't, ensure that the flywheel ring gear is intact. If the gear is undamaged, replace the starter drive.	3.1
2.2—Determine whether ignition override switches are functioning properly (clutch start switch, neutral safety switch), by connecting a jumper across the switch(es), and turning the ignition switch to "start".	If starter operates, adjust or replace switch:	3.1
	If the starter doesn't operate:	2.3
2.3—Check the ignition switch "start" position: Connect a 12V test lamp or voltmeter between the starter post of the solenoid (or relay) and ground. Turn the ignition switch to the "start" position, and jiggle the key.	If the lamp doesn't light or the meter needle doesn't move when the switch is turned, check the ignition switch for loose connections, cracked insulation, or broken wires. Repair or replace as necessary:	3.1
	If the lamp flickers or needle moves when the key is jiggled, replace the ignition switch.	3.3

Checking the ignition switch "start" position

STARTER RELAY (IF EQUIPPED)

Test and Procedure	Results and Indications	Proceed to
2.4—Remove and bench test the starter, according to specifications in the engine electrical section.	If the starter does not meet specifications, repair or replace as needed:	3.1
	If the starter is operating properly:	2.5
2.5—Determine whether the engine can turn freely: Remove the spark plugs, and check for water in the cylinders. Check for water on the dipstick, or oil in the radiator. Attempt to turn the engine using an 18″ flex drive and socket on the crankshaft pulley nut or bolt.	If the engine will turn freely only with the spark plugs out, and hydrostatic lock (water in the cylinders) is ruled out, check valve timing:	9.2
	If engine will not turn freely, and it is known that the clutch and transmission are free, the engine must be disassembled for further evaluation:	Chapter 3

Section 3—Primary Electrical System

Test and Procedure	Results and Indications	Proceed to
3.1—Check the ignition switch "on" position: Connect a jumper wire between the distributor side of the coil and ground, and a 12V test lamp between the switch side of the coil and ground. Remove the high tension lead from the coil. Turn the ignition switch on and jiggle the key.	If the lamp lights:	**3.2**
	If the lamp flickers when the key is jiggled, replace the ignition switch:	**3.3**
	If the lamp doesn't light, check for loose or open connections. If none are found, remove the ignition switch and check for continuity. If the switch is faulty, replace it:	**3.3**

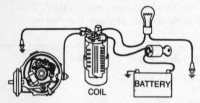

Checking the ignition switch "on" position

3.2—Check the ballast resistor or resistance wire for an open circuit, using an ohmmeter. See Chapter 3 for specific tests.	Replace the resistor or resistance wire if the resistance is zero. **NOTE:** *Some ignition systems have no ballast resistor.*	**3.3**

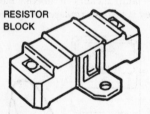

Two types of resistors

3.3—On point-type ignition systems, visually inspect the breaker points for burning, pitting or excessive wear. Gray coloring of the point contact surfaces is normal. Rotate the crankshaft until the contact heel rests on a high point of the distributor cam and adjust the point gap to specifications. On electronic ignition models, remove the distributor cap and visually inspect the armature. Ensure that the armature pin is in place, and that the armature is on tight and rotates when the engine is cranked. Make sure there are no cracks, chips or rounded edges on the armature.	If the breaker points are intact, clean the contact surfaces with fine emery cloth, and adjust the point gap to specifications. If the points are worn, replace them. On electronic systems, replace any parts which appear defective. If condition persists:	**3.4**

Test and Procedure	Results and Indications	Proceed to
3.4—On point-type ignition systems, connect a dwell-meter between the distributor primary lead and ground. Crank the engine and observe the point dwell angle. On electronic ignition systems, conduct a stator (magnetic pickup assembly) test. See Chapter 3.	On point-type systems, adjust the dwell angle if necessary. **NOTE:** *Increasing the point gap decreases the dwell angle and vice-versa.*	**3.6**
	If the dwell meter shows little or no reading;	**3.5**
	On electronic ignition systems, if the stator is bad, replace the stator. If the stator is good, proceed to the other tests in Chapter 3.	

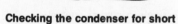

Dwell is a function of point gap

3.5—On the point-type ignition systems, check the condenser for short: connect an ohmmeter across the condenser body and the pigtail lead.	If any reading other than infinite is noted, replace the condenser	**3.6**

Checking the condenser for short

3.6—Test the coil primary resistance: On point-type ignition systems, connect an ohmmeter across the coil primary terminals, and read the resistance on the low scale. Note whether an external ballast resistor or resistance wire is used. On electronic ignition systems, test the coil primary resistance as in Chapter 3.	Point-type ignition coils utilizing ballast resistors or resistance wires should have approximately 1.0 ohms resistance. Coils with internal resistors should have approximately 4.0 ohms resistance. If values far from the above are noted, replace the coil.	**4.1**

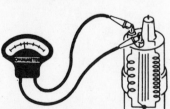

Check the coil primary resistance

Section 4—Secondary Electrical System
See Chapters 2–3 for service procedures

Test and Procedure	Results and Indications	Proceed to
4.1—Check for spark: Hold each spark plug wire approximately ¼″ from ground with gloves or a heavy, dry rag. Crank the engine, and observe the spark.	If no spark is evident:	**4.2**
	If spark is good in some cylinders:	**4.3**
	If spark is good in all cylinders:	**4.6**

Check for spark at the plugs

4.2—Check for spark at the coil high tension lead: Remove the coil high tension lead from the distributor and position it approximately ¼″ from ground. Crank the engine and observe spark. **CAUTION: This test should not be performed on engines equipped with electronic ignition.**	If the spark is good and consistent:	**4.3**
	If the spark is good but intermittent, test the primary electrical system starting at 3.3:	**3.3**
	If the spark is weak or non-existent, replace the coil high tension lead, clean and tighten all connections and retest. If no improvement is noted:	**4.4**
4.3—Visually inspect the distributor cap and rotor for burned or corroded contacts, cracks, carbon tracks, or moisture. Also check the fit of the rotor on the distributor shaft (where applicable).	If moisture is present, dry thoroughly, and retest per 4.1:	**4.1**
	If burned or excessively corroded contacts, cracks, or carbon tracks are noted, replace the defective part(s) and retest per 4.1:	**4.1**
	If the rotor and cap appear intact, or are only slightly corroded, clean the contacts thoroughly (including the cap towers and spark plug wire ends) and retest per 4.1: If the spark is good in all cases:	**4.6**
	If the spark is poor in all cases:	**4.5**

Inspect the distributor cap and rotor

Test and Procedure	Results and Indications	Proceed to
4.4—Check the coil secondary resistance: On point-type systems connect an ohmmeter across the distributor side of the coil and the coil tower. Read the resistance on the high scale of the ohmmeter. On electronic ignition systems, see Chapter 3 for specific tests.	The resistance of a satisfactory coil should be between 4,000 and 10,000 ohms. If resistance is considerably higher (i.e., 40,000 ohms) replace the coil and retest per 4.1. **NOTE:** *This does not apply to high performance coils.*	

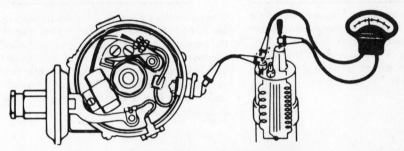

Testing the coil secondary resistance

4.5—Visually inspect the spark plug wires for cracking or brittleness. Ensure that no two wires are positioned so as to cause induction firing (adjacent and parallel). Remove each wire, one by one, and check resistance with an ohmmeter.	Replace any cracked or brittle wires. If any of the wires are defective, replace the entire set. Replace any wires with excessive resistance (over 8000 Ω per foot for suppression wire), and separate any wires that might cause induction firing.	**4.6**

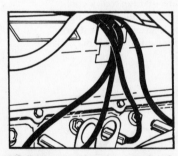

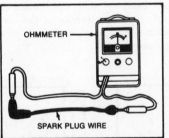

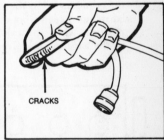

Misfiring can be the result of spark plug leads to adjacent, consecutively firing cylinders running parallel and too close together	**On point-type ignition systems, check the spark plug wires as shown. On electronic ignitions, do not remove the wire from the distributor cap terminal; instead, test through the cap**	**Spark plug wires can be checked visually by bending them in a loop over your finger. This will reveal any cracks, burned or broken insulation. Any wire with cracked insulation should be replaced**

4.6—Remove the spark plugs, noting the cylinders from which they were removed, and evaluate according to the color photos in the middle of this book.	See following.	**See following.**

Test and Procedure	Results and Indications	Proceed to
4.7—Examine the location of all the plugs.	The following diagrams illustrate some of the conditions that the location of plugs will reveal.	4.8

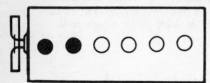

Two adjacent plugs are fouled in a 6-cylinder engine, 4-cylinder engine or either bank of a V-8. This is probably due to a blown head gasket between the two cylinders

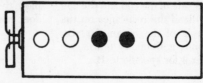

The two center plugs in a 6-cylinder engine are fouled. Raw fuel may be "boiled" out of the carburetor into the intake manifold after the engine is shut-off. Stop-start driving can also foul the center plugs, due to overly rich mixture. Proper float level, a new float needle and seat or use of an insulating spacer may help this problem

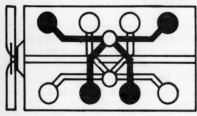

An unbalanced carburetor is indicated. Following the fuel flow on this particular design shows that the cylinders fed by the right-hand barrel are fouled from overly rich mixture, while the cylinders fed by the left-hand barrel are normal

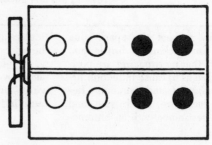

If the four rear plugs are overheated, a cooling system problem is suggested. A thorough cleaning of the cooling system may restore coolant circulation and cure the problem

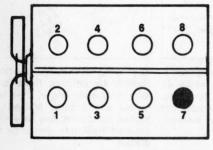

Finding one plug overheated may indicate an intake manifold leak near the affected cylinder. If the overheated plug is the second of two adjacent, consecutively firing plugs, it could be the result of ignition cross-firing. Separating the leads to these two plugs will eliminate cross-fire

Occasionally, the two rear plugs in large, lightly used V-8's will become oil fouled. High oil consumption and smoky exhaust may also be noticed. It is probably due to plugged oil drain holes in the rear of the cylinder head, causing oil to be sucked in around the valve stems. This usually occurs in the rear cylinders first, because the engine slants that way

Test and Procedure	Results and Indications	Proceed to
4.8—Determine the static ignition timing. Using the crankshaft pulley timing marks as a guide, locate top dead center on the compression stroke of the number one cylinder.	The rotor should be pointing toward the No. 1 tower in the distributor cap, and, on electronic ignitions, the armature spoke for that cylinder should be lined up with the stator.	**4.8**
4.9—Check coil polarity: Connect a voltmeter negative lead to the coil high tension lead, and the positive lead to ground (**NOTE:** *Reverse the hook-up for positive ground systems*). Crank the engine momentarily. **Checking coil polarity**	If the voltmeter reads up-scale, the polarity is correct: If the voltmeter reads down-scale, reverse the coil polarity (switch the primary leads):	**5.1** **5.1**

Section 5—Fuel System
See Chapter 4 for service procedures

Test and Procedure	Results and Indications	Proceed to
5.1—Determine that the air filter is functioning efficiently: Hold paper elements up to a strong light, and attempt to see light through the filter.	Clean permanent air filters in solvent (or manufacturer's recommendation), and allow to dry. Replace paper elements through which light cannot be seen:	**5.2**
5.2—Determine whether a flooding condition exists: Flooding is identified by a strong gasoline odor, and excessive gasoline present in the throttle bore(s) of the carburetor. **If the engine floods repeatedly, check the choke butterfly flap**	If flooding is not evident: If flooding is evident, permit the gasoline to dry for a few moments and restart. If flooding doesn't recur: If flooding is persistent:	**5.3** **5.7** **5.5**
5.3—Check that fuel is reaching the carburetor: Detach the fuel line at the carburetor inlet. Hold the end of the line in a cup (not styrofoam), and crank the engine. **Check the fuel pump by disconnecting the output line (fuel pump-to-carburetor) at the carburetor and operating the starter briefly**	If fuel flows smoothly: If fuel doesn't flow (**NOTE:** *Make sure that there is fuel in the tank*), or flows erratically:	**5.7** **5.4**

Test and Procedure	Results and Indications	Proceed to
5.4—Test the fuel pump: Disconnect all fuel lines from the fuel pump. Hold a finger over the input fitting, crank the engine (with electric pump, turn the ignition or pump on); and feel for suction.	If suction is evident, blow out the fuel line to the tank with low pressure compressed air until bubbling is heard from the fuel filler neck. Also blow out the carburetor fuel line (both ends disconnected):	5.7
	If no suction is evident, replace or repair the fuel pump: NOTE: *Repeated oil fouling of the spark plugs, or a no-start condition, could be the result of a ruptured vacuum booster pump diaphragm, through which oil or gasoline is being drawn into the intake manifold (where applicable).*	5.7
5.5—Occasionally, small specks of dirt will clog the small jets and orifices in the carburetor. With the engine cold, hold a flat piece of wood or similar material over the carburetor, where possible, and crank the engine.	If the engine starts, but runs roughly the engine is probably not run enough. If the engine won't start:	5.9
5.6—Check the needle and seat: Tap the carburetor in the area of the needle and seat.	If flooding stops, a gasoline additive (e.g., Gumout) will often cure the problem:	5.7
	If flooding continues, check the fuel pump for excessive pressure at the carburetor (according to specifications). If the pressure is normal, the needle and seat must be removed and checked, and/or the float level adjusted:	5.7
5.7—Test the accelerator pump by looking into the throttle bores while operating the throttle.	If the accelerator pump appears to be operating normally:	5.8
	If the accelerator pump is not operating, the pump must be reconditioned. Where possible, service the pump with the carburetor(s) installed on the engine. If necessary, remove the carburetor. Prior to removal:	5.8

Check for gas at the carburetor by looking down the carburetor throat while someone moves the accelerator

Test and Procedure	Results and Indications	Proceed to
5.8—Determine whether the carburetor main fuel system is functioning: Spray a commercial starting fluid into the carburetor while attempting to start the engine.	If the engine starts, runs for a few seconds, and dies:	5.9
	If the engine doesn't start:	6.1

Test and Procedure	Results and Indications	Proceed to
5.9—Uncommon fuel system malfunctions: See below:	If the problem is solved: If the problem remains, remove and recondition the carburetor.	6.1

Condition	Indication	Test	Prevailing Weather Conditions	Remedy
Vapor lock	Engine will not restart shortly after running.	Cool the components of the fuel system until the engine starts. Vapor lock can be cured faster by draping a wet cloth over a mechanical fuel pump.	Hot to very hot	Ensure that the exhaust manifold heat control valve is operating. Check with the vehicle manufacturer for the recommended solution to vapor lock on the model in question.
Carburetor icing	Engine will not idle, stalls at low speeds.	Visually inspect the throttle plate area of the throttle bores for frost.	High humidity, 32–40° F.	Ensure that the exhaust manifold heat control valve is operating, and that the intake manifold heat riser is not blocked.
Water in the fuel	Engine sputters and stalls; may not start.	Pump a small amount of fuel into a glass jar. Allow to stand, and inspect for droplets or a layer of water.	High humidity, extreme temperature changes.	For droplets, use one or two cans of commercial gas line anti-freeze. For a layer of water, the tank must be drained, and the fuel lines blown out with compressed air.

Section 6—Engine Compression
See Chapter 3 for service procedures

Test and Procedure	Results and Indications	Proceed to
6.1—Test engine compression: Remove all spark plugs. Block the throttle wide open. Insert a compression gauge into a spark plug port, crank the engine to obtain the maximum reading, and record.	If compression is within limits on all cylinders: If gauge reading is extremely low on all cylinders: If gauge reading is low on one or two cylinders: (If gauge readings are identical and low on two or more adjacent cylinders, the head gasket must be replaced.)	7.1 6.2 6.2

Checking compression

Test and Procedure	Results and Indications	Proceed to
6.2—Test engine compression (wet): Squirt approximately 30 cc. of engine oil into each cylinder, and retest per 6.1.	If the readings improve, worn or cracked rings or broken pistons are indicated: If the readings do not improve, burned or excessively carboned valves or a jumped timing chain are indicated: NOTE: *A jumped timing chain is often indicated by difficult cranking.*	See Chapter 3 7.1

Section 7—Engine Vacuum
See Chapter 3 for service procedures

Test and Procedure	Results and Indications	Proceed to
7.1—Attach a vacuum gauge to the intake manifold beyond the throttle plate. Start the engine, and observe the action of the needle over the range of engine speeds.	See below.	See below

INDICATION: normal engine in good condition

Proceed to: 8.1

Normal engine
Gauge reading: steady, from 17–22 in./Hg.

INDICATION: sticking valves or ignition miss

Proceed to: 9.1, 8.3

Sticking valves
Gauge reading: intermittent fluctuation at idle

INDICATION: late ignition or valve timing, low compression, stuck throttle valve, leaking carburetor or manifold gasket

Proceed to: 6.1

Incorrect valve timing
Gauge reading: low (10–15 in./Hg) but steady

INDICATION: improper carburetor adjustment or minor intake leak.

Proceed to: 7.2

Carburetor requires adjustment
Gauge reading: drifting needle

INDICATION: ignition miss, blown cylinder head gasket, leaking valve or weak valve spring

Proceed to: 8.3, 6.1

Blown head gasket
Gauge reading: needle fluctuates as engine speed increases

INDICATION: burnt valve or faulty valve clearance. Needle will fall when defective valve operates

Proceed to: 9.1

Burnt or leaking valves
Gauge reading: steady needle, but drops regularly

INDICATION: choked muffler, excessive back pressure in system

Proceed to: 10.1

Clogged exhaust system
Gauge reading: gradual drop in reading at idle

INDICATION: worn valve guides

Proceed to: 9.1

Worn valve guides
Gauge reading: needle vibrates excessively at idle, but steadies as engine speed increases

White pointer = steady gauge hand   Black pointer = fluctuating gauge hand

Test and Procedure	Results and Indications	Proceed to
7.2—Attach a vacuum gauge per 7.1, and test for an intake manifold leak. Squirt a small amount of oil around the intake manifold gaskets, carburetor gaskets, plugs and fittings. Observe the action of the vacuum gauge.	If the reading improves, replace the indicated gasket, or seal the indicated fitting or plug:	**8.1**
	If the reading remains low:	**7.3**
7.3—Test all vacuum hoses and accessories for leaks as described in 7.2. Also check the carburetor body (dashpots, automatic choke mechanism, throttle shafts) for leaks in the same manner.	If the reading improves, service or replace the offending part(s):	**8.1**
	If the reading remains low:	**6.1**

Section 8—Secondary Electrical System
See Chapter 2 for service procedures

Test and Procedure	Results and Indications	Proceed to
8.1—Remove the distributor cap and check to make sure that the rotor turns when the engine is cranked. Visually inspect the distributor components.	Clean, tighten or replace any components which appear defective.	**8.2**
8.2—Connect a timing light (per manufacturer's recommendation) and check the dynamic ignition timing. Disconnect and plug the vacuum hose(s) to the distributor if specified, start the engine, and observe the timing marks at the specified engine speed.	If the timing is not correct, adjust to specifications by rotating the distributor in the engine: (Advance timing by rotating distributor opposite normal direction of rotor rotation, retard timing by rotating distributor in same direction as rotor rotation.)	**8.3**
8.3—Check the operation of the distributor advance mechanism(s): To test the mechanical advance, disconnect the vacuum lines from the distributor advance unit and observe the timing marks with a timing light as the engine speed is increased from idle. If the mark moves smoothly, without hesitation, it may be assumed that the mechanical advance is functioning properly. To test vacuum advance and/or retard systems, alternately crimp and release the vacuum line, and observe the timing mark for movement. If movement is noted, the system is operating.	If the systems are functioning:	**8.4**
	If the systems are not functioning, remove the distributor, and test on a distributor tester:	**8.4**
8.4—Locate an ignition miss: With the engine running, remove each spark plug wire, one at a time, until one is found that doesn't cause the engine to roughen and slow down.	When the missing cylinder is identified:	**4.1**

Section 9—Valve Train
See Chapter 3 for service procedures

Test and Procedure	Results and Indications	Proceed to
9.1—Evaluate the valve train: Remove the valve cover, and ensure that the valves are adjusted to specifications. A mechanic's stethoscope may be used to aid in the diagnosis of the valve train. By pushing the probe on or near push rods or rockers, valve noise often can be isolated. A timing light also may be used to diagnose valve problems. Connect the light according to manufacturer's recommendations, and start the engine. Vary the firing moment of the light by increasing the engine speed (and therefore the ignition advance), and moving the trigger from cylinder to cylinder. Observe the movement of each valve.	Sticking valves or erratic valve train motion can be observed with the timing light. The cylinder head must be disassembled for repairs.	**See Chapter 3**
9.2—Check the valve timing: Locate top dead center of the No. 1 piston, and install a degree wheel or tape on the crankshaft pulley or damper with zero corresponding to an index mark on the engine. Rotate the crankshaft in its direction of rotation, and observe the opening of the No. 1 cylinder intake valve. The opening should correspond with the correct mark on the degree wheel according to specifications.	If the timing is not correct, the timing cover must be removed for further investigation.	**See Chapter 3**

Section 10—Exhaust System

Test and Procedure	Results and Indications	Proceed to
10.1—Determine whether the exhaust manifold heat control valve is operating: Operate the valve by hand to determine whether it is free to move. If the valve is free, run the engine to operating temperature and observe the action of the valve, to ensure that it is opening.	If the valve sticks, spray it with a suitable solvent, open and close the valve to free it, and retest. If the valve functions properly: If the valve does not free, or does not operate, replace the valve:	10.2 10.2
10.2—Ensure that there are no exhaust restrictions: Visually inspect the exhaust system for kinks, dents, or crushing. Also note that gases are flowing freely from the tailpipe at all engine speeds, indicating no restriction in the muffler or resonator.	Replace any damaged portion of the system:	11.1

CHILTON'S
AUTO BODY
REPAIR TIPS

Tools and Materials • Step-by-Step Illustrated Procedures
How To Repair Dents, Scratches and Rust Holes
Spray Painting and Refinishing Tips

With a little practice, basic body repair procedures can be mastered by any do-it-yourself mechanic. The step-by-step repairs shown here can be applied to almost any type of auto body repair.

TOOLS & MATERIALS

You may already have basic tools, such as hammers and electric drills. Other tools unique to body repair — body hammers, grinding attachments, sanding blocks, dent puller, half-round plastic file and plastic spreaders — are relatively inexpensive and can be obtained wherever auto parts or auto body repair parts are sold. Portable air compressors and paint spray guns can be purchased or rented.

Auto Body Repair Kits

The best and most often used products are available to the do-it-yourselfer in kit form, from major manufacturers of auto body repair products. The same manufacturers also merchandise the individual products for use by pros.

Kits are available to make a wide variety of repairs, including holes, dents and scratches and fiberglass, and offer the advantage of buying the materials you'll need for the job. There is little waste or chance of materials going bad from not being used. Many kits may also contain basic body-working tools such as body files, sanding blocks and spreaders. Check the contents of the kit before buying your tools.

BODY REPAIR TIPS

Safety

Many of the products associated with auto body repair and refinishing contain toxic chemicals. Read all labels before opening containers and store them in a safe place and manner.

• Wear eye protection (safety goggles) when using power tools or when performing any operation that involves the removal of any type of material.

• Wear lung protection (disposable mask or respirator) when grinding, sanding or painting.

Sanding

1 Sand off paint before using a dent puller. When using a non-adhesive sanding disc, cover the back of the disc with an overlapping layer or two of masking tape and trim the edges. The disc will last considerably longer.

2 Use the circular motion of the sanding disc to grind *into* the edge of the repair. Grinding or sanding away from the jagged edge will only tear the sandpaper.

3 Use the palm of your hand flat on the panel to detect high and low spots. Do not use your fingertips. Slide your hand slowly back and forth.

WORKING WITH BODY FILLER

Mixing The Filler

Cleanliness and proper mixing and application are extremely important. Use a clean piece of plastic or glass or a disposable artist's palette to mix body filler.

1 Allow plenty of time and follow directions. No useful purpose will be served by adding more hardener to make it cure (set-up) faster. Less hardener means more curing time, but the mixture dries harder; more hardener means less curing time but a softer mixture.

2 Both the hardener and the filler should be thoroughly kneaded or stirred before mixing. Hardener should be a solid paste and dispense like thin toothpaste. Body filler should be smooth, and free of lumps or thick spots.

Getting the proper amount of hardener in the filler is the trickiest part of preparing the filler. Use the same amount of hardener in cold or warm weather. For contour filler (thick coats), a bead of hardener twice the diameter of the filler is about right. There's about a 15% margin on either side, but, if in doubt use less hardener.

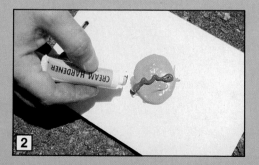

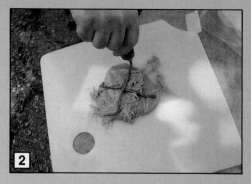

3 Mix the body filler and hardener by wiping across the mixing surface, picking the mixture up and wiping it again. Colder weather requires longer mixing times. Do not mix in a circular motion; this will trap air bubbles which will become holes in the cured filler.

Applying The Filler

1 For best results, filler should not be applied over ¼" thick.

Apply the filler in several coats. Build it up to above the level of the repair surface so that it can be sanded or grated down.

The first coat of filler must be pressed on with a firm wiping motion.

Apply the filler in one direction only. Working the filler back and forth will either pull it off the metal or trap air bubbles.

REPAIRING DENTS

Before you start, take a few minutes to study the damaged area. Try to visualize the shape of the panel before it was damaged. If the damage is on the left fender, look at the right fender and use it as a guide. If there is access to the panel from behind, you can reshape it with a body hammer. If not, you'll have to use a dent puller. Go slowly and work the metal a little at a time. Get the panel as straight as possible before applying filler.

1 This dent is typical of one that can be pulled out or hammered out from behind. Remove the headlight cover, headlight assembly and turn signal housing.

2 Drill a series of holes ½ the size of the end of the dent puller along the stress line. Make some trial pulls and assess the results. If necessary, drill more holes and try again. Do not hurry.

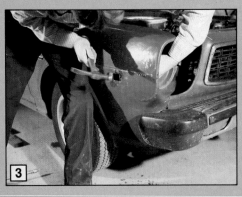

3 If possible, use a body hammer and block to shape the metal back to its original contours. Get the metal back as close to its original shape as possible. Don't depend on body filler to fill dents.

4 Using an 80-grit grinding disc on an electric drill, grind the paint from the surrounding area down to bare metal. Use a new grinding pad to prevent heat buildup that will warp metal.

5 The area should look like this when you're finished grinding. Knock the drill holes in and tape over small openings to keep plastic filler out.

6 Mix the body filler (see Body Repair Tips). Spread the body filler evenly over the entire area (see Body Repair Tips). Be sure to cover the area completely.

7 Let the body filler dry until the surface can just be scratched with your fingernail. Knock the high spots from the body filler with a body file ("Cheese-grater"). Check frequently with the palm of your hand for high and low spots.

8 Check to be sure that trim pieces that will be installed later will fit exactly. Sand the area with 40-grit paper.

9 If you wind up with low spots, you may have to apply another layer of filler.

10 Knock the high spots off with 40-grit paper. When you are satisfied with the contours of the repair, apply a thin coat of filler to cover pin holes and scratches.

11 Block sand the area with 40-grit paper to a smooth finish. Pay particular attention to body lines and ridges that must be well-defined.

12 Sand the area with 400 paper and then finish with a scuff pad. The finished repair is ready for priming and painting (see Painting Tips).

Materials and photos courtesy of Ritt Jones Auto Body, Prospect Park, PA.

REPAIRING RUST HOLES

There are many ways to repair rust holes. The fiberglass cloth kit shown here is one of the most cost efficient for the owner because it provides a strong repair that resists cracking and moisture and is relatively easy to use. It can be used on large and small holes (with or without backing) and can be applied over contoured areas. Remember, however, that short of replacing an entire panel, no repair is a guarantee that the rust will not return.

1 Remove any trim that will be in the way. Clean away all loose debris. Cut away all the rusted metal. But be sure to leave enough metal to retain the contour or body shape.

2 Grind away all traces of rust with a 24-grit grinding disc. Be sure to grind back 3-4 inches from the edge of the hole down to bare metal and be sure all traces of paint, primer and rust are removed.

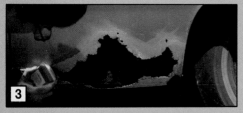

3 Block sand the area with 80 or 100 grit sandpaper to get a clear, shiny surface and feathered paint edge. Tap the edges of the hole inward with a ball peen hammer.

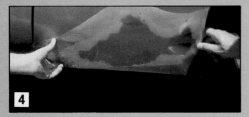

4 If you are going to use release film, cut a piece about 2-3″ larger than the area you have sanded. Place the film over the repair and mark the sanded area on the film. Avoid any unnecessary wrinkling of the film.

5 Cut 2 pieces of fiberglass matte to match the shape of the repair. One piece should be about 1″ smaller than the sanded area and the second piece should be 1″ smaller than the first. Mix enough filler and hardener to saturate the fiberglass material (see Body Repair Tips).

6 Lay the release sheet on a flat surface and spread an even layer of filler, large enough to cover the repair. Lay the smaller piece of fiberglass cloth in the center of the sheet and spread another layer of filler over the fiberglass cloth. Repeat the operation for the larger piece of cloth.

7 Place the repair material over the repair area, with the release film facing outward. Use a spreader and work from the center outward to smooth the material, following the body contours. Be sure to remove all air bubbles.

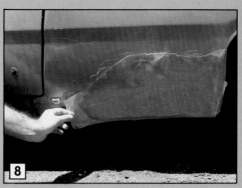

8 Wait until the repair has dried tack-free and peel off the release sheet. The ideal working temperature is 60°-90° F. Cooler or warmer temperatures or high humidity may require additional curing time. Wait longer, if in doubt.

9 Sand and feather-edge the entire area. The initial sanding can be done with a sanding disc on an electric drill if care is used. Finish the sanding with a block sander. Low spots can be filled with body filler; this may require several applications.

10 When the filler can just be scratched with a fingernail, knock the high spots down with a body file and smooth the entire area with 80-grit. Feather the filled areas into the surrounding areas.

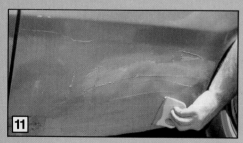

11 When the area is sanded smooth, mix some topcoat and hardener and apply it directly with a spreader. This will give a smooth finish and prevent the glass matte from showing through the paint.

12 Block sand the topcoat smooth with finishing sandpaper (200 grit), and 400 grit. The repair is ready for masking, priming and painting (see Painting Tips).

Materials and photos courtesy Marson Corporation, Chelsea, Massachusetts

PAINTING TIPS

Preparation

1 SANDING — Use a 400 or 600 grit wet or dry sandpaper. Wet-sand the area with a ¼ sheet of sandpaper soaked in clean water. Keep the paper wet while sanding. Sand the area until the repaired area tapers into the original finish.

2 CLEANING — Wash the area to be painted thoroughly with water and a clean rag. Rinse it thoroughly and wipe the surface dry until you're sure it's completely free of dirt, dust, fingerprints, wax, detergent or other foreign matter.

3 MASKING — Protect any areas you don't want to overspray by covering them with masking tape and newspaper. Be careful not get fingerprints on the area to be painted.

4 PRIMING — All exposed metal should be primed before painting. Primer protects the metal and provides an excellent surface for paint adhesion. When the primer is dry, wet-sand the area again with 600 grit wet-sandpaper. Clean the area again after sanding.

Painting Techniques

P aint applied from either a spray gun or a spray can (for small areas) will provide good results. Experiment on an old piece of metal to get the right combination before you begin painting.

SPRAYING VISCOSITY (SPRAY GUN ONLY) — Paint should be thinned to spraying viscosity according to the directions on the can. Use only the recommended thinner or reducer and the same amount of reduction regardless of temperature.

AIR PRESSURE (SPRAY GUN ONLY) — This is extremely important. Be sure you are using the proper recommended pressure.

TEMPERATURE — The surface to be painted should be approximately the same temperature as the surrounding air. Applying warm paint to a cold surface, or vice versa, will completely upset the paint characteristics.

THICKNESS — Spray with smooth strokes. In general, the thicker the coat of paint, the longer the drying time. Apply several thin coats about 30 seconds apart. The paint should remain wet long enough to flow out and no longer; heavier coats will only produce sags or wrinkles. Spray a light (fog) coat, followed by heavier color coats.

DISTANCE — The ideal spraying distance is 8"-12" from the gun or can to the surface. Shorter distances will produce ripples, while greater distances will result in orange peel, dry film and poor color match and loss of material due to overspray.

OVERLAPPING — The gun or can should be kept at right angles to the surface at all times. Work to a wet edge at an even speed, using a 50% overlap and direct the center of the spray at the lower or nearest edge of the previous stroke.

RUBBING OUT (BLENDING) FRESH PAINT — Let the paint dry thoroughly. Runs or imperfections can be sanded out, primed and repainted.

Don't be in too big a hurry to remove the masking. This only produces paint ridges. When the finish has dried for at least a week, apply a small amount of fine grade rubbing compound with a clean, wet cloth. Use lots of water and blend the new paint with the surrounding area.

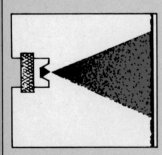

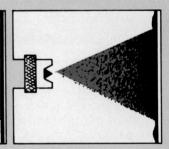

WRONG

CORRECT

WRONG

Thin coat. Stroke too fast, not enough overlap, gun too far away.

Medium coat. Proper distance, good stroke, proper overlap.

Heavy coat. Stroke too slow, too much overlap, gun too close.

Section 11—Cooling System
See Chapter 3 for service procedures

Test and Procedure	Results and Indications	Proceed to
11.1—Visually inspect the fan belt for glazing, cracks, and fraying, and replace if necessary. Tighten the belt so that the longest span has approximately ½″ play at its midpoint under thumb pressure (see Chapter 1).	Replace or tighten the fan belt as necessary:	**11.2**

Checking belt tension

Test and Procedure	Results and Indications	Proceed to
11.2—Check the fluid level of the cooling system.	If full or slightly low, fill as necessary:	**11.5**
	If extremely low:	**11.3**
11.3—Visually inspect the external portions of the cooling system (radiator, radiator hoses, thermostat elbow, water pump seals, heater hoses, etc.) for leaks. If none are found, pressurize the cooling system to 14–15 psi.	If cooling system holds the pressure:	**11.5**
	If cooling system loses pressure rapidly, reinspect external parts of the system for leaks under pressure. If none are found, check dipstick for coolant in crankcase. If no coolant is present, but pressure loss continues:	**11.4**
	If coolant is evident in crankcase, remove cylinder head(s), and check gasket(s). If gaskets are intact, block and cylinder head(s) should be checked for cracks or holes.	
	If the gasket(s) is blown, replace, and purge the crankcase of coolant:	**12.6**
	NOTE: *Occasionally, due to atmospheric and driving conditions, condensation of water can occur in the crankcase. This causes the oil to appear milky white. To remedy, run the engine until hot, and change the oil and oil filter.*	
11.4—Check for combustion leaks into the cooling system: Pressurize the cooling system as above. Start the engine, and observe the pressure gauge. If the needle fluctuates, remove each spark plug wire, one at a time, noting which cylinder(s) reduce or eliminate the fluctuation.	Cylinders which reduce or eliminate the fluctuation, when the spark plug wire is removed, are leaking into the cooling system. Replace the head gasket on the affected cylinder bank(s).	

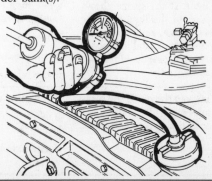

Pressurizing the cooling system

Test and Procedure	Results and Indications	Proceed to
11.5—Check the radiator pressure cap: Attach a radiator pressure tester to the radiator cap (wet the seal prior to installation). Quickly pump up the pressure, noting the point at which the cap releases.	If the cap releases within ± 1 psi of the specified rating, it is operating properly:	**11.6**
	If the cap releases at more than ± 1 psi of the specified rating, it should be replaced:	**11.6**

Checking radiator pressure cap

11.6—Test the thermostat: Start the engine cold, remove the radiator cap, and insert a thermometer into the radiator. Allow the engine to idle. After a short while, there will be a sudden, rapid increase in coolant temperature. The temperature at which this sharp rise stops is the thermostat opening temperature.	If the thermostat opens at or about the specified temperature:	**11.7**
	If the temperature doesn't increase: (If the temperature increases slowly and gradually, replace the thermostat.)	**11.7**
11.7—Check the water pump: Remove the thermostat elbow and the thermostat, disconnect the coil high tension lead (to prevent starting), and crank the engine momentarily.	If coolant flows, replace the thermostat and retest per 11.6:	**11.6**
	If coolant doesn't flow, reverse flush the cooling system to alleviate any blockage that might exist. If system is not blocked, and coolant will not flow, replace the water pump.	

Section 12—Lubrication
See Chapter 3 for service procedures

Test and Procedure	Results and Indications	Proceed to
12.1—Check the oil pressure gauge or warning light: If the gauge shows low pressure, or the light is on for no obvious reason, remove the oil pressure sender. Install an accurate oil pressure gauge and run the engine momentarily.	If oil pressure builds normally, run engine for a few moments to determine that it is functioning normally, and replace the sender.	—
	If the pressure remains low:	**12.2**
	If the pressure surges:	**12.3**
	If the oil pressure is zero:	**12.3**
12.2—Visually inspect the oil: If the oil is watery or very thin, milky, or foamy, replace the oil and oil filter.	If the oil is normal:	**12.3**
	If after replacing oil the pressure remains low:	**12.3**
	If after replacing oil the pressure becomes normal:	—

Test and Procedure	Results and Indications	Proceed to
12.3—Inspect the oil pressure relief valve and spring, to ensure that it is not sticking or stuck. Remove and thoroughly clean the valve, spring, and the valve body.	If the oil pressure improves: If no improvement is noted:	— **12.4**
12.4—Check to ensure that the oil pump is not cavitating (sucking air instead of oil): See that the crankcase is neither over nor underfull, and that the pickup in the sump is in the proper position and free from sludge.	Fill or drain the crankcase to the proper capacity, and clean the pickup screen in solvent if necessary. If no improvement is noted:	**12.5**
12.5—Inspect the oil pump drive and the oil pump:	If the pump drive or the oil pump appear to be defective, service as necessary and retest per 12.1: If the pump drive and pump appear to be operating normally, the engine should be disassembled to determine where blockage exists:	**12.1** **See Chapter 3**
12.6—Purge the engine of ethylene glycol coolant: Completely drain the crankcase and the oil filter. Obtain a commercial butyl cellosolve base solvent, designated for this purpose, and follow the instructions precisely. Following this, install a new oil filter and refill the crankcase with the proper weight oil. The next oil and filter change should follow shortly thereafter (1000 miles).		

TROUBLESHOOTING EMISSION CONTROL SYSTEMS

See Chapter 4 for procedures applicable to individual emission control systems used on specific combinations of engine/transmission/model.

TROUBLESHOOTING THE CARBURETOR

See Chapter 4 for service procedures

Carburetor problems cannot be effectively isolated unless all other engine systems (particularly ignition and emission) are functioning properly and the engine is properly tuned.

Condition	Possible Cause
Engine cranks, but does not start	1. Improper starting procedure 2. No fuel in tank 3. Clogged fuel line or filter 4. Defective fuel pump 5. Choke valve not closing properly 6. Engine flooded 7. Choke valve not unloading 8. Throttle linkage not making full travel 9. Stuck needle or float 10. Leaking float needle or seat 11. Improper float adjustment
Engine stalls	1. Improperly adjusted idle speed or mixture **Engine hot** 2. Improperly adjusted dashpot 3. Defective or improperly adjusted solenoid 4. Incorrect fuel level in fuel bowl 5. Fuel pump pressure too high 6. Leaking float needle seat 7. Secondary throttle valve stuck open 8. Air or fuel leaks 9. Idle air bleeds plugged or missing 10. Idle passages plugged **Engine Cold** 11. Incorrectly adjusted choke 12. Improperly adjusted fast idle speed 13. Air leaks 14. Plugged idle or idle air passages 15. Stuck choke valve or binding linkage 16. Stuck secondary throttle valves 17. Engine flooding—high fuel level 18. Leaking or misaligned float
Engine hesitates on acceleration	1. Clogged fuel filter 2. Leaking fuel pump diaphragm 3. Low fuel pump pressure 4. Secondary throttle valves stuck, bent or misadjusted 5. Sticking or binding air valve 6. Defective accelerator pump 7. Vacuum leaks 8. Clogged air filter 9. Incorrect choke adjustment (engine cold)
Engine feels sluggish or flat on acceleration	1. Improperly adjusted idle speed or mixture 2. Clogged fuel filter 3. Defective accelerator pump 4. Dirty, plugged or incorrect main metering jets 5. Bent or sticking main metering rods 6. Sticking throttle valves 7. Stuck heat riser 8. Binding or stuck air valve 9. Dirty, plugged or incorrect secondary jets 10. Bent or sticking secondary metering rods. 11. Throttle body or manifold heat passages plugged 12. Improperly adjusted choke or choke vacuum break.
Carburetor floods	1. Defective fuel pump. Pressure too high. 2. Stuck choke valve 3. Dirty, worn or damaged float or needle valve/seat 4. Incorrect float/fuel level 5. Leaking float bowl

Condition	Possible Cause
Engine idles roughly and stalls	1. Incorrect idle speed 2. Clogged fuel filter 3. Dirt in fuel system or carburetor 4. Loose carburetor screws or attaching bolts 5. Broken carburetor gaskets 6. Air leaks 7. Dirty carburetor 8. Worn idle mixture needles 9. Throttle valves stuck open 10. Incorrectly adjusted float or fuel level 11. Clogged air filter
Engine runs unevenly or surges	1. Defective fuel pump 2. Dirty or clogged fuel filter 3. Plugged, loose or incorrect main metering jets or rods 4. Air leaks 5. Bent or sticking main metering rods 6. Stuck power piston 7. Incorrect float adjustment 8. Incorrect idle speed or mixture 9. Dirty or plugged idle system passages 10. Hard, brittle or broken gaskets 11. Loose attaching or mounting screws 12. Stuck or misaligned secondary throttle valves
Poor fuel economy	1. Poor driving habits 2. Stuck choke valve 3. Binding choke linkage 4. Stuck heat riser 5. Incorrect idle mixture 6. Defective accelerator pump 7. Air leaks 8. Plugged, loose or incorrect main metering jets 9. Improperly adjusted float or fuel level 10. Bent, misaligned or fuel-clogged float 11. Leaking float needle seat 12. Fuel leak 13. Accelerator pump discharge ball not seating properly 14. Incorrect main jets
Engine lacks high speed performance or power	1. Incorrect throttle linkage adjustment 2. Stuck or binding power piston 3. Defective accelerator pump 4. Air leaks 5. Incorrect float setting or fuel level 6. Dirty, plugged, worn or incorrect main metering jets or rods 7. Binding or sticking air valve 8. Brittle or cracked gaskets 9. Bent, incorrect or improperly adjusted secondary metering rods 10. Clogged fuel filter 11. Clogged air filter 12. Defective fuel pump

TROUBLESHOOTING FUEL INJECTION PROBLEMS

Each fuel injection system has its own unique components and test procedures, for which it is impossible to generalize. Refer to Chapter 4 of this Repair & Tune-Up Guide for specific test and repair procedures, if the vehicle is equipped with fuel injection.

TROUBLESHOOTING ELECTRICAL PROBLEMS

See Chapter 5 for service procedures

For any electrical system to operate, it must make a complete circuit. This simply means that the power flow from the battery must make a complete circle. When an electrical component is operating, power flows from the battery to the component, passes through the component causing it to perform its function (lighting a light bulb), and then returns to the battery through the ground of the circuit. This ground is usually (but not always) the metal part of the car or truck on which the electrical component is mounted.

Perhaps the easiest way to visualize this is to think of connecting a light bulb with two wires attached to it to the battery. If one of the two wires attached to the light bulb were attached to the negative post of the battery and the other were attached to the positive post of the battery, you would have a complete circuit. Current from the battery would flow to the light bulb, causing it to light, and return to the negative post of the battery.

The normal automotive circuit differs from this simple example in two ways. First, instead of having a return wire from the bulb to the battery, the light bulb returns the current to the battery through the chassis of the vehicle. Since the negative battery cable is attached to the chassis and the chassis is made of electrically conductive metal, the chassis of the vehicle can serve as a ground wire to complete the circuit. Secondly, most automotive circuits contain switches to turn components on and off as required.

Every complete circuit from a power source must include a component which is using the power from the power source. If you were to disconnect the light bulb from the wires and touch the two wires together (don't do this) the power supply wire to the component would be grounded before the normal ground connection for the circuit.

Because grounding a wire from a power source makes a complete circuit—less the required component to use the power—this phenomenon is called a short circuit. Common causes are: broken insulation (exposing the metal wire to a metal part of the car or truck), or a shorted switch.

Some electrical components which require a large amount of current to operate also have a relay in their circuit. Since these circuits carry a large amount of current, the thickness of the wire in the circuit (gauge size) is also greater. If this large wire were connected from the component to the control switch on the instrument panel, and then back to the component, a voltage drop would occur in the circuit. To prevent this potential drop in voltage, an electromagnetic switch (relay) is used. The large wires in the circuit are connected from the battery to one side of the relay, and from the opposite side of the relay to the component. The relay is normally open, preventing current from passing through the circuit. An additional, smaller, wire is connected from the relay to the control switch for the circuit. When the control switch is turned on, it grounds the smaller wire from the relay and completes the circuit. This closes the relay and allows current to flow from the battery to the component. The horn, headlight, and starter circuits are three which use relays.

It is possible for larger surges of current to pass through the electrical system of your car or truck. If this surge of current were to reach an electrical component, it could burn it out. To prevent this, fuses, circuit breakers or fusible links are connected into the current supply wires of most of the major electrical systems. When an electrical current of excessive power passes through the component's fuse, the fuse blows out and breaks the circuit, saving the component from destruction.

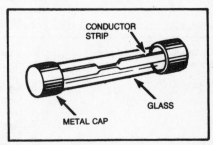

Typical automotive fuse

A circuit breaker is basically a self-repairing fuse. The circuit breaker opens the circuit the same way a fuse does. However, when either the short is removed from the circuit or the surge subsides, the circuit breaker resets itself and does not have to be replaced as a fuse does.

A fuse link is a wire that acts as a fuse. It is normally connected between the starter relay and the main wiring harness. This connection is usually under the hood. The fuse link (if installed) protects all the

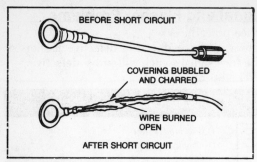

Most fusible links show a charred, melted insulation when they burn out

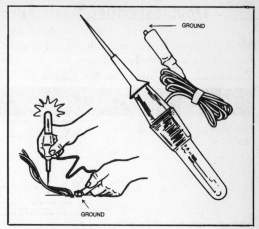

The test light will show the presence of current when touched to a hot wire and grounded at the other end

chassis electrical components, and is the probable cause of trouble when none of the electrical components function, unless the battery is disconnected or dead.

Electrical problems generally fall into one of three areas:

1. The component that is not functioning is not receiving current.

2. The component itself is not functioning.

3. The component is not properly grounded.

The electrical system can be checked with a test light and a jumper wire. A test light is a device that looks like a pointed screwdriver with a wire attached to it and has a light bulb in its handle. A jumper wire is a piece of insulated wire with an alligator clip attached to each end.

If a component is not working, you must follow a systematic plan to determine which of the three causes is the villain.

1. Turn on the switch that controls the inoperable component.

2. Disconnect the power supply wire from the component.

3. Attach the ground wire on the test light to a good metal ground.

4. Touch the probe end of the test light to the end of the power supply wire that was disconnected from the component. If the component is receiving current, the test light will go on.

NOTE: *Some components work only when the ignition switch is turned on.*

If the test light does not go on, then the problem is in the circuit between the battery and the component. This includes all the switches, fuses, and relays in the system. Follow the wire that runs back to the battery. The problem is an open circuit between the

battery and the component. If the fuse is blown and, when replaced, immediately blows again, there is a short circuit in the system which must be located and repaired. If there is a switch in the system, bypass it with a jumper wire. This is done by connecting one end of the jumper wire to the power supply wire into the switch and the other end of the jumper wire to the wire coming out of the switch. If the test light lights with the jumper wire installed, the switch or whatever was bypassed is defective.

NOTE: *Never substitute the jumper wire for the component, since it is required to use the power from the power source.*

5. If the bulb in the test light goes on, then the current is getting to the component that is not working. This eliminates the first of the three possible causes. Connect the power supply wire and connect a jumper wire from the component to a good metal ground. Do this with the switch which controls the component turned on, and also the ignition switch turned on if it is required for the component to work. If the component works with the jumper wire installed, then it has a bad ground. This is usually caused by the metal area on which the component mounts to the chassis being coated with some type of foreign matter.

6. If neither test located the source of the trouble, then the component itself is defective. Remember that for any electrical system to work, all connections must be clean and tight.

Troubleshooting Basic Turn Signal and Flasher Problems
See Chapter 5 for service procedures

Most problems in the turn signals or flasher system can be reduced to defective flashers or bulbs, which are easily replaced. Occasionally, the turn signal switch will prove defective.

F = Front   R = Rear   ● = Lights off   ○ = Lights on

Condition	Possible Cause
Turn signals light, but do not flash	Defective flasher
	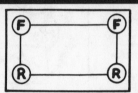
No turn signals light on either side	Blown fuse. Replace if defective. Defective flasher. Check by substitution. Open circuit, short circuit or poor ground.
	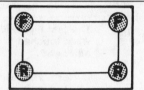
Both turn signals on one side don't work	Bad bulbs. Bad ground in both (or either) housings.
	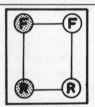
One turn signal light on one side doesn't work	Defective bulb. Corrosion in socket. Clean contacts. Poor ground at socket.
	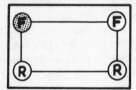
Turn signal flashes too fast or too slowly	Check any bulb on the side flashing too fast. A heavy-duty bulb is probably installed in place of a regular bulb. Check the bulb flashing too slowly. A standard bulb was probably installed in place of a heavy-duty bulb. Loose connections or corrosion at the bulb socket.
	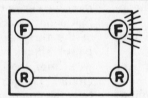
Indicator lights don't work in either direction	Check if the turn signals are working. Check the dash indicator lights. Check the flasher by substitution.

One indicator light doesn't light	On systems with one dash indicator: See if the lights work on the same side. Often the filaments have been reversed in systems combining stoplights with taillights and turn signals. Check the flasher by substitution. On systems with two indicators: Check the bulbs on the same side. Check the indicator light bulb. Check the flasher by substitution.

Troubleshooting Lighting Problems

See Chapter 5 for service procedures

Condition	Possible Cause
One or more lights don't work, but others do	1. Defective bulb(s) 2. Blown fuse(s) 3. Dirty fuse clips or light sockets 4. Poor ground circuit
Lights burn out quickly	1. Incorrect voltage regulator setting or defective regulator 2. Poor battery/alternator connections
Lights go dim	1. Low/discharged battery 2. Alternator not charging 3. Corroded sockets or connections 4. Low voltage output
Lights flicker	1. Loose connection 2. Poor ground. (Run ground wire from light housing to frame) 3. Circuit breaker operating (short circuit)
Lights "flare"—Some flare is normal on acceleration—If excessive, see "Lights Burn Out Quickly"	High voltage setting
Lights glare—approaching drivers are blinded	1. Lights adjusted too high 2. Rear springs or shocks sagging 3. Rear tires soft

Troubleshooting Dash Gauge Problems

Most problems can be traced to a defective sending unit or faulty wiring. Occasionally, the gauge itself is at fault. See Chapter 5 for service procedures.

Condition	Possible Cause
COOLANT TEMPERATURE GAUGE	
Gauge reads erratically or not at all	1. Loose or dirty connections 2. Defective sending unit. 3. Defective gauge. To test a bi-metal gauge, remove the wire from the sending unit. Ground the wire for an instant. If the gauge registers, replace the sending unit. To test a magnetic gauge, disconnect the wire at the sending unit. With ignition ON gauge should register COLD. Ground the wire; gauge should register HOT.
AMMETER GAUGE—TURN HEADLIGHTS ON (DO NOT START ENGINE). NOTE REACTION	
Ammeter shows charge Ammeter shows discharge Ammeter does not move	1. Connections reversed on gauge 2. Ammeter is OK 3. Loose connections or faulty wiring 4. Defective gauge

Condition	Possible Cause

OIL PRESSURE GAUGE

Gauge does not register or is inaccurate	1. On mechanical gauge, Bourdon tube may be bent or kinked. 2. Low oil pressure. Remove sending unit. Idle the engine briefly. If no oil flows from sending unit hole, problem is in engine. 3. Defective gauge. Remove the wire from the sending unit and ground it for an instant with the ignition ON. A good gauge will go to the top of the scale. 4. Defective wiring. Check the wiring to the gauge. If it's OK and the gauge doesn't register when grounded, replace the gauge. 5. Defective sending unit.

ALL GAUGES

All gauges do not operate All gauges read low or erratically All gauges pegged	1. Blown fuse 2. Defective instrument regulator 3. Defective or dirty instrument voltage regulator 4. Loss of ground between instrument voltage regulator and frame 5. Defective instrument regulator

WARNING LIGHTS

Light(s) do not come on when ignition is ON, but engine is not started Light comes on with engine running	1. Defective bulb 2. Defective wire 3. Defective sending unit. Disconnect the wire from the sending unit and ground it. Replace the sending unit if the light comes on with the ignition ON. 4. Problem in individual system 5. Defective sending unit

Troubleshooting Clutch Problems

It is false economy to replace individual clutch components. The pressure plate, clutch plate and throwout bearing should be replaced as a set, and the flywheel face inspected, whenever the clutch is overhauled. See Chapter 6 for service procedures.

Condition	Possible Cause
Clutch chatter	1. Grease on driven plate (disc) facing 2. Binding clutch linkage or cable 3. Loose, damaged facings on driven plate (disc) 4. Engine mounts loose 5. Incorrect height adjustment of pressure plate release levers 6. Clutch housing or housing to transmission adapter misalignment 7. Loose driven plate hub
Clutch grabbing	1. Oil, grease on driven plate (disc) facing 2. Broken pressure plate 3. Warped or binding driven plate. Driven plate binding on clutch shaft
Clutch slips	1. Lack of lubrication in clutch linkage or cable (linkage or cable binds, causes incomplete engagement) 2. Incorrect pedal, or linkage adjustment 3. Broken pressure plate springs 4. Weak pressure plate springs 5. Grease on driven plate facings (disc)

Troubleshooting Clutch Problems (cont.)

Condition	Possible Cause
Incomplete clutch release	1. Incorrect pedal or linkage adjustment or linkage or cable binding 2. Incorrect height adjustment on pressure plate release levers 3. Loose, broken facings on driven plate (disc) 4. Bent, dished, warped driven plate caused by overheating
Grinding, whirring grating noise when pedal is depressed	1. Worn or defective throwout bearing 2. Starter drive teeth contacting flywheel ring gear teeth. Look for milled or polished teeth on ring gear.
Squeal, howl, trumpeting noise when pedal is being released (occurs during first inch to inch and one-half of pedal travel)	Pilot bushing worn or lack of lubricant. If bushing appears OK, polish bushing with emery cloth, soak lube wick in oil, lube bushing with oil, apply film of chassis grease to clutch shaft pilot hub, reassemble. NOTE: Bushing wear may be due to misalignment of clutch housing or housing to transmission adapter
Vibration or clutch pedal pulsation with clutch disengaged (pedal fully depressed)	1. Worn or defective engine transmission mounts 2. Flywheel run out. (Flywheel run out at face not to exceed 0.005") 3. Damaged or defective clutch components

Troubleshooting Manual Transmission Problems
See Chapter 6 for service procedures

Condition	Possible Cause
Transmission jumps out of gear	1. Misalignment of transmission case or clutch housing. 2. Worn pilot bearing in crankshaft. 3. Bent transmission shaft. 4. Worn high speed sliding gear. 5. Worn teeth or end-play in clutch shaft. 6. Insufficient spring tension on shifter rail plunger. 7. Bent or loose shifter fork. 8. Gears not engaging completely. 9. Loose or worn bearings on clutch shaft or mainshaft. 10. Worn gear teeth. 11. Worn or damaged detent balls.
Transmission sticks in gear	1. Clutch not releasing fully. 2. Burred or battered teeth on clutch shaft, or sliding sleeve. 3. Burred or battered transmission mainshaft. 4. Frozen synchronizing clutch. 5. Stuck shifter rail plunger. 6. Gearshift lever twisting and binding shifter rail. 7. Battered teeth on high speed sliding gear or on sleeve. 8. Improper lubrication, or lack of lubrication. 9. Corroded transmission parts. 10. Defective mainshaft pilot bearing. 11. Locked gear bearings will give same effect as stuck in gear.
Transmission gears will not synchronize	1. Binding pilot bearing on mainshaft, will synchronize in high gear only. 2. Clutch not releasing fully. 3. Detent spring weak or broken. 4. Weak or broken springs under balls in sliding gear sleeve. 5. Binding bearing on clutch shaft, or binding countershaft. 6. Binding pilot bearing in crankshaft. 7. Badly worn gear teeth. 8. Improper lubrication. 9. Constant mesh gear not turning freely on transmission mainshaft. Will synchronize in that gear only.

Condition	Possible Cause
Gears spinning when shifting into gear from neutral	1. Clutch not releasing fully. 2. In some cases an extremely light lubricant in transmission will cause gears to continue to spin for a short time after clutch is released. 3. Binding pilot bearing in crankshaft.
Transmission noisy in all gears	1. Insufficient lubricant, or improper lubricant. 2. Worn countergear bearings. 3. Worn or damaged main drive gear or countergear. 4. Damaged main drive gear or mainshaft bearings. 5. Worn or damaged countergear anti-lash plate.
Transmission noisy in neutral only	1. Damaged main drive gear bearing. 2. Damaged or loose mainshaft pilot bearing. 3. Worn or damaged countergear anti-lash plate. 4. Worn countergear bearings.
Transmission noisy in one gear only	1. Damaged or worn constant mesh gears. 2. Worn or damaged countergear bearings. 3. Damaged or worn synchronizer.
Transmission noisy in reverse only	1. Worn or damaged reverse idler gear or idler bushing. 2. Worn or damaged mainshaft reverse gear. 3. Worn or damaged reverse countergear. 4. Damaged shift mechanism.

TROUBLESHOOTING AUTOMATIC TRANSMISSION PROBLEMS

Keeping alert to changes in the operating characteristics of the transmission (changing shift points, noises, etc.) can prevent small problems from becoming large ones. If the problem cannot be traced to loose bolts, fluid level, misadjusted linkage, clogged filters or similar problems, you should probably seek professional service.

Transmission Fluid Indications

The appearance and odor of the transmission fluid can give valuable clues to the overall condition of the transmission. Always note the appearance of the fluid when you check the fluid level or change the fluid. Rub a small amount of fluid between your fingers to feel for grit and smell the fluid on the dipstick.

If the fluid appears:	It indicates:
Clear and red colored	Normal operation
Discolored (extremely dark red or brownish) or smells burned	Band or clutch pack failure, usually caused by an overheated transmission. Hauling very heavy loads with insufficient power or failure to change the fluid often result in overheating. Do not confuse this appearance with newer fluids that have a darker red color and a strong odor (though not a burned odor).
Foamy or aerated (light in color and full of bubbles)	1. The level is too high (gear train is churning oil) 2. An internal air leak (air is mixing with the fluid). Have the transmission checked professionally.
Solid residue in the fluid	Defective bands, clutch pack or bearings. Bits of band material or metal abrasives are clinging to the dipstick. Have the transmission checked professionally.
Varnish coating on the dipstick	The transmission fluid is overheating

TROUBLESHOOTING DRIVE AXLE PROBLEMS

First, determine when the noise is most noticeable.

Drive Noise: Produced under vehicle acceleration.

Coast Noise: Produced while coasting with a closed throttle.

Float Noise: Occurs while maintaining constant speed (just enough to keep speed constant) on a level road.

External Noise Elimination

It is advisable to make a thorough road test to determine whether the noise originates in the rear axle or whether it originates from the tires, engine, transmission, wheel bearings or road surface. Noise originating from other places cannot be corrected by servicing the rear axle.

ROAD NOISE

Brick or rough surfaced concrete roads produce noises that seem to come from the rear axle. Road noise is usually identical in Drive or Coast and driving on a different type of road will tell whether the road is the problem.

TIRE NOISE

Tire noise can be mistaken as rear axle noise, even though the tires on the front are at fault. Snow tread and mud tread tires or tires worn unevenly will frequently cause vibrations which seem to originate elsewhere; *temporarily, and for test purposes only,* inflate the tires to 40–50 lbs. This will significantly alter the noise produced by the tires, but will not alter noise from the rear axle. Noises from the rear axle will normally cease at speeds below 30 mph on coast, while tire noise will continue at lower tone as speed is decreased. The rear axle noise will usually change from drive conditions to coast conditions, while tire noise will not. Do not forget to lower the tire pressure to normal after the test is complete.

ENGINE/TRANSMISSION NOISE

Determine at what speed the noise is most pronounced, then stop in a quiet place. With the transmission in Neutral, run the engine through speeds corresponding to road speeds where the noise was noticed. Noises produced with the vehicle standing still are coming from the engine or transmission.

FRONT WHEEL BEARINGS

Front wheel bearing noises, sometimes confused with rear axle noises, will not change when comparing drive and coast conditions. While holding the speed steady, lightly apply the footbrake. This will often cause wheel bearing noise to lessen, as some of the weight is taken off the bearing. Front wheel bearings are easily checked by jacking up the wheels and spinning the wheels. Shaking the wheels will also determine if the wheel bearings are excessively loose.

REAR AXLE NOISES

Eliminating other possible sources can narrow the cause to the rear axle, which normally produces noise from worn gears or bearings. Gear noises tend to peak in a narrow speed range, while bearing noises will usually vary in pitch with engine speeds.

Noise Diagnosis

The Noise Is:	Most Probably Produced By:
1. Identical under Drive or Coast	Road surface, tires or front wheel bearings
2. Different depending on road surface	Road surface or tires
3. Lower as speed is lowered	Tires
4. Similar when standing or moving	Engine or transmission
5. A vibration	Unbalanced tires, rear wheel bearing, unbalanced driveshaft or worn U-joint
6. A knock or click about every two tire revolutions	Rear wheel bearing
7. Most pronounced on turns	Damaged differential gears
8. A steady low-pitched whirring or scraping, starting at low speeds	Damaged or worn pinion bearing
9. A chattering vibration on turns	Wrong differential lubricant or worn clutch plates (limited slip rear axle)
10. Noticed only in Drive, Coast or Float conditions	Worn ring gear and/or pinion gear

Troubleshooting Steering & Suspension Problems

Condition	Possible Cause
Hard steering (wheel is hard to turn)	1. Improper tire pressure 2. Loose or glazed pump drive belt 3. Low or incorrect fluid 4. Loose, bent or poorly lubricated front end parts 5. Improper front end alignment (excessive caster) 6. Bind in steering column or linkage 7. Kinked hydraulic hose 8. Air in hydraulic system 9. Low pump output or leaks in system 10. Obstruction in lines 11. Pump valves sticking or out of adjustment 12. Incorrect wheel alignment
Loose steering (too much play in steering wheel)	1. Loose wheel bearings 2. Faulty shocks 3. Worn linkage or suspension components 4. Loose steering gear mounting or linkage points 5. Steering mechanism worn or improperly adjusted 6. Valve spool improperly adjusted 7. Worn ball joints, tie-rod ends, etc.
Veers or wanders (pulls to one side with hands off steering wheel)	1. Improper tire pressure 2. Improper front end alignment 3. Dragging or improperly adjusted brakes 4. Bent frame 5. Improper rear end alignment 6. Faulty shocks or springs 7. Loose or bent front end components 8. Play in Pitman arm 9. Steering gear mountings loose 10. Loose wheel bearings 11. Binding Pitman arm 12. Spool valve sticking or improperly adjusted 13. Worn ball joints
Wheel oscillation or vibration transmitted through steering wheel	1. Low or uneven tire pressure 2. Loose wheel bearings 3. Improper front end alignment 4. Bent spindle 5. Worn, bent or broken front end components 6. Tires out of round or out of balance 7. Excessive lateral runout in disc brake rotor 8. Loose or bent shock absorber or strut
Noises (see also "Troubleshooting Drive Axle Problems")	1. Loose belts 2. Low fluid, air in system 3. Foreign matter in system 4. Improper lubrication 5. Interference or chafing in linkage 6. Steering gear mountings loose 7. Incorrect adjustment or wear in gear box 8. Faulty valves or wear in pump 9. Kinked hydraulic lines 10. Worn wheel bearings
Poor return of steering	1. Over-inflated tires 2. Improperly aligned front end (excessive caster) 3. Binding in steering column 4. No lubrication in front end 5. Steering gear adjusted too tight
Uneven tire wear (see "How To Read Tire Wear")	1. Incorrect tire pressure 2. Improperly aligned front end 3. Tires out-of-balance 4. Bent or worn suspension parts

HOW TO READ TIRE WEAR

The way your tires wear is a good indicator of other parts of the suspension. Abnormal wear patterns are often caused by the need for simple tire maintenance, or for front end alignment.

Excessive wear at the center of the tread indicates that the air pressure in the tire is consistently too high. The tire is riding on the center of the tread and wearing it prematurely. Occasionally, this wear pattern can result from outrageously wide tires on narrow rims. The cure for this is to replace either the tires or the wheels.

This type of wear usually results from consistent under-inflation. When a tire is under-inflated, there is too much contact with the road by the outer treads, which wear prematurely. When this type of wear occurs, and the tire pressure is known to be consistently correct, a bent or worn steering component or the need for wheel alignment could be indicated.

Feathering is a condition when the edge of each tread rib develops a slightly rounded edge on one side and a sharp edge on the other. By running your hand over the tire, you can usually feel the sharper edges before you'll be able to see them. The most common causes of feathering are incorrect toe-in setting or deteriorated bushings in the front suspension.

When an inner or outer rib wears faster than the rest of the tire, the need for wheel alignment is indicated. There is excessive camber in the front suspension, causing the wheel to lean too much putting excessive load on one side of the tire. Misalignment could also be due to sagging springs, worn ball joints, or worn control arm bushings. Be sure the vehicle is loaded the way it's normally driven when you have the wheels aligned.

Cups or scalloped dips appearing around the edge of the tread almost always indicate worn (sometimes bent) suspension parts. Adjustment of wheel alignment alone will seldom cure the problem. Any worn component that connects the wheel to the suspension can cause this type of wear. Occasionally, wheels that are out of balance will wear like this, but wheel imbalance usually shows up as bald spots between the outside edges and center of the tread.

Second-rib wear is usually found only in radial tires, and appears where the steel belts end in relation to the tread. It can be kept to a minimum by paying careful attention to tire pressure and frequently rotating the tires. This is often considered normal wear but excessive amounts indicate that the tires are too wide for the wheels.

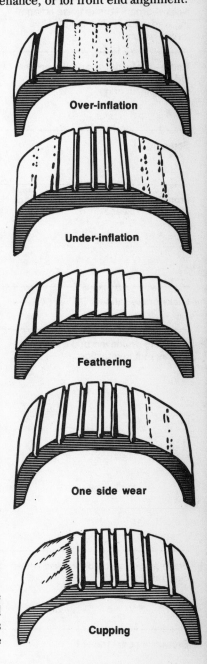

Over-inflation

Under-inflation

Feathering

One side wear

Cupping

Second-rib wear

Troubleshooting Disc Brake Problems

Condition	Possible Cause
Noise—groan—brake noise emanating when slowly releasing brakes (creep-groan)	Not detrimental to function of disc brakes—no corrective action required. (This noise may be eliminated by slightly increasing or decreasing brake pedal efforts.)
Rattle—brake noise or rattle emanating at low speeds on rough roads, (front wheels only).	1. Shoe anti-rattle spring missing or not properly positioned. 2. Excessive clearance between shoe and caliper. 3. Soft or broken caliper seals. 4. Deformed or misaligned disc. 5. Loose caliper.
Scraping	1. Mounting bolts too long. 2. Loose wheel bearings. 3. Bent, loose, or misaligned splash shield.
Front brakes heat up during driving and fail to release	1. Operator riding brake pedal. 2. Stop light switch improperly adjusted. 3. Sticking pedal linkage. 4. Frozen or seized piston. 5. Residual pressure valve in master cylinder. 6. Power brake malfunction. 7. Proportioning valve malfunction.
Leaky brake caliper	1. Damaged or worn caliper piston seal. 2. Scores or corrosion on surface of cylinder bore.
Grabbing or uneven brake action—Brakes pull to one side	1. Causes listed under "Brakes Pull". 2. Power brake malfunction. 3. Low fluid level in master cylinder. 4. Air in hydraulic system. 5. Brake fluid, oil or grease on linings. 6. Unmatched linings. 7. Distorted brake pads. 8. Frozen or seized pistons. 9. Incorrect tire pressure. 10. Front end out of alignment. 11. Broken rear spring. 12. Brake caliper pistons sticking. 13. Restricted hose or line. 14. Caliper not in proper alignment to braking disc. 15. Stuck or malfunctioning metering valve. 16. Soft or broken caliper seals. 17. Loose caliper.
Brake pedal can be depressed without braking effect	1. Air in hydraulic system or improper bleeding procedure. 2. Leak past primary cup in master cylinder. 3. Leak in system. 4. Rear brakes out of adjustment. 5. Bleeder screw open.
Excessive pedal travel	1. Air, leak, or insufficient fluid in system or caliper. 2. Warped or excessively tapered shoe and lining assembly. 3. Excessive disc runout. 4. Rear brake adjustment required. 5. Loose wheel bearing adjustment. 6. Damaged caliper piston seal. 7. Improper brake fluid (boil). 8. Power brake malfunction. 9. Weak or soft hoses.

Troubleshooting Disc Brake Problems (cont.)

Condition	Possible Cause
Brake roughness or chatter (pedal pumping)	1. Excessive thickness variation of braking disc. 2. Excessive lateral runout of braking disc. 3. Rear brake drums out-of-round. 4. Excessive front bearing clearance.
Excessive pedal effort	1. Brake fluid, oil or grease on linings. 2. Incorrect lining. 3. Frozen or seized pistons. 4. Power brake malfunction. 5. Kinked or collapsed hose or line. 6. Stuck metering valve. 7. Scored caliper or master cylinder bore. 8. Seized caliper pistons.
Brake pedal fades (pedal travel increases with foot on brake)	1. Rough master cylinder or caliper bore. 2. Loose or broken hydraulic lines/connections. 3. Air in hydraulic system. 4. Fluid level low. 5. Weak or soft hoses. 6. Inferior quality brake shoes or fluid. 7. Worn master cylinder piston cups or seals.

Troubleshooting Drum Brakes

Condition	Possible Cause
Pedal goes to floor	1. Fluid low in reservoir. 2. Air in hydraulic system. 3. Improperly adjusted brake. 4. Leaking wheel cylinders. 5. Loose or broken brake lines. 6. Leaking or worn master cylinder. 7. Excessively worn brake lining.
Spongy brake pedal	1. Air in hydraulic system. 2. Improper brake fluid (low boiling point). 3. Excessively worn or cracked brake drums. 4. Broken pedal pivot bushing.
Brakes pulling	1. Contaminated lining. 2. Front end out of alignment. 3. Incorrect brake adjustment. 4. Unmatched brake lining. 5. Brake drums out of round. 6. Brake shoes distorted. 7. Restricted brake hose or line. 8. Broken rear spring. 9. Worn brake linings. 10. Uneven lining wear. 11. Glazed brake lining. 12. Excessive brake lining dust. 13. Heat spotted brake drums. 14. Weak brake return springs. 15. Faulty automatic adjusters. 16. Low or incorrect tire pressure.

Condition	Possible Cause
Squealing brakes	1. Glazed brake lining. 2. Saturated brake lining. 3. Weak or broken brake shoe retaining spring. 4. Broken or weak brake shoe return spring. 5. Incorrect brake lining. 6. Distorted brake shoes. 7. Bent support plate. 8. Dust in brakes or scored brake drums. 9. Linings worn below limit. 10. Uneven brake lining wear. 11. Heat spotted brake drums.
Chirping brakes	1. Out of round drum or eccentric axle flange pilot.
Dragging brakes	1. Incorrect wheel or parking brake adjustment. 2. Parking brakes engaged or improperly adjusted. 3. Weak or broken brake shoe return spring. 4. Brake pedal binding. 5. Master cylinder cup sticking. 6. Obstructed master cylinder relief port. 7. Saturated brake lining. 8. Bent or out of round brake drum. 9. Contaminated or improper brake fluid. 10. Sticking wheel cylinder pistons. 11. Driver riding brake pedal. 12. Defective proportioning valve. 13. Insufficient brake shoe lubricant.
Hard pedal	1. Brake booster inoperative. 2. Incorrect brake lining. 3. Restricted brake line or hose. 4. Frozen brake pedal linkage. 5. Stuck wheel cylinder. 6. Binding pedal linkage. 7. Faulty proportioning valve.
Wheel locks	1. Contaminated brake lining. 2. Loose or torn brake lining. 3. Wheel cylinder cups sticking. 4. Incorrect wheel bearing adjustment. 5. Faulty proportioning valve.
Brakes fade (high speed)	1. Incorrect lining. 2. Overheated brake drums. 3. Incorrect brake fluid (low boiling temperature). 4. Saturated brake lining. 5. Leak in hydraulic system. 6. Faulty automatic adjusters.
Pedal pulsates	1. Bent or out of round brake drum.
Brake chatter and shoe knock	1. Out of round brake drum. 2. Loose support plate. 3. Bent support plate. 4. Distorted brake shoes. 5. Machine grooves in contact face of brake drum (Shoe Knock). 6. Contaminated brake lining. 7. Missing or loose components. 8. Incorrect lining material. 9. Out-of-round brake drums. 10. Heat spotted or scored brake drums. 11. Out-of-balance wheels.

Troubleshooting Drum Brakes (cont.)

Condition	Possible Cause
Brakes do not self adjust	1. Adjuster screw frozen in thread. 2. Adjuster screw corroded at thrust washer. 3. Adjuster lever does not engage star wheel. 4. Adjuster installed on wrong wheel.
Brake light glows	1. Leak in the hydraulic system. 2. Air in the system. 3. Improperly adjusted master cylinder pushrod. 4. Uneven lining wear. 5. Failure to center combination valve or proportioning valve.

Mechanic's Data

General Conversion Table

Multiply By	To Convert	To	
LENGTH			
2.54	Inches	Centimeters	.3937
25.4	Inches	Millimeters	.03937
30.48	Feet	Centimeters	.0328
.304	Feet	Meters	3.28
.914	Yards	Meters	1.094
1.609	Miles	Kilometers	.621
VOLUME			
.473	Pints	Liters	2.11
.946	Quarts	Liters	1.06
3.785	Gallons	Liters	.264
.016	Cubic inches	Liters	61.02
16.39	Cubic inches	Cubic cms.	.061
28.3	Cubic feet	Liters	.0353
MASS (Weight)			
28.35	Ounces	Grams	.035
.4536	Pounds	Kilograms	2.20
—	To obtain	From	Multiply by

Multiply By	To Convert	To	
AREA			
.645	Square inches	Square cms.	.155
.836	Square yds.	Square meters	1.196
FORCE			
4.448	Pounds	Newtons	.225
.138	Ft./lbs.	Kilogram/meters	7.23
1.36	Ft./lbs.	Newton-meters	.737
.112	In./lbs.	Newton-meters	8.844
PRESSURE			
.068	Psi	Atmospheres	14.7
6.89	Psi	Kilopascals	.145
OTHER			
1.104	Horsepower (DIN)	Horsepower (SAE)	.9861
.746	Horsepower (SAE)	Kilowatts (KW)	1.34
1.60	Mph	Km/h	.625
.425	Mpg	Km/1	2.35
—	To obtain	From	Multiply by

Tap Drill Sizes

National Coarse or U.S.S.

Screw & Tap Size	Threads Per Inch	Use Drill Number
No. 5	40	.39
No. 6	32	.36
No. 8	32	.29
No. 10	24	.25
No. 12	24	.17
1/4	20	8
5/16	18	F
3/8	16	5/16
7/16	14	U
1/2	13	27/64
9/16	12	31/64
5/8	11	17/32
3/4	10	21/32
7/8	9	49/64

National Coarse or U.S.S.

Screw & Tap Size	Threads Per Inch	Use Drill Number
1	8	7/8
1 1/8	7	63/64
1 1/4	7	1 7/64
1 1/2	6	1 11/32

National Fine or S.A.E.

Screw & Tap Size	Threads Per Inch	Use Drill Number
No. 5	44	.37
No. 6	40	.33
No. 8	36	.29
No. 10	32	.21

National Fine or S.A.E.

Screw & Tap Size	Threads Per Inch	Use Drill Number
No. 12	28	.15
1/4	28	3
6/16	24	1
3/8	24	Q
7/16	20	W
1/2	20	29/64
9/16	18	33/64
5/8	18	37/64
3/4	16	11/16
7/8	14	13/16
1 1/8	12	1 3/64
1 1/4	12	1 11/64
1 1/2	12	1 27/64

Drill Sizes In Decimal Equivalents

Inch	Decimal	Wire	mm	Inch	Decimal	Wire	mm	Inch	Decimal	Wire & Letter	mm	Inch	Decimal	Letter	mm	Inch	Decimal	mm
1/64	.0156		.39		.0730	49			.1614		4.1		.2717		6.9		.4331	11.0
	.0157		.4		.0748		1.9		.1654		4.2		.2720	I		7/16	.4375	11.11
	.0160	78			.0760	48			.1660	19			.2756		7.0		.4528	11.5
	.0165		.42		.0768		1.95		.1673		4.25		.2770	J		29/64	.4531	11.51
	.0173		.44	5/64	.0781		1.98		.1693		4.3		.2795		7.1	15/32	.4688	11.90
	.0177		.45		.0785	47			.1695	18			.2810	K			.4724	12.0
	.0180	77			.0787		2.0	11/64	.1719		4.36	9/32	.2812		7.14	31/64	.4844	12.30
	.0181		.46		.0807		2.05		.1730	17			.2835		7.2		.4921	12.5
	.0189		.48		.0810	46			.1732		4.4		.2854		7.25	1/2	.5000	12.70
	.0197		.5		.0820	45			.1770	16			.2874		7.3		.5118	13.0
	.0200	76			.0827		2.1		.1772		4.5		.2900	L		33/64	.5156	13.09
	.0210	75			.0846		2.15		.1800	15			.2913		7.4	17/32	.5312	13.49
	.0217		.55		.0860	44			.1811		4.6		.2950	M			.5315	13.5
	.0225	74			.0866		2.2		.1820	14			.2953		7.5	35/64	.5469	13.89
	.0236		.6		.0886		2.25		.1850	13	19/64	.2969		7.54		.5512	14.0
	.0240	73			.0890	43			.1850		4.7		.2992		7.6	9/16	.5625	14.28
	.0250	72			.0906		2.3		.1870		4.75		.3020	N			.5709	14.5
	.0256		.65		.0925		2.35	3/16	.1875		4.76		.3031		7.7	37/64	.5781	14.68
	.0260	71			.0935	42			.1890	12			.3051		7.75		.5906	15.0
	.0276		.7	3/32	.0938		2.38		.1890		4.8		.3071		7.8	19/32	.5938	15.08
	.0280	70			.0945		2.4		.1910	11			.3110		7.9	39/64	.6094	15.47
	.0292	69			.0960	41			.1929		4.9	5/16	.3125		7.93		.6102	15.5
	.0295		.75		.0965		2.45		.1935	10			.3150		8.0	5/8	.6250	15.87
	.0310	68			.0980	40			.1960	9			.3160	O			.6299	16.0
1/32	.0312		.79		.0981		2.5		.1969		5.0		.3189		8.1	41/64	.6406	16.27
	.0315		.8		.0995	39			.1990	8			.3228		8.2		.6496	16.5
	.0320	67			.1015	38			.2008		5.1		.3230	P		21/32	.6562	16.66
	.0330	66			.1024		2.6		.2010	7			.3248		8.25		.6693	17.0
	.0335		.85		.1040	37		13/64	.2031		5.16		.3268		8.3	43/64	.6719	17.06
	.0350	65			.1063		2.7		.2040	6		21/64	.3281		8.33	11/16	.6875	17.46
	.0354		.9		.1065	36			.2047		5.2		.3307		8.4		.6890	17.5
	.0360	64			.1083		2.75		.2055	5			.3320	Q		45/64	.7031	17.85
	.0370	63		7/64	.1094		2.77		.2067		5.25		.3346		8.5		.7087	18.0
	.0374		.95		.1100	35			.2087		5.3		.3386		8.6	23/32	.7188	18.25
	.0380	62			.1102		2.8		.2090	4			.3390	R			.7283	18.5
	.0390	61			.1110	34			.2126		5.4		.3425		8.7	47/64	.7344	18.65
	.0394		1.0		.1130	33			.2130	3	11/32	.3438		8.73		.7480	19.0
	.0400	60			.1142		2.9		.2165		5.5		.3445		8.75	3/4	.7500	19.05
	.0410	59			.1160	32		7/32	.2188		5.55		.3465		8.8	49/64	.7656	19.44
	.0413		1.05		.1181		3.0		.2205		5.6		.3480	S			.7677	19.5
	.0420	58			.1200	31			.2210	2			.3504		8.9	25/32	.7812	19.84
	.0430	57			.1220		3.1		.2244		5.7		.3543		9.0		.7874	20.0
	.0433		1.1	1/8	.1250		3.17		.2264		5.75		.3580	T		51/64	.7969	20.24
	.0453		1.15		.1260		3.2		.2280	1			.3583		9.1		.8071	20.5
	.0465	56			.1280		3.25		.2283		5.8	23/64	.3594		9.12	13/16	.8125	20.63
3/64	.0469		1.19		.1285	30			.2323		5.9		.3622		9.2		.8268	21.0
	.0472		1.2		.1299		3.3		.2340	A			.3642		9.25	53/64	.8281	21.03
	.0492		1.25		.1339		3.4	15/64	.2344		5.95		.3661		9.3	27/32	.8438	21.43
	.0512		1.3		.1360	29			.2362		6.0		.3680	U			.8465	21.5
	.0520	55			.1378		3.5		.2380	B			.3701		9.4	55/64	.8594	21.82
	.0531		1.35		.1405	28			.2402		6.1		.3740		9.5		.8661	22.0
	.0550	54		9/64	.1406		3.57		.2420	C		3/8	.3750		9.52	7/8	.8750	22.22
	.0551		1.4		.1417		3.6		.2441		6.2		.3770	V			.8858	22.5
	.0571		1.45		.1440	27			.2460	D			.3780		9.6	57/64	.8906	22.62
	.0591		1.5		.1457		3.7		.2461		6.25		.3819		9.7		.9055	23.0
	.0595	53			.1470	26			.2480		6.3		.3839		9.75	29/32	.9062	23.01
	.0610		1.55		.1476		3.75	1/4	.2500	E	6.35		.3858		9.8	59/64	.9219	23.41
1/16	.0625		1.59		.1495	25			.2520		6.		.3860	W			.9252	23.5
	.0630		1.6		.1496		3.8		.2559		6.5		.3898		9.9	15/16	.9375	23.81
	.0635	52			.1520	24			.2570	F		25/64	.3906		9.92		.9449	24.0
	.0650		1.65		.1535		3.9		.2598		6.6		.3937		10.0	61/64	.9531	24.2
	.0669		1.7		.1540	23			.2610	G			.3970	X			.9646	24.5
	.0670	51		5/32	.1562		3.96		.2638		6.7		.4040	Y		31/32	.9688	24.6
	.0689		1.75		.1570	22		17/64	.2656		6.74	13/32	.4062		10.31		.9843	25.0
	.0700	50			.1575		4.0		.2657		6.75		.4130	Z		63/64	.9844	25.0
	.0709		1.8		.1590	21			.2660	H			.4134		10.5	1	1.0000	25.4
	.0728		1.85		.1610	20			.2677		6.8	27/64	.4219		10.71			

AIR/FUEL RATIO: The ratio of air to gasoline by weight in the fuel mixture drawn into the engine.

AIR INJECTION: One method of reducing harmful exhaust emissions by injecting air into each of the exhaust ports of an engine. The fresh air entering the hot exhaust manifold causes any remaining fuel to be burned before it can exit the tailpipe.

ALTERNATOR: A device used for converting mechanical energy into electrical energy.

AMMETER: An instrument, calibrated in amperes, used to measure the flow of an electrical current in a circuit. Ammeters are always connected in series with the circuit being tested.

AMPERE: The rate of flow of electrical current present when one volt of electrical pressure is applied against one ohm of electrical resistance.

ANALOG COMPUTER: Any microprocessor that uses similar (analogous) electrical signals to make its calculations.

ARMATURE: A laminated, soft iron core wrapped by a wire that converts electrical energy to mechanical energy as in a motor or relay. When rotated in a magnetic field, it changes mechanical energy into electrical energy as in a generator.

ATMOSPHERIC PRESSURE: The pressure on the Earth's surface caused by the weight of the air in the atmosphere. At sea level, this pressure is 14.7 psi at 32°F (101 kPa at 0°C).

ATOMIZATION: The breaking down of a liquid into a fine mist that can be suspended in air.

AXIAL PLAY: Movement parallel to a shaft or bearing bore.

BACKFIRE: The sudden combustion of gases in the intake or exhaust system that results in a loud explosion.

BACKLASH: The clearance or play between two parts, such as meshed gears.

BACKPRESSURE: Restrictions in the exhaust system that slow the exit of exhaust gases from the combustion chamber.

BAKELITE: A heat resistant, plastic insulator material commonly used in printed circuit boards and transistorized components.

BALL BEARING: A bearing made up of hardened inner and outer races between which hardened steel ball roll.

BALLAST RESISTOR: A resistor in the primary ignition circuit that lowers voltage after the engine is started to reduce wear on ignition components.

BEARING: A friction reducing, supportive device usually located between a stationary part and a moving part.

BIMETAL TEMPERATURE SENSOR: Any sensor or switch made of two dissimilar types of metal that bend when heated or cooled due to the different expansion rates of the alloys. These types of sensors usually function as an on/off switch.

BLOWBY: Combustion gases, composed of water vapor and unburned fuel, that leak past the piston rings into the crankcase during normal engine operation. These gases are removed by the PCV system to prevent the build-up of harmful acids in the crankcase.

BRAKE PAD: A brake shoe and lining assembly used with disc brakes.

BRAKE SHOE: The backing for the brake lining. The term is, however, usually applied to the assembly of the brake backing and lining.

BUSHING: A liner, usually removable, for a bearing; an anti-friction liner used in place of a bearing.

BYPASS: System used to bypass ballast resistor during engine cranking to increase voltage supplied to the coil.

CALIPER: A hydraulically activated device in a disc brake system, which is mounted straddling the brake rotor (disc). The caliper contains at least one piston and two brake pads. Hydraulic pressure on the piston(s) forces the pads against the rotor.

CAMSHAFT: A shaft in the engine on which are the lobes (cams) which operate the valves. The camshaft is driven by the crankshaft, via a belt, chain or gears, at one half the crankshaft speed.

CAPACITOR: A device which stores an electrical charge.

CARBON MONOXIDE (CO): a colorless, odorless gas given off as a normal byproduct of combustion. It is poisonous and extremely dangerous in confined areas, building up slowly to toxic levels without warning if adequate ventilation is not available.

CARBURETOR: A device, usually mounted on the intake manifold of an engine, which mixes the air and fuel in the proper proportion to allow even combustion.

CATALYTIC CONVERTER: A device installed in the exhaust system, like a muffler, that converts harmful byproducts of combustion into carbon dioxide and water vapor by means of a heat-producing chemical reaction.

CENTRIFUGAL ADVANCE: A mechanical method of advancing the spark timing by using flyweights in the distributor that react to centrifugal force generated by the distributor shaft rotation.

CHECK VALVE: Any one-way valve installed to permit the flow of air, fuel or vacuum in one direction only.

CHOKE: A device, usually a moveable valve, placed in the intake path of a carburetor to restrict the flow of air.

CIRCUIT: Any unbroken path through which an electrical current can flow. Also used to describe fuel flow in some instances.

CIRCUIT BREAKER: A switch which protects an electrical circuit from overload by opening the circuit when the current flow exceeds a predetermined level. Some circuit breakers must be reset manually, while other reset automatically

COIL (IGNITION): A transformer in the ignition circuit which steps of the voltage provided to the spark plugs.

COMBINATION MANIFOLD: An assembly which includes both the intake and exhaust manifolds in one casting.

COMBINATION VALVE: A device used in some fuel systems that routes fuel vapors to a charcoal storage canister instead of venting

them into the atmosphere. The valve relieves fuel tank pressure and allows fresh air into the tank as fuel level drops to prevent a vapor lock situation.

COMPRESSION RATIO: The comparison of the total volume of the cylinder and combustion chamber with the piston at BDC and the piston at TDC.

CONDENSER: 1. An electrical device which acts to store an electrical charge, preventing voltage surges.
2. A radiator-like device in the air conditioning system in which refrigerant gas condenses into a liquid, giving off heat.

CONDUCTOR: Any material through which an electrical current can be transmitted easily.

CONTINUITY: Continuous or complete circuit. Can be checked with an ohmmeter.

COUNTERSHAFT: An intermediate shaft which is rotated by a mainshaft and transmits, in turn, that rotation to a working part.

CRANKCASE: The lower part of an engine in which the crankshaft and related parts operate.

CRANKSHAFT: The main driving shaft of an engine which receives reciprocating motion from the pistons and converts it to rotary motion.

CYLINDER: In an engine, the round hole in the engine block in which the piston(s) ride.

CYLINDER BLOCK: The main structural member of an engine in which is found the cylinders, crankshaft and other principal parts.

CYLINDER HEAD: The detachable portion of the engine, fastened, usually, to the top of the cylinder block, containing all or most of the combustion chambers. On overhead valve engines, it contains the valves and their operating parts. On overhead cam engines, it contains the camshaft as well.

DEAD CENTER: The extreme top or bottom of the piston stroke.

DETONATION: An unwanted explosion of the air fuel mixture in the combustion chamber caused by excess heat and compression, advanced timing, or an overly lean mixture. Also referred to as "ping".

DIAPHRAGM: A thin, flexible wall separating two cavities, such as in a vacuum advance unit.

DIESELING: A condition in which hot spots in the combustion chamber cause the engine to run on after the key is turned off.

DIFFERENTIAL: A geared assembly which allows the transmission of motion between drive axles, giving one axle the ability to turn faster than the other.

DIODE: An electrical device that will allow current to flow in one direction only.

DISC BRAKE: A hydraulic braking assembly consisting of a brake disc, or rotor, mounted on an axle, and a caliper assembly containing, usually two brake pads which are activated by hydraulic pressure. The pads are forced against the sides of the disc, creating friction which slows the vehicle.

DISTRIBUTOR: A mechanically driven device on an engine which is responsible for electrically firing the spark plug at a predetermined point of the piston stroke.

DOWEL PIN: A pin, inserted in mating holes in two different parts allowing those parts to maintain a fixed relationship.

DRUM BRAKE: A braking system which consists of two brake shoes and one or two wheel cylinders, mounted on a fixed backing plate, and a brake drum, mounted on an axle, which revolves around the assembly. Hydraulic action applied to the wheel cylinders forces the shoes outward against the drum, creating friction and slowing the vehicle.

DWELL: The rate, measured in degrees of shaft rotation, at which an electrical circuit cycles on and off.

ELECTRONIC CONTROL UNIT (ECU): Ignition module, module, amplifier or igniter. See Module for definition.

ELECTRONIC IGNITION: A system in which the timing and firing of the spark plugs is controlled by an electronic control unit, usually called a module. These systems have not points or condenser.

ENDPLAY: The measured amount of axial movement in a shaft.

ENGINE: A device that converts heat into mechanical energy.

EXHAUST MANIFOLD: A set of cast passages or pipes which conduct exhaust gases from the engine.

FEELER GAUGE: A blade, usually metal, of precisely predetermined thickness, used to measure the clearance between two parts. These blades usually are available in sets of assorted thicknesses.

F-Head: An engine configuration in which the intake valves are in the cylinder head, while the camshaft and exhaust valves are located in the cylinder block. The camshaft operates the intake valves via lifters and pushrods, while it operates the exhaust valves directly.

FIRING ORDER: The order in which combustion occurs in the cylinders of an engine. Also the order in which spark is distributed to the plugs by the distributor.

FLATHEAD: An engine configuration in which the camshaft and all the valves are located in the cylinder block.

FLOODING: The presence of too much fuel in the intake manifold and combustion chamber which prevents the air/fuel mixture from firing, thereby causing a no-start situation.

FLYWHEEL: A disc shaped part bolted to the rear end of the crankshaft. Around the outer perimeter is affixed the ring gear. The starter drive engages the ring gear, turning the flywheel, which rotates the crankshaft, imparting the initial starting motion to the engine.

FOOT POUND (ft.lb. or sometimes, ft. lbs.): The amount of energy or work needed to raise an item weighing one pound, a distance of one foot.

FUSE: A protective device in a circuit which prevents circuit overload by breaking the circuit when a specific amperage is present. The device is constructed around a strip or wire of a lower amperage rating than the circuit it is designed to protect. When an amperage higher than that stamped on the fuse is present in the circuit, the strip or wire melts, opening the circuit.

GEAR RATIO: The ratio between the number of teeth on meshing gears.

GENERATOR: A device which converts mechanical energy into electrical energy.

HEAT RANGE: The measure of a spark plug's ability to dissipate heat from its firing end. The higher the heat range, the hotter the plug fires.

HUB: The center part of a wheel or gear.

HYDROCARBON (HC): Any chemical compound made up of hydrogen and carbon. A major pollutant formed by the engine as a byproduct of combustion.

HYDROMETER: An instrument used to measure the specific gravity of a solution.

INCH POUND (in.lb. or sometimes, in. lbs.): One twelfth of a foot pound.

INDUCTION: A means of transferring electrical energy in the form of a magnetic field. Principle used in the ignition coil to increase voltage.

INJECTION PUMP: A device, usually mechanically operated, which meters and delivers fuel under pressure to the fuel injector.

INJECTOR: A device which receives metered fuel under relatively low pressure and is activated to inject the fuel into the engine under relatively high pressure at a predetermined time.

INPUT SHAFT: The shaft to which torque is applied, usually carrying the driving gear or gears.

INTAKE MANIFOLD: A casting of passages or pipes used to conduct air or a fuel/air mixture to the cylinders.

JOURNAL: The bearing surface within which a shaft operates.

KEY: A small block usually fitted in a notch between a shaft and a hub to prevent slippage of the two parts.

MANIFOLD: A casting of passages or set of pipes which connect the cylinders to an inlet or outlet source.

MANIFOLD VACUUM: Low pressure in an engine intake manifold formed just below the throttle plates. Manifold vacuum is highest at idle and drops under acceleration.

MASTER CYLINDER: The primary fluid pressurizing device in a hydraulic system. In automotive use, it is found in brake and hydraulic clutch systems and is pedal activated, either directly or, in a power brake system, through the power booster.

MODULE: Electronic control unit, amplifier or igniter of solid state or integrated design which controls the current flow in the ignition primary circuit based on input from the pickup coil. When the module opens the primary circuit, the high secondary voltage is induced in the coil.

NEEDLE BEARING: A bearing which consists of a number (usually a large number) of long, thin rollers.

OHM: (Ω) The unit used to measure the resistance of conductor to electrical flow. One ohm is the amount of resistance that limits current flow to one ampere in a circuit with one volt of pressure.

OHMMETER: An instrument used for measuring the resistance, in ohms, in an electrical circuit.

OUTPUT SHAFT: The shaft which transmits torque from a device, such as a transmission.

OVERDRIVE: A gear assembly which produces more shaft revolutions than that transmitted to it.

OVERHEAD CAMSHAFT (OHC): An engine configuration in which the camshaft is mounted on top of the cylinder head and operates the valve either directly or by means of rocker arms.

OVERHEAD VALVE (OHV): An engine configuration in which all of the valves are located in the cylinder head and the camshaft is located in the cylinder block. The camshaft operates the valves via lifters and pushrods.

OXIDES OF NITROGEN (NOx): Chemical compounds of nitrogen produced as a byproduct of combustion. They combine with hydrocarbons to produce smog.

OXYGEN SENSOR: Used with the feedback system to sense the presence of oxygen in the exhaust gas and signal the computer which can reference the voltage signal to an air/fuel ratio.

PINION: The smaller of two meshing gears.

PISTON RING: An open ended ring which fits into a groove on the outer diameter of the piston. Its chief function is to form a seal between the piston and cylinder wall. Most automotive pistons have three rings: two for compression sealing; one for oil sealing.

PRELOAD: A predetermined load placed on a bearing during assembly or by adjustment.

PRIMARY CIRCUIT: Is the low voltage side of the ignition system which consists of the ignition switch, ballast resistor or resistance wire, bypass, coil, electronic control unit and pick-up coil as well as the connecting wires and harnesses.

PRESS FIT: The mating of two parts under pressure, due to the inner diameter of one being smaller than the outer diameter of the other, or vice versa; an interference fit.

RACE: The surface on the inner or outer ring of a bearing on which the balls, needles or rollers move.

REGULATOR: A device which maintains the amperage and/or voltage levels of a circuit at predetermined values.

RELAY: A switch which automatically opens and/or closes a circuit.

RESISTANCE: The opposition to the flow of current through a circuit or electrical device, and is measured in ohms. Resistance is equal to the voltage divided by the amperage.

RESISTOR: A device, usually made of wire, which offers a preset amount of resistance in an electrical circuit.

RING GEAR: The name given to a ring-shaped gear attached to a differential case, or affixed to a flywheel or as part a planetary gear set.

ROLLER BEARING: A bearing made up of hardened inner and outer races between which hardened steel rollers move.

ROTOR: 1. The disc-shaped part of a disc brake assembly, upon which the brake pads bear; also called, brake disc.
2. The device mounted atop the distributor shaft, which passes current to the distributor cap tower contacts.

SECONDARY CIRCUIT: The high voltage side of the ignition system, usually above 20,000 volts. The secondary includes the ignition coil, coil wire, distributor cap and rotor, spark plug wires and spark plugs.

SENDING UNIT: A mechanical, electrical, hydraulic or electromagnetic device which transmits information to a gauge.

SENSOR: Any device designed to measure engine operating conditions or ambient pressures and temperatures. Usually electronic in nature and designed to send a voltage signal to an on-board computer, some sensors may operate as a simple on/off switch or they may provide a variable voltage signal (like a potentiometer) as conditions or measured parameters change.

SHIM: Spacers of precise, predetermined thickness used between parts to establish a proper working relationship.

SLAVE CYLINDER: In automotive use, a device in the hydraulic clutch system which is activated by hydraulic force, disengaging the clutch.

SOLENOID: A coil used to produce a magnetic field, the effect of which is produce work.

SPARK PLUG: A device screwed into the combustion chamber of a spark ignition engine. The basic construction is a conductive core inside of a ceramic insulator, mounted in an outer conductive base. An electrical charge from the spark plug wire travels along the conductive core and jumps a preset air gap to a grounding point or points at the end of the conductive base. The resultant spark ignites the fuel/air mixture in the combustion chamber.

SPLINES: Ridges machined or cast onto the outer diameter of a shaft or inner diameter of a bore to enable parts to mate without rotation.

TACHOMETER: A device used to measure the rotary speed of an engine, shaft, gear, etc., usually in rotations per minute.

THERMOSTAT: A valve, located in the cooling system of an engine, which is closed when cold and opens gradually in response to engine heating, controlling the temperature of the coolant and rate of coolant flow.

TOP DEAD CENTER (TDC): The point at which the piston reaches the top of its travel on the compression stroke.

TORQUE: The twisting force applied to an object.

TORQUE CONVERTER: A turbine used to transmit power from a driving member to a driven member via hydraulic action, providing changes in drive ratio and torque. In automotive use, it links the driveplate at the rear of the engine to the automatic transmission.

TRANSDUCER: A device used to change a force into an electrical signal.

TRANSISTOR: A semi-conductor component which can be actuated by a small voltage to perform an electrical switching function.

TUNE-UP: A regular maintenance function, usually associated with the replacement and adjustment of parts and components in the electrical and fuel systems of a vehicle for the purpose of attaining optimum performance.

TURBOCHARGER: An exhaust driven pump which compresses intake air and forces it into the combustion chambers at higher than atmospheric pressures. The increased air pressure allows more fuel to be burned and results in increased horsepower being produced.

VACUUM ADVANCE: A device which advances the ignition timing in response to increased engine vacuum.

VACUUM GAUGE: An instrument used to measure the presence of vacuum in a chamber.

VALVE: A device which control the pressure, direction of flow or rate of flow of a liquid or gas.

VALVE CLEARANCE: The measured gap between the end of the valve stem and the rocker arm, cam lobe or follower that activates the valve.

VISCOSITY: The rating of a liquid's internal resistance to flow.

VOLTMETER: An instrument used for measuring electrical force in units called volts. Voltmeters are always connected parallel with the circuit being tested.

WHEEL CYLINDER: Found in the automotive drum brake assembly, it is a device, actuated by hydraulic pressure, which, through internal pistons, pushes the brake shoes outward against the drums.

ABBREVIATIONS AND SYMBOLS

A: Ampere

AC: Alternating current

A/C: Air conditioning

A-h: Ampere hour

AT: Automatic transmission

ATDC: After top dead center

µA: Microampere

bbl: Barrel

BDC: Bottom dead center

bhp: Brake horsepower

BTDC: Before top dead center

BTU: British thermal unit

C: Celsius (Centigrade)

CCA: Cold cranking amps

cd: Candela

cm^2: Square centimeter

cm^3, cc: Cubic centimeter

CO: Carbon monoxide

CO_2: Carbon dioxide

cu.in., in^3: Cubic inch

CV: Constant velocity

Cyl.: Cylinder

DC: Direct current

ECM: Electronic control module

EFE: Early fuel evaporation

EFI: Electronic fuel injection

EGR: Exhaust gas recirculation

Exh.: Exhaust

F: Fahrenheit

F: Farad

pF: Picofarad

µF: Microfarad

FI: Fuel injection

ft.lb., ft. lb., ft. lbs.: foot pound(s)

gal: Gallon

g: Gram

HC: Hydrocarbon

HEI: High energy ignition

HO: High output

hp: Horsepower

Hyd.: Hydraulic

Hz: Hertz

ID: Inside diameter

in.lb.; in. lb.; in. lbs: inch pound(s)

Int.: Intake

K: Kelvin

kg: Kilogram

kHz: Kilohertz

km: Kilometer

km/h: Kilometers per hour

kΩ: Kilohm

kPa: Kilopascal

kV: Kilovolt

kW: Kilowatt

l: Liter

l/s: Liters per second

m: Meter

mA: Milliampere

mg: Milligram

mHz: Megahertz

mm: Millimeter

mm^2: Square millimeter

m^3: Cubic meter

$M\Omega$: Megohm

m/s: Meters per second

MT: Manual transmission

mV: Millivolt

μm: Micrometer

N: Newton

N-m: Newton meter

NOx: Nitrous oxide

OD: Outside diameter

OHC: Over head camshaft

OHV: Over head valve

Ω: Ohm

PCV: Positive crankcase ventilation

psi: Pounds per square inch

pts: Pints

qts: Quarts

rpm: Rotations per minute

rps: Rotations per second

R-12: A refrigerant gas (Freon)

SAE: Society of Automotive Engineers

SO_2: Sulfur dioxide

T: Ton

t: Megagram

TBI: Throttle Body Injection

TPS: Throttle Position Sensor

V: 1. Volt; 2. Venturi

μV: Microvolt

W: Watt

∞: Infinity

<: Less than

>: Greater than

Index